ERIC BUTTERWORTH was born in Leeds and educated at Leeds Grammar School. He graduated from the University of Cambridge in 1953. From 1953 to 1956 he worked in the Ministry of Labour. Since then he has lectured in the University of Leeds and in the University of York, where he is, at present, Reader in Community Work. His publications include *A Muslim Community in Britain* (1967), *Social Problems of Modern Britain* (1972), which he co-edited with David Weir, and *Social Welfare in Modern Britain* (1975), which he co-edited with Robert Holman.

DAVID WEIR was born in 1939 and educated at Bradford Grammar School and at Queen's College, Oxford. He subsequently held the post of research sociologist at Aberdeen University (1961–2) and from 1962 to 1963 was attached to the Extra-Mural Department of Leeds University. He then joined the Sociology Department of Hull University as research assistant and subsequently assistant lecturer (1963–5) and from 1966 to 1971 was lecturer in the Sociology Department of Manchester University. From 1971 to 1974 he was lecturer and subsequently senior lecturer in Sociology at Manchester Business School. He is at present Professor of Organizational Behaviour at Glasgow University. Among his other publications are *Men and Work in Modern Britain* (1973) and *Social Problems of Modern Britain* (1972), which he co-edited with Eric Butterworth.

Eric Butterworth and David Weir are the general editors of the Fontana Modern Britain series.

Edited by
Eric Butterworth and David Weir

The Sociology of Modern Britain

Revised Edition

An Introductory Reader

Fontana/Collins

First published in Fontana 1970
Revised edition 1976
Second Impression August 1976
Third Impression February 1977

Copyright © in the introduction and original material
Eric Butterworth and David Weir 1970, 1975

Made and printed in Great Britain by
William Collins Sons & Co Ltd. Glasgow

Contents

Preface to the Revised Edition

The Sociology of Modern Britain was originally published in 1970 as the first of a series of introductory readers on contemporary British life and society. This foundation book has since been followed by *Social Problems of Modern Britain* (1972), *Men and Work in Modern Britain* (1973), *Cities in Modern Britain* (1975) and *Social Welfare in Modern Britain* (1975).

Clearly, many of our original expectations of the readers and students to whom these readers would appeal have been met, as has been shown by the letters and comments that we have received. And the principles that we originally adopted, and have applied subsequently in the later books – for example, of providing a frame of reference for the study of British society, of selecting readings from a variety of sources not exclusively restricted to sociological writings, and of making links between the themes – have proved helpful.

But now, some five years after the original publication, we did feel that a revised edition was called for. With four other books available in the series, it was possible to redefine the priorities, for clearly some topics no longer required separate treatment, while others needed to be introduced or expanded. More recent work needed to be taken into consideration, especially in those areas to which, in hindsight, we had devoted insufficient attention in the original edition. For usefulness, too, the suggestions for Further Reading and the Textbook and reference section also required to be brought up to date.

New material, then, has been introduced into all the chapters, but their organization and the introductory sections at the beginning of each are largely unaltered, except to include references to the new readings. But we have not changed the extracts or articles simply to include more recent material, but because the new pieces represent important standpoints and distinctive views that need to be taken into consideration as we move into the second half of the 1970s. With these changes we hope that *The Sociology of Modern Britain* and the Modern Britain series will become available to an even wider range of students and readers.

It is pleasant to be able to record our thanks to all those friends, colleagues and critics (and some who appear in two or all of those guises) who have in numerous ways helped us to reshape this reader. In particular we would like to thank Noreen Davey, Joan Handforth and Jane Fenton who undertook the secretarial and administrative duties to prepare the book for publication, and our wives, Ann Butterworth and Mary Weir, who are owed a special debt.

November 1974

ERIC BUTTERWORTH
DAVID WEIR

Introduction to the Modern Britain Series

The main purpose of this series of readers is to introduce students to the study of their own society. We hope to do this by presenting material within a sociological frame of reference. Sociology is a word that has many overtones but in its broadest sense it refers to an attempt to study society in a disciplined and systematic way. There are many specific theories within the subject area of sociology, just as there are in any field of knowledge, even physics, chemistry or engineering; and of course, not all sociologists would agree with each and every theory which any other sociologist would put forward. But nonetheless we are now in a situation where an impressive amount of research and writing has been undertaken within British society especially since the last war. One of the results of this kind of work is that it becomes possible to examine many familiar aspects of our own society in new and unfamiliar ways. This is a characteristic consequence of studying sociology, in fact, that it provides a focus for studying events and suggests criteria of relevance which allows us to 'make sense' of at least part of the bewildering mosaic of social phenomena. Sociology provides a frame of reference, an approach, which allows us to make some sense of our society even where it would be impossible to consider more than a fraction of the mass of material which is being produced about it.

As everybody has an interest in being informed and in understanding how their own society works, this series of books is intended in a real sense for the general reader, but perhaps more particularly for those who are undertaking some relatively structured learning about Britain today.

An increasing number of people are taking courses on 'British society' which have a bearing on their training or reflect their concern to understand social processes and social functions. For many, given the reading available, this may reflect a heavy diet of factual material (the number of households, rate of divorce, circulation of newspapers and the like) which becomes largely concerned with what *is* rather than with *how* or *why*. It tends to lose out on sociological perspective and relevance. The result of an attempt to absorb an undifferentiated mass of unrelated statistics is twofold. In the first place we tend to suffer from a sort of mental indigestion – 'Did 14·375 per cent of red-haired Glaswegians vote Conservative in the 1964 General Election . . . or did Pinza win the Derby in 1953? . . . Does it matter? . . .' – which may lead us to the even more disturbing conclusion that *all* statistics are equally meaningless. Such learning is possibly easily absorbed for examination purposes, but equally quickly forgotten afterwards if it cannot be assimilated to any more general framework of understanding.

For some others the first introduction to the work of the social sciences is at a more rarefied level and their intellectual diet may become excessively rich in the esoteric ramifications of some currently fashionable theories. This presents problems of a different kind. For this produces a tendency to rule out of consideration any 'facts', findings or insights that don't happen to fit the theory, and thus valuable learning possibilities may be lost.

It is our view that the two approaches mentioned are equally unsatisfactory for the student who is a beginner. But we need to distinguish different senses in which we use the term 'beginner'. It is true that a particular person may have previously had no intensive contact with the social sciences. So in that sense he is starting from scratch. But in another sense he is already something of an expert, for he has lived in this society, or one similar to it, all his life. This then must constitute the starting point of the process of learning. In the first place the teacher has to begin where the student happens to be, with a particular experience of life and a system of beliefs and attitudes which help him to explain that experience. He already has views about his society, although they may be misinformed or based on untenable assumptions about how things happen. In this situation, it seems to us he requires material which allows him to examine some of his preconceptions. As Walter Lippmann, the American writer, has said: 'For the most part we do not first see, and then define, we define first and then see. We are told about the world before we see it. We imagine most things before we experience them. And these preconceptions, unless education has made us acutely aware, govern deeply the whole process of perception.' Aneurin Bevan made a similar point when he wrote: 'It is inherent in our intellectual activity that we seek to imprison reality in our description of it. Soon, long before we realize it, it is we who become the prisoners of the description. From that point on, our ideas degenerate into a kind of folklore which we pass to each other, fondly thinking we are still talking of the reality around us.' Of course, sociologists have their 'folklore' just as do any other group in society and we would not wish to claim any more for this series of books of readings than that they may stimulate the student to consider *alternative* perceptions and constructions of social reality to those which he brings to the study of his own society. With this basis the enquiring student, of whatever age or background, may go in one of several directions. He may perhaps undertake systematic study or reading about some other society or culture on the basis of the concepts and perceptions he has found useful in the study of his own, or he may begin to examine some specific aspect of society, say the extended family system, in more depth and detail.

Our decision to compile the first book in this series – the first edition of *The Sociology of Modern Britain* – arose from our experience in teaching a wide range of students, many of whom were adults, in university extra-mural and on undergraduate and postgraduate courses, on professional courses of many kinds, and in several educational institutions. We recognized a number of factors which made the courses on this theme less satisfactory than they might have been. Our series is an attempt to remedy some of these deficiencies. In our experience of introductory courses, much original and relevant work never finds its way to the student body, even though it may be mentioned in the reading lists. University libraries may have only single copies of a journal containing an article recommended to many students. The problems are much worse in other educational settings. For the general reader, the public library may represent a treasure house of material and documentation, but it may also present a façade of baffling impenetrability to the reader who is interested in a particular topic – say the educational system – but doesn't quite know what he wants. Faced with a row of books all of which apparently contain information of some relevance to the topic, how is he to choose between them? One or two bad choices, a few wasted visits, and the initial enthusiasm may be dissipated in a puzzled frustration which may create a permanent antipathy to the subject. Often these problems may be compounded by teachers who are not themselves trained in the subject and who feel equally in need of a frame of reference. Systematic teaching demands this. Too often, perhaps, subjects may be introduced to students as a series of disconnected episodes of merely intrinsic interest.

It is clear that the audience we have aimed at covers a wide range. There are members of the general public whose interest in the nature of their society may have been stimulated by television programmes, colour supplements and the like. These may or may not move on to adult classes, or courses of study such as those provided by the Open University, Extra-Mural Departments, the WEA, and by local authorities. Many students at Colleges of Education, Technical colleges, and Colleges of Further Education, undertake general introductory courses in sociology, much of the content of which relates to Britain, and these are beginning to develop in the sixth forms of some schools. Professional or pre-professional courses of training, in-service and refresher courses for such groups as hospital administrators, managers and social workers, are more and more common. As the amount of this provision in the social sciences increases, the problems of teaching it and gaining access to relevant material become, if anything, greater than they have been before.

This, like others in the series, is an *introductory* reader. An attempt has been made to introduce a range of topics and approaches with a balance between what is descriptive and what is analytical and conceptual. Had we been trying to meet the needs of university students near the end of their courses our selection would have been quite different in a number of respects.

Every chapter has an introductory section which is designed to pose some of the important questions which arise in the particular context of our readings without providing a detailed commentary on all the relevant sociological concepts and issues. These introductory sections attempt also to link certain pertinent themes, which are not dealt with in specific extracts, to further reading. This book can be used profitably in conjunction with one of the textbooks in current use. The Textbook Reference section at the end contains detailed page references to the most relevant themes that the courses for which we are catering will wish to cover.

The readings follow the introductory section in each chapter. Because of the audience it was felt unnecessary to reproduce the detailed footnotes and references many of them contained. As far as possible many of the most important references in the text to authors or books have been included in the Further Reading at the end of the relevant chapter. The common practice of numbering tables according to their place in the particular reading rather than their place in the work from which they are taken has been followed. Most of the readings are, of course, edited or abbreviated versions of the original texts, which inevitably repay fuller and more detailed study if time permits.

As far as further reading is concerned, we concentrate on books which are reasonably easy to obtain. Many are in paperback and using our source books it would be possible to obtain a wide range of material quite cheaply. Others will lead the student to utilize libraries.

Several criteria have guided us in the course of our selection of readings. Readability is one of these, and although the extracts vary in difficulty it is hoped that the most difficult can be tackled successfully with the help of the references and discussion of major points in the chapter introductions. The variations in the level of the readings, and the different approaches to be found in them, are not fortuitous: they are designed to pose questions from which every student must start. Some are deliberately short, lending themselves to class discussion; others may be more properly studied independently. In some cases the readings deal with similar material from different points of view, and this is a deliberate policy to make links between themes which cut across the boundaries of chapters, and reinforce, for example, the sense of inter-relationships between social institutions and an awareness of the cumulative consequences of social change. We have chosen work which is not on the whole readily available to the student, often from journals and books to which he is unlikely to have access. We have tended to avoid choosing from paperbacks though in one or two cases books have reappeared in paperback after our original selection was made.

There are many personal elements which arise in making a choice of readings and we have tried to be explicit about some of them, but our focus throughout has been upon the specific needs and requirements of the students taking introductory courses, largely in non-university settings, and of general readers outside of the major educational institutions.

It is hoped that this series of source books of readings will go some way to meeting some of the needs of students and teachers involved in the kinds of courses we have mentioned. We hope also that they will prove interesting in their own right to general readers and that they may lead into a more systematic examination of some of the issues we have attempted to raise here.

Their value will depend on the extent to which they are used. They are above all intended to assist interested readers in the process of initially learning about the nature of their own society. Though it is hoped to cover all or most of the major aspects of contemporary society in this series, of course, any one book stands on its own. They are not intended to promote any particular sectarian or theoretically purist position. In our experience of textbook and other one-sided approaches this is an unnecessary attempt to do the teacher's job for him and is anyway fairly rapidly seen through by students. We have been very much encouraged and helped by feedback from students and teachers about the first edition of *The Sociology of Modern Britain* and *Social Problems of Modern Britain,* the first two books in the series. Above all we welcome comments and criticisms from all those teaching and studying in this field, at whatever level.

ERIC BUTTERWORTH
DAVID WEIR

1 Family

The word family means many things to different people. It is
usual to think of it as composed of husband, wife and their
children. This is the *nuclear* family which is the normal household unit in Britain. Members of this family are usually
biologically related, though this is not invariably the case: the
institution of adoption provides the same legal basis as for
any other family. There are differences in the way the term
nuclear family is used: in most cases it refers to parents and
children living together but sometimes it is used to describe
members of a nuclear family wherever they might happen to
be.

Most people are members of two families during their lives.
The first is the family of *origin* (or orientation) in which our
earliest experiences take place. The second is the family of
marriage (or procreation) in which we play the roles of parents.
The functions of the family involve on the one hand internal
processes, the ways in which the family operates as a system
of relationships and on the other those which relate to the
wider society.

In common with other advanced industrial societies of the
West the nuclear family is the primary unit but the extended
family can still remain important. This term refers to a
grouping which is wider than the nuclear family but involves
those related by marriage or kinship. The studies of Bethnal
Green by Young and Willmott and Townsend provide interesting evidence for the continuing vitality of one kind of extended
family. Among some immigrant groups to Britain, for example
Pakistanis and Indians, the norm remains the joint family
based on the authority, for certain defined purposes, of the
head of this three-generation grouping, but in practice more
and more begin to live in modified forms of the nuclear family,
possibly with certain relatives present in the household unit.
The definition of household used in the ten-yearly census is:
'one person living alone or a group of persons living together,
partaking of meals prepared together and benefiting from a
common housekeeping.'

It is important to see social institutions such as the family not in monolithic terms but as changing rapidly in certain ways. Advertising portrays the image of what Dr Leach in his 1967 Reith Lectures on the family and marriage referred to as 'the cereal packet norm' – the family which includes young children.

The need to study the family from an historical perspective is the assumption behind the reading from **Young and Willmott** which starts our chapter. Three stages of family life, from the pre-industrial to the present day, are outlined. In the first, the pre-industrial stage, the family was usually the unit of production, working together in a number of complementary or similar roles. After industrialization the members of the family were more likely to become individual wage-earners, and this was a process likely, it is suggested, to tear apart the working-class family. In the present stage the unity of the family has been restored around the functions of consumption as opposed to the functions of production in Stage 1.

Certain characteristics of the modern, or Stage 3, family are suggested, among which are 'home-centredness', especially when the children are young; the greater importance of the nuclear family as opposed to the extended family (of relatives); and finally the diminishing segregation of the roles of the sexes. These points may be linked with those made by Bott in another reading in this chapter. There are class aspects of the extent to which families are to be formed with the characteristics of Stage 3, and it is suggested in the reading that examples of all three stages are still to be found. Two trends are discernible in Stage 3: one is the extent to which women work outside the home, and the other is the large amount of work now done in the home by men. These trends are so advanced that there is no kind of work in the home which is strictly reserved for the wives, and sharing of tasks is probably increasing. Information from the sample of families indicated that time, too, is shared much more – less so if only the weekdays are taken into account. If weekends are included more time is spent in the family situation than at work.

Technology and greater living space for family members have led to more comfort and more inclination for adults to be in the home. Activities previously of a communal kind, or which almost inevitably involved contact with neighbours, such as drawing water or using the wash-house, are now provided

for in the home. Light and heat are much more efficiently
supplied to the home, and higher living standards and smaller
families have a bearing on these changes. What has been
achieved, in the opinion of the authors, is a new sort of
integration arising from the historical experience and social
changes such as the limitation of families and the extension of
women's rights.

The next reading arises from research undertaken by **Rosser
and Harris** in the Swansea area which demonstrates that the
period during which family life revolves around young children
takes up less than half of the normal cycle of family life. In
future this stage of procreation (phase II) will take up a smaller
proportion of the family cycle because of changes which result
from earlier ages of marriage, fewer children born within a
shorter period, and greater expectation of life. As Rosser and
Harris point out, each phase of the cycle has its characteristic
patterns of household composition, family behaviour and
social participation in the life of the community.

The work of **Bott** is taken from her intensive study of
twenty families in London reflecting different structures and
forms of organization. As she points out, all three of the types
of organization she discusses were found in all families but
the relative amounts varied considerably. She relates the type
of organization which predominates in a family to the external
social relationships of its members. One implication from her
work is that if the family moves from the area where husband
and wife have connected social networks and segregated roles
to perform to another where they are on their own as a nuclear
family this is likely to have consequences for their roles and
their way of life. The move from Bethnal Green to Greenleigh
in Young and Willmott's *Family and Kinship* illustrates this
from a rather different point of view.

The relationships which develop within the family are
influenced by the experience and expectations of its members
and the kind of work, for example, which its adult members
undertake. **Tunstall,** on the Hull fisherman, shows how much
the husband's job influences relationships between members of
his family and how attitudes to pay shaped within the family
carry over to labour-management relationships.

Another example of the close-knit comradeship of a group
which, like the fishermen, arises from their contact not only in
the work-situation but also in the neighbourhood and in their

leisure activities is to be found in the study of Featherstone, a mining district in Yorkshire, featured in the reading in Chapter 4 by Dennis, Henriques and Slaughter. A contrast with these working-class situations is provided in part of the reading by Hubert later in this chapter when she discusses the independence, before marriage, of the middle-class girl.

The thesis put forward by **Dennis** in the second reading about relationships is that the family is the only social institution in an increasingly specialized society in which people are perceived and valued as whole persons, and marriage the only place where the individual can expect esteem and love. The emphasis upon this and upon sociability helps to account for the increasing popularity of marriage even when the divorce rates are rising. It is suggested that romantic love becomes the only valid basis for marriage, unlike the situation which prevails among minorities from Asia living in Britain where marriage is to be viewed as an alliance between families of roughly equivalent social status.

The discussion of romantic love is taken further by **Little.** He shows how the link between love and marriage which is now taken for granted is the product of historical circumstances and what functions this has in delimiting the area of responsibility for the individual more successfully than is possible in societies whose kinship patterns reflect much more detailed and wide-ranging obligations to a wider range of kinsfolk.

A substantial number of people do not experience a 'normal' family situation, either as children or adults, for a variety of reasons. **Illsley and Thompson** show the varieties of experience and structure which may be collected together under the unsatisfactory blanket term 'broken homes'. Among the factors which have to be taken into account are how the home was broken, the ages of the children, and the diversity of their subsequent upbringing. Some effects were social and others economic or psychological. One of the findings of the authors on this evidence from Aberdeen is that the conditions were least favourable as a whole for children who were illegitimate, those brought up in institutions, and children of separated and divorced parents.

Among the broken homes were those which were a consequence of the death of a parent. The next reading is concerned with the loss of a husband for widows with young children and the consequences for them in terms not only of economic position but also of their social situation. **Marris** provides a sensitive and perceptive view of the condition of widowhood that can be compared with other forms of singleness, whether voluntary or enforced. His sample was drawn from those areas of London mentioned in connection with the books by Young and Willmott. He concludes that the adjustment to widowhood is more a concern to achieve an independent status rather than remarriage or other forms of companionship available to the widow.

The recent rise in the divorce rate is the subject of widespread and often uninformed speculation. That there has been a substantial growth is undeniable, and **Chester** considers this in relation to the complex of factors which involve both personal relationships and expectations and social conditions. He concludes that contemporary marriages are more vulnerable to divorce than wartime marriages and that the differentials are increasing (i.e. that marriages of the late 1960s, for example, will be more prone to divorce). Two main questions are considered: are contemporary couples having more divorces or divorces earlier in marriage (since the British evidence contrasts with that from the United States in that a majority of those divorcing in the past thirty years have been married for over ten years)? Are couples experiencing more marriage breakdown or merely resorting more readily to divorce in the event of breakdown? It is suggested that in the future there will be more divorce and earlier divorce, with perhaps one marriage in eight ending in this way.

Chester shows how divorce is not to be taken as an index of marriage breakdown. In the experience since 1900 separation often became an alternative to divorce whereas more recently those who separate may go on to divorce, thereby appearing twice in the figures (and leading the unwary to declarations of doom about the future of the family – an issue which is touched upon in the reading by McGregor in Chapter 7).

Finally, divorce is related to statistics of other forms of personal behaviour and experience which relate to moral norms: to illegitimate births, venereal disease, crime and others. It is made abundantly clear that the statistics have to be treated with great care in the way in which they are interpreted, and that changes in personal and social values are of great relevance.

Kinship and the wider bonds of family are seen in two

contrasting settings. **Loudon** deals with an area in the Vale of Glamorgan and the way in which shared kinship connections and gossip provide a social cement for the established, setting them off from newcomers who are unaware of kinship links. His reference to 'affines' (the spouse and other relatives in law) raises the question of the terminology of kinship. Although it has been assumed that kinship among the middle class is less important than among working-class groups there is evidence to suggest that despite the fact that kinship may involve different things for the middle classes it remains important. **Hubert** suggests that frequency of contact, for instance, cannot, among the middle class, be taken in isolation as the criterion of a close relationship. In her sample from Highgate in London it was not possible to assume that ties of affection were unimportant even where contact was infrequent. The interchange of daily services played little part in the lives of those interviewed.

Although restricted to certain middle-class groups, what has been called the 'dual career family' has made its appearance recently. The Rapoports consider the extent to which this pursuit of individual careers by both heads of households, whilst maintaining a family life together, will become more pervasive. The satisfaction from the pursuit of a career is seen as extending to more and more people, in consequence of affluence, and in particular to women. The pattern of dual *worker* families has been more obvious, and this non-career type is to be found traditionally where husbands and wives work in industries such as textiles.

The women graduates who were studied in the research showed three major groups of work and family patterns: the *conventional*, whereby the woman drops her career on marriage and does not return to it; the *interrupted*, where she intends to resume when her children grow older; and the *continuous*, where the career is interrupted through childbirth either minimally or not at all. The forces which produce the dual career family are discussed in a broad context, since they involve relationships within the family, and the social and cultural environment in which it is set. They have many implications for issues which are raised in this chapter: for example, there are common issues which arise from the reading by Ann Oakley and from that by Young and Willmott which relate to the position of women, and the way in which it is perceived, and the network of relationships is on a 'couple' basis rather than an individual one. The women appear to gain from their opportunities for self-expression. In this sample, children, despite problems raised by mothers having careers, were reported as showing independence and resourcefulness and contributing to meeting overall family needs.

The starting point of **Oakley**'s reading is that sex is 'an organizing principle of social structure, and it plays a great part in determining social roles'. She quotes Anthony Storr, a psychiatrist, on the emotional problems created by women's freedom and the effects these have on relationships within marriage. A consideration follows of the definition of occupation by gender, and some figures are quoted from a number of countries in Western society to illustrate differentiation by sex and the disproportionate share that men have in jobs carrying prestige with high levels of skill required and high incomes. Ann Oakley suggests that the consistency between countries has much to do with Western definitions of masculinity and femininity. The position of women in such societies is the subject of the reading by Juliet Mitchell in Chapter 7. The differentiation between men and women may have increased in recent years. Women's careers are characteristically discontinuous, with the consequence discussed by the Rapoports that after the break women are unlikely to get far in their careers. Opportunities are also linked to traditions and prejudices about 'masculine' or 'feminine' types of occupation or characteristics. The education that a woman has will bear on her opportunities, and it is still the case that as education is more important for a boy than a girl, so the culture of our society, the argument runs, predetermines the boundaries of the possible for women and restricts opportunities in ways that the biological differences between the sexes cannot explain.

The Symmetrical Family

M. Young and P. Willmott

Reprinted with permission from M. Young and P. Willmott, *The Symmetrical Family*, Routledge & Kegan Paul, 1973, pp. 27–32, 93–100

On our main subject there has been no full history. 'It is a sad comment on British historiography that while we have a great many studies of political parties, trade unions and religious bodies, there is not a single history of the basic social institution of British life, the family. Until some attempt has been made to fill this gap it is impossible to write with assurance about family life in the nineteenth century, or to do more than hazard a few guesses at the nature of the impact of industrialism upon the home.' After Harrison wrote that statement, Anderson went some way towards filling the gap by documenting kinship patterns in one town, Preston, as well as in rural Lancashire and Ireland. The fourfold scheme that we put forward in this book will obviously become more differentiated, the interpretations more sophisticated, when the whole job has been done by historians, rather than sociologists, and changes in family structure related in all their complexity to demography.

But we believe enough is already known to allow a partial reconstruction to be made. The process of change, as we are interpreting it, has so far proceeded through three stages. Even though there is so much in common between family life at each stage, and even though the boundaries between one stage and another are somewhat arbitrary, the rough-and-ready division seems to us useful, as does the generalization, even though it cannot any more than most generalizations do justice to all the evidence. In the first stage, the pre-industrial, the family was usually the unit of production. For the most part, men, women and children worked together in home and field. This type of economic partnership was, for working-class people, supplanted after a bitter struggle by the Stage 2 family, whose members were caught up in the new economy as individual wage-earners. The collective was undermined. Stage 2 was the stage of disruption. One historian has pointed the contrast in this way:

Women became more dependent upon the employer or the labour market, and they looked back to a 'golden' period in which home earnings from spinning, poultry and the like, could be gained around their own door. In good times the domestic economy, like the peasant economy, supported a way of life centred upon the home, in which inner whims and compulsions were more obvious than external discipline. Each stage in industrial differentiation and specialization struck also at the family economy, disturbing customary relations between man and wife, parents and children, and differentiating more sharply between 'work' and 'life'. It was to be a full hundred years before this differentiation was to bring returns, in the form of labour-saving devices, back into the working woman's home. Meanwhile, the family was roughly torn apart each morning by the factory bell.

The process affected most the families of manual workers (and not all of these by any means). The trends were different in the middle-class family, where the contrasts for both husbands and wives were somewhat less sharp than they had been in the past. But as working-class people were preponderant most families were probably 'torn apart' by the new economic system. In the third stage the unity of the family has been restored around its functions as the unit not of production but of consumption.

It is clearly not possible, since social history is unlike political or military history, to do more by way of dating than to indicate in a rough manner when the successive waves of change started moving through the social structure. The Stage 1 family lasted until the new industry overran it in a rolling advance which went on from the eighteenth well into the nineteenth century. The development of the new industry was uneven as between different parts of the country, coming much later to London than to the industrial north. It also outmoded the old techniques of production more slowly in some occupations than in others. But come it did, eventually, along with many other forms of employment which shared one vital feature, that the employees worked for wages. This led to the Stage 2 family. The third stage started earlier in the twentieth century and is still working its way downwards. At any one period there were, and still are, families representing all three stages. But as first one wave and then another has been set in motion, the proportions in Stage 2 increased in the nineteenth century and in Stage 3 in the twentieth.

The new kind of family has three main characteristics which differentiate it from the sort which prevailed in Stage 2. The first is that the couple, and their children, are very much centred on the home, especially when the children are young. They can be so much together, and share so much together, because they spend so much of their time together in the same space. Life has, to use another term, become more 'privatized'. We shall argue in the next chapter that this trend has been supported by the form taken by technological change.

The second characteristic is that the extended family (consisting of relatives of several different degrees to some extent sharing a common life) counts for less and the immediate, or nuclear, family for more. We have not been able to discover much documentary evidence about kinship patterns in nineteenth-century England. People certainly often lived with or near relatives, and we would expect that daughters more often maintained close links with their parents, and particularly with their mothers, than sons did with theirs. Extended families must have been used for mutual aid. But we doubt, along with Anderson, whether they became so pervasive and so much the arena of women's lives until this century. Our belief is that since the second war, in particular, there has been a further change and that the nuclear family has become relatively more isolated in the working as in other classes.

The third and most vital characteristic is that inside the family of marriage the roles of the sexes have become less segregated. The difference between two contemporary families of the 1950s, with and without segregated roles, has been well described by Bott.

There was considerable variation in the way husbands and wives performed their conjugal roles. At one extreme was a family in which the husband and wife carried out as many tasks as possible separately and independently of each other. There was a strict division of labour in the household, in which she had her tasks and he had his. He gave her a set amount of housekeeping money, and she had little idea of how much he earned or how he spent the money he kept for himself. In their leisure time, he went to cricket matches with his friends, whereas she visited her relatives or went to a cinema with a neighbour. With the exception of festivities with relatives, this husband and wife spent very little of their leisure time together. They did not consider that they were unusual in this respect. On the contrary, they felt their behaviour was typical of their social circle. At the other extreme was a family in which husband and wife shared as many activities and spent as much time together as possible. They stressed that husband and wife should be equals: all major decisions should be made together, and even in minor household matters they should help one another as much as possible. This norm was carried out in practice. In their division of labour, many tasks were shared or inter-changeable. The husband often did the cooking and sometimes the washing and ironing. The wife did the gardening and often the household repairs as well. Much of their leisure time was spent together, and they shared similar interests in politics, music, literature, and in entertainment. Like the first couple, this husband and wife felt their behaviour was typical of their social circle, except that they carried the inter-changeability of tasks a little further than most people.

Bott was writing fifteen years ago, and not many families have yet got as far as the second couple. Power has not been distributed equally in more than a few families. Division of labour is still the rule, with the husband doing the 'man's' work and the wife taking prime responsibility for the housekeeping and the children. We believe that this applies to the majority of families. But the direction of change has, we believe, been from Bott's first to her second type.

Many different terms have been used for the new kind of family that is emerging. Since it has so many facets to it, a single apt word is not easy to find. Burgess and Locke said, a quarter of a century ago, that the family had moved from 'institution to companionship', and their words 'companionship family' have sometimes found favour, although not with us. The members of a family are more (or less) than companions. For the same reason we do not like 'companionate', as employed by Goldthorpe and his colleagues. We have ourselves talked about 'partnership' and the 'home-centred' family, but these words too are open to objection, the former because it is so general as to be applicable to all forms of marriage, and the latter because, although it stresses one of the distinguishing characteristics we have just mentioned, it does not now seem to us to stress the most important of them, the de-segregation of roles. The new family could be labelled simply egalitarian. But that would not square with the marked differences that still remain in the human rights, in the work opportunities and generally in the way of life of the two sexes. The term which is best, in our view, is the one used by Gorer, the 'symmetrical family', although the emphasis we want to give is not the same as his. He said that, 'In a symmetrical relationship A responds to B as B responds to A; the differences of temperament, of function, of skills are all minimized.' We think it is closer to the facts of the situation as it is now to preserve the notion of difference but ally it to a measure of egalitarianism. In this context the essence of a symmetrical relationship is that it is opposite but similar. If all segregation of roles ever disappeared (apart from that minimum prescribed by the dictatorship of a biology from which there is for most people no escape) then one might properly talk about egalitarian marriage. But to be fair to what has happened in this century a term is needed which can describe the majority of families in which there is some role-segregation along with a greater degree of equality than at Stage 2.

We must make it clear, in case we have failed to do so up to now, that we do not think that the Principle of Stratified Diffusion applied until the second half of the nineteenth century to family structure or indeed to much else. It had to wait until the new ideas of democracy had freed people's aspirations and the new products of industry had satisfied some of them. So the middle classes did not lead the movement from the first to the second stage. Their families were not broken up in the way that Thompson described, nor were those of many skilled workers. But the middle classes were the first to enter the third stage, reducing the numbers of their children and adopting other features of the new family. They have been followed by successive strata of the population. The main question posed by the 1970 survey is whether a new, fourth phase is now being initiated in the same class to ripple its way with the same wave-motion through the structure of society in the next century.

Less segregation of roles

These various historical processes are still working their way through the social structure which means that, in many if not all respects, they have had a fuller effect on the families of richer than poorer people, and of younger rather than older. With poorer and with older people the vestiges of Stage 2 are still very much apparent. But the great majority of married people in our sample were members of the dominant type of new family.

In Stage 2 families there was segregation of roles in many more ways than those to do with money. If husbands did any 'work' at all at home the tasks that they, and their wives, thought proper to them were those to which male strength and male manual skill lent themselves. It was not a man's place to do woman's work any more than the other way round. All that has now changed. Wives are working outside the home in what is much less of a man's world than it used to be.

Husbands also do a lot of work in the home, including many jobs which are not at all traditional men's ones – which is one reason why the distinction between work and leisure is now a great deal less clear for men than it used to be. It never was very distinct for women. There is now no sort of work in the home strictly reserved for 'the wives'; even clothes-washing and bed-making, still ordinarily thought of as women's jobs, were frequently mentioned by husbands as things they did as well. The extent of the sharing is probably still increasing. The latest reading that we have is recorded in Table 1. What husbands did in detail varied according to occupational class. The people at the top helped rather less than others with house-cleaning, for instance. But taking all forms of help into account it was still true that fewer semi-skilled and unskilled workers contributed at all in this sort of way.

The relationship can also be looked at in another way. Table 2 shows that on weekdays men spent more time with colleagues than they did with family. But take account of the weekend and the picture changes. If the week is treated as a whole the immediate family wins out in the competition for time against its main rival, people at work.

They shared their work; they shared their time. But if the trend was towards it, most married couples were obviously still a long way from the state of unisex that some young people had arrived at. There were many roles which were still primarily the prerogative of one sex or another, particularly in the classes which were not so far on in the process of change. In 1970 the general rule in working-class families with cars was still that the husbands were the drivers and the wives passengers, like the children. But this role, too, was well on the way to being shared. Mr Barwick,

Table 1. Occupational class and husband's help in the home (main sample: married men working full-time)

Reported help to wife at least once a week	Professional and managerial	Clerical	Skilled	Semi-skilled and unskilled	All
None	14%	13%	14%	24%	15%
Washing up only	16%	7%	13%	12%	13%
Other tasks (cleaning, cooking, child care etc.), with or without washing up	70%	80%	73%	64%	72%
Total %	100%	100%	100%	100%	100%
Number	171	70	236	107	585

Table 2. Average hours spent with immediate family compared to others (diary sample: married men aged 30 to 49)

	Weekday	Saturday	Sunday	Total for week
Family	5·7	8·7	9·5	46·7
Family together with friends or relatives	0·5	1·9	2·3	6·7
Total with family	6·2	10·6	11·8	53·4
Work colleagues without family	7·1	2·6	1·0	39·1
Friends or relatives without family	0·7	1·1	0·8	5·4
Alone	2·1	1·1	0·7	12·3
Total waking hours accounted for	16·1	15·4	14·3	110·2
Number of men	203	197	197	—

In this and later tables time is expressed not in hours and minutes but in hours and tenths of hours. The total for the week has been calculated by multiplying the sample weekday by five and adding the two weekend days. Time has been excluded for which there was no record about who was present with the diarist.

a carpenter in Sutton, described what he did at 7 p.m. one Saturday.

> I took Beryl out for a driving lesson just to polish up on turns in the road etc. The kids enjoy Mum driving for a change. Beryl's driving is a bit of a thing in the family at the moment. There is a bit of a competition going on with Dot, one of our friends who is learning as well. There was the usual inquest on the phone tonight after the lessons they had both had.

Just as it was in some families still thought rather strange for women to be drivers, it was in virtually all not expected that men should do more than *help* their wives at the work of child-rearing and housekeeping. The primary responsibilities for home and work were still firmly with one sex or the other.

Miniaturization of machines

The symmetrical family would not have developed as it has without the aid of technology, which has been responsible for the last change we want to mention. If technology had made it impossible to operate within the small frame of the home – if it had turned out that consumption had to be, like production, organized in large groups such as Robert Owen thought could be the salvation of mankind in his mill at New Lanark and in his community at New Harmony in Hampshire, and the builders of the *kibbutzim* in Israel likewise in this century – then the family would perhaps have bent to technical necessity. As it is, technology has played new tunes on the same old theme of the primacy of the primordial.

It was not like that in Stage 2 of our scheme. People were thrust into an industrial economy before the houses and consumer goods to put in them had properly arrived. Almost the only luxury was provided in the tavern, and this was largely reserved for men. Along with their work-mates they could find in the warmth and conviviality of the pub some comfort to compensate them for the harshness of their working conditions, as well as abatement for the thirst which the hardness of the work stimulated. The weekends could, as incomes grew, be so uproarious that absenteeism on 'St Monday', as it was known even in the nineteenth century, was much higher than on any other day. The homes could not compete. They were small. They were full of wailing infants, at any rate where the parents did not keep them quiet (and sometimes stunt them for life) by feeding them with the opium-derived 'Godfrey's Cordial'. The Temperance Reformers, whether religious or secular, sometimes had success with their fearful stories of nemesis for the drinker which were the nineteenth-century counterpart of the statistics about lung cancer which the doctors and their allies have been producing in this. But often not. The space that mattered most for the husband used to be the collective space of the alehouse. As the amount of private space has increased there has been more physical room for the husband at home, more comfort and more room for receiving friends.

The water, before it was piped into an individual supply, used to come from a collective well or stand-pipe in the street or on the landing of one of the tenements built by the Peabody, Guinness, Sutton and other philanthropic housing trusts. The washing was done in communal wash-places. If people took baths at all, they did so in the public slipper-baths. The entertainments were also collective long after a public hanging on Tyburn Hill, near where the Marble Arch now stands, ceased to be the greatest sight in London, drawing crowds of a hundred thousand. The street-markets were an entertainment, as they and football and horse-racing, almost alone of the collective spectacles of the past, still are. The city burst out on Bank Holidays as it had long before when archery practice had been compulsory. Transport was collective. The music hall was collective, as was its successor, the cinema. And for a time it looked as though the big would go on getting bigger, outside as well as at work. In the 1930s Llewellyn Smith drew from his survey the conclusion that:

the supply of some of the more important forms of amusement has become mechanized, with consequent results which, *mutatis mutandis*, bear some analogy to those which follow the mechanization of industrial processes. The most characteristic instrument of popular entertainment today is the cinema, of which the first beginnings under the name of the 'bioscope' were referred to by Charles Booth. Today the 258 cinemas within the County of London, with their 344,000 seats and their repeated performances, are capable of entertaining a quarter of the whole population on any one day.

The extent of the change is obvious. What kept people out of the home (and especially husbands with their superiority of command over the money) was the absence of attraction within it. A city of small workshops was also a city of mass life. In this century a city of large factories and offices is also a city of miniature life on the family scale. It is as though the giant of technology has laboured only with one end, to produce tiny reproductions of itself, like the car of the last chapter, and so to make up for the damage it did to the family in the past. Gas-light and electric light were inventions as crucial as piped water; at least husbands could see the faces of their wives after dark without too great an expense. The fractional horse-power motor was another key invention, powering home-laundries, home ice-makers, tiny cold stores, floor cleaners and cooking aids. The average housewife has been given 'about the same amount of mechanical assistance (about two horsepower) as was deployed by the average industrial worker around 1914'. These inventions have, perhaps, done more for the wife than for the husband. But he has been just as absorbed as she by the machines which have brought entertainment into the home, starting with the gramophone and ending (so far) with colour television, and more so than she by the new style of do-it-yourself handicraft production with its power tools and extension ladders and stick-on tiles and emulsion paints. All in all, the machine has by mimicking man, from his fingers to his brain, enabled modern man to mimic his forbears. A partnership in leisure has therefore succeeded a partnership in work.

We do not know how much time people used to spend in and out of the home. But we do know what people who completed the diaries said about their custom in 1970. The figures are in Table 3. We very much doubt whether, before homes became Home, men at any rate would have passed more than half their time there.

We have been sketching out the manner in which family patterns have changed in the last two centuries. The pre-industrial family in which husbands, wives and children were partners in production (if far from equal partners) was in the end unable to resist the force of a much wider division of labour than could be managed within its tiny compass. The new economy did not smoothly incorporate the old or produce a new moral or any other sort of order by which the family could be sustained. Only slowly, and after a great deal of suffering of which women and children were the victims even more than men, has a different

Table 3. Proportion of total time spent at home by husbands and wives (diary sample: married men and women aged 30 to 49: total number of people shown in brackets)

	Weekday	Saturday	Sunday
Men	55% (203)	66% (197)	76% (197)
Women working outside the home	71% (132)	75% (127)	83% (127)
Women not working outside the home	87% (76)	82% (73)	87% (74)

sort of integration been achieved around the functions of the family as a unit of consumption rather than production. Various changes, starting first in the middle classes, have been both interacting causes and consequences of the general transformation. The struggle for women's rights has gradually changed the mental climate, as well as bringing material benefits like family allowances to the aid of wives and children; and each victory has set off a campaign for another. Just because their husbands have been willing to co-operate in the process, the limitation of families has emancipated women more than anything else, and as success has been achieved both wives and children have become more rewarding to co-operate with. The acquisition of better homes has (except for those left out of the general advance) made it more worthwhile for husbands to spend money on them, and their occupants. There is then less reason for a sharp segregation of incomes. And if contraception and more tolerant husbands enable wives to go out to work, they can win for themselves a measure of financial independence.

Family Structure

C. Rosser and C. C. Harris

Reprinted with permission from C. Rosser and C. C. Harris, *The Family and Social Change*, London, Routledge & Kegan Paul, 1965, pp. 164–7

So far we have been examining the composition of the households in which our subjects lived at the time of our survey. For purposes of analysis and exposition, we have classified these into a series of 'household types', following the categories used by Young and Willmott in their study of Bethnal Green. The result is an essentially static, 'snap-shot' view of Swansea at a particular point in time. We must now emphasize the somewhat obvious, but neglected, point that from the point of view of individual families these are not separate 'household types' but phases in a continuous cycle of development. Domestic groups are 'born' at marriage, expand with births, reach a sort of climax as the period of procreation is passed and as the children grow to maturity, and decline as the children marry and 'leave the nest' to found elementary families (and separate domestic groups) of their own. The original domestic group finally disintegrates with the death of one or both of the original partners. This is the normal and universal familial process. With each phase of the cycle, the composition of the domestic group alters – as children are born, or as they leave home on marriage (or bring in their spouses to form composite households). This natural and continuous rhythm of the successive generations must obviously underlie any discussion either of household composition or of family relationships external to the individual household. Here in this endless process are the essential dynamics of family life. It is of course a continuous process within each individual family, though it can without great difficulty be divided into a series of arbitrary but recognizable phases, much as can the life-span of a particular individual. As there are 'seven ages of man', so there seem to be four ages of the family. In the table, we show the phases into which we have divided this continuous and repetitive cycle of growth and decline, together with the numbers and proportions of the persons in our Swansea sample who fell by our definitions into each phase (taking married persons only of course, since marriage is the starting point of the cycle):

Table 1. The Family Cycle

Family Phase	Definition	Numbers in our Sample	Percentage of total
Phase I: Home-Making	From marriage to the birth of the first child	297	17
Phase II: Procreation	From the birth of first child to the marriage of the first child	808	47
Phase III: Dispersion	From the marriage of the first child to the marriage of the last child	262	16
Phase IV: Final	From marriage of last child to death of original partners	358	20
Total		1,725	100

We have taken these particular beginning and ending points for the four phases because they can be easily identified for the persons in our sample, and because of course they do represent clear and distinct milestones in the progress of an individual family through this typical cycle. In the average case, with marriage about the age of 23, the first phase lasts about two years, the second about twenty-three years (since it is from the birth to marriage of the first child). The length of the final two phases depends on the number of children born and on the facts of longevity. There have been dramatic changes in this average and normal family cycle over the last half-century or so with the striking decline in family size and the marked improvement in life-expectancies. And it is useful in order to clarify and emphasize these changes, particularly those in family size, to divide Phase II which we have called the Phase of Procreation into two subphases – 'child-bearing' during which births are actually occurring, and 'child-rearing' in which the children born are growing to maturity. It is the very great shortening of the actual period of child-bearing, comparing say the present generation of women with that of their grandmothers, which has produced the most marked change in this family cycle.

Each age or phase has its characteristic pattern of household composition, of family behaviour, and of social participation in the life of the community of which the family concerned is a component. The dominant social characteristic of the first phase is that it is a period of very considerable adjustments and re-arrangements in relationships, particularly with the sudden arrival on the scene of a new set of relatives – the in-laws. Our survey revealed that the majority of marriages begin with the newly-married couple living temporarily with relatives, more often than not in the home of the bride's parents. Hence charac-teristically this first phase of the family cycle is often spent wholly or partly in a composite household. In the second phase of the cycle, the characteristic domestic group for the larger part of this period consists of parents and dependent children, though towards the end of this phase it is not uncommon for a composite household covering three generations to be again formed with an elderly parent or parents from either the wife's or the husband's side (more usually the former) coming to live with the family.

The Phase of Dispersion begins with the marriage of the first child and continues until all the children are married. As the children marry and leave home, the domestic group goes through a period of declining size, though commonly the size of the group may expand temporarily as one or other of the married children starts off marriage by bringing the spouse into the parental household. The partial rupture of relationships characteristic of this phase may thus be softened by the formation of a temporary composite household. When all the children have in fact married, even if they have not all left home, the family concerned has entered the last phase of the cycle – and in most cases the original couple find themselves on their own once more.

This, briefly expressed, is of course a model of the life-cycle covering the normal or typical case. There are, it scarcely needs to be emphasized, numerous variations in practice on this general model of the four ages of the family. Some persons never marry and thus never enter on this cycle. Others marry but never have any children and are thus permanently halted as it were in the first phase. In other cases the cycle is abnormal through the death of one or both partners early in the marriage, or through 'broken homes' produced by separations or divorces (though these latter accounted for only 1·5 per cent of the cases in our sample). In yet others, one or more of the children may never marry and remain permanently in the parental home – the case for example of the spinster daughter living with and caring for her elderly father and mother, or of the bachelor son maintaining the home for his widowed mother. In some cases the couple concerned may have well above the 'normal' number of children which will affect in their case the length of the two final phases. These many variations are, however, minority instances. In the vast majority of cases the process that we have outlined above does in fact represent the pattern of family development over the succeeding generations.

Family Activities
E. Bott

Reprinted with permission from E. Bott, *Family and Social Network*, London, Tavistock Publications, 1957, pp. 52–61

The organization of familial activities can be classified in many ways. I find it useful to speak of 'complementary', 'independent', and 'joint' organization. In complementary organization, the activities of husband and wife are different and separate but fitted together to form a whole. In independent organization, activities are carried out separately by husband and wife without reference to each other, in so far as this is possible. In joint organization, activities are carried out by husband and wife together, or the same activity is carried out by either partner at different times.

All three types of organization were found in all families. In fact, familial tasks could not be carried out if this were not so. But the relative amounts of each type of organization varied from one family to another. The phrase *segregated conjugal role-relationship* is here used for a relationship in which complementary and independent types of organization predominate. Husband and wife have a clear differentiation of tasks and a considerable number of separate interests and activities. They have a clearly defined division of labour into male tasks and female tasks. They expect to have different leisure pursuits, and the husband has his friends outside the home and the wife has hers. The phrase *joint conjugal role-relationship* is here used for a relationship in which joint organization is relatively predominant. Husband and wife expect to carry out many activities together with a minimum of task differentiation and separation of interests. They not only plan the affairs of the family together but also exchange many household tasks and spend much of their leisure time together.

Among the research couples, there were some general resemblances in the type of organization characteristically followed in a particular type of activity but, within these broad limits, there was a great deal of variation. Thus in all families there was a basic division of labour, by which the husband was primarily responsible for supporting the family financially and the wife was primarily responsible for housework and childcare; each partner made his own differentiated but complementary contribution to the welfare of the family as a whole. But within this general division of labour, there was considerable variation of detail. Some wives worked, others did not. Some families had a very flexible division of labour in housework and childcare by which many tasks were shared or interchangeable, whereas other families had a much stricter division into the wife's tasks and the husband's tasks.

Similarly, there were some activities, such as making important decisions that would affect the whole family, that tended to be carried out jointly by husband and wife. But here too there was considerable variation. Some husbands and wives placed great emphasis on joint decision, whereas others hardly mentioned it. Couples who stressed the importance of joint decisions also had many shared and interchangeable tasks in housework and childcare.

In activities such as recreation, including here entertaining and visiting people as well as hobbies, reading, going to the cinema, concerts, and so forth, there was so much variation that it is impossible to say that one form of organization was consistently dominant in all families.

The research couples made it clear that there had been important changes in their degree of conjugal segregation during their married life. In the first phase, before they had children, all couples had had far more joint activities, especially in the form of shared recreation outside the home. After their children were born the activities of all couples had become more sharply differentiated and they had had to cut down on joint external recreation. Data from the group discussions with wives in the third phase, when the children were adolescent and leaving home, suggest that most husbands and wives do not return to the extensive joint organization of the first phase even when the necessity for differentiation produced by the presence of young children is no longer great.

But the differences in degree of segregation of conjugal roles among the research families cannot be attributed to differences in phase development, because all the families were in more or less the same phase. Early in the research, it seemed likely that these differences were related in some way or another to forces in the social environment of the families. In first attempts to explore these forces an effort was made to explain conjugal segregation in terms of social class. This attempt was not very successful. The husbands who had the most segregated role-relationships with their wives had manual occupations, and the husbands who had the most joint role-relationships with their wives were professional or semi-professional people; but there were several working-class families that had relatively little segregation, and there were professional families in which segregation was considerable. Having a working-class occupation is a necessary but not a sufficient cause of the most marked degree of conjugal segregation. An attempt was also made to relate degree of segregation to the type of local area in which the family lived, since the data suggested that the families with most segregation lived in homogeneous areas of low population turnover, whereas the families with predominantly joint role-relationships lived in heterogeneous areas of high population turnover. Once again, however, there were several exceptions.

Because I could not understand the relationship between conjugal segregation, social class, and neighbourhood composition, I put social class and neighbourhood composition to one side for the time being and turned to look more closely at the immediate environment of the families, that is, at their actual external relationships with friends, neighbours, relatives, clubs, shops, places of work, and so forth. This approach proved more fruitful.

First it appeared that the external social relationships of all families assumed the form of a network rather than the form of an organized group. In an organized group, the component individuals make up a larger social whole with common aims, interdependent roles, and a distinctive subculture. In network formation, on the other hand, only some, not all, of the component individuals have social relationships with one another. For example, supposing that a family, X, maintains relationships with friends, neighbours, and relatives who may be designated as A, B, C, D, E, F . . . N, one will find that some but not all of these external persons know one another. They do not form an organized group in the sense defined above. B might know A and C but none of the others; D might know F without knowing A, B, or E. Furthermore, all of these persons will have friends, neighbours, and relatives of their own who are not known by family X. In a network the component external units do not make up a larger social whole; they are not surrounded by a common boundary.

Second, although all the research families belonged to networks rather than to groups, there was considerable variation in the 'connectedness' of their networks. By connectedness, I mean the extent to which the people known by a family know and meet one another independently of the family. I use the word 'close-knit' to describe a network in which there are many relationships among the component units, and the word 'loose-knit' to describe a network in which there are few such relationships. Strictly speaking, 'close-knit' should read 'close-knit relative to the networks of the other research families,' and 'loose-knit' should read 'loose-knit relative to the networks of the other research families.' The shorter terms are used to simplify the language, but it should be remembered that they are shorthand expressions of relative degrees of connectedness and that they are not intended to be conceived as polar opposites.

A qualitative examination of the research data suggests that the degree of segregation of conjugal roles is related to the degree of connectedness in the total network of the family. Those families that had a high degree of segregation in the role-relationship of husband and wife had a close-knit network; many of their friends, neighbours, and relatives knew one another. Families that had a relatively joint role-relationship between husband and wife had a loose-knit network; few of their relatives, neighbours, and friends knew one another. There were many degrees of variation between these two extremes. On the basis of our data, I should therefore like to put forward the following hypothesis: the degree of segregation in the role-relationship of husband and wife varies directly with the connectedness of the family's social network. The more connected the network, the greater the degree of segregation between the roles of husband and wife. The less connected the network, the smaller the degree of segregation between the roles of husband and wife.

At first sight this seems to be an odd relationship, for it is hard to see why the social relationship of other people with one another should affect the relationship of husband and wife. What seems to happen is this. When many of the people a person knows interact with one another – that is, when the person's network is close-knit – the members of his network tend to reach consensus on norms and they exert consistent informal pressure on one another to conform to the norms, to keep in touch with one another, and, if need be, to help one another. If both husband and wife come to marriage with such close-knit networks, and if conditions are such that the previous pattern of relationships is continued, the marriage will be super-imposed on these pre-existing relationships, and both spouses will continue to be drawn into activities with people outside their own elementary family (family of procreation). Each will get some emotional satisfaction from these external relationships and will be likely to demand correspondingly less of the spouse. Rigid segregation of conjugal roles will be possible because each spouse can get help from people outside.

But when most of the people a person knows do not interact with one another, that is, when his network is loose-knit, more variation on norms is likely to develop in the network, and social control and mutual assistance will be more fragmented and less consistent. If husband and wife come to marriage with such loose-knit networks or if conditions are such that their networks become loose-knit after marriage, they must seek in each other some of the emotional satisfactions and help with familial tasks that couples in close-knit networks can get from outsiders. Joint organization becomes more necessary for the success of the family as an enterprise.

Relationships 1

J. Tunstall

Reprinted with permission from J. Tunstall, *The Fisherman*, London, MacGibbon & Kee, 1962, pp. 160–5

For three-quarters of her days the fisherman's wife is apart from her husband. Her main preoccupation is usually children and she is likely to have a slightly larger family than those of other working-class women. For instance, in sixty fishing families where the husband was in his thirties, the average number of children was over three – and many of the wives would, of course, later have more children.

While he is at sea the fisherman arranges for a regular weekly amount of money to be sent to his wife. The man can choose any amount he likes but any fisherman who allots his wife less than the whole of his basic wage is likely to become an object of derision to his mates. Many men allot their wives as much as £10 a week. In addition, husbands tend to buy substantial items like furniture and children's clothing.

A fisherman's wife, therefore, tends to be slightly better off than her neighbour – particularly since she does not have to feed her husband for a large part of the time. That she has comparatively more money than her neighbours, and probably more children, both contribute to the fact that few fishermen's wives go out to work.

The fishermen themselves are invariably against their wives working. When ashore, a fisherman likes to have all his meals cooked by his wife, and since his turn-round time between trips is more often than not in the middle of the week, this alone prevents his wife going out to work. But even in the fish processing houses, which are often willing to let women come and go very casually, and would not object to a woman taking three days off every three weeks, few fishermen's wives are found at work. Fishermen often think it is an insult to their capacity, or perhaps to their status as men, if their wives go out to work. What is the point of his sacrifice, his willingness to go fishing and to accept its hardships in order to get money, if his wife then decides to go out to work as well? Fishermen say quite frankly that they are jealous of their wives going out and meeting men – which would of course happen at work. Similarly, most fishermen while at sea discourage their wives from going out in the evenings. They are often critical too of the extent to which their wives visit their own mothers. But they accept mothers-in-law at worst as a necessary evil.

When her husband is at sea the wife needs understanding, companionship, help with her children, and a chance of escaping sometimes from what is otherwise the prison of her home. In the majority of cases these needs are satisfied by her mother. It seems to be usually only when the mother is dead, or does not live in Hull, or herself goes out to work, that the woman has to turn to a sister, perhaps, or a neighbour. When the woman's own family begins to grow up – especially when her eldest daughter is old enough to help in the house and to become a female gossip-partner – she may see less of her mother; although fishermen's wives are far from neglectful when their mother's help in domestic tasks is no longer required. Without exception, every fisherman's wife I interviewed, who had at least two children under ten years of age, and a mother alive in Hull, saw the mother regularly.

The fisherman's wife organizes her life around the task of bringing up her children – and this inevitably becomes in many ways more important than her other main task of looking after her husband during the ninety days or so each year when he is ashore.

The fisherman remains something of a stranger to his children. Men at sea talk a good deal about their 'bairns' but the attitude seems disinterested and more like that of an uncle than a father. Some men try to compensate for their absence by giving lavish presents to their children. One fisherman, complaining he was seldom home, said: 'The wife told me not long ago that my little daughter asked, "Mummy, who's that man who comes to stay with us?"'

During the last decade fishermen made up about 2½ per cent of the working men of Hull and East Riding, but accounted for about 5 per cent of the divorces. This is hardly surprising in view of the strains inevitably imposed on the fisherman's marriage.

In many cases, it seems to be at the beginning of (or immediately before) the marriage that the conflict between the man and the woman is greatest. The fisherman does not usually have many interests in common with his wife. Some men quickly come to regard their wives merely as providers of sexual and cooking services, in return for a weekly wage. With the passage of time, however, conflict tends to be reduced.

Among fishermen a rough agreement exists as to what is reasonable behaviour for a fisherman in his marriage. It is widely believed that during a turn-round time of three days between trips, a man should spend some time with his wife apart from eating and sleeping with her. On the other hand it is regarded as unusual for a fisherman to spend all three evenings with his wife. Men who only go out drinking when accompanied by their wives tend to regard themselves as unusually virtuous.

Strain is exerted on the marriage by the contrast between what happens when a fisherman has three days' turn-round time and when he has three weeks or more out of a ship. Wives say that a husband, who the last time home spent £40 in three days, now begs for money to buy cigarettes.

Fishing homes usually show evidence of recent decorating, painting, wallpapering – and wives usually report that this has been done by the man. Most fishermen find themselves doing such jobs, behaving indeed like the prototype 'companion' husband. But even though many fishermen at such times adopt more humble roles in the home, it seems to be during these periods that conflict really develops. We have already seen that when a fisherman comes home he disrupts the normal routine. At first this is welcome, he comes bearing gifts for the children. His coming is the main event by which the passage of time in the home is marked, he brings the family into focus.

The fisherman's marriage is shaped by his occupation. The very sequence of his presence and absence is determined by his trawler trips. But also his marriage comes to shape his attitude to work. The motives which sent a boy fishing in the first place are different from those which continue to make a man go fishing in later years. These motives are inevitably bound up with his marriage. After he has been ashore a while the fisherman feels that certain pressures are being exerted on him to go back. Money is shorter. 'Dole and rebate' usually is only roughly the same as the weekly 'wage' the wife receives when he is at sea, and the total sum declines progressively. The man inevitably finds himself differently regarded by his wife after a week or two from how she regarded him after a day or two.

As he goes back to sea again he cannot help feeling that these two things – the smaller amount of cash and his wife's different attitude – are suspiciously closely related. Does the wife only want him when he has money? When he is there more than a few days why does she grow weary of him? Why is he going to sea just to pay that ungrateful wife and her children? 'Legalized prostitution.' One sees the point and it explains why fishermen say so often and so savagely that women are just 'money-grabbing bitches' and less polite things. 'My wife is all "Gimme, Gimme",' one man commented.

The consequences of his marriage feed back into the structure of the industry a number of important implications. Though the fisherman may give more than just his basic wage to his wife, there still remains the belief that the basic wage is hers and the rest is his. This is why the fisherman says that his pay has never been put up for years. (The poundage payment between 1947 and 1960 has changed only from 11s 6d to 12s 9d per £100 of the catch's auction price.) If you point out that the basic rate has gone up a number of times the fisherman says that the basic goes to his wife.

Thus fishermen come to distrust increases in the basic, and might distrust even more a large negotiated increase in the basic rates to compensate a drop in the poundage. In this way attitudes to pay, which are shaped in the context of the family, carry over into the field of trade unionism and labour-management relations.

Relationships 2
N. Dennis

Reprinted with permission from *International Journal of Comparative Sociology*, Vol. II, 1962, pp. 86–8

The need which can be satisfied *outside* the family with increasing difficulty only is the need to participate in a relationship where people are perceived and valued as whole persons.

In urban industrial society it is necessary to collaborate with one set of people in order to earn a living, with another to worship, with a third set to be educated, with a fourth for amusement, with a fifth in seeing to the affairs of the neighbourhood, and so on. Minute differentiation of function is the secret of productivity. But the one thing which this type of organization of roles cannot 'produce' are the values of what Toennies called 'mutual furtherance and affirmation'. In the elaboration of modern social institutions, marriage has become the only place in which the individual can demand and expect esteem and love. Adults have no one on whom they have a right to lean for this sort of support at all comparable to their right to lean on their spouse. The marriage relation, to a far greater extent than in systems where communal type solidarities exist between fellow-workmen, neighbours, and extended kin categories, is in a strategic position in this respect.

In contributing to one another love, dignity and emotional support in spite of failures in specific roles or particular tasks, the spouses are fundamentally alike. Yet this is a special case of cooperation where likeness of contribution nevertheless produces great interdependence. This is so for two reasons. Unlike, say, housework, where the task could be carried out by a single person, and more than one person does it for reasons of convenience, sociability essentially requires the interplay of feelings for its fruition. The man and woman give each other something they could not provide for themselves. Unlike, say, sexual intercourse, which is possible in casual liaisons, companionship needs time and conditions suited to the emergence of primary-type ties, and these conditions do not flourish outside the family. James Thurber's 'One is a Wanderer' well describes the futility in the big city of the search for companionship outside of the family setting. Not only is it practically difficult to find communal satisfactions in modern society. The norms do not allow men and women not married to one another to indulge in tender companionate relationships. Any friendship between males tends to be stigmatized by attributing to it a homosexual basis. These rules are functional. They prevent obligations arising in communal type relationships from contaminating complex and fractionalized utilitarian relationships in the economy and in society at large.

The changing grounds of recruitment to the role of spouse support this interpretation. Sentiments turn increasingly towards the notion of romantic love as not just preferable but as the inevitable and only valid basis for marriage. Values emphasize personal response to the exclusion of economic advancement or social standing. A second tendency has been the increased obscurity of standards of choice where these are not connected with the romantic motif. 'In all the conversation about courtship there appears to be a lack of any definite criteria for liking or disliking . . . expectations which are vague and diffuse are more easily met and adjustment between husband and wife . . . may therefore be less difficult than in cases where both partners know exactly what they want.'

The divorce figures themselves support this interpretation. Primary relations which are sought for themselves, as contrasted with those which emerge as the by-product of other cooperative activities, are difficult to sustain. The well documented and much discussed 'loss of functions' of the family has reduced the possible volume of by-product primary group satisfactions. It is not surprising therefore that the divorce figures should have reached their present level. When people marry under the influence of romantic love, as Bertrand Russell has said, 'each imagines the other to be possessed of more than mortal perfections and conceives that marriage is going to be one long dream of bliss . . . In America, where the romantic view of marriage has been taken more seriously than anywhere else, and where law and custom alike are based on the dreams of spinsters, the result has been an extreme prevalence of divorce and an extreme rarity of happy marriages.' In so far as companionship, a close, durable, intimate, and unique relationship with one member of the opposite sex becomes the prime necessity in marriage, a failure in this respect becomes sufficient to lead to its abandonment. But it is significant that divorced people nevertheless remarry at about the rate at which bachelors and spinsters marry. They are discontented with a particular spouse. They cannot do without marriage if their primary social needs are to be met.

The spouse relationship, as has been indicated, is reorganized around this new balance of functions. Getting a living and making a comfortable and beautiful home are subordinated to companionship. Raising a family is also assessed within this context.

The Basis of Marriage

K. Little

Reprinted with permission from K. Little, 'The Strange Case of Romantic Love', *The Listener*, April 7, 1966

I call romantic love 'strange' because in some societies a strong love attraction is socially viewed as a laughable and tragic aberration. Individual love relationships seem to occur everywhere; but a romantic complex is entirely absent from many societies, and our own Western civilization is almost unique in this respect. I mean by this the idea that falling in love is a highly desirable basis of courtship and marriage.

This special feature of our culture can be traced back to feudalism during the eleventh century. Among the ruling class at that time marriage was a mere commercial enterprise, an assignment forced upon the two interested parties by their overlords and guardians. It was destitute of love. Indeed, the wife of the knight or baron has been described as a serf and a chattel whom he kept in order by such corporal chastisement as circumstances might require.

With the ending of the struggle between Christendom and the pagan or infidel invaders, the castle became the centre of social intercourse. The knight who was now free to remain at home instituted a court. This gave women a chance to express feminine interests and graces.

This change of attitude, which lifted the woman of noble birth from conditions of savagery, was associated with the troubadours. They effected her rescue not by encouraging wives to love their husbands or husbands to cherish their wives but by propounding a code of gallantry. This required knights and squires, as part of their chivalric duty, to gain the favour of a lady, and having won it to make it the lodestone of their lives. The relationship was supposed to be restrained on the physical side, rapturous, beautiful, and tender but entirely extra-marital. Marriage was regarded as the most formidable obstacle and dangerous enemy of love.

The medieval concept had drawn a line between the spiritual

and the sexual aspects of love. The court society of the baroque and the rococo periods rewarded the gallant's deeds and duels with carnal favours. This integrated love and sex, though only outside marriage.

The idea that love and sex could be combined then filtered down from the castle to the city. It appealed to the rising merchant classes, but illicit relationships did not square with puritanism and thrift. Consequently, the verbiage of courtly love was now addressed not to the married women but to the marriageable maiden. This meant that between engagement and marriage the man was expected to court the girl and display emotional fervour. Association with the opposite sex was not supposed to take place before the betrothal. Nevertheless, the aim at last was to integrate love and marriage. Young people were to make their own choice of partner on the basis of their feelings. Thus, for the first time, the spirituality of love and the marital sex relationship became the same. The conjugal union was to be sanctified by the former.

I have explained that romance first connoted love outside marriage. Marriage was arranged, hence it was assumed that only extra-maritally could people make true love choices. The significant change is that romance has come to be the predominant factor. The connubial state as well as courtship should be rapturous. At first romance was monopolized by aristocratic ladies and by conveying the idea that amorous dalliance was a mark of noble birth, gave to love-making a high social status. It encouraged courtship among the bourgeois family, placing its women members on a special pedestal. Their duty, by the middle of the nineteenth century, was to keep alive virtues and graces that the sterner sex had no chance of developing. The latter – the sons of manufacturers – had to be converted into gentlemen. So, protected from vice and from danger, protected even from serious work, the wife or daughter symbolized her menfolk's aspirations. She was their surrogate in the upper-class world of gentility.

How, then, did romance manage to survive the subsequent emancipation of women? George Bernard Shaw has given part of the answer. His plays show clearly how romance has adapted to feminine needs. Girls, he declares, are right to choose their own spouses; it enables them to deal with the opposite sex as equals. The ethic laid it down that love is profaned by marrying for money, but there is nothing wrong about marrying for love: on the contrary, it is everyone's simple duty. So popular proved this theme that with the development of mass media of communication it became the principal stock-in-trade of major industries. In other words, not only were the traditional barriers down, but the wheel had turned full circle. Who could question this when, as it appeared, thrones were abdicated and royal families did not deny commoners as suitors – all for the sake of romantic love?

I exaggerate, but only because some psychologists have dismissed this emotion as adolescent frenzy. Instead, perhaps romantic love is one of society's methods of rationalizing changes in the organization of marriage. Abstractions come easier in the context of a different culture and so, finally, an example from West Africa. Traditionally, among the people there the bride is chosen by the family, who expect her to produce children and help economically. There, unlike here, even in monogamy a man's closest relationship is not with his wife but with his kinsfolk.

Nowadays, however, educated young West Africans have discovered the alleged virtues of romantic love. They stress the idea of marriage being a true union of husband and wife as well as an economic partnership. Love will be the most important thing when they marry. These younger people have new opportunities in West Africa today. Particularly if educated, there are careers in which they can often rise quickly. But to advance individualistically may seriously offend respected older kinsfolk and relatives. Having partly paid for a man's education, they will expect a return and to share in his subsequent prosperity. It is difficult for him to refuse, because this wide family system has ingrained deep feelings of obligation. He has somehow to square personal interests – his ambition – with kinship sentiment.

Western marriage, therefore, may be an emotional solution. It emphasizes love for a single partner and so reduces the extent of moral obligation customarily felt. This is what I meant by romantic love having a rationalizing function. It helps in the dilemma described to ease an otherwise guilty conscience.

Broken Homes

R. Illsley and B. Thompson

Reprinted with permission from R. Illsley and B. Thompson, 'Women from Broken Homes', *Sociological Review*, March 1961, Keele, University College of North Staffordshire, pp. 27–8, 48–50, 51–2

'Broken home' is only one of many terms used to describe abnormal family circumstances in which children are deprived of continuous care from two parents. The variety of terminology, 'abnormal upbringing', 'disturbed home', 'parental deprivation', 'deprived children', often reflects differences in definition and in underlying concept. In some studies illegitimate children are automatically included in the abnormal category, in others they are ignored. Sometimes the emphasis is on parental loss by death, separation or divorce, sometimes the term is widened to include marital disharmony, child neglect or extreme poverty. Distinctions are sometimes drawn between children whose homes were broken at different ages but more often than not the age at which the break occurred is not reported.

Equally important, however, is the omission to differentiate between homes broken in different ways (death of father or mother, divorce, desertion, illegitimate birth) and between different types of upbringing following the break. One might reasonably expect that a child whose father had died and who was brought up by a mother and grandparents would differ in some respects from a child whose mother deserted the family and who was subsequently reared in a number of temporary homes.

Little is known about the incidence and social distribution of broken homes in a general population. Most of our knowledge derives from the experience of pathological groups and their controls. Closely matched controls for a series of delinquent, promiscuous or psychotic individuals, are unlikely to be a true cross-section of the population. The position is well summarized by Wootton in a review of hypotheses and research into the connection between delinquency and broken homes: 'Attempts to assess the significance of their findings are thwarted, first by the absence of precise definition of what constitutes the "breaking" of a home, and, second, by lack of any information as to the frequency of the broken home amongst the population in general'. The material on this most popular hypothesis is, in fact, quite exceptionally difficult to sort out.

The term 'broken home', however, is imprecise and any consideration of possible traumatic effects must take account of the different ways in which a home may be broken, the ages of the children and the great diversity of their subsequent upbringing. The commonest cause of a broken home, the father's death, has least repercussion on the unity of the family. Dispersal of the family is more frequent when the mother dies or leaves the home; much depends in these circumstances on the availability of older sisters and other kin, but in general the father finds it difficult to look after very young children who may therefore be brought up apart from the family. The young child, on the other hand, often finds a permanent and stable home for the rest of its childhood whereas the older children are faced with domestic responsibilities and recurring family crises as makeshift arrangements break down.

A distinction must also be drawn between social, economic and psychological effects. The father's death may cut the family's standard of living but need not drastically change its domestic habits, its cultural values or its relationship with neighbours, friends or kin; the mother may become preoccupied with outside work and domestic worries but this need not amount to maternal deprivation. On the other hand, parental disharmony leading ultimately to separation could have a profound effect on the child's personality and its later social and sexual life.

Despite such diversity of experiences a few general conclusions may be drawn. Where the father dies but the home remains otherwise intact, the daughters, as adult women, differ little from other women reared in intact homes; such differences as do occur are not necessarily the result of paternal deprivation but might easily result from the slightly lower level of such families before and after the break. The father's death or absence might have greater repercussions on boys than on girls. This possibility warrants further study for more fathers than mothers die young and more boys than girls become delinquents; Andry suggests that young male delinquents are more likely to have a defective relationship with their father than their mother.

Judged by their educational and occupational experience, the social class of their husbands and their high rates of extra-marital conception, conditions of upbringing were least favourable for illegitimate children, those brought up in foster-homes and institutions and the children of separated and divorced parents – particularly where the final break was preceded by prolonged estrangement or periods of temporary separation. Unstable conditions, lack of continuous care and consequent insecurity were common factors in the lives of such children and it is difficult to disentangle such influences from the effect of parental deprivation per se. It seems significant in this respect, however, that children brought up by relatives and apart from both parents fared much better on all our criteria, being very little different from children brought up by their mother following the father's death. Nearly two-thirds of the children brought up by relatives were under five at the time of the break and most of them received continuous care from their relatives subsequent to the break. The circumstances leading to a broken home and the continuity and quality of care following the break seem, on this evidence, to be more important than parental loss itself.

Children from broken homes are demographically abnormal for they inevitably contain a higher than average proportion of youngest children and of those brought up as only children. An excess of youngest and only children in populations of delinquent or mentally ill individuals from broken homes does not necessarily mean that family break-up has a more disturbing effect on them than on children with different positions in the family. Indeed, if our findings are generally applicable it seems likely that youngest children may be comparatively fortunate in their conditions of upbringing after the break, for many are resettled in stable homes and receive continuous care from a parent or parent substitute for the rest of their childhood. Roughly a third of only children came from broken homes – twice as many as in other family sizes. A number of investigators have reported a high incidence of youngest or only children among delinquents and psychiatric patients and the indirect effect of family break-up and its aftermath may contribute towards this.

Early parental death is less common than a generation ago; divorce is much more common. Recent studies of young families show that more homes are now broken by separation or divorce than by death. Although, in our study, the children of separated and divorced parents appear to have fared worse than those whose parents died, a higher divorce rate does not necessarily mean more unhappy children. Many unsuccessful marriages which now end in divorce were preserved intact a generation ago and the children grew up in an unhappy rather than a broken home. In this study of adult women such cases are included in the category 'intact home' and their inclusion in that category may have dulled the contrast between broken and intact homes; in a contemporary study of young children they would be included among broken homes.

With our present limited understanding of family habits and their impact on child personality and behaviour the net effect of these changes is incalculable.

The changing composition of broken homes, the relative decrease of parental loss and the greater frequency of divorce reinforces the need, revealed throughout this study, to treat the general concept of the broken home with extreme caution. Broken homes do not possess a monopoly of marital disharmony and childhood unhappiness – many children from intact homes suffer from family insecurity and emotional deprivation. Conversely many children from broken homes lead a happy normal life. This is particularly true in post-war Britain where social services and concern for child welfare have softened many of the harsher consequences of parental loss.

Widowhood

P. Marris

Reprinted with permission from P. Marris, *Widows and their Families*, London, Routledge & Kegan Paul, 1958, pp. 124–8

At first the loss of her husband seems to spread a pervasive mood of frustration over all a widow's interests. For a while she may become indifferent even to the care of her children: her home, her future, her family – nothing matters any more. Bewildered by her loss, she can hardly at first believe it. She still hears his footsteps on the stairs, his voice calling, finds herself waiting for him at the door when the men come home from work, and as each habitual expectation is unfulfilled, she begins to realize the meaning of his death. Then she may cling all the more desperately to her memories, to his possessions, trying to deny that he is really gone, only to feel grief all the more poignantly when the power of illusion fails. Or she may try to escape from everything that reminds her of the past. But this seems a betrayal of the dead, and in its turn arouses all her latent anxieties about the sincerity of her love, the fear that she is in some way responsible for his death, even absurdly wished it. And she may defend herself against these self-accusations by an obsessive assertion of her grief. Thus bereavement seems to involve a conflict between the desire to acquire an indifference which the loss has no power to hurt, and to idealize the happiness of which it deprived her. But whether she tries to live in the past, or live as if it had never been, she cannot avoid grief, and she bitterly resents her fate. She looks for someone or something to accuse, and envies the good fortune of others.

It may take two years or more to become reconciled to bereavement, and the working out of grief seems to proceed uneasily, by contradictory impulses, isolating the grief-stricken in a struggle that they cannot share. Mourning itself seems to ease the conflict. The funeral, placing a memorial, wearing black, visiting the grave are tributes to the dead, and also continue a relationship with him that does not deny his death. As the mourner accepts her loss, as she gains assurance that she has established her loyalty beyond reproach, as her other interests revive, putting her loss in proportion, these conventional observances can be gradually discontinued. Mourning articulates grief, and gives it expression.

Grief, by its nature, seems to yield very reluctantly to consolation. The profound discouragement of bereavement tends for a while to devalue all relationships except that which has been lost, so that a widow, instead of turning to her children, her parents or her friends with all the more affection, becomes at times almost indifferent towards them. Moreover, there seems to be a need to mourn the dead, to show how much the loss has meant, and consolation must wait until this tribute has been paid. Hence it is difficult for friends or relatives to help a widow overcome her grief. Sympathy may only aggravate distress: exhortations to be practical and look to the future seem glib and insensitive, solicitousness seems officious – the comforters seem to fuss ineffectually outside a conflict that they cannot understand, when all she wants is to be left alone. They can best guide her recovery by encouraging her patiently to feel that she has mourned enough.

The apathy and withdrawal that follow bereavement tend to

isolate a widow from social life. Her indifference and depression make her poor company. When she meets old friends, she is painfully reminded of former meetings when her husband was beside her. She envies married couples their mutual companionship, and feels awkward going out with them by herself. And she seems to project her indifference and bitterness onto others, believing that she is unwanted or neglected. However sympathetic people may be, there is always something humiliating in misfortune, a sense of being pitied or patronized. Hence the attraction of relationships where she does not feel inferior – with her children, companions at work, remarriage. Here she need not feel accepted only out of charity, but can give as much to the relationship as she takes from it.

But if relatives and friends cannot do much to ease the pain of grief, nor even at times to relieve a widow's loneliness, their practical help is invaluable. Minding the children and the sick, getting meals and shopping, advising, dealing with officials, helping out with a loan or a present of clothes, holiday expenses, a television set – family life in the East End of London provides a system of mutual services that spreads the burden on each household. It is useful at any time, and especially valuable to a widowed mother, who must be relieved of part of her household routine if she is to earn a livelihood for herself and her children. Not that the nature of these services changes so much in widowhood: she probably received the same kind of help, for the most part, when her husband was alive. But now she depends upon it more. Only in certain household jobs, and practical advice, does it seem that a brother, a cousin or a son may, in the most literal sense, sometimes take the dead man's place. If the nature of the help her relatives give her otherwise changes very little in widowhood, this is partly because at all times it provides insurance against just such hardship.

Her relationships with her husband's family are more radically affected. A man is more usually drawn into his wife's family than she into his. He visits his old home on his own, after work of an evening perhaps, or on Sunday morning with the children. When he dies, the common bond is broken. And where, before, there was rivalry between wife and mother-in-law, the conflict may break out in open recrimination, inflamed by the bitterness of grief. But even where there is no resentment, she tends to see less of her husband's family: there is no longer much obligation to overcome a mutually protective reserve that has always characterized the relationship. Only occasionally, having, perhaps, few close relatives of her own, or her husband's people living much nearer, may she be drawn to them by a mutual sympathy in their bereavement.

On the whole, therefore, widowhood tends to impoverish social life. A widow can take little pleasure in entertainment, feels awkward with her old friends, loses the only strong tie with her husband's family, and has moods in which her lonely struggle to master grief, her apathy and repudiation of consolation, isolate her even from her own family. These tendencies are reinforced because now she is poorer. She has less money to spend on entertainment, less for fares to visit her friends and relations, and less time, too, since she is more than ever dependent on her earnings. Poverty, besides, makes her sensitive, and she fears to be thought a tiresome poor relation, whose visits will be interpreted as a begging mission. Perhaps there is always a sense of failure in misfortune, however undeserved, and the more so when the misfortune involves poverty.

It would be wrong, therefore, to conclude that when her husband dies, his place must necessarily be taken, as if social relationships were organized like an army, closing its ranks about the fallen. Only in the day to day management of a household economy must a substitute be found, and his widow may prefer to provide this substitute by her own efforts. The love and companionship of a successful marriage are hard to replace at best, and grief, for the reasons I have tried to describe, makes it harder. Hence his widow seems rather to try to reconcile herself to the loss, to find consolation in the memory of her married life until the pain of bereavement sinks in time below the threshold of consciousness.

If this is true, then the adjustment to widowhood is not, most characteristically, to find in a second husband, parents, children, brothers or sisters someone to restore companionship and a secure livelihood, but rather to establish an independent status. But so long, at least, as women are paid less than men, it is likely to seem an inferior status. If a widow has children, her income will be less in proportion to her responsibilities even than a single woman, who besides will have had more opportunity to pursue a career. Thus a widow cannot maintain her standard of living after her husband dies merely by going out to work, because she cannot earn a man's wage.

Divorce

Robert Chester

Reprinted with permission from Robert Chester, 'Divorce in the Nineteen Sixties', *Marriage Guidance*, Vol. 14, No. 2, 1972, pp. 35–9

Between 1959 and 1969 the annual number of petitions for divorce and annulment in England and Wales increased by 133 per cent. This represents an average growth of 9 per cent per annum compound, and the rise in numbers was from 26,000 to 61,000. The trend shows no sign of levelling off, and the growth rate is likely to be given at least a temporary acceleration by the new divorce law operating from January 1971. It is necessary, of course, to allow for the increase in the number of marriages during the period, and the *divorce rate* per 1,000 married population shows an increase of 100 per cent (against the 133 per cent increase for petitions). During the 1960s, that is to say, the divorce rate doubled. At the 1969 rate, almost four million adults will have the experience of divorce during the remaining three decades of this century, and perhaps two million children under school leaving age will be affected. Clearly divorce is now a mass experience, and it is possible that these estimates understate the future magnitude.

Divorce has not been very much studied by social scientists in England. When they have studied it, the tendency has been to explain the historical increase (from under 1,000 per annum at the turn of the century) in terms of population growth, the disturbing effects of war, and the increased availability of divorce. Certainly availability has been increased by such measures as sex-equalization in 1923, extensions of grounds in 1937, and the provisions of the Legal Aid Act 1949. Factors of this kind, however, can hardly be responsible for the recent great increase in divorce, and it has become necessary to look elsewhere for an explanation. It begins to seem probable that changes in social conditions developing throughout the post-war years are now being reflected in the statistics of various kinds of personal behaviour, and that there have been changes in the norms of marriage. The study of contemporary divorce is in part a study of social change, and closer analysis of recent divorce trends reveals some suggestive patterns.

Analysis by cohort

Some light can be thrown on changing behaviour by the method which is technically known as cohort analysis. The idea underlying this procedure is basically very simple. In carrying it out, all the members of a particular 'generation' – say, all those who were born or married in a particular year – are followed through to see what their total experience has been at different points in time. It is possible, for instance, to take all the marriages in 1960, and to calculate the proportion which have ended in divorce by each successive anniversary of the marriage. We can then have a running account of their experience, and the people in this group can be compared with those who married earlier or later to see if there are any changes in behaviour between the cohorts or 'generations'. Calculations for each annual marriage cohort of the 1960s are shown in the table, together with the figures for those who married in 1942/43. The latter figures are included because these wartime marriages were supposed to be peculiarly vulnerable to breakdown and had accumulated historically record figures for divorce.

Percentage of Successive Marriage Cohorts Divorced at Various Durations of Marriage. England and Wales

Those married in the year	Duration of marriage in years					
	4	5	6	7	8	9
1960	0·70	1·54	2·37	3·22	4·05	4·89
1961	0·76	1·62	2·52	3·38	4·35	—
1962	0·85	1·80	2·73	3·73	—	—
1963	0·95	2·00	3·10	—	—	—
1964	1·03	2·20	—	—	—	—
1965	1·19	—	—	—	—	—
1942/43	—	1·08	1·98	2·73	3·44	4·01

To compare the experience of cohorts, readings should be made *down* the columns, and it will immediately be seen that each successive marriage group shows a higher incidence of divorce than its predecessor at any given duration of marriage. For instance, those who married in 1960 show 1·54 per cent divorced at the end of five years of marriage, whereas by the time *they* had been married five years the couples of 1964 show 2·20 per cent, an increase of one-third. Similarly, after six years of marriage 2·37 per cent of the 1960 couples had divorced, but the figure for those marrying in 1963 is 3·10 per cent. Of the 1960 marriages almost 5 per cent had divorced before ten years of marriage, and those marrying later in the decade seem set to exceed this, probably quite considerably in the case of the most recent marriages. The universal tendency is for each marriage group to have higher divorce figures than the one before, and there is no evidence that the upward trend is diminishing.

A further point shown by the table is that even the lowest divorce figures for marriages of the sixties (those for 1960) are greater than those for the highest wartime figure. That is, as measured by this technique, contemporary marriages are more vulnerable to divorce than war marriages. At nine years' duration the 1960 marriages had accumulated 4·89 per cent divorced, against 4·01 per cent for the war marriages, an excess of more than one-fifth, and on the evidence of the table the marriages of the late 1960s will experience much wider differentials still.

There is another trend which can be shown by cohort analysis, and this relates to youthful marriages. It is possible for any given year to divide marriages into those where the bride is a teenager and those where she is 20 or more, and to follow each group separately. When this is done it can be seen both that the younger marriages are most prone to divorce and that this group shares the pattern of increasingly higher figures successively throughout the decade. Of the teenage girls marrying in 1960 (82,000), approximately 9 per cent had become divorced by the end of 1969, and later marriage groups seem certain to exceed this. The relationship between young age at marriage and marital instability is not well understood, but clearly such marriages are very hazardous.

In seeking to interpret the figures so far given, two questions in particular seem to need exploring, viz:

(1) Are contemporary couples having more divorces, or are they merely having divorce earlier in marriage?

(2) If having more divorces, are modern couples also experiencing more *marriage breakdown*, or merely resorting more readily to divorce in the event of breakdown?

More divorce or only earlier divorce?

Obviously contemporary cohorts are experiencing more early divorce, but there is no way of relating the percentage of a marriage group divorced by any particular anniversary to the percentage of that group which will divorce in the long run. It could be that the more recent couples are having most of their divorces in the early years of marriage, and that ultimately no greater proportion will be divorced. This seems unlikely, however. In the past, divorcing has continued up to advanced durations of marriage, with rather more than half occurring later than the tenth anniversary. After a twenty-year period in which petitions have first halved and then more than doubled it would be foolish to dogmatize on this point, and the new law will in any case create a 'bulge' which will temporarily obscure the trend. But whichever way it is measured divorce is increasing fast, and it seems unlikely that statistics in the next decade will show other than a modern propensity to have more divorce as well as earlier divorce. While only guesswork is possible, it may be that as many as one in eight, or even more, of contemporary marriages will end in divorce.

More breakdown or only more divorce?

Rising divorce figures are viewed with concern by many people because it is assumed that divorce provides an index of marriage breakdown. The relationship between divorce and the total volume of marriage breakdown, however, is a very uncertain one, both because of the difficulty of defining marriage breakdown and the impossibility of measuring all its components. Some would want to include in marriage breakdown those unions where the couple continue to cohabit, but only in deep disharmony and failure of emotional support. In practice we know nothing of the dimensions of this group of marriages, and we must measure breakdown only in terms of situations where there is deliberate absence of a spouse through divorce, annulment, separation or desertion. Marriages, that is, which have broken up as well as broken down.

Even here, however, accurate numbers of breakdowns cannot be given, because only some components are exactly known. Divorce and annulment figures are reliable, because marriages can be dissolved only by public processes. Figures for separated spouses, however, are currently a mystery. Some couples part purely informally, and the numbers and trends of these are completely unknown. Figures are available for breakdowns which are dealt with in the Magistrates' Courts, and these have remained roughly stable throughout the 1960s at approximately 32,000 per annum. These numbers, however, cannot simply be added to divorces to give an annual total of legally recorded breakdowns, because some who separate via lower courts go on to divorce later on, thus presenting a problem of double-counting. Probably about half of those obtaining magistrate's orders go on to divorce, although this is only a 'best estimate'. On the basis of a number of assumptions which are fully explained elsewhere, it seems possible that the annual numbers of *recorded* breakdowns increased during the 1960s by about 65 per cent, against 100 per cent for the divorce rate, and 133 per cent for the number of petitions. These figures indicate the unreliability of divorce figures alone in the estimation of marriage breakdown, and of course they leave out of account the category of informally broken marriages. It might be expected that modern couples would be more ready than others in the past to regularize unsatisfactory marital situations, and that the number of un-recorded breakdowns has been falling. If such is the case, this would reduce still further the total increase of marriage break-down from the 65 per cent suggested above. In other words, if fewer couples part informally, then recorded breakdowns come to be a truer reflection of the total, and increases therein would not necessarily indicate a commensurate increase in marital instability. At the very minimum, however, current figures suggest a greater propensity than in the past to dissolve a failed union. Contemporary marriages certainly have higher *recorded* breakdown rates, and they very probably have higher total breakdown rates, although the latter conclusion should be regarded as tentative.

Estimating the future is a hazardous exercise, but it may be worthwhile to speculate what proportion of contemporary marriages may ultimately succumb to one form or another of marriage breakdown. It seems possible that 12–15 per cent of marriages may come to an end via application to the divorce court or to magistrates. This leaves unaccounted for both unrecorded separations, and empty but legally intact marriages if a fuller definition of marriage breakdown is employed. One estimate puts the figure at 5–10 per cent of marriages for both kinds of breakdown combined, and adding these to recorded breakdowns it seems possible that between one-sixth and one-quarter of contemporary marriages may experience failure through termination, separation, or internal collapse. We cannot be certain that such high rates are historically new, and in any case historical comparisons may be unwise or misleading when people in the periods concerned have very different conceptions and expectations of marriage. What we can be certain of is that marriage difficulties are very widespread in modern society.

Conclusion

Since the mid-1950s there have been increases in the recorded statistics of various forms of personal behaviour and experience which relate to moral norms. Apart from divorce, such increases are seen, for instance, in illegitimate births, legitimate births premaritally conceived, venereal disease, crimes known to the police and (possibly) attempted suicide. As with marriage breakdown, there are problems concerning the compilation and verification of all these statistics, and they must be treated with caution. Nevertheless, the coincidence of timing and trend might plausibly indicate a shift in personal and social values commencing with the second decade after the war. It is not intended here to explore the changes in social conditions which may cumulatively have led to changes in the values of individuals and social groups, and it is certainly not the intention to deplore the 'permissive' or 'affluent' society. Such stereotyped catch phrases have very doubtful usefulness for serious social analysis, and the issues involved are so new and complex that no-one can yet pretend to fully understand them.

Nevertheless, many observers have commented that the 1960s saw a breakthrough into a new kind of society, based on a relative if uneven affluence, and possessing a more *laissez-faire* approach to matters of personal behaviour. Social change is always likely to make most impact on the young, and those born since the late 1930s have matured into a world in which many orthodoxies have been challenged or overthrown, and many previously tractable groups have become self-consciously assertive, not least young people themselves, and women. There has been a general revolution of rising expectations, and such a situation is unlikely to leave unchanged the previous norms of marriage behaviour and family relationships. Our information is incomplete and unsatisfactory in many ways, but it seems to indicate that high manifest levels of marital instability should be expected to become an integral feature of individual and social experience.

Kinship 1
J. B. Loudon

Reprinted with permission from J. B. Loudon, 'Kinship and Crisis in South Wales', *British Journal of Sociology*, Vol. 12, No. 4, 1961, pp. 347–9

It is on ceremonial occasions that people reveal the extent to which they are aware not only of the details of their own kin ties but of those of members of other 'families'. One of the chief difficulties facing newcomers is their lack of knowledge of the key kinship connections between their long-settled neighbours. This is not only or chiefly because they are liable in their ignorance to ally themselves irrevocably with the wrong people when they arrive, or with members of one or other faction in a long-standing local feud. The real point is that without some knowledge of kin ties they can take little part in local gossip.

Gossip is undoubtedly the most important channel for constant reaffirmation of shared values about behaviour. Those who cannot join in gossip about their neighbours, friends and relatives, especially gossip which requires that kind of intricate map-reading of kinship connections which comes as second nature to those with lifelong familiarity with the local genealogical landscape, soon find themselves excluded from conversations at local gatherings. Nuances of expression escape them when discussion turns on the relevance to the speaker's long held opinion of a particular family of the latest example of the behaviour of one of its members. Even where the individual under discussion is referred to by more than his Christian name, more often than not it is by one of half a dozen common Welsh surnames or by the name of a house or farm; and his behaviour may well be related to that of members of earlier generations of his family now all dead.

Conversely, the newcomer tends to be treated by his neighbours with that reserve which is appropriate towards people who
have no easy way of expressing, in relation to particular individuals and instances familiar to their audience, their general
ideas about what is right and wrong, still less of showing that
they share the expectations of their neighbours regarding customary behaviour in specific contexts. It should not be thought
that kinship as a means of evaluating behaviour and placing
people is primarily employed by women. It is true that, in
general, women appear to have a more detailed and systematic
knowledge of kin ties than men do, in the Vale as elsewhere in
Britain. Men's knowledge of genealogical connections, while
usually pragmatic, is often no less extensive than that of women.
People who live in small rural neighbourhoods in the Vale and
who cannot be identified in terms of local kin ties are often
regarded with latent suspicion by their neighbours.

The importance of this process is obviously dependent on the
proportion of the inhabitants who have local kinship connections.
In one typical village in the Vale there are 112 people living in 31
households. Only 5 households, comprising 21 individuals, lack
kin ties with people living less than 10 miles away. A further 5
households, comprising 19 individuals, are linked through
kinship with people living in neighbouring parishes. Each of the
remaining 21 households, comprising 72 individuals, have kin
ties with other households in the village as well as with other
people living elsewhere in the Vale. It is sometimes said by
informants that people who have moved into the Vale never
'belong' until at least one of their children has married a member
of a local family. In general, informants have no clear definition
of what they mean by a local family, though those who consider
themselves to be members of one often differentiate between
what they call 'real Vale people' and others in discussing marriage
preferences. Such preferences, colloquially expressed in a variety
of ways, oblique, derisive or simply practical, are often best
identified by reference to the informant's evaluation of exceptions
rather than in looking for statements of rules. A woman is said
by her husband's kin and neighbours to be a successful farmer's
wife in spite of the fact that she is not a farmer's daughter and
was born and brought up in a town. A rich member of a long-
established gentry family marries, as his second wife, a woman
who was originally a servant in his household and his relatives

say: 'But she's really a decent little woman and Freddy has never been looked after so well in his life', or the envious say, with a sigh, of a marriage between people much better off than themselves, 'Well, money marries money, doesn't it?'

Impressions gained from such items of gossip may be confirmed by survey material. The vast majority of farmers' wives are, in fact, the daughters of farmers. Most members of the upper class, however defined, marry members of the upper class. Affinal ties tend to reinforce business connections between entrepreneurs.

The evaluative function of kinship is of particular importance in any study of the ways in which members of a local community identify and deal with unusual behaviour. The social roles, including kinship roles, filled by an individual actor are related to the readiness with which his family, friends and neighbours regard certain kinds of behaviour on his part as unusual. Furthermore, the readiness with which some kinds of unusual behaviour are recognized as evidence of mental disorder, by doctors as well as others, is related to the perceived social status of the individual. In relatively small communities, especially among what have been described as the highly homogeneous sections of the local population, kin ties are often more important than factors such as occupation, education and economic resources in the perception of social status in certain contexts. Where an individual has no extensive local network of kin ties, evaluation of unusual behaviour is often in terms of general or 'national' norms of expectation regarding the performance, for example, of occupational or 'social class' roles. Unusual behaviour on the part of those with 'close-knit' networks is more likely to be assessed in terms of flexible local norms which are adaptable to particular circumstances.

Kinship 2

J. Hubert

Reprinted with permission from *International Journal of Comparative Sociology*, 1966, pp. 61, 63–5, 79–80

This paper deals with a small sector of the results of research in progress among a set of middle-class families in London. The object of the study is to analyse the structure and estimate the magnitude and social significance of the kinship systems of British middle-class families.

It started with a pilot investigation of 30 families living on a private housing estate in North London, generally considered to be a 'good middle-class area', and having a high proportion of professional people living on it. Following the pilot survey, a random sample of 60 households was taken of the total population of electors' households on the estate (about 250 in all). This sample was heterogeneous in terms of marital status, family stage, age, religion and occupation, though the majority of individuals are married with children, Protestant, and the occupations of the heads of households fall within the broad band of 'middle-class' occupations . . .

The majority of the individuals in the Highgate sample are not born Londoners. Twenty-two out of 60 were born in London, the rest elsewhere. This is not surprising since one might expect a metropolitan population to be drawn from all over the country. But it contrasts with the origins of the working-class informants in Young and Willmott's survey of Bethnal Green, where 85 per cent of men and 85 per cent of women were born in London. Taking very crude geographical areas, a similar number of the Highgate individuals were born in the south (including the south-west) of England, and the north of England – 11 in each; 6 were born in Scotland, 1 in Ireland, and none in either Wales or East Anglia. A surprising number, 9 out of 38 non-Londoners, were born abroad, but only in rare cases were they born of foreign parents – in most cases their parents were living abroad, which in itself has some kinship relevance.

Most of the Highgate informants are thus migrants to London, and come from a wide range of different areas. By definition, all 30 married couples now live in London, and over two-thirds of them also first met their spouses in London; of the 21 pairs who met there, in only 5 cases were both born there; only 2 couples first met in any other 'home town' of either of them, the rest elsewhere in the country or abroad. Thus there was in nearly every case some degree of mobility before marriage, on the part of both men and women. Spouses were not, on the whole, drawn from a home environment and very few met either directly or indirectly through kin.

The 2 couples who met in their home town first met as children, which may or may not be considered to be meeting through kin. Of the others, only 4 couples met through relatives of some kind. Eleven couples met through their training, or in connection with their work, the other 13 either socially or in some indeterminate way. The high proportion of couples who met through college and work is perhaps typical of a professional group of people.

The fact that most informants married spouses from different areas implies that either their parents moved from the place they were born, or that the informants themselves left home before marriage. In fact in most cases both men and women had been living away from home for some time before they were married. This is not unexpected in the case of the men, but is so with the high proportion of women. Exactly two thirds of the wives were living away from home before they married, all of them for over a year, and the majority of them for five or more years.

What emerges from this is that the informants, and in particular the women, were independent of their parents before they married, at least in terms of residence. This contrasts with the working-class situation usually described, in which a girl lives at home until she marries and possibly for some time after she marries, until the couple can afford a place of their own. This early independence of girls from their parents, and especially from their mothers, is significant because it affects the type of relationship they have with their mothers, and attitude towards them, in adult life. Certainly we have not found situations at all like those described by Young and Willmott in Bethnal Green, where married daughters depend on their mothers not only for day-to-day services in the house, but also for emotional support in their daily life. The fact that this does not commonly occur in Highgate does not mean that the young wives do not have strong affective ties with their mothers, but residential independence long before marriage, combined with professional training and general independence of outlook, must lead to at least a different sort of relationship between married daughters and their mothers; one expressed not in terms of daily contact and moral support, but in perhaps maturer ways, with dependence only in times of crisis, e.g. in confinements and illness, not in the daily running of their lives.

Independence from parents is not merely an accidental concomitant of professional life. In most cases there is explicit agreement that children should be independent of their parents. This is manifested in earlier life by the willingness to send children to boarding schools. This attitude is apparent, when their children marry, in the strong preference on both sides for the young couple to set up house on their own, and in order that this should be possible parents will provide money towards a house rather than let them have to move in with them.

This stress on independence is significant as one of the main factors in the formation and development of kin relationships and attitudes. It means that young people can choose to live where they like, or where their work takes them, because the sort of relationship they grow up to have with their parents, and thus with their other kin, does not depend on frequent and intense contact of any kind. From childhood onwards there are different attitudes and expectations of parent-child behaviour, and different ways of expressing emotion.

This fact makes the assessment of relationships with kin somewhat more difficult. It means that frequency of contact cannot be taken in isolation as the criterion of a close relationship, and in fact it may sometimes be misleading as an indication of the strength of an affective tie between two kinsmen.

The relative freedom, in intellectual and emotional terms, of children from their parents, is important in various ways in their subsequent relationships with extra-familial kin in general. In one respect merely being residentially independent, especially in order to get professional training of some kind, enables persons to widen the scope of their contacts, and to meet people with whom they have things in common, e.g. similar training and intellectual disciplines. Young people will be freer to choose as friends people they like, and this may extend to members of the family as well. 'Community of interest' is often quoted as one of the most important things in the choice of friends from within the family. These people, by virtue of their background, education and occupation, have additional criteria to apply in their selection of kin. In fact one might have expected far fewer and less intense relationships with kin than is the case. What is surprising is not the paucity of kin relationships, but the number and richness of them considering the alternatives open to these individuals, and in many cases the lack of common interests between them.

To return to residential independence – it can be seen that it is not only our informants that have moved from their parental home or home area, but the majority of their kin have scattered too, in this and previous generations.

This does *not* mean that relationships are ineffective or necessarily distant between parents and children, or between other sorts of kin. The expected patterns of behaviour are based on strong affective ties which are not, however, expressed in frequent and intense interchange of contact and services or mutual dependence. Just because there is not frequent and intense contact does not mean that the affective tie does not exist. Nor that, in certain circumstances, kin are not called upon for assistance or advice. It is significant that certain services are given regardless of the geographical distance between kin. For example, one of the situations in which mothers are most frequently called in to help is at the birth of a baby. Nearly all the young wives had their mothers to stay in the house at least during one confinement, i.e. when she herself was in hospital. Many mothers travelled from great distances to do this, one or two even from abroad. Thus it can be seen that distance is no barrier to the sort of services these sort of people tend to need. Neither mothers nor daughters expect or want daily exchange of household services in normal circumstances, neither do they generally want constant contact with each other.

The type of relationship between parents and children obviously determines to a large extent the sort of relationships an individual will have with the rest of his or her kin. If a relationship with a parent is not manifested in constant interaction then two things result. Firstly, the ideology and attitudes with which a child is brought up will be of such a kind that he does not expect a close relationship with his extra-familial kin, and secondly, because of relatively infrequent contact with parents and siblings, genealogically more distant kin will enter into his life even less, and ties even with relatives who may be in constant contact with a parent may be dropped or maintained according to individual preferences. In this sense geographical distance may enable ties to be dropped without, generally, upsetting the relationships between other kin.

Considering a wide divergence of occupations and cultural interests and, in some cases, of class background, a great many ties are maintained with relatives. Generally, contact is not frequent, but this seems to bear little direct relation to geographical distance except insofar as the latter acts as an extreme limiting factor. Where people want to see their kin, wide distances are covered relatively often. Expectations of extra-familial kin behaviour do not usually demand frequent contact, even when proximity allows it. With closer kin, specifically parents and siblings, there is more evidence to support the hypothesis (often held for all kin) that as much interaction will take place as possible at all times. Even for parents and siblings this is not entirely so, but here behaviour approximates more to this hypothesis, and this is so in spite of the ideology of independence with which children grow up, and the complex set of circumstances arising out of a wide range of occupations and cultural interests.

Ties with kin outside the family of origin are maintained on a more selective basis, and they are often manifested only in contact of an intermittent nature. Partly, this is because these ties are not often of a very strong kind – it is fair to say that to a great extent these people function independently of the majority of their kin. But it is also partly because more overt behaviour patterns of any more intense nature are not expected between members of these families.

Sex Roles in Western Society
Ann Oakley

Reprinted with permission from Ann Oakley, *Towards a New Society: Sex, Gender and Society*, Maurice Temple Smith, 1972, pp. 150–7

In Western societies today, sex *is* an organizing principle of social structure, and, despite popular belief to the contrary, it plays a great part in determining social roles. So it is not surprising to find that a great deal of anxiety in Western culture has its roots in the demands made by gender roles. Psychiatrists tell us that a great deal of our security as adults comes from staying within the boundaries of these roles – that we must stay within them if mental health is to be preserved. The psychiatrist Anthony Storr writes:

> ...in Western civilization at the present time, men who consult a psychiatrist on account of emotional problems very commonly show too little aggression, whereas their feminine counterparts often exhibit too much... the pattern of the too-compliant male and the over-dominant female is so common that it accounts for a great deal of marital disharmony... Neurotic men complain of their wives' dominance, neurotic women of the husbands' lack of it... In such a marriage, each partner will generally show characteristics belonging to the opposite sex and will have failed to demarcate and define their respective roles in a partnership where the boundaries between male and female are blurred rather than accentuated... The emancipation of women is an inescapable fact... but we are far from having solved the problems created by women's freedom... A confident belief in one's own masculinity or femininity is a fundamental part of human identity.

This fear certainly echoes the fears of ordinary people. For example, studies of attitudes towards the employment of women show that, bound up with people's beliefs about appropriate behaviour, is a fear that women will become 'masculinized' by employment, that they will become aggressive and dominant, and that family discord or breakdown will result. A UNESCO study found that 'The women themselves distrust their own aggressiveness which reveals itself when they acquire their new status – the harmony between man and wife is at stake, the possibility of true love seems to be less certain.'

As in the past, these fears arise at a time when changes in the roles of the sexes are seen to be imminent. In modern industrial society changes tend to be especially visible, since there is an emphasis on change rather than on the endurance of tradition; but in fact, despite 'emancipation' and despite the appearance of change in sex roles, fundamental differences between male and female work roles persist. Even where there is change, people often hold to traditional ways of thinking and behaving.

In all industrialized countries there is a marked differentiation by gender of most if not all occupations. One basic occupation in particular, that of housewife, is exclusively feminine. (The definition of 'housewife' here is 'the person in a household who is mainly responsible for the domestic duties'.) In Great Britain, 76 per cent of all employed women are housewives, and so are 93 per cent of non-employed women. The high percentage of housewives among the non-employed women is accounted for by the fact that many of them have children – nearly 60 per cent, with 28 per cent having children under two. Child care is, of course, an almost exclusively feminine task, both in the home and out of it. Mothers are responsible for the daily care of children, not fathers; females staff playgroups, nurseries, primary schools and (to a lesser extent) secondary schools; nurses, including child nurses, are almost all females (the figure is 90 per cent in Germany, Austria, Great Britain, Denmark, Norway, Switzerland, Finland and Greece). In fact most professional women are either nurses or teachers. In the United States females make up 86 per cent, and in Great Britain 80 per cent, of all primary school teachers.

Within industry there is a great deal of differentiation by sex. Most women, in all industrialized countries, are concentrated in textile and clothing manufacture and in food processing – usually between a third and two thirds of all working women are found in these industries. Since the Second World War, however, there has been spectacular growth in the employment of women in offices, so that in America, for instance, about 60 per cent of working women are in white-collar jobs. These secretarial jobs require a relatively short and inexpensive training and the behaviour they demand fits with the traditional female role: a male secretary except in certain high-level occupations such as the Civil Service, would be unthinkable in most countries. (Similarly, of course, the employment of women in factories producing domestic goods – textiles, clothes and food – reflects their conventional role.)

On the whole, males command the majority of jobs carrying high prestige, high skill and high income, and this is true throughout the industrial world. For example, of all professional scientific and technical qualifications gained by full-time students in Great Britain in 1969, men took 77 per cent and women 7 per cent. In the engineering and electrical industries in Britain in 1968, 17 per cent of the men employed worked in semi-skilled jobs, but 48 per cent of the women. Of all managers of large establishments tabulated for Britain in 1966, 87 per cent were men and 13 per cent women: of all foremen and supervisors 82 per cent were men and 18 per cent women. Women make up 3 per cent of all barristers in the USA, 4 per cent in Great Britain, and 7 per cent in Sweden. A mere 0·06 per cent of all engineers are female in Britain, 0·07 per cent in the USA and 3·7 per cent in France. While women in the professions receive the same rates of pay as men, in other jobs they do not: thus skill, prestige, financial reward and gender are interrelated in a complex but consistent fashion.

An index of this consistency – which has much to do with Western definitions of masculinity and femininity – is that in the United States in 1950 seven tenths of all working women were in twenty occupations, clustered around domestic and clerical work, nursing, teaching, and unskilled factory work. In Sweden, a country with a very contrasting history, the proportion in 1962 was exactly the same. In these twenty occupations in the United States only 12 per cent of men were to be found; in Sweden, twelve years later, 11·9 per cent. In both countries, and also in Britain, Belgium, Denmark, France, Germany, Italy, the Netherlands and Norway, two-fifths of all working women were in five occupations. Much of the differentiation indicated by these figures has remained stable or even increased in recent years, despite the widespread belief that the sexes are becoming interchangeable through equal access to many occupations.

Apart from the jobs that men and women take up, there are other ways in which the statistics of employment show the impact of sex on social role.

Women's careers are characteristically discontinuous, whereas men's are not. A significant proportion of the female industrial labour force consists of part-time workers – at least 10 per cent in Canada and Federal Germany, 18 per cent in Britain, and more than 20 per cent in Sweden, Denmark and the United States. The tendency to choose part-time work is a reflection of women's domestic responsibilities; in one sample, 18 per cent of women working full time had children under sixteen, against 53 per cent of those working part time. Domestic responsibility usually means that a woman has to give up work completely for several years at a time, and only return to it gradually. Pauline Pinder, in a survey undertaken for Political and Economic Planning in 1969, described the difference between the careers of men and women:

The average man's working life extends uninterruptedly from the end of school or training until retirement; but the average woman is increasingly likely to have a three phase working life: the first, from leaving school to the birth of her first child, when she will normally work full time; the second, while her children are young, when she may withdraw wholly or partly from the labour force; the third, from the time the youngest child goes to school until she reaches the age of retirement, during which she will probably return to full-time work.

It is not just in the rhythms of their careers that men and women differ. There are extensive differences bound up with the general roles of the sexes and with the expectations and opportunities they lead to. Tradition and prejudice continue to affect these opportunities, so that jobs which are traditionally feminine tend to remain so – usually through some rationalization about their suitability for women. The young woman deciding on a job or career will tend to reject (or be rejected by) 'masculine' occupations and consider only those to which she has easy access as potential sources of satisfaction. Here she will be greatly influenced by her upbringing, which will equip her better for jobs that demand the sort of 'feminine' character traits that are likely to be instilled in her. The effect of this is made still stronger by the fact that breaking into a man's occupation in itself demands a good share of the 'masculine' virtues of initiative, effort and aggressiveness.

Finally there is her education – a more potent factor in forming sex differences than most people are ready to admit. In theory, education is supposed to be equally available to males and females in our contemporary industrial society, and this is thought to be one of the most concrete effects of post-war democratic ideology and of twentieth-century female emancipation. What are the facts?

At the primary and secondary levels the number of girls at school is nearly (though not quite) in proportion to their numbers in the population as a whole. In North America in 1963, for example, girls made up 48·4 per cent of primary school pupils and 49·4 per cent of secondary school pupils although females outnumber males as a whole.

At the lowest end of education there is a persistent tendency for illiteracy to be more frequent in females than in males. In Greece, 30 per cent of women are illiterate compared with 8 per cent of men; in Yugoslavia, 34 per cent of women and 12 per cent of men; in Spain, 18 per cent of women and 8 per cent of men.

But it is at the highest levels of education that the disparity is most marked. For every hundred people aged twenty to twenty-four in higher education in 1965 there were 6·6 females in the United Kingdom, 5·3 in Denmark, 2·3 in Switzerland and 15·2 in Bulgaria. While women made up about two-fifths of the intake of university students in Britain in 1967, women take less than a third of all final degrees and only about one-ninth of all higher degrees.

These facts clearly reflect the belief that education is more important for a boy than it is for a girl – as indeed it is in a society where 'work' is the activity of all adult men but only some women. And it is not merely in the numbers receiving an education that gender plays a part: it also influences the subjects they study. In the United States in 1964, 46 per cent of Masters' degrees in education were gained by women but only 10 per cent of these in science. Of all those studying medicine, dentistry and health in Britain in 1967, two-thirds were men. Similar disproportions can be found elsewhere.

To sum up, then, we can say that the chief importance of biological sex in determining social roles is in providing a universal and obvious division around which other distinctions can be organized. In deciding which activities are to fall on each side of the boundary, the important factor is culture. In early upbringing, in education and in their adult occupations, males and females are pressed by our society into different moulds. At the end of this process it is not surprising that they come to regard their distinctive occupations as predetermined by some general law, despite the fact that in reality the biological differences between the sexes are neither so large nor so invariable as most of us suppose, and despite the way in which other cultures have developed sex roles quite different from our own, which seem just as natural and just as inevitable to them as ours do to us.

Further Reading: **Family**

† N. W. BELL AND E. F. VOGEL (Eds.): *A Modern Introduction to the Family*, The Free Press, 1960.
* M. FARMER: *The Family*, Longmans, 1970.
* R. FLETCHER: *The Family and Marriage*, Penguin Books, 1962 (and 2nd edn.).
* C. C. HARRIS: *The Family*, Allen & Unwin, 1969.
  A. MYRDAL AND V. KLEIN: *Women's Two Roles*, Routledge & Kegan Paul, 2nd edn., 1968.
* J. AND E. NEWSON: *Patterns of Infant Care*, Penguin Books, 1965.
* R. AND R. RAPOPORT: 'The Dual Career Family', *Human Relations*, Vol. 24, No. 6.
* P. TOWNSEND: *The Family Life of Old People*, Routledge & Kegan Paul, 1957 (and abridged, Penguin Books, 1963).
* P. WILLMOTT AND M. YOUNG: *Family and Class in a London Suburb*, Routledge & Kegan Paul, 1960 (and Penguin Books).
† R. F. WINCH: *The Modern Family*, 3rd edn., Holt Rinehart & Winston, 1971.
* M. YOUNG AND P. WILLMOTT: *Family and Kinship in East London*, Routledge & Kegan Paul, 1957 (and Penguin Books).

* Available in paperback
† Reference

2 Community

It is difficult to find an acceptable definition of the term community because it is used in so many different ways: for example, to describe an area on the one hand where all the inhabitants are able to have face-to-face contacts, or on the other hand an area the size of a large city. For some the boundaries of their area may reflect merely administrative convenience; for others they may represent strong feelings of common interest. Community tends to be a God word. In many circumstances, when it is mentioned, we are expected to abase ourselves before it rather than attempt to define it. It contains some or all of the following: a territorial area, a complex of institutions within an area, and a sense of 'belonging'.

The notion of territorial area is present in most definitions of community, though even here qualifications have to be made. The word has been used to describe groups of people, physicians, lawyers, and others, who are in the same kind of occupational or professional position. Locality is relevant in all the readings which follow for one reason or another. Within the distinct area which it covers, the boundaries of which may be blurred for all kinds of reasons, the community contains certain types of institutions which lead to the development of distinctive sets of social relationships.

Communities vary a good deal in the ways in which they are independent of, or dependent upon, close ties with other communities. Isolation in Britain tends to exist only in remote rural areas, and the character of the fifth of the population living in rural areas is influenced by the increasing presence of former town dwellers who come to live in the country though often continuing to work in the towns. The sense of community, of belonging, is not confined to those living in close-knit villages: it has been documented in the studies of East London, by Young, Willmott and others. In his consideration of the characteristics of the city, Wirth emphasizes a set of social conditions, notably the size of the population, the density of settlement, and the heterogeneity of the inhabitants.

Certain factors help to determine the nature of the development of a community. They include: time and common residence, shared activities and the degree of involvement in them, the characteristics of members (especially where they come from), and the kinds of leadership which are present. Frankenberg provides a useful continuum of communities, from 'truly rural' to examples drawn from housing estates and central areas of cities. In some cases the feeling of community may be only a residue after the bonds which kept the community together begin to disintegrate.

A classification by Curle of villages in Devon into four types of social sub-system is discussed in Sprott's *Human Groups*. It provides a useful frame of reference, distinguishing as it does between two types which are 'closed' and two which are 'open'. Closed but integrated is the relatively static traditional type whereas closed but disintegrating represents its decay and loss of vitality (in part because of the age structure) in the interaction between the inhabitants. Open but not integrated reflects the 'atomized' pattern of new suburbs transported to a rural setting, whereas open and integrated suggests open and flexible but equipped with common standards and a strong sense of community.

The first two readings relate to the 'common bonds' which members of a community share. These are considered, by Morris and Mogey in the first, in relation to five basic roles, of new householder, tenant, neighbour, parent, together with a residential community role, which assume different degrees of importance with the passage of time or because of the changed family circumstances of the inhabitants. Berinsfield, where the survey was conducted, is an untypical example of a new housing development in that most of the inhabitants previously lived together in a hutted group of buildings where levels of amenity were low. Their previous acquaintance made for certain differences, as did the scheme for rehousing whereby no pair of neighbours was housed together, but the bonds can be considered, with others, in relation to any neighbourhood.

Since 1919 a larger and larger proportion of the population have been housed in public housing on 'estates'. The reading about Watling relates to one of the first of these developments raising questions about the community life which develops and the pressures which affect the forms it takes. In particular, brief reference here is made to the factors leading to differentiation, among them the growth of organizations and the economic standing of the families. One of the crucial points is the way in which the sense of community which originally arose from facing common problems dissipated itself when new and sectional loyalties began to develop.

Questions about the journey to work and the mobility of the population, and the effect of these on the level of commitment to any 'community', arise from the study since Watling and their life there 'belonged to only part of their day, and merely to a passing period of their lives'.

Cohen focuses upon the East End of London as a 'reception centre' for newcomers, with each group bringing distinctive traditions and cultural values. A good deal of current writing about minorities focuses upon processes of assimilation or accommodation but, as he points out, there was no question for these subcommunities of assimilation into a dominant indigenous culture. It was a pattern of integration which, until recently, meant newcomers starting as outsiders and becoming insiders later by dissociating themselves from more conspicuous outsiders. The process has gone on through conflict rather than harmony. The three social factors which underpinned the integration are seen as: the extended kinship structures, regulating socialization in each subcommunity; the ecological structure of the working-class neighbourhood; and the structure of the local economy, all of which interacted with each other. With their elimination, Cohen suggests, the present state of tension has developed. He identifies three distinct strata within both the community as a whole and the subcommunities: the socially mobile elite, the respectables, and the lumpen.

The changes began to gather momentum from the 1950s, when new towns and estates were built and large-scale redevelopment took place, leading to the entry of new minorities such as West Indians and Pakistanis. Families leave, firms move out and property speculators enter, and the neighbourhood changes its nature. Trends in industry that developed affected the craft industries and small-scale production in the East End, and the situation is made worse by what is seen as a crisis of indigenous leadership. The East End is a large area to generalize about but the analysis indicates clearly the interrelationship of the different elements in the life of communities of this kind and their changing patterns of life.

In some respects **Raban,** in the next reading, projects a view of the city and in particular of metropolitan life which echoes sociologists such as Durkheim, Wirth and others who stressed the anonymity, impersonality, and segregation of the city. But he does identify the gathering together of a group, or 'a community of people' as he calls them, who share ideas: 'narrow, passionate *cognoscenti* bolstered by received ideas, given to clubs and cliques and intense sectarian debates'. He sees them as part of the essence of city life, drawn together by political or religious beliefs, common-interest groups, keeping the outside world at bay. Raban suggests it would be easy to see beliefs such as those of the Krishna people as merely grotesque, but that they are a response to the unreality and diversity of the city. They are symptoms of serious urban conditions: clubs, cliques, cells and the wire are all 'foxholes for all those whom the city has isolated, for whom no longer reality is habitable'. The city is a place to live out the dream.

Mobility within the urban setting, and in particular the different rates of turnover of the population in different kinds of areas, is one theme of the study of a redevelopment area in central Liverpool by Vereker and Mays. It is not fortuitous that areas of high mobility are reception areas for immigrants, and often have been traditionally so because of the combination of type of house and accommodation, level of amenities, and other factors. Rex and Moore's book on Sparkbrook is the best-known study of an 'immigrant' area.

The reading from **Illsley, Finlayson and Thompson,** documents the movement of young adults into and out of Aberdeen. Its relevance to the community is in drawing attention to factors from outside, such as the demands of the occupational structure, which bring about movement and influence the commitment that is felt towards the place people live. Differences between the social groups emerge very clearly.

The reading from **Stacey,** about the small town of Banbury in Oxfordshire documents the movement of immigrants into the town and how this arose from changes in the social and economic structure. In consequence of the growth of the town and the entry of new kinds of inhabitants a distinction arises between traditionalists and non-traditionalists, each with distinct systems of values and ways of life. This has implications not only for the organizations in the town but also for its social class and its political divisions.

Mobility, and the confrontation of 'old' and 'new', may lead to changes in the structure of power. **Elias and Scotson,** in the first reading on the theme of leadership, discuss what they call the quality of 'sociological oldness' whereby working-class families living for a long time in the same area may exercise power by monopolizing key positions in local institutions rather than by the inheritance of property. This arises, the authors suggest, from the greater cohesion and solidarity, and the greater uniformity of norms of the group. The study was undertaken in a rural area of Leicestershire where the old-established 'villagers' came into conflict with the inhabitants of the new estate grafted on to the old village. This is shown to be the result of becoming interdependent as neighbours. Finally, the stereotyped image of the Estate in the minds of the villagers was reinforced by a minority of Estate youngsters whose behaviour was bad.

The tensions and conflicts which arise in the main from social class, leading in this case to the erection of a wall between old and new housing development (also owner-occupier and tenant respectively) is documented in a fascinating way in Collison's *The Cutteslowe Walls*. There is also material in it about the ways in which common residence and shared social class affiliations tend to go together.

Like the material on Banbury that on Glossop, by **Birch,** provides a historical perspective which helps to show how changes in the social structure have led to new sources of leadership. In the past high status, influence and political power went together in a clear hierarchical structure but now the leaders of industry, for instance, are not rooted in the community in the same way, nor do they play a prominent part in it. There is now no established elite. The opening of new avenues of social advancement by education have had disadvantages, it is suggested, for small towns like Glossop.

Miller, in the third reading on leadership, provides a comparative focus on three cities, two in America and one, Bristol, in Britain, with regard to the influence of different groups on community decision-making. The differences are striking, notably the way in which the 'Key Influentials' in 'English City' come from a broad spectrum of community life.

It is suggested tentatively that a different occupational prestige system and a different local political system explain the variations between 'Key Influentials' in the cities discussed.

The reading from the **Buchanan** Report on Traffic in Towns raises some general questions about aspects of the urban environment. In particular the problems arising from the presence of cars in larger and larger numbers are discussed, since they are responsible for a great deal of noise, as well as danger and anxiety generally. Consequences for the planning of particular neighbourhoods and for patterns of shopping and play are among the issues which arise. Altogether the reading emphasizes the importance not only of looking at the situation as it is at the present time but anticipating the changes which will take place, and the problems they create from the point of view of amenity and quality of life, in the future.

There is a world-wide crisis in the technology of city development, a crisis which worries the inhabitants more than the technologists. The whole question of urban change is the subject of the reading by **Page** which links with that by Buchanan. It is one in which people affected are more and more likely to want to act to prevent redevelopment. Physical deterioration is considered in relation to redevelopment and change, and the effects on people nearby, and to 'new urban hardware' which leads to increased noise, pollution and the like. Planning practice is hung up on a kind of utopian fallacy that one day the city will be complete and transitory development problems will suddenly disappear.

Changing patterns of energy use are considered, and both their favourable and unfavourable consequences. The growth in transport indicates an enormous increase in the consumption of energy per head by the end of the century. Although official reports on the environment have indicated the problems and the kinds of action that are necessary, the *laissez-faire* approach continues. Whereas a lead might be expected from statutory undertakings they have failed for the most part to accept their responsibilities. The reading concludes with a plea for urgent action to anticipate the threats to our urban environment and establish acceptable and necessary standards for urban living.

Common Bonds 1
R. N. Morris and J. Mogey

Reprinted with permission from R. N. Morris and J. Mogey, *The Sociology of Housing*, London, Routledge & Kegan Paul, 1965, pp. 44–53

Informants perceived five common bonds which could be expressed in role terms. Firstly, all were new-house dwellers. The 'householder role' covers all references to problems of gardening, and the maintenance and furnishing of the new house. Secondly, all were tenants of the same local authority. The 'tenant role' covers activities in this role-set: notably the payment of rent and complaints about the house and amenities, in so far as these were actually voiced corporately through the tenants' association. Thirdly, everyone had to adjust to new neighbours, as no pair of old neighbours was rehoused together. 'Neighbour roles' include adjustments to the neighbours, and the establishment of norms of neighbourly behaviour.

Fourthly, nearly all informants had young children. 'Parental roles' comprised those needs which were related to the children's behaviour, or suggested provisions for their welfare. Finally, many families felt the need to join with other residents in organizing social activities and entertainments, or in providing other services, designed to benefit all adults. 'Residential community roles' includes all references to the residential community as a whole. Most of these references were to the social centre, the need for more amenities, or to the provision of social events for the adults.

The common bonds of the householder role were mainly intangible. There was, firstly, widespread excitement and pride occasioned by living in a new house, after experience of a hut or of life with in-laws. This normally found expression through delight with the running hot water, the bathroom and the w.c. These correlated consistently and highly with house satisfaction. One respondent assured us that her ten-year-old son was so thrilled that he had insisted on taking a bath every day since they had moved into their new home. At the time of the interview, this remarkable performance had been maintained for three months.

Similarly, many families took a new pride in themselves and their appearance.

The second common bond of the householder role concerned the process of adjustment to the new home – finding the appropriate furniture and cultivating the garden:

> This is the first place where we could take an interest in the garden and surroundings and home.

For the first few months, this process was so universal that whenever a householder looked out of the window he could see others coping with the same problems. New furnishings and appliances were a constant source of interest:

> The usual way – you start off with a pushbike and finish up with a car.
> Everyone's trying to be better, buying new furniture.

The interest was not simply part of the competition for status which occurs in any relatively new group; it was also an attempt to establish new norms of equipment and behaviour which would be appropriate for their role as dwellers in a new house. Whenever a resident went out, or paused for breath in the garden, he could see neighbours engaged in the same activities, and glad to exchange a grumble or a tip.

The tenant role offered a second important potential link between families, for all came within the responsibility of the same local authority. This bond has usually been important in leading to the formation of a tenants' association to request and sometimes agitate for the rapid installation of important services; but in Berinsfield the situation was more complex. The history of the hutted camp had been marked by sporadic and sometimes open conflict with the RDC, and by intervals of sullen non-cooperation. In July 1958, only half the respondents believed that the council's allocation policy would be fair and open. In November 1958, about 70 per cent of the rehoused families thought that the council had been fair; but very few of the families still in huts retained this view.

In the first set of interviews, references to the tenant role were mostly concerned with the problem of finding the extra rent for the new house. For most families the increase was between 30s and 40s (£1·50 and £2) per week. Later, when most families had adjusted to the increase, this problem received references only from the most recent arrivals. There was little spontaneous suggestion of a cooperative campaign for lower rents, or of help for families who had difficulty in meeting the extra commitments. The rent issue was quickly overshadowed by references to the open front gardens; and to the desire for a tenants' association which would ensure a prompt response to tenants' complaints.

The 'open fronts' were the major point of conflict in November 1958 between the council and the rehoused families. The council's insistence on this feature of the plan meant that most families had no separate front gardens, and little defence against any children who chose to stare through their windows. This threat to privacy was reinforced by a fear that the standard of maintenance applied by the RDC to the open fronts would fall below the tenants' aspirations. Our tape recordings of the tenants' association meetings for this period illustrate the importance of the open fronts controversy in the later months of 1958. The open fronts still gave rise to quite a few complaints in the following July:

> They should have put proper fences up in the beginning.
> They should give us front gardens, more privacy.
> They should do the front gardens; have a little wall in front, or railings.

One family went further, and expressed the view that:

> Half the rent you pay should be for privacy.

The neighbour role was also crucial at first, and of diminishing importance subsequently. The 'respectables' voiced the fear that the new houses might be allotted to 'scruffy' families; and some wished that families had been grouped according to this standard:

> They tried hard to put people who were in bad conditions into a house. The only thing I think is wrong is to put all those rough people in. They should have been put all together – I don't think they will change.
> If they wanted a model village, they got the wrong people – people who do not care how they live.

Rehousing gave every family a new pair of next-door neighbours; most families had previously been acquainted only superficially with their new neighbours. As the neighbour role is usually of crucial significance on a new estate, it was to be expected in the first two sets of interviews that neighbour roles would be critical. Satisfaction with the neighbours consistently implied satisfaction with the residential community; while dissatisfaction with the neighbours almost always meant dissatisfaction with the residential community.

The importance of the neighbours was not, however, as striking on this analysis as had been expected. Since most families were previously acquainted, less status competition was necessary to crystallize the village's social structure. Prior acquaintance reduced the importance of nearness and unavoidable contact in determining relationships; from this point of view, Berinsfield was not a normal housing estate.

When families are tied to their homes, their range of acquaintances is very limited. They will tend to expect the immediate neighbours to fill the roles of both neighbour and friend. These two roles, however, may be interpreted in a variety of ways. If the families' expectations are compatible, they will generally play both roles towards each other, and the primary social relationships of phase one will then develop. These two roles are not completely compatible, however; if families' expectations are different, they will tend to play a narrow range of roles towards each other, and the secondary relationships of phase two will develop. When two families are already acquainted, the first exploratory phase may be unnecessary. This argument would account for the lack of evidence of obvious 'phase one' behaviour at Berinsfield, especially among the locals; for there was no indication that mutual help, borrowing and lending increased as families tried to adjust to their new environment.

The fourth common bond was the parental role. Unlike the first three, this tended to grow in importance with the passage of time. Respondents quickly noticed the lack of amenities for the children, and the need for cooperative action to discipline the more unruly ones. These were complementary, for it was hoped that good amenities would alleviate and in the long run remove the nuisance which the children represented to some residents. Many of the children from Field Farm had grown accustomed to roaming and playing wherever they chose; protests were largely futile:

My children are getting out of hand since we moved up here:
I want to get out.

Many respondents hoped that this behaviour would not persist
in the new village, for they regarded tidiness and the preservation
of trees and grass as the most important means of making
Berinsfield beautiful. There were also requests for a bus to take
the younger children to their school, about two miles from the
village. This request was met, through the efforts of the tenants'
association, at the beginning of the 1959–60 school year; previously the children had had to walk along a very muddy path,
or along the edge of a fast and dangerous main road.

The role of the children in determining the nature of the contacts between neighbours was also important. Their behaviour
and needs may produce either cooperation or conflict: much will
depend on the adjustment which the parents have already made
to each other. The age of the children is important in determining
the radius of their influence as a common bond. When they are
young, it tends to operate within the neighbourhood. As they
grow older, it tends to move to the residential community, and
then farther afield. Disciplinary action at the community level
was accordingly sought in relation to the older children; while
trouble with the neighbours was the main threat represented by
the younger ones.

Residential community roles represented the fifth common
bond. References were mainly to social events for the adults and
to the need for amenities, and occasionally a parish council, for
the whole village. These references tended to become of greater
importance as families adapted themselves to their new homes
and neighbours. Social events were offered regularly by the social
centre during the year of our survey; yet in spite of the relative
success of bingo and jumble sales, the organizers felt that the
centre attracted little sustained interest and support. At the time
of the move, they assured us that attendance by the locals had
become negligible; and very few of the strangers ever attended.
In this respect, too, the phase hypothesis applied only weakly to
Berinsfield.

Residential community roles had nevertheless become the
most important category by the end of the research, and social
events for the adults were one of the principal manifest needs of
the village. There was thus a contrast between the expressed need
for residential community roles and the limited use made of the

available opportunities. This may reflect simply the absence of facilities to perform desired roles, such as those of shopper, church member and drinker. In part, it may be due to ignorance of the opportunities available. It may also, however, be related to the community centre's normal function of crystallizing differences within the residential community, which will alienate some groups and lead to a demand for activities which the centre cannot provide, or for existing activities in more congenial company. Finally, since the centre, like the general store, was still housed in a dilapidated hut, it may have lost status through its inability to acquire a new home.

Common Bonds 2
Ruth Durant

Reprinted with permission from Ruth Durant, *Watling, A Social Survey*, London, P. S. King & Son, 1939, pp. 42–9

At the end of this early period, in the summer of 1931, the Estate had acquired much of the likeness of a town and had lost much of its earlier resemblance to an intimate community of people. The people themselves had become more like strangers to each other. In other words, a housing estate which is faced with its specific problems is more likely to develop social consciousness and keenness for local unity than a modern town pursuing its daily routine.

But it has to be remembered that a housing estate will never exactly resemble an ordinary town; a number of important differences remain which at least offer the possibility of its being favourably distinguished by the intensity of local social life. Indeed, so far as Watling is concerned, this seems to have been achieved. Its development was positive as compared, firstly, with the institutional bareness of Watling's early life, and secondly, as compared with the dreary social existence of suburbia. It was negative when its temper and tempo are set against Watling's early keenness on its own behalf. Whilst new instruments of corporate activity had been created, the old communal enthusiasm had markedly waned.

One set of causes had been primarily responsible for this

result: forces inherent in the development of the Estate itself were destructive of community life. Growth of local organizations necessarily means decline of ambition to secure them. This is an obvious fact which needs no elaboration. Moreover, at first the desire to equip the Estate with amenities was common. There was no difficulty in getting various groups of people to agree on a plan of campaign. Later, it was more difficult for them to agree on the administration of existing amenities especially since new residents had arrived who had not shared the failures and successes of the early struggle. Moreover, there was no institution whose authority was recognized by all people and to which a final appeal could be addressed.

Economic and social differentiation was a further result of Watling's growth. In the early period the major difficulties were common to all people. For many, however, adjustment to their environment meant to become acutely aware of their individual worries. The financial burden of higher rent, more fares and instalment fees on furniture weighed heavily. The weariness of long train journeys made itself felt. Poverty loomed larger than loneliness. People were too worried to develop social interests, and often too tired to seek entertainment. Just when communal life was most in need of their support, when local societies were in their infancy, the economic crisis set in and endangered the existence of innumerable households. For at least one-quarter of all families the margin of comfort was extremely small. That means that illness or unemployment, or the loss of a wage-earner, completely upsets their carefully balanced budgets. Hence the crisis not only enhanced the difficulties of needy families but it also pushed more households into that category.

Simultaneously, it sharpened the cleavage between poor and well-to-do people on the Estate. There were amongst the small families of the Civil Servants, transport workers and other people in secure positions, a considerable number who were not immediately affected by external influences, such as the crisis. In fact, they profited from the fall in prices and felt richer, whilst the others became poorer. Thus complaints about snobbishness and also apathy were repeatedly heard during the same period. None of these tendencies was very beneficial to social development.

A further factor created and accentuated differentiation. From 1928 immigration to the Estate slowed down; it became subject to vacancies only. Although large in total, immigration henceforth became an individual event, problems of adjustment to the Estate an individual experience for each particular family, and their solutions became extremely individualistic too. People either completely shut themselves up in their homes or they went to one of the existing local societies which competed for their favour. Each of these, whether it provided politics, garden seeds or nursing services, was now a closed unit. Hence, by joining, the newly acquired member was not hindered from himself becoming self-contained.

Moreover, it became increasingly difficult for the residents to identify this place with their existence. They realized that, sooner rather than later, they would have to leave it again: the individual family was so mobile. During the ten years which have passed since the first houses were occupied the total number of families who have lived on the Estate is nearly twice its maximum capacity. One out of every two families which have ever come to the Estate moved elsewhere before the end of ten years. Almost half of all families stayed there less than five years. Watling belonged to only one part of their day, and merely to a passing period of their lives.

Subcultural Conflict and Working-Class Community
Phil Cohen

Reprinted with permission from Phil Cohen, *Subcultural Conflict and Working-Class Community*, Working Paper in Cultural Studies, Centre for Contemporary Culture, University of Birmingham, 1972, pp. 9–21

Since the very beginning of the industrial revolution the East End has provided a kind of unofficial 'reception centre' for a succession of immigrant communities, in flight from religious persecution or economic depression. First came the Huguenots, spinners and weavers, at the end of the seventeenth century, and still today their presence survives in surnames, and place names in the area. Then, throughout the nineteenth century there was a constant immigration of Irish, mostly labourers, and small traders from Central Europe, and in the last two decades of course Pakistanis, and to a lesser extent West Indians and Greek

Cypriots. Today the East End is indeed like 'five parts of the world, put in one place'.

Each subcommunity brought with it not just specific skills, but also of course its own traditions, and cultural values. There was no question of assimilation into a dominant indigenous culture – either that of the 'native' dockland community, or of the English ruling class. What in fact happened, until recently, was that each new subcommunity, in turn, and over time became an accepted, but differentiated part of the 'East End' by allying itself with the longer established sections of the community against another, later subcommunity. The outsiders become established, become insiders, by dissociating themselves from an even more conspicuous set of outsiders. Perhaps it is a natural human tendency to draw the line under one's own feet; at any rate in the East End integration has proceeded by means of conflict, rather than by dissolving it.

There are three main social factors underpinning this pattern of integration: the extended kinship structures which regulate socialization in each subcommunity; secondly the ecological structure of the working-class neighbourhood; and finally the structure of the local economy. In reality these factors interact and reinforce each other – but it is important to understand them, because it is precisely the elimination of these factors, the transformation of these structures which has caused the present state of tension in the area. So let's look at them briefly, one by one.

Extended kinship networks

This is a system by which the family of marriage remains linked by an intricate web of rights and obligations to the respective families of origin, and serves as a link between them. Based in the first instance on maintaining the close relationship between mother and daughter, so that when she gets married the daughter will continue to live as close as she can to 'mum', and extending in widening circles to include uncles and aunts, grandparents, nephews and nieces, and their relations, this system virtually turns the family into a micro-community, and in fact provides for many of the functions of mutual aid and support that are elsewhere carried out by agencies in the community. Obviously such a system makes for cultural continuity and stability; it reduces generational conflict to a minimum – leaving home and getting married do not become life and death issues as they do in the nuclear family. Firstly because the extended family constitutes a much richer and more diversified human environment for the child; secondly children tend to stay at home until they get married, or to put it another way, only leave in order to do so; thirdly getting married does not involve any divorce between the young couple and their families, but rather recruits new members into the kinship network. And although the extended family preserves historical traditions of the subcommunity, handing them on from generation to generation, it does not serve to insulate it from the 'outside world'. On the contrary it serves as the basis for eventual integration. For the family both becomes firmly anchored in a given locality (matrilocal residence as it's technically called) and the network is continually expanding outwards; the net result is that over time the ties of neighbourhood are extended into ties of kinship and vice versa. If everybody knows everybody else in traditional neighbourhoods it is not because they are related through interlocking kinship networks, but that schoolmates, workmates, pubmates while they may or may not be related to relatives of one's own, will tend to be related to other mates, or mates to other relatives of one's own. But this can't be explained simply in terms of the internal dynamic of kinship, the ecology of the neighbourhood also plays a part.

Ecology of the working-class neighbourhood

The close-packed back to backs, facing each other across alley-ways or narrow streets, corner shops and local pubs, the turning, all this helps to shape and support the close textures of traditional working-class life, its sense of solidarity, its local loyalties and traditions. And this in turn is underpinned by the extended kinship networks of the traditional working-class family, which have been so well observed in Bethnal Green.

But how does the ecology of the neighbourhood work in practice? Let's take the street as an example. In these neighbourhoods the street forms a kind of 'communal space', a mediation between the totally private space of the family, with its intimate involvements, and the totally public space e.g. parks, thoroughfares, etc., where people relate to each other as strangers, and with indifference. The street, then, is a space where people can relate as neighbours, can express a degree of involvement with others, who are outside the family, but yet not as strangers; it maintains an intricate social balance between rights and obligations, distance and relation in the community. It also serves to generate an informal system of social controls. For where the street is played in, talked in, sat out in, constantly spectated as a source of neighbourly interest, it is also policed, and by the people themselves. Nothing much can happen – however trivial (a child falling, a woman struggling with heavy parcels, etc.), without it becoming a focus of interest and intervention. The presence of corner shops and pubs in the turning also serves to generate social interaction at street level, as well as providing natural settings for 'gossip cliques', which if they do nothing else constantly reaffirm the reality of neighbourhood ties!

The net result is that neighbours as well as relatives are available to help cope with the day to day problems that arise in the constant struggle to survive under the conditions of the working-class community. And in many areas, including the East End, institutions such as loans clubs, holiday clubs and the like developed to supplement family mutual aid, and formalize the practices of 'neighbouring'.

The local economy

Perhaps the most striking feature of the traditional East End economy is its diversity; dockland, the many distributive and service trades linked to it, the craft industries, notably tailoring and furniture making, the markets. This diversity meant that people lived and worked in the East End – there was no need for them to go outside in search of jobs. The extended family remains intrinsic to the recruitment of the labour force and even to the work process itself; son followed father into the same trade or industry while many of the craft and service trades were organized into 'family concerns'. As a result of this, the situation of the work place, its issues and interests, remained tied to the situation outside work – the issues and interests of the community.

There was a direct connection between the position of the producer and the consumer. The fierce pride of being an East Ender was often linked to the equally fierce pride of craftmanship and skilled labour. And it was from this section of the working class – sometimes called the labour aristocracy – that the indigenous leadership was drawn; politically conscious and highly articulate in defence of local interest, both at the community level and at the point of production. This elite group was also the most socially mobile, tending to re-emigrate from the East End to the outer ring of the middle-class suburbs; as Jewish people used to put it: the distance from Bethnal Green to Golders Green was two generations. Yet their ranks were continuously replenished as new subcommunities established themselves as part of the respectable working class. There were also those less fortunate who, for a variety of reasons, fell by the wayside, and remained permanent 'outsiders' *vis à vis* the 'established'. They were relegated to the ranks of the labouring poor caught in a vicious circle of poverty, ill-health, unemployment and lack of education. This residual group was doubly excluded – unskilled and lacking union organization they had little or no bargaining power on the labour market; and stigmatized as 'pariahs' by the rest of the community, the scapegoat for its problems, and denied any effective voice in their solution.

At any given time, then, the social structure of the community as a whole, and of the subcommunities within it tended to be polarizing into three distinct strata: the socially mobile elite who monopolize leadership; the respectables, who form the 'staple backbone' of the community; and the lumpen (so called) who are often driven to petty criminal activity to survive. And incidentally there is not a better example of the overriding importance of the extended kinship structure on the pattern of East End life than the fact that when this lowest strata began to evolve a kind of lumpen aristocracy, based on criminal activity, it was the small family 'firm' that was taken as the model for its social organization!

The Future Perfect versus the Historical Present

The social structure we've described held until the early fifties; and then, slowly at first, but with gathering momentum it began to change, and the pattern of social integration that had traditionally characterized the East End began, dramatically, to break down. Without going into a long argument about cause and effect, it is possible to say that this breakdown coincided with the wholesale redevelopment of the area, and the process of chain reactions which this triggered. The redevelopment was in two phases, the first spanning the decade of the fifties, the second from the early sixties to the present; let's examine the impact of each in turn.

The fifties saw the development of new towns and large estates on the outskirts of East London, Dagenham, Greenleigh etc., and a large number of families from the worst slums of the East End were rehoused in this way. The East End, one of the highest density areas in London, underwent a gradual depopulation. But as it did so, certain areas underwent a repopulation, as they were rapidly colonized by a large influx of West Indians, and Pakistanis. One of the reasons why these communities were attracted (in the weak sense of the word) to such areas is often called 'planning blight'. This concept has been used to describe what happens in the take-off phase of comprehensive redevelopment in the inner residential zones of large urban centres. The typical pattern is that as redevelopment begins, land values inevitably rise, and rental values fall; the most dynamic elements in local industry, who are usually the largest employers of labour, tend to move out, alongside the migrating families, and are often offered economic incentives to do so; much of the existing dilapidated property in the area is bought up cheaply by property speculators and Rachman-type landlords, who are only interested in the maximum exploitation of their assets – the largest profits in the shortest time; as a result the property is often not maintained and becomes even further dilapidated. Immigrant families, with low incomes, and excluded from council housing, naturally gravitate to these areas, and their own trades and service industries begin to penetrate the local economy. This in turn accelerates the migration of the indigenous community to the new towns and estates. The only apparent exception to planning blight, in fact proves the rule. For those few areas which are linked to invisible assets – such as possessing houses of 'character' i.e. late Georgian or early Victorian, or amenities such as parks – are actually bought up and improved, renovated for the new middle class, students, young professionals, who require easy access to the commercial and cultural centre of the city. The end result on the local community is the same; whether the neighbourhood is upgraded or downgraded, long-resident working-class families move out.

As the worst effects of the first phase both on those who moved, and on those who stayed behind, became apparent, the planning authorities decided to reverse their policy. Everything was now concentrated on building new estates on slum sites within the East End. But far from counteracting the social disorganization of the area, this merely accelerated the process. In analysing the impact of redevelopment on the community,

D

these two phases can be treated as one. No one is denying that redevelopment brought an improvement in material conditions for those fortunate enough to be rehoused (there are still thousands on the housing list). But while this removed the tangible evidence of poverty, it did nothing to improve the real economic situation of many families, and those with low incomes may, despite rent rebate schemes, be worse off. But to this was added a new poverty – the impoverishment of working-class culture. Redevelopment meant the destruction of the neighbourhood, the breakdown of the extended kinship network, which as we've seen combined to exert a powerful force for social cohesion in the community. I now think perhaps I've overstated the extent to which the community structures have broken down, as this paper was originally the basis of a proposal for funding the Project.

The first effect of the high density, high rise schemes, was to destroy the function of the street, the local pub, the corner shop, as articulations of communal space. Instead there was only the privatized space of the family unit, stacked one on top of each other, in total isolation, juxtaposed with the totally public space which surrounded it, and which lacked any of the informal social controls generated by the neighbourhood. The streets which serviced the new estates became thoroughfares, their users 'pedestrians', and by analogy so many bits of human traffic, and this irrespective of whether or not they were separated from motorized traffic. It's indicative of how far the planners failed to understand the human ecology of the working-class neighbourhood that they could actually talk about building 'vertical streets'! The people who had to live in them weren't fooled. As one put it – they might have running hot water, and central heating but to him they were still prisons in the sky. Inevitably the physical isolation, the lack of human scale and sheer impersonality of the new environment was felt worst by people living in the new tower blocks which have gradually come to dominate the East End landscape.

The second effect of redevelopment was to destroy what we have called 'matrilocal residence'. Not only was the new housing designed on the model on the nuclear family with little provision for large low income families (usually designated as problem families!) and none at all for groups of young single people, but the actual pattern of distribution of the new housing tended to disperse the kinship network; families of marriage were separated from their families of origin, especially during the first phase of the redevelopment. The isolated family unit could no longer call on the resources of wider kinships network, or of the neighbourhood, and the family itself became the sole focus of solidarity. This meant that any problems were bottled up within the immediate interpersonal context which produced them; and at the same time family relationships were invested with a new intensity, to compensate for the diversity of relationships previously generated through neighbours and wider kin. The trouble was that although the traditional kinship system which corresponded to it, had broken down, the traditional patterns of socialization (of communication and control) continued to reproduce themselves in the interior of the family. The working-class family was thus not only isolated from the outside, but undermined from within. There is no better example of what we are talking about than the plight of the so called 'housebound mother'. The street or turning was no longer available as a safe playspace, under neighbourly supervision. Mum, or Auntie, was no longer just round the corner to look after the kids for the odd morning. Instead the task of keeping an eye on the kids fell exclusively to the young wife, and the only safe playspace was the 'safety of the home'. Feeling herself cooped up with the kids, and cut off from the outside world, it wouldn't be surprising if she occasionally took out her frustration on those nearest and dearest! Only market research and advertising executives imagine that the housebound mother sublimates everything in her G-plan furniture, her washing machine or non-stick frying pans.

Underlying all this however there was a more basic process of change going on in the community, a change in the whole economic infrastructure of the East End.

In the late fifties, the British economy began to recover from the effect of the war, and to apply the advanced technology developed during this period to the more backward sectors of the economy. Craft industries, and small scale production in general were the first to suffer; automated techniques replaced the traditional hand skills and their simple division of labour. Similarly the economies of scale provided for by the concentration of capital resources meant that the small scale family business was no longer a viable unit. Despite a long rearguard action many of the traditional industries, tailoring, furniture making, many of the service and distributive trades linked to the docks, rapidly declined, or were bought out. Symbolic of this was the disappearance of the corner shop; where these were not demolished by redevelopment, they were replaced by the larger supermarkets often owned by large combines. Even where corner shops were offered places in the redevelopment area often they could not afford the high rents. There was a gradual polarization in the structure of the labour force: on the one side the highly specialized, skilled and well-paid jobs associated with the new technology, and the high growth sectors that employed them; on the other the routine, dead end, low paid and unskilled jobs associated with the labour intensive sectors, especially the service industries. As might be expected, it was the young people, just out of school, who got the worst of the deal. Lacking openings in their fathers' trades, and lacking the qualifications for the new industries, they were relegated to jobs as vanboys, office boys, packers, warehousemen, etc., and long spells out of work. More and more people, young and old, had to travel out of the community to their jobs, and some eventually moved out to live elsewhere, where suitable work was to be found. The local economy as a whole contracted, became less diverse. The only section of the community which was unaffected by this was dockland, which retained its position in the labour market, and with it, its traditions of militancy. It did not, though remain unaffected by the breakdown of the pattern of integration in the East End as a whole, *vis à vis* its sub-community structure. Perhaps this goes some way to explain the paradoxical fact that within the space of twelve months, the dockers could march in support of Enoch Powell, and take direct action for community control in the Isle of Dogs!

If someone should ask why the plan to 'modernize' the pattern of East End life should have been such a disaster, perhaps the only honest answer is that, given the macro-social forces acting on it, given the political, ideological, and economic framework within which it operated, the result was inevitable. For example many local people wonder why the new environment should be the way it is. The reasons are complex; they are political in so far as the system does not allow for any effective participation by local working-class community in the decision-making process at any stage or level of planning. The clients of the planners are simply the local authority or commercial developer who employs them. They are ideological in so far as the plans are unconsciously modelled on the structure of the middle-class environment, which is based on the concept of *property*, and *private ownership*, on individual differences of status, wealth etc.; whereas the structure of the working-class environment is based on the concept of community, or collective identity, common lack of ownership, wealth etc. Similarly needs were assessed on the norms of the middle-class nuclear family, rather than the extended working-class family etc. But underpinning both these sets of reasons lie the basic economic factors involved in comprehensive redevelopment. Quite simply – faced with the task of financing a large housing programme, the local authorities were forced to borrow large amounts of capital, and also to design schemes which would attract capital investment to the area. This means that they have to borrow at the going interest rates, which in this country are very high, and that to subsidize housing, certain of the best sites have to be earmarked for commercial developers. A further and perhaps decisive factor is the cost of land, since very little of it is publicly owned and land values rise as the area develops.

All this means that planners have to reduce the cost of production to a minimum, through the use of capital intensive techniques – prefabricated and standardized components, allowing for semi-automated processes in construction. The attraction of high rise developments (tower blocks outside the trade) is not only that they meet these requirements, but they allow for certain economies of scale, such as the input costs of essential services, which can be grouped around a central core. As to 'non essential' services i.e. ones that don't pay, such as playspace, community centres, youth clubs and recreational facilities, these often have to be sacrificed to the needs of commercial developers, who of course have quite different priorities. Perhaps the best example of this happening is the notorious St Catherine's Dock Scheme. This major contribution towards solving the East End's housing problem includes a yachting marina, a luxury hotel, luxury apartment blocks, and various cultural amenities for their occupants plus – a small section of low-income accommodation, presumably to house the families of the low paid staff who will service the luxury amenities. And lest anyone becomes too sentimental about the existing site, Telfords warehouses etc., it should be mentioned that the original development was by the East India Company in the early nineteenth century, involved the destruction of the homes of thousands of poor families in the area, and met with such stiff opposition from them that it eventually required an Act of Parliament to get the scheme approved!

The situation facing East Enders at present, then, is not new. When the first tenements went up in the nineteenth century they raised the same objections from local people, and for the same very good reasons, as their modern counterparts – the tower blocks. What *is* new is that in the nineteenth century the voice of the community was vigorous and articulate on these issues, whereas today, just when it needs it most, the community is faced with a crisis of indigenous leadership.

The reasons for this are already implicit in the analysis above. The labour aristocracy, traditional source of leadership, has virtually disappeared along with the artisan mode of production. At the same time there has been a split in consciousness between the spheres of production and consumption. More and more East Enders are forced to work outside the area; young people especially are less likely to follow family traditions in this respect. As a result the issues of the work place are no longer experienced as directly linked to community issues. Of course there has always been a 'brain drain' of the most articulate, due to social mobility. But not only has this been intensified as a result of the introduction of comprehensive schools, but the recruitment of fresh talent from the strata below – i.e. from the ranks of the respectable working class, has also dried up. For this strata, traditionally the social cement of the community, is also in a state of crisis.

Soft City
Jonathan Raban

Reprinted with permission from Jonathan Raban, *Soft City*, Hamish Hamilton, 1974, pp. 112–23

People often complain of metropolitan life that it coarsens thought, that the intellect is held cheaply, that serious issues degenerate into trends of the moment and the coterie. From the judicious distance of a provincial university town, London and New York often look like circuses, their intelligentsias as sleek as performing seals. So much of talk is fashion and frippery; its buzz of new ideas is brazenly decorative, there to adorn the talker and to protect him from the incursions of the world. When an idea becomes a commodity, readily transmittable and exchangeable in the bazaar of society at large, it takes on the characteristics of other commodities. It may be unpalatable to think of ideas as if they could have the same function as house-fronts, cars or handbags but it is surely true that they very often do so. People gather behind them, for private and highly partial reasons. The inexpensive synthesis, of the kind that can be extracted from ecology, or structuralism, or *The Gutenberg Galaxy*, or *One Dimensional Man*, comforts and assuages those who embrace it. It makes the world simpler, gives a thrust of direction and authority to the individual living in a prolix and confusing city. We are not so far here from Gissing's Thomas Bird, picking himself out from the crowd with his treasured private knowledge of the geography of Polynesia.

These narrow, passionate *cognoscenti* bolstered by received ideas, given to clubs and cliques and intense sectarian debates, are part of the essence of city life. For the member of an urban guerrilla cell, or an ecological watchdog organization, or a neo-mystical commune, or one of the countless coffee-and-discussion groups that are always springing up in big cities, his ideology is a *route*, a consecrated path through the unintelligible scatter of city streets. A sense of community, and the perspective which we acquire as one of the privileges of belonging to a community, are hard to come by in the city. Neither the street nor the neighbour-hood (except in some of the leafier suburbs and odd clusters of besieged roads of working-class terraces) confers a sufficient sense of membership on its residents. The turnover of owners and tenants is too rapid, and the sheer physical density with which metropolitan space is occupied makes for a warren of private cubicles in which people jealously and secretively protect their own patches. Ideas, unlike neighbours, are chosen; and a com-munity of people who share an idea, a craze, a belief is perhaps the most precious of all the associations which a man may make in a city. There is a café around the corner from where I live which is a nest of coteries in the long dull middle of the afternoon. Italian *au pair* girls go there, so do folk music enthusiasts and loitering record collectors. But there is also a curious group of young men in fishermen's jerseys who have the activist's look of glinting, mildly fanatical anaemia. One day I learned how to make a bomb; and the technical jargon of revolution spills from their table in single overheard phrases. I am not a party to their beliefs, nor do I know what they are (Trotskyists . . . anarchists . . . People's Democracy . . . midnight slogan painters . . . colour-ful fantasizing about the lives of other people is a chronic urban habit); and this very quality of unknownness scares me. But there is a real resemblance between this tableful of revolutionaries, if that is in fact what they are up to, and some of the less exotic coterie-milieux which I know better. I sometimes go to a pub in Soho with a corner full of book reviewers, and one catches the same note there: the same pitch of voice, the technical talk, the possessive hunch over the table of people making a close, improvised, temporary community in the middle of a city of strangers. Communities like this, which come to life around an idea, are constantly dissolving; they are not fixed in place or time, although membership of them is a permanently defining feature of one's identity.

A large city is a honeycomb of such groups. To the outsider, they are likely to seem silly or sinister, and certainly evanescent. For every group which establishes itself with capital and property in a quarter, there are many whose outward and visible signs are known and valued only by their members. Their most important possessions are their ideas, and these are preserved for fellow-initiates, not exposed to the hostile examination of the world outside. They communicate by rumour and the telephone; they meet in public places – in halls, in parks, in pubs and cafés, and on streets and squares. Like their members, they are in a state of constant locomotion in the city. One or two established organizations – the Salvation Army is the prime example – have borrowed the motile structure of these groups; grasping, as General Booth grasped, that the most effective institutions in a big city must keep on the move with the people.

Sometimes such a group will suddenly move into visibility and claim the attention of outsiders in the crowd with its extreme and bizarre public symbols. In New York, Los Angeles and London, there is a wandering tribe of street folk; they live in Radha Krishna temples, their heads are shaved except for a scrubby tuft on their crowns, they process through the streets in sandals and saffron-dyed sheets, chanting the 'Hare Krishna' mantra and beating on tambourines. On Oxford Street, motorists caught in the continual traffic jam yell cheerful obscenities at these outlandish communards. They seem indifferent. Their vegetarian diet and life of indoor meditation have pulled the skins of their faces away from their lips and eyes so that they have a curiously protuberant, root-vegetable look. Yet they are not without dignity: their voices are gentle, hazed, their accents invariably English urban, and patches of Manchester and Stepney show through their stiff, devoted impersonation of the mystic east.

They are keen to evangelize, and methodically explain themselves with the rehearsed precision of a telephone answering service. I sat in my socks in a basement, sharing their bowl of grated oranges and vegetables, as they talked at me earnestly, not expecting to be believed, knowing, I suspect, that many of their visitors only come to smirk and peer. They are solemn, courteous, and extremely ugly: their scraped turnip faces nod slowly under the naked 200-watt bulb, which itself looks rather like another communard. Each word and gesture is reverently drawn out; everything here is ritual theatre – self-consciousness is elevated to mystical consciousness of the self, and everyday life turns into a studied allegory.

The International Society for Krishna Consciousness promotes a rural peasant culture as a spiritual antidote to and romantic release from city life. It recruits the disaffiliated young from the streets, offering them spartan communes and a simple, hokum-scientific doctrine of mind power. Like nineteenth-century spiritualism, of which it is a less sophisticated replica, it preaches an ethic of impoverished literalism. The movement's *swami*, in a characteristic booklet called *Easy Journey to Other Planets*, invites you to join a bargain coach-trip to the spiritual world:

> The material world is only a shadow representation of the anti-material world, and intelligent men who are clean in heart and habit will be able to learn, in a nutshell, all the details of the anti-material world from the text of the *Gita*, and these are in actuality more exhaustive than material details . . .
>
> . . . The gross materialist may try to approach the anti-material worlds by endeavouring with spaceships, satellites, rockets, etc., which he throws into outer space, but by such means he cannot even approach the material planets in the higher regions of the material sky, and what to speak of those planets situated in the anti-material sky, which is far beyond the material universe . . . Master *yogis* who control the anti-material particle within the material body by practice of mystic powers can give up their material bodies at will at any given moment and can thus enter the anti-material worlds through a specific thoroughfare which connects the material and anti-material worlds.

This is a sad piece of writing; barely literate twaddle in which the jargon of popular science is treated with a superstitious reverence. Reading it, one suffocates in the appalling intellectual constriction of its vision of the world, and senses, too, in its ramshackle and reduced vocabulary and grammar, some of the sheer difficulty which its intended audience must experience when they try to think about the world at all. (A more unpleasant, because more grandly commercialized version of the same style, may be found in the work of Ron L. Hubbard and the Scientologists – another group of urban evangelists who operate in London from a shop in the Tottenham Court Road, and have had some success in converting people off the streets of the city.) The liberation of spirit which it purports to offer is a liberation into chains; it drops one into a mental abyss in which the simplest of ideas, the most elementary of rational processes, is impossibly large, foreign and unwieldy.

But when the *swami* writes of a 'thoroughfare', he indicates a route for believers which goes not so much to the stars as through the city streets. For the devotee, London becomes legible by being relegated to a plane of inferior consciousness. It turns into a chimera: the 'material' city is there to be transcended by home-made mysticism and holy gobbledygook. The chanting, the amazing dress, the razored skulls of these young men are there as a fierce announcement – they have seen through the illusory life of shops and automobiles; for them, the city we inhabit does not exist. In their city, the stars are under their feet, and the cosmos has blacked-out Bourne and Hollingsworth; they process through the chimerical void to the unearthly tinkling of their tambourines.

Krishna Consciousness presents its ideas as uniquely expensive commodities: but they are freely available to anyone who is prepared to pay for them with self-abasement, discipline, and by wearing the proud stigmata of robes and tonsure. One of the most significant features of the movement is the way in which it embraces the caste system; it promises the status of a *brahmana* to the believer. 'The caste system', writes the *swami*, 'is very scientific'; but the castes of which he writes are fundamentally different from real castes in that anybody may elect himself to the caste which he considers himself fit to belong to. We are instructed to search our hearts for signs of 'spiritual advancement', and if we find ourselves qualified, then, automatically, we become brahmans. Status is a matter not of external circumstances but of the deliberate exercise of will over consciousness. It is inside our heads that we are aristocrats; the impersonal world, represented by the judgements and deferences of society at large, is, in the rhetoric of Krishna Consciousness, an irrelevant delusion.

It might be consoling to see the beliefs of the Krishna people as merely grotesque or dotty – the extreme responses of faddish, under-educated, under-employed young people to the unassimilable scatter of the city. But there is something more to them than that. Every western metropolis is at present swarming with bands of devotees, some flying political colours, some resurrecting or inventing exotic religions, some committed to eccentric hobbies and crazes. Some are as harmless as the radio-controlled model glider enthusiasts who foregather every Saturday on a corner of Richmond Park, cocooned from public inquisitiveness by their impressive technicalities, their talk of thermals and wavelengths and launching-ropes, mightily oblivious of the dogs and children who scamper among their balsa wood aeroplanes. They have a weekend world of their own, a private city which is invisible to the uninitiated. But at the other extreme, there are the revolutionary cells, and gangs like the Envies; people who have – like the members of the Hare Krishna Temple – concocted elaborate philosophies to prove that the city is a bead-curtain of illusion. The convicted conspirators of the English 'Angry Brigade', who had been accused of planting bombs in a number of public institutions and in the London house of a cabinet minister, subscribed to the theories of the Paris Situationists – who speak of the 'spectacle' or 'façade' of capitalism, and of revolution as imagination liberated from hierarchical modes of thought and behaviour. There can surely be no doubt that the unreality of the city, its prolixity and illegibility, its capacity to exceed all the imaginative shapes we try to impose upon it, enables its citizens to treat it with a terrifying arbitrariness. Georg Simmel, the nineteenth-century German sociologist, identified the characteristic urban habit of mind as *blasé*; Engels saw the city's major evil in the lack of curiosity shown by members of the crowd for each other. When the city becomes a mere façade, when Oxford Street ceases to exist, when violence can be casually inflicted by one metropolitan group upon another, then realism – a respect for detail, objects, independent and various lives – becomes the most pressing of all necessities.

At the Radha Krishna temple near the British Museum in Bloomsbury, a pale communard with a Glaswegian accent pointed to a man with a droopy moustache who was sitting next to me. 'Telex operator, right?' said the communard. The man stopped turning the pages of *Krsna Consciousness: the Topmost Yoga System*, and nodded slowly, reverently. 'To me', said the communard, 'he is pure consciousness. We do not see a person's job, or his clothes, or his house and family. We see his soul.' The man with the soul looked grateful; few other telex operators can visit distant planets or turn, like magic pumpkins, into brahmans, the ultimate aristocrats of the world-soul. He was leaving the street outside far behind; its dense puzzles, its intricate social networks, its inequalities, its confusion of noises and smells, were, he had learned, just dull impediments from which he could liberate himself at a blink.

Such subjective inspirational clairvoyance is a hallmark of these isolated groups within the city. It is shared by Weathermen, Diggers, Sufists, Envies, by moralistic thugs and by placid vegetarian contemplatives. Each holds an idea, an idiom and a uniform in common; and each believes that the city is a 'façade', easily transcended by an act of will, a trick of the mind, or the lit fuse of a bomb. The word 'consciousness', whether employed by the revolutionary or the religiomane, is a shorthand-notation: it conveys the notion that the intuitive self might actually come to replace the edifice of society – that the world on the ground might be moulded into the shape of a totalitarian world inside the head.

It is a dangerous kind of dreaming, this solemn, simple mentalism. It releases the dreamer into a domain of total possibility in which his reality is as inventive, psychotic or banal as his own imagination. He imagines himself a brahman . . . he is a brahman. If a toolmaker's apprentice from West Ham wants to turn into an Asian mystic, he may do so simply by rigging himself out in the appropriate uniform and chanting the prescribed abracadabra. If one shifts from group to group, one watches London dissolving; from a paddy field of disembodied souls, to a systematic capitalist conspiracy of banks, police stations, court-houses and monuments, to a range of Cuban hills where fellow guerrillas squat in waiting wearing patched jeans and ex-W.D. windcheaters, to the gothic, magical city of signs prophesied in the writings of Nostradamus.

In a television interview transmitted the day after her conviction in the 'Angry Brigade' trial in 1972, Anna Mendelson talked in what is increasingly becoming a characteristic idiom of our time; a style in which familiar words are pronounced as if they were components of an arcane code. She spoke distractedly in a dream-monotone: phrases like 'working class', 'conspiracy', 'change of consciousness' came out rounded as pebbles, but what they meant to me was clearly not what they meant to her. When she was asked whether the bombings had had any tangible effect on the progress of the revolution in England, she stared mildly, apparently incomprehendingly at her interviewer and said, 'I suppose they must have . . . yes . . . they must have, mustn't they . . .' so vaguely that one felt that one had trespassed illicitly over the far side of her dream.

These intense, private groups, compacted around a core of symbolic objects and ideas are very serious symptoms of a metropolitan condition. They may or may not be politically important in themselves; and when they take a religious turn they may indicate nothing about the spiritual awakening which fond members of the clerisy enjoy forecasting. But the club, the clique, the cell, the commune, the code are proliferating forms in the city. Huddled, defensive, profoundly complacent in their indifference or hostility to the rest of the city, they are the foxholes for all those whom the city has isolated, for whom no larger reality is habitable. Mayhew saw the illegible mass of the nine-teenth-century city as a network of tight castes, each one operating independently of the others and of society at large. Money, education and social welfare provisions have largely released the castes of the modern city from thraldom to their occupations. Just as the poor can render themselves invisible in cheap fashion-styled clothes so they can acquire ideas and identities of a much wilder and grander kind than could Mayhew's costermongers and mudlarks. In our city, it is easy to drift into a privacy of symbols, a domain of subjective illusions made concrete by the fact that two or three people have gathered together to conspire in them.

It is impossible to miss the crackle of tribal hostilities in London and New York today. What is most worrying is the subtlety, narrowness and parochialism with which the lines are drawn. The fierce antagonism between blacks and whites, between haves and have-nots, is tragically comprehensible. What is not so easy to understand is the continual barrage of explosions from wars so small that only the participants can explain which sides are fighting them. *Gay News* reports vicious factional quarrels between opposed groups of London homosexuals, with smashed typewriters and bloody noses. A party for the opening of the Women's Lib magazine *Spare Rib* ended in an internecine brawl. Like the cross-hatching of bitchery which keeps literary coteries (themselves highly-developed examples of self-conscious caste groups) alive, the malevolent buzz of city life is a way of marking boundaries of taste, staking out the ever-more-question-able frontier between us and them. People in one postal district despise those in the next; the owner of the baby Renault reproves the driver of the expensive Jensen; the revolutionary dismisses the Buddhist, the Buddhist the revolutionary. It is a war of ideas and epigrams, in which objects are called on to play the parts of ideas, to express the ideologies of their owners; and its local battles are passionately territorial in nature. Each party has its own city, its own version of the self, its own route through that other, endlessly malleable city of fact.

Structure and Change

R. Illsley, A. Finlayson and B. Thompson

Reprinted with permission from 'The Motivation and Characteristics of Internal Migrants', *Millbank Memorial Fund Quarterly*, Vol. XLI, No. 3, July 1963

This paper documents the movement of young adults into and out of the city of Aberdeen in the post-war years. Fifty-nine husbands had come to Aberdeen before marriage. Of these, ten came with their parental families as dependent adolescents. As with the premarital migration of women two distinct reasons are discernible: (1) the father's promotion, change of job or retire-ment; (2) the family migration consequent on parental death or marital breakdown.

Most of the others came to Aberdeen independently as adolescents or young adults.

The composition of this group of young job-migrants clearly reflects the relation between migration and the structure of professional and managerial careers. For example, 32 per cent of this group of premarital immigrants had Class I or II occupa-tions (i.e. professional or managerial), compared with 13 per cent in the whole sample. Two promotion mechanisms are apparent, each involving migration and each of roughly equal importance. On the one hand are those who move within the same organization: bankers, insurance officials, industrial managers, salaried employees of large-scale organizations with many branches, for whom promotion means a larger branch, often in another town; unwillingness to move in these circumstances is often tantamount to withdrawal from the promotion race. For the other group, promotion is obtained by a move from one organization to another, each move representing a step up the professional ladder. In our sample this group included university lecturers, teachers, local government officials, newspaper reporters, lawyers and some industrial and commercial managers. It might be said that since migration for these men generally involves formal application for a job, it has more of the character of a voluntary act than it has for those who move within an organization; nevertheless, disinclination to move often means losing opportunities of promotion and, consequently, migration has become a generally accepted part of the way of life for many in these professions.

The impulse towards migration is regulated by two factors, the pulling power of the new place of residence and the strength of ties with the old. In this type of survey and analysis the positive element is easy to detect; men say 'I came here because I was transferred by my office', 'because I was appointed as a lecturer', or 'because there were plenty of jobs in my line in Aberdeen'.

With out-migration, as with in-migration, the motives are complex and we are aware that a broad sociological analysis gives only part of the picture. The factors, however, which emerge as important at this level of analysis are: the social and industrial geography of the area; the places of origin of husband and wife; and the husband's occupation. This last factor is discussed more fully below.

The data on out-migration in this study refer to the 5-year period following the birth of the first child. At this stage most wives are not employed outside the home and the wife's job or career has little bearing on family decisions. The husband's occupation automatically assumes greater importance in that he is the sole wage-earner and the family's standard of living is directly dependent upon him. Many young middle-class men are still at the beginning of a career which may entail further geographical and hierarchical moves; most manual workers, on the other hand, have reached the peak of earnings in their occupation and further advance may be obtained only by change of occupation or by moving to an area with higher wages. The occupational basis of migration was still very evident in our population at this stage. The highest rate of out-migration occurred in Social Class I – 63 per cent within the 5 years; the rate fell sharply with decreasing status – to 33 per cent in Class II, 19 per cent in Class III and 10 per cent in Classes IV and V. Broad class differences, however, conceal some of the most interesting industrial and occupational differences.

Two of the highest rates occurred in 'occupational' groups which are intrinsically mobile – university students and members of the armed forces; they assume prominence in this study only because Aberdeen is a university city and because military conscription was in force at the time. The high rate among university-trained or professionally-qualified workers, however, has a more general relevance, for it indicates a way of life and a career structure current in a large and increasing section of society. It is in sharp distinction to the rate among men in managerial occupations, the group most similar in income and responsibilities; within this latter group the migration rate is high only among the employees of large-scale national organizations; it is lowest in the peculiarly local industries such as fishing, fish handling and granite working which require skills unprized in other centres, or in small business (catering, retail distribution) in which success depends on a stable clientele or a local reputation. Somewhat similar considerations apply to clerical workers whose rate of out-migration is identical, for here, too, it is the employees of large organizations (banks, insurance companies) who are most likely to move.

Among manual workers in our population the most mobile were skilled mechanics, fitters and electricians, their rate of out-migration in fact exceeding that of the remaining non-manual workers. This is probably in part a local phenomenon stemming from the relatively limited outlets for their skill compared with the opportunities available to them in larger industrial centres in England and abroad. Educationally, socially, and physically, however, these engineers are the aristocrats of local manual work and they may be particularly susceptible to the attractions of a higher standard of living elsewhere when they find their occupational pathway blocked locally. They are very largely Aberdonian in origin, not earlier in-migrants from the countryside. They differ sharply in their rate of out-migration from other skilled engineers in the city, many of whom are employed in shipbuilding, an industry which is stationary or declining throughout the country and which is not conspicuously more prosperous in other areas than in Aberdeen. The engineering industry thus provides an excellent example of the impact of both local and national conditions on rates of migration, of the push-pull forces which have received so much attention in migration research.

The other manual-worker industry experiencing relatively high rates of migration in Aberdeen is transport, particularly railway transport. Here again, the national character of the industry is important, for transference within the organization is possible and may be the quickest method of obtaining promotion; the habit of long-distance travel, cheaper and easier communications and familiarity with other centres may possibly help to break down resistance to geographical movement.

The lowest rate of out-migration occurs in the fishing industry, which is largely manned by local workers. Employment in the same industry or occupation is available at only a few British ports, so that the incentive to move is low. It is probably relevant that this industry has had a low status locally and has not been attractive to workers with high social and economic aspirations. In terms of education, housing, and various aspects of reproductive behaviour and health, the members of this industry tend to rank lower than Social Class V and it seems likely that limited cultural outlook and aspirations heavily influence the low rate of migration.

The out-migration material confirms the earlier analysis based on in-migration statistics in showing that mobility is part of the way of life of young professional people. Mobility is less common in the lower white-collar occupations where skills are less specialized and where local candidates are more readily available. At lower occupational levels, the position is more complex and the volume and character of occupational migration is relatively more affected, not only by personal and family factors, but also by the relationship between opportunities at the local and national level. Knowledge of the local context is consequently crucial to an understanding of the occupational drives towards migration; analysis on a national or even regional scale may, by an averaging process, conceal motivation.

Tradition and Change

M. Stacey

Reprinted with permission from M. Stacey, *Tradition and Change, A Study of Banbury*, Oxford University Press, 1960, pp. 12–20

According to the findings of the schedule inquiry, immigrants now make up about half the adult population of the town, as Table 1 shows. True immigrants, those who were at least seven years old when they came to Banbury, outnumber born Banburians by nearly 4 per cent. But when these are reinforced by those born in the district and by those who came in early childhood, the local people outnumber the immigrants in the ratio 11:9.

Table 1
Proportion of Banburians and Immigrants

	%
1. Born Banburians	41·4
2. Secondary Banburians	3·5
3. District born	10·0
4. True immigrants	45·1

Many of the immigrants coming from great industrial cities, and particularly those who came from the north, found it difficult to adapt themselves to Banbury. Some found it unsociable. One Lancashire woman described how, in her first months in the town, she used to sit down and cry: 'I thought I'd never get to know anyone; they're so much more friendly at home.' Others found it self-centred and self-important: 'If they get a shower of rain in Banbury they think it's raining all over the world.' Many remarked on the slow tempo of life: 'I even found I was walking faster than anyone else.'

Banburians consider the industrial immigrants 'foreign' because they came with values and customs greatly different from those of the town. Many of the men were used to working in large-scale industry for absentee owners; they had been brought up to take it for granted that a worker belonged to a trade union. One said that the Banbury workers were 'like sheep'; another, anxious to build his union, that they were 'pigs to organize'.

Professional people of a kind new to Banbury came too, men who were graduates in metallurgy or engineering. Banbury could not place them: many of them were not 'Oxford or Cambridge', but came from provincial universities. They did not hold time-honoured positions as the priest and the doctor did.

As the town grew, and later the war came and the welfare state was further developed, new government offices were opened and old ones enlarged and rehoused, bringing with them more executive and clerical civil servants. The schools were extended and there were more posts for qualified teachers.

So today in Banbury and district there are traditionalists: those who are part of the traditional social structure and who live by the traditional values and customs of old Banbury. There are others, the non-traditionalists, who do not belong to the traditional social structure and do not accept its values and customs; they do not share any common social system or system of values and customs for they are composed of many different, and sometimes opposed, groups; they include those who have come in with quite other systems of values and customs and those who are developing new ways to meet the changed circumstances of their life and work.

The traditionalists still judge people by 'who they are', by reference to their social status, their family and social background as well as their occupations. They are actively aware of fine status divisions. They accept their position and behave with the manners appropriate to it.

They all, for example, look up to Sir William, who comes of an old local family and who has lived in the same village, just outside Banbury, for the past thirty years. They acknowledge his public service and his work for charity. Sir William accepts his status. He is an active county councillor because he regards 'public service as a duty which a man in (his) position owes'. He feels, too, that he should 'set an example' and is, therefore, punctilious in his dress and manners. He is a member of the Church Council in the village and reads the lessons at Matins.

In the town itself, Mr Shaw, a prosperous tradesman who owns a business, which has been in the family for three generations and in which his son also works, is an acknowledged leader. He, too, knows where he stands in the old-town society and accepts his position. Like Sir William, he considers that 'service to the community' is a duty. He has been Mayor of the town and gives freely to local charity. Mr Grey, another of the leading tradespeople, is very like him in his social position and in many of his attitudes. But Grey is a 'pillar of the Methodist Church' and a Liberal in politics, while Shaw is a sidesman at the parish church and a member of the Conservative Association.

George is an example of a traditional worker in Banbury. He has been employed at one of the old family businesses for twenty-five years. He accepts the leadership of Sir William and of the Shaws and the Greys in the town. For he feels that 'the ordinary working man hasn't got the education' and that 'it's better to leave things like that to people who know about them'. So he does not belong to a trade union and avoids political discussions. He votes Conservative and is 'Church', but his neighbour, a native like himself with a similar job, is a staunch Baptist and a Liberal.

Accepting time-honoured status divisions, traditionalists like these find associations in the town and district which cater for their 'own sort'. They join according to their interests, but it is by the social side of an association's activities that they judge it. They would feel uncomfortable in one which catered for a different 'class' from their own; the sociability of the association would suffer, the relations would be too formal.

Thus, Sir William rides with the hunt. Shaw and Grey play bowls with the Chestnuts, while George and his neighbour belong to the Borough Bowls. Shaw drinks at the 'White Lion' in the town centre, but George goes to the pub at the end of his street. Grey, like George's neighbour, does not drink. George is a member of the British Legion (Sir William is its President).

These traditionalists, too, are all closely associated with the town and district. Men of the upper class, like Sir William, divide their associations between those which are local and those of their class which are national. Many of the traditionalists are natives as are the men in the examples. But by no means all of them are. Some are people who have come into the town from similar social backgrounds to follow traditional occupations, or who have accepted enough of Banbury's traditions to fit into it and to make their life in the locality, with Banbury as their principal frame of reference. They, as much as the Banbury-born traditionalists, rely on the local papers as essential sources of information about the fortunes and misfortunes of local people and families and of the clubs and societies.

In all these respects, the life, the values, and attitudes of the traditionalists are similar to what was described for the town before 1930 by informants like X. But, in those days traditionalists like these probably made up the greater part of the town. This they no longer do. Although they do not all know each other, it is possible to think of traditionalists as belonging to one social system. For traditional society is made up of a network of face-to-face groups, based on family, neighbours, occupations, associations, and status.

This is not true of the non-traditionalists who now make up a considerable and increasing part of the town. Non-traditionalists, as the name implies, have for the most part only negative characteristics in common: in one way or another they do not follow the traditional pattern of life. They are composed of two broad groups: those for whom the traditional structure has no place and those who reject that structure.

Many non-traditionalists do no apply 'Who is he?' as a test of a man's social acceptability. Their test is rather 'What does he do?', judging him on his merits as an individual both at work and at home, rather than on his family connections and original social background. And on this basis they wish to be judged. Occupation is, therefore, more important for them than it is for the traditionalist. Furthermore, they do not belong to, or they do not accept, the status structure of Banbury. This is not to say that they do not recognize status. They do, and, in one way or another, are deeply concerned with it.

Sir William is matched, for example, by Lord A. who is chairman of a group of engineering companies. Lord A. owns a Hall in the district, but he is not often there because his work takes him to various parts of the country, to London, and to the United States. He has no roots in the locality and belongs rather to an international society, for he has face-to-face relations with people in and from all parts of the world. He does not belong to the traditional status system, for he derives his status, not from his family as Sir William does, but from his position in industry. He 'made his own way in the world' and, although he sent his son to a major public school, he expects him to make his own way too. His son had a post in Lord A.'s company, but he subsequently left.

Similarly, in the middle class, in the town itself, there are many who do not have a place in its traditional status system for there is no answer to the question 'Who is he?' in the way that Banbury understands it. Mr Brown, for example, is a technologist on the staff of the aluminium factory. He is a graduate from a provincial university. Like Lord A. he did not inherit his position but has earned it on merit. He came to Banbury to work and, if he does not get promotion in the factory, he will apply for a better post elsewhere: his social aspirations are more closely linked to his job than to the status 'sets' of Banbury.

The second broad group are those who not only do 'not fit in' to Banbury society, but who actively reject its traditional standards. They follow a system of values and customs of an altogether different sort – in another place they might be traditionalists. George is matched today by people like Ted, who was brought up in an industrial city. He, like his father, has been a 'union man' ever since he started work. He is a Labour councillor. The class system for him is a matter of worker or not worker ('the boss class'). He accepts his status as a worker and is proud of it, but, unlike George, he will not receive patronage from his 'betters'. 'The workers look after their own,' he says. He does not accept that he has 'betters' and rejects the leadership of people like Sir William, Shaw, and Grey. He supports the Labour Party. He wants to improve the lot and the chances of the workers as a class.

Many non-traditionalists had difficulty in finding associations to suit them in the town and district and have created or tried to create new ones. Some middle-class non-traditionalists have interests which are more intellectual than those of old Banbury. Brown, for example, is an active member of the Banbury players, a new organization which is supported by immigrant non-traditionalists and which has also considerable support from the old-town society. But his friends who are interested in music and painting find it difficult to get people together for them.

The trade unionists found that there was no union in the aluminium factory and that, when they tried to form one, they had to meet in secret for fear of victimization. Indeed, they were not successful until the war and Ernest Bevin came and 'changed all that'. Now the factory has nearly 100 per cent membership and relations with the management are said to be good. They found, too, that the Labour Party was weak. But their activities there were sufficiently successful for the Conservative majority to be reduced to less than 2,000 votes at the 1945 election.

Furthermore, non-traditionalists found that the associations which catered for their interests had values they did not appreciate. Many non-traditionalists are, for example, less interested in the social side of a sports club than in the standard of play. In one tennis club there was serious friction as a result of this between non-traditionalists who wanted the social atmosphere preserved. As a result, Brown, who was at one time a member, and others resigned.

Most non-traditionalists claim membership of one of the Christian denominations, but, in general, they are less active in the life of church or chapel than the traditionalists. Religious differences are not an important basis of grouping among them.

While many of the non-traditionalists are immigrants, by no means all of them are, any more than all traditionalists were born in the town. There are Banbury-born workers, for example, who have joined a trade union and vote for the Labour Party. Other Banburians have accepted the merit basis of judging people (perhaps because they do not wish to be tied to the position of their family). Others, again, are less concerned with church and chapel than they used to be. All these have, to a greater or lesser extent, joined the ranks of non-traditionalists. But perhaps the majority of non-traditionalists are immigrants, as emigrants from Banbury might also be found to be if enough of them could be traced.

The traditionalists themselves, although in many ways they still live by the customs and values of the period before 1930, have not been unchanged by the activities of the non-traditionalists and by the social and economic changes that have been going on around them. In the middle class, for example, people like Shaw and Grey, the tradesmen, are closer together than they used to be. They agree that 'private enterprise' means a business owned by an individual or a family. This agreement seems more important now that they are faced with international companies which run factories in their own town and with a growing number of 'company shops'; faced also with a large and active trade-union movement, a Labour Party branch, and the Co-operative Society. They are united in their anti-socialism, which now seems more important than their disagreements about conservatism and liberalism. Indeed, Grey, although he is a Liberal, has appeared at recent general elections on the platform of the Conservative candidate. In their opposition to the Labour Party they are joined by the middle-class non-traditionalists (like Brown) who dislike socialism as much as they do. Furthermore, traditionalists belong to some of the newer organizations, like the Rotary Club, where they meet non-traditionalists.

In short, Banbury today is a mixture of old and new and all its inhabitants are influenced by the old and the new. Its established practices and customs, its institutions and the values associated with them are being modified by men who practise new techniques and new forms of organization. This division between old and new is not one between Banburian and immigrant so much as between traditionalist and non-traditionalist. The former cling, so far as they can, to the old values based on personal face-to-face relationships, preferring the small organization to the large. For the latter the old ways are irrelevant. Non-traditionalists judge people as individuals, are not afraid of large-scale organization and abstract ideas, and belong to groups (industrial hierarchies and nation-wide trade unions, for example) which extend beyond Banbury.

But a deeper division than this, for traditionalist and non-traditionalist alike, is the division into social classes. It is a division looked upon and operated differently by the two groups but which affects each as profoundly. A traditional worker like George accepts a total status system. He accords leadership to the gentry and to the business men on all counts, social, economic, political, and religious. Non-traditional 'trade-union-minded' workers like Ted concede the economic power of owners and managers, 'the boss class', but do not concede them a 'divine right' of social or political leadership. The middle-class non-traditionalist has a status in relation to his occupation of which Banbury is not the arbiter, for his status follows from the hierarchy of industry (be it aluminium processing or government department). He has also a status which he has made for himself in Banbury among the neighbours and friends. But it is not a total status position as it is for the traditional middle class. For them many factors count towards one final social-status position: occupation, income, manner of life, reputation, and by no means least, family background, in the sense not only of the start their family gave them, but of lineage. Nevertheless, in terms of how and where they live and in their assumptions about the 'right' way to behave in everyday living, George, the traditional worker, and Ted, the non-traditional worker, have a great deal more in common than they have with middle-class traditionalists like Shaw and Grey or middle-class non-traditionalists like Brown.

Furthermore, social status, looked at broadly in terms of major social-class divisions, is allied to political divisions and cuts across the frontier between traditional and non-traditional. The alignment of Conservative and Liberal against Labour draws most of the non-traditional middle class together with traditionalists of all classes in opposition to the non-traditional (for Banbury) Labour working class. The widest gap, therefore, lies between the traditional middle class and the non-traditional working class.

Leadership 1

N. Elias and J. L. Scotson

Reprinted with permission from N. Elias and J. L. Scotson, *The Established and the Outsiders*, London, Frank Cass & Co., 1965, pp. 130–2, 152–3, 155–9

For a very long time groups of families could only acquire the sociological quality of 'oldness' if they rose above the lower orders who had no or little property to transmit. The 'village' of Winston Parva seems to indicate that property is no longer as essential a condition of sociological 'oldness' as it used to be. Old peasant families based on the inheritance of land have of course been known in the past; so have old craftsmen families whose 'oldness' was based on the monopolized transmission of special skills. 'Old' working-class families appear to be characteristic of our own age. Whether they are a freak or an omen remains to be seen. Because sociological oldness in their case is not noticeably connected with inheritance of property certain other conditions of power which are normally to be found in other cases too, but which in other cases are less conspicuous, stand out more clearly in their case, particularly the power derived from the monopolization of key positions in local institutions, from greater cohesion and solidarity, from greater uniformity and elaboration of norms and beliefs and from the greater discipline, external and internal, which went with them. Greater cohesion, solidarity, uniformity of norms and self-discipline helped to maintain monopolization, and this in turn helped to reinforce these group characteristics. Thus the continued chance of 'old groups' to stand out; their successful claim to a higher social status than that of other interdependent social formations and the satisfactions derived from them, go hand in hand with specific differences in the personality structure which play their part, positive or negative as the case may be, in the perpetuation of an old families' network.

That 'old families' are known to each other and have strong ties with each other, however, does not mean that they necessarily like each other. It is only in relation to outsiders that they tend to stand together. Among themselves they may, and almost invariably do, compete, mildly or wildly according to circumstances, and may, often by tradition, heartily dislike or even hate one another. Whichever it is, they exclude outsiders. A good deal of common family lore is floating in the air of every circle of 'old families' enriched by each generation as it comes and goes. Like other aspects of the common tradition it creates an intimacy – even between people who dislike each other – which newcomers cannot share.

'Oldness' in a sociological sense thus refers to social relationships with properties of their own. They give a peculiar flavour to enmities and to friendships. They tend to produce a marked exclusivity of sentiment, if not of attitude, a preference for people with the same sensibilities as oneself, strengthening the common front against outsiders. Although individual members may turn away and may even turn against the group, the intimate familiarity of several generations gives to such 'old' groups for a while a degree of cohesion which other less 'old' groups lack. Born from a common history that is remembered it forms another strong element in the configuration of chances they have to assert and to maintain for a while their superior power and status in relation to other groups. Without their power the claim to a higher status and a specific charisma would soon decay and sound hollow whatever the distinctiveness of their behaviour. Rejecting gossip, freezing-out techniques, 'prejudice' and 'discrimination' would soon lose their edge; and so would any other of the manifold weapons used to protect their superior status and their distinction.

Thus, concentrated in the form of a model, the configuration found at Winston Parva in miniature shows more clearly its implications for a wider field. The task is not to praise and to blame; it is rather to help towards a better understanding and a better explanation of the interdependencies which trapped two groups of people in Winston Parva in a configuration not of their own making and which produced specific tensions and conflicts between them. The tensions did not arise because one side was wicked or overbearing and the other was not. They were inherent in the pattern which they formed with each other. If one had asked the 'villagers' they would probably have said they did not want an Estate at their doorstep, and if one had asked the Estate people they would probably have said they would rather not settle near an older neighbourhood such as the 'village'. Once they were thrown together they were trapped in a conflict situation which none of them could control and which one has to understand as such if one wants to do better in other similar cases. The 'villagers' naturally behaved to the newcomers as they were used to behave to deviants in their own neighbourhood. The immigrants on their part quite innocently behaved in their new place of residence in the manner which appeared natural to them. They were not aware of the existence of an established order with its power differentials and an entrenched position of the core group of leading families in the older part. Most of them did not understand at all why the older residents treated them with contempt and kept them at a distance. But the role of a lower status group in which they were placed and the indiscriminate discrimination against all people who settled on the Estate must have early discouraged any attempt to establish closer contacts with the older groups. Both sides acted in that situation without much reflection in a manner which one might have foreseen. Simply by becoming interdependent as neighbours they were thrust into an antagonistic position without quite understanding what was happening to them and most certainly without any fault of their own.

This, as has already been said, was a small-scale conflict not untypical of processes of industrialization. If one looks at the world at large one cannot fail to notice many configurations of a similar kind though they are often classified under different headings. Broad trends in the development of contemporary societies appear to lead to situations such as this with increasing frequency. Differences between sociologically 'old' and 'new' groups can be found today in many parts of the world. They are, if one may use this word, normal differences in an age in which people can travel with their belongings from one place to another more cheaply under more comfortable conditions at greater speed over wider distances than ever before, and can earn a living in many places apart from that where they have been born. One can discover variants of the same basic configuration, encounters between groups of newcomers, immigrants, foreigners and groups of old residents all over the world. The social problems created by these migratory aspects of social mobility, though varying in details, have a certain family similarity. Sometimes they are simply conceived as geographical aspects. All that happens it seems is that people move physically from one place to another. In reality, they always move from one social group to another. They always have to establish new relationships with already existing groups. They have to get used to the role of newcomers who seek entry into, or are forced into inter-dependence with, groups with already established traditions of their own and have to cope with the specific problems of their new role. Often enough they are cast in the role of outsiders in relation to the established and more powerful groups whose standards, beliefs, sensibilities and manners are different from theirs.

If the migrants have different skin colour and other hereditary physical characteristics different from those of the older residents, the problems created by their own neighbourhood formations and by their relations with the inhabitants of older neighbourhoods are usually discussed under the heading 'racial problems'. If the newcomers are of the same 'race' but have different language and different national traditions, the problems with which they and the older residents are confronted are classified as problems of 'ethnic minorities'. If social newcomers are neither of a different 'race', or of a different 'ethnic group', but merely of a different 'social class', the problems of social mobility are discussed as 'class problems', and, often enough, as problems of 'social mobility' in a narrower sense of the word. There is no ready-made label which one can attach to the problems that arose in the microcosm of Winston Parva because there the newcomers and the old residents, at least in the 'village', were neither of a different 'race', nor, with one or two exceptions, of different 'ethnic descent' or of a different 'social class'. But some of the basic problems arising from the encounter of established and outsider groups in Winston Parva were not very different from those which one can observe in similar encounters elsewhere, though they are often studied and conceptualized under different headings.

In all these cases the newcomers are bent on improving their position and the established groups are bent on maintaining theirs. The newcomers resent, and often try to rise from, the inferior status attributed to them and the established try to preserve their superior status which the newcomers appear to threaten. The newcomers cast in the role of outsiders are perceived by the established as people 'who do not know their place'; they offend the sensibilities of the established by behaving in a manner which bears in their eyes clearly the stigma of social inferiority, and yet, in many cases, newcomer groups quite innocently are apt to behave, at least for a time, as if they were the equals of their new neighbours. The latter show the flag; they fight for their superiority, their status and power, their standards and beliefs, and they use in that situation almost everywhere the same weapons, among them humiliating gossip, stigmatizing beliefs about the whole group modelled on observations of its worst section, degrading code words and, as far as possible, exclusion from all chances of power – in short, the features which one usually abstracts from the configuration in which they occur under headings such as 'prejudice' and 'discrimination'. As the established are usually more highly integrated and, in general, more powerful, they are able to mutual induction and ostracism of doubters to give a very strong backing to their beliefs. They can often enough induce even the outsiders to accept an image of themselves which is modelled on a 'minority of the worst' and an image of the established which is modelled on a 'minority of the best', which is an emotional generalization from the few to the whole. They can often impose on newcomers the belief that they are not only inferior in power but inferior by 'nature' to the established group. And this internalization by the socially inferior group of the disparaging belief of the superior group as part of their own conscience and self-image powerfully reinforces the superiority and the rule of the established group.

The 'bad behaviour' of a minority of Estate youngsters which reinforced again and again the 'villagers'' stereotyped image of the Estate was not confined to branches of sex morality. One of the standard complaints of the 'village' people was that about the bad behaviour of the 'swarms of children' from the Estate. Tales were constantly repeated about the 'masses' of children who grew up to be delinquents and criminals and who destroyed the 'old peace' of the 'village'.

Complaints about the 'swarms of children' who disturbed the peace of the 'village' were not entirely unjustified, but it was not so much the actual number of children on the Estate which mattered as the conditions under which they lived. The children who roamed the streets and disturbed the peace of the 'villagers' came from the minority of 'notorious' families which has already been mentioned. Living as they did in relatively small houses, children from these large families had nowhere else to go but the streets after school or work. Those who tried to join the older youth clubs were soon shown that they were not welcome. They had learned a certain reserve on the Estate and applied it, as it seemed, quite easily to their relations with 'village' youngsters. But a minority of youngsters from the Estate, mostly children of the problem families, reacted differently. They enjoyed embarrassing the people who rejected them. The vicious circle, the see-saw process, in which the old and new neighbourhoods, the established and the outsiders, were involved ever since they had become interdependent, showed its full force in the relations between their young people. The children and adolescents of the despised Estate minority were shunned, rejected and 'frozen out' by their 'respectable' contemporaries from the 'village' even more firmly and cruelly than were their parents because the 'bad example' they set threatened their own defences against the unruly urges within; and because the wilder minority of younger people felt rejected, they tried to get their own back by behaving badly with greater deliberation. The knowledge that by being noisy, destructive and offensive they could annoy those by whom they were rejected and treated as outcasts, acted as an added incentive, and perhaps, as the major incentive, for 'bad behaviour'. They enjoyed doing the very things for which they were blamed as an act of revenge against those who blamed them.

Some groups of this type, mainly composed of boys aged between 14 and 18, 'got a kick out of' trying to enter one of the church or chapel clubs. They would enter the club noisily, shouting, singing and laughing. When a club official approached them one of them would ask to join the club while the others stood around grinning. The boys knew beforehand that they would be asked to agree to attend church services regularly. When this provision was put to them they would begin to groan and to shout in protest. Then they were usually asked to leave, though in some instances they were allowed to stay for one evening in order to see what advantages club life had to offer them. The request that they should leave was the anticipated climax of the performance for the group. They expected to be asked to conform to the established standards of behaviour as laid down by the churches; they expected to be rejected or to be accepted only on terms of their complete acceptance of 'village' standards. When this stage was reached the group would leave noisily, shouting abuse, slamming doors and then gathering in the street to shout and to sing for a while. Sometimes a group might agree to stay for the evening and would then 'make a nuisance' of themselves by knocking over chairs, by 'being rough with the girls', or by making loud obscene comments about club activities.

Leadership 2
A. H. Birch

Reprinted with permission from A. H Birch, *Small-Town Politics*, London, Oxford University Press, 1959, pp. 34–5, 37–40

Looking back, it seems as if the social structure of the town fifty years ago was fairly clear-cut. At the very peak of the social hierarchy, in a category by themselves, were the members of the Howard family, the only people in the town who would be ranked as aristocratic in the wider society of the county or the nation. Beneath the Howards were the industrialists who comprised the town's upper class. They were wealthy men, some of them wealthier than the Howards and some even millionaires, who had either grown up in Glossop or moved into it at an early age, and who owed both their fortunes and their social status to their success in developing the town's industries. At the bottom of the hierarchy were the great mass of factory hands and their dependents who comprised the working class. In an intermediate position were a relatively small number of shopkeepers, professional people, and office workers. The only clear way to rise in the social scale was to make money in business. Given the right qualities, however, this was not particularly difficult, and if success was achieved there were no cultural barriers to social acceptance. Some of the millowners had themselves come from humble origins, and in Glossop nobody thought any the worse of them for that.

The structure of influence and political power in the town corresponded almost exactly with this social structure. The Howards had great potential influence but by the last years of the nineteenth century they had become rather aloof from local affairs. The real rulers of the town were the industrialists, who dominated its political and social organizations. They led the political parties, controlled the Borough Council, took turns to be mayor, and competed with each other to represent the constituency in Parliament. They also played a major part in the life of the churches, the sports clubs, and the charitable organizations. Their common leadership in business, social, and political affairs served to unify the community.

Today the social system is a good deal more complicated. The departure of nearly all the leading industrialists has left a gap which nobody has filled in the same way, and the present leaders of industry play a much less active part in social and political affairs. To explain this we must mention two aspects of the social revolution that England has experienced in the first half of the twentieth century.

The first of these is the development of new avenues of social mobility. Fifty years ago the standard way to get on in the world was to leave school at fourteen, go into industry or commerce, and rise to fortune by a combination of hard work, bright ideas, and good luck. People who succeeded in this way generally made their careers in the towns in which they were brought up, and they were normally keen to raise their status in the community by participating fully in its civic life.

In recent years this avenue of advancement has been largely replaced by the examination system. The way to grammar school and university is now open to all children who can pass the required examinations, and the importance of this is not lessened by the fact that the proportion of middle-class children who pass is higher than the proportion of working-class children who do so. At the same time, formal education has become a requisite for economic advancement in more and more fields. To an increasing extent, it is the educational system itself which now selects the people who will fill positions of responsibility in industry and commerce, and the main stepping-stones to a successful career are the selection for grammar school at the age of eleven, the selection for technical college or university at the age of eighteen, and the academic and professional qualifications that are subsequently acquired.

From the national point of view, this development has been almost wholly advantageous: it has opened a new avenue of social advancement for the children of poorer families and it has widened the field of recruitment to managerial and professional occupations. However, from the point of view of small- and medium-sized towns, it has been a mixed blessing. For although intelligent young people in such places have greater opportunities than ever before, most of those who benefit move to other parts of the country and thereby deprive their home towns of their services. People who get ahead in this way tend to become geographically as well as socially mobile, and to join the increasingly large class of professional and managerial workers who do not have strong roots in any local community.

The sample survey we conducted indicates that something like 60 per cent of the professional and managerial workers are immigrants to the town, compared with only 35 per cent of the adult population as a whole. If only the persons in the most influential positions are included – the chief industrialists, the senior public officials, the clergymen, the headmasters – the proportion is higher still. Our estimate, based not on the sample survey but on our discussions with local people, is that about four-fifths of these people are immigrants.

In the industrial field, the wealthy millowners of the past have been replaced by men of two types. In the first place, there are the owners of the seven or eight small firms that have moved into the town in the past twenty-five years, several of them central Europeans who came to England during the age of Hitler. Secondly, there are a larger number of salaried managers of the factories that are owned by combines, some of whom may move on to other branches in the future. When posts fall vacant in these firms, they are advertised over a wide area and the local man does not have any appreciable advantage over the outsider.

One of the results of this situation is that the present leaders of industry are not rooted in the community in the way that their predecessors were, and they do not play a prominent part in its social and political life. The consequence is, however, that the influence of the leaders of industry is largely confined to their own firms and they play very little part in the public life of the community as a whole.

The people of managerial and professional rank, although accorded superior status by the rest of the townsfolk, do not constitute an established elite as did the industrialists of a generation ago. Since most of them are immigrants and they do not play a prominent role in civic affairs, this is not surprising, but two other elements in the situation need to be noted. One is that these people are not so wealthy as their predecessors and do not spend money so conspicuously, either for their own or for the public benefit. The other is that although the economic gap between them and the industrial workers of the town is much smaller than it was, the cultural gap is somewhat greater. Most people in the managerial and professional groups have enjoyed a higher education, and in consequence have developed interests which are not generally shared by people who left school at the age of fourteen. One result of this is that there is much less contact between people of different economic groups in their sparetime activities than used to be the case.

Leadership 3

D. C. Miller

Reprinted with permission from 'Industry and Community Power Structure – A Comparative Study of an English and American City', *American Sociological Review*, Vol. XXIII, 1958, pp. 9–15

The role of business leaders within a local community poses some challenging questions about the on-going processes of community decision making. Why do business leaders take an active interest in community affairs? What is the extent of their influence in the community? How do they exercise this influence?

The purpose of this paper is to describe and analyse the characteristics of decision makers in an American and an English city. It has been repeatedly asserted that business men (manufacturers, bankers, merchants, investment brokers, and large real estate holders) exert predominant influence in community decision making. This is the central hypothesis under test.

Research Design

Two cities with similar economic, demographic, and educational characteristics were selected. 'Pacific City' is located in the Pacific Northwest, USA, 'English City' in South-western England. Both are comparable in many features with Hunter's Southern City. The following summary shows the close similarity of the three cities.

> Southern Regional City in 1950 had a population of 331,000. It serves as the commercial, financial, and distributive centre for the South-eastern section of the United States. It manufactures aircraft, textiles, and cotton waste products; is a transportation centre of rail, air, bus, and truck lines; and is a centre of education possessing a large university and many small colleges.
>
> Pacific City had a population of 468,000 in 1950. It is the commercial, financial, and distribution centre for the Pacific Northwest. Major transportation lines are centred in the city and it has a fine port. The city is the largest educational centre of the region with a state university and many small colleges.
>
> English City, also a regional city, serves as the commercial, financial, and distributive centre of the West of England. Its population in 1950 was 444,000. The major manufactures are airplanes, ships, beer, cigarettes, chocolate, machinery, and paper. It possesses an ocean port. The city houses a provincial (state) university and many private grammar schools.

The Community Power Structure is composed of key influentials, top influentials, the community power complex, and those parts of the institutionalized power structure of the community that have come into play when activated by a community issue. When not active, the community power structure remains in a latent state. In this paper attention is centred upon the role of the top influentials and the key influentials as representative of a significant part of the community power structure.

The Top Influentials (T.I.) are persons from whom particular members are drawn into various systems of power relations according to the issue at stake.

The Key Influentials (K.I.) are the socio-metric leaders among the top influentials.

Table 1. Key Influentials as Selected by Top Influentials and Ranked by Status as Influential Policy Makers

Pacific City	English City	Southern City
1. Manufacturing executive	1. Labour party leader	1. Utilities executive
2. Wholesale owner and investor	2. University president	2. Transport executive
3. Mercantile executive	3. Manufacturing executive	3. Lawyer
4. Real estate owner – executive	4. Bishop, Church of England	4. Mayor
5. Business executive (woman)	5. Manufacturing executive	5. Manufacturing executive
6. College president	6. Citizen party leader	6. Utilities executive
7. Investment executive	7. University official	7. Manufacturer owner
8. Investment executive	8. Manufacturer owner	8. Mercantile executive
9. Bank executive – investor	9. Labour leader	9. Investment executive
10. Episcopalian bishop	10. Civil leader (woman)	10. Lawyer
11. Mayor (lawyer)	11. Lawyer	11. Mercantile executive
12. Lawyer	12. Society leader	12. Mercantile owner

Business representation: 67 per cent	Business representation: 25 per cent	Business representation: 75 per cent

This marked difference between the American cities and English City raises questions about community organization. Why should two labour leaders be among the outstanding leaders in English City while not one labour leader appears among the key influentials of the two American cities?

Evidence for the influence of the K.I. was sought by establishing measures of actual behaviour for all the T.I. These measures included the activity of T.I. in committee work as reported in the newspapers over a two year period, and by their own statements of committee participation. Likewise, we sought evidence of their activity as spokesmen in community life as reported by the newspapers.

K.I. are very active in community affairs. However, this activity may not be reflected in newspaper accounts. There is no significant correlation in Pacific City between committee choice status and newspaper mentions of community activities; in English City there is a low negative correlation indicating that K.I. have received less newspaper publicity than T.I. This lack of publicity is in keeping with two features of civic activity as engaged in by K.I.: (1) much of their activity is policy making and is carried on quietly, and (2) there is a social convention that 'key' leaders do not seek publicity. In England, a deliberate effort is made by some K.I. to keep their names from the newspaper as a role requirement of their social class. The similarities exhibited by K.I. in the two cities suggest that there are many common role patterns. The influentials participate widely in social, civic, and professional organizations.

Business men appear to exert a predominant influence in community decision making in Pacific City and Southern City. However, in English City the hypothesis is rejected. The K.I. come from a broad representation of the institutional sectors of community life. Why should this difference exist between the two American cities and the English City? Two major factors seem to explain much of this difference. The first is the difference in occupational prestige values between the United States and England. In contrast to the United States 'the social status of industry in England, and so of its captains is low by comparison with the law, medicine, and the universities'. Top business managers are recruited from the universities (and upper-class families) where the tradition of a liberal education predominates, and this kind of education emphasizes humanistic values and minimizes the business orientation that characterizes the social climate of the typical American university campus. Many top business leaders, educated at Oxford and Cambridge, reported during interviews that they regarded business life as a very useful activity but did not view it as occupying the whole man. They expressed a respect for scholarly pursuits. Indeed, specialized courses in business administration in the University are very few, and the tradition continues that business management is learned by experience within the firm. This value system plays a role in the selection of community leaders in English City just as the larger emphasis and prestige of business leadership influences the selection of community leaders in the two American cities.

A second major factor is the structure of city government. In Pacific City the city council is composed of nine members elected at large on a non-partisan ballot.

A background of small business predominates. None of the council members was chosen as a top influential by our panel raters or by top influentials. There is every indication that the top community leaders do not regard the council as a strong centre of community power. The council tends to make decisions on community issues after a relatively long period of debate and after power mobilization has taken place in the community. During this period such groups as the Chamber of Commerce, the Labour Council, Municipal League, Parent-Teachers Association, and Council of Churches take stands. Council members may be approached and appeals made to them. Newspaper editors write articles. K.I. may make open declarations for or against the current issues and use their influence with the 'right persons or groups'. The mayor as administrative head and an elective official is both relatively powerful as patronage dispenser, and, at the same time, exposed to pressure from citizens to whom he may be indebted for his position either in the past or in the future. In contrast to this pattern, English City has a city council composed of 112 members. When the council is organized, members are appointed to committees that meet once or twice a week. Issues that arise in any part of the community are quickly brought to the Council's attention. The city clerk is the administrative head of the city government. He is a civil servant appointed by the council on the basis of his administrative ability and serves under a requirement of impartiality as elections come and political parties change in power. The members of the Council are released by their employers from work at the time of meetings. They are paid a stipend by the local government for time lost from work and for any personal expenses incurred in attending meetings within or outside the city. Table 2 shows the occupational composition of 110 members (2 vacant seats) of English City Council in 1955.

The Council is composed of three major groups, trade union members (32 per cent), business members (30 per cent), and other community members (37 per cent). Five of the twelve K.I. of the community are members and play major roles in their respective parties. The council is the major arena of community decision. Issues reach it directly, are investigated by Council

Table 2. Occupational Composition of English City Council in 1955

32 Per Cent Trade Union Members N=37	30 Per Cent Business Group Members N=33	37 Per Cent Other Community Sectors N=40
2 Foremen	4 Manufacturers	2 Solicitors
16 Skilled workers	7 Wholesale and retail owners	1 Doctor
5 Semi-skilled workers	1 Cinema owner	1 Dentist
8 Clerical workers	4 Contractors	1 Engineer
4 Trade union officials	8 Company directors and secretaries	1 Accountant
2 Unskilled workers	1 Bank official	1 Auctioneer
	8 Insurance officials	1 Teacher
		2 Ministers
		3 Political party organizing secretaries
		3 National government officials
		12 Housewives
Note: two vacant seats		12 Retired workers

committees, and are decided upon by a vote taken in the full council. Community organizations play important roles in debating the issues, but these are definitely secondary or supplementary activities. The community value system condemns any pressure tactics on the Council as 'bad taste'. However, in the council a caucus of elected party leaders is held before any important vote and a position is taken by the leaders for the party. The 'whip' is applied and members are expected to vote as instructed. Such action is rationalized as necessary for responsible party government.

Two factors, a different occupational prestige system and a different council-community power complex, seem to explain the variation in the composition of key influentials who come to power in Pacific City and English City.

Urban Environment
Buchanan Report

Reprinted with permission from *Traffic in Towns*, London, Her Majesty's Stationery Office, 1963, pp. 19-22

Whilst delays in traffic jams, and difficulties of parking have already caught public attention, and whilst road accidents have become the subject of a steadily mounting campaign to try to catch public attention, the deterioration of our urban surroundings under the growing weight of traffic has passed almost unnoticed. Part of the explanation is doubtless the fact that we have all grown up with the motor vehicle, and it has grown up with us, so we tend to take it and its less desirable effects very much for granted.

Of all the influences which the motor vehicle has on the environment the question of safety should be put foremost. It is not really possible to separate this from the matter of accidents, which has already been discussed. To be safe, to feel safe at all times, to have no serious anxiety that husbands, wives or children will be involved in a traffic accident, are surely prerequisites for civilized life. Against this standard, subjective though it may be, the conditions in our towns resulting from the use of motor vehicles obviously leave a great deal to be desired. There are now virtually no urban streets that are completely safe. Even ten years ago there were residential streets where few people owned cars, and where the only traffic was the occasional coal lorry or furniture van, but now most domestic deliveries are made by motor vehicles, and many of the residents have cars. These changes have resulted in continuous movement of vehicles up and down the street; and where, as is so often the case, there are no private garages, the cars stand in the street and create additional hazards for children. Moreover, as main roads have become congested with traffic, drivers have sought alternative routes, only too often using streets unsuitable for the purpose, or invading areas which by any standard should have a measure of peace and quiet about them. Some of this infiltration has taken place by drivers on their own initiative, in other cases it is the result of official policies for expediting the movement of traffic.

In addition to danger and anxiety, the motor vehicle is responsible for a great deal of noise. This is a matter which has recently been under consideration, along with other aspects of noise, by an official committee set up under the Minister for Science. In their Report, the Committee concluded that 'in London (and no doubt this applies to other large towns as well) road traffic is, at the present time, the predominant source of annoyance, and no other single noise is of comparable importance'. They discerned three possible lines of attack on the nuisance of traffic noise:

(1) *Reducing the noise emitted by vehicles*
The Committee concluded that, while there was clear evidence that amongst certain classes of vehicle the noise levels were higher than they need be having regard to the knowledge available to manufacturers, there were nevertheless considerable difficulties in reducing the noise levels from the most frequent offenders – namely diesel-engined buses and heavy commercial vehicles.

(2) *Smoothing the traffic flow*
Vehicles produce their maximum noise when accelerating in low gear. Therefore anything that can be done to keep traffic moving smoothly will tend to reduce noise.

(3) *Reducing traffic flows past any given spot*
This would be done by diversionary roads and other measures of a town planning nature.

The Committee considered that the better sound insulation of buildings against external noise could be achieved only at the expense of modern methods of building, such as light cladding and they concluded therefore that it would be unwise to look to better insulation for any great contribution towards the mitigation of the problem of external noise.

We accept the Committee's general conclusion that traffic noise is now the predominant noise nuisance in towns. The Committee found little evidence to show that noise causes direct physical ill-effects on people, or mental or nervous illness, but they concluded that one of the commonest and most undesirable effects is the interference with communication based on sound (e.g. conversation, teaching). Our own conclusion, based on observation and many discussions, is that traffic noise is steadily developing into a major nuisance, seriously prejudicial to the general enjoyment of towns, destructive of the amenities of dwellings on a wide scale, and interfering in no small degree with efficiency in offices and other business premises. But again, this is something which people have mostly grown up with and so tend to take very much for granted.

The conclusions of the Committee that not a great deal can be expected towards the abatement of traffic noise either from the improved design of heavy vehicles, or from the better insulation of buildings, are extremely important. They suggest that the long-term remedy must lie with town planning, encompassing at one extreme the diversion of heavy traffic flows from areas where people live, to the detailed layout of buildings and building groups at the other. At every turn in our consideration of traffic problems, we have been impressed by the need for vehicle users to be aware of their responsibilities to the rest of the community.

Fumes and smell constitute a further unpleasant by-product of the motor vehicle. Fumes are emitted mainly from engine exhausts, but also from ventilation holes in carburettors and tanks, and from 'breathers' in crankcases. They contain, amongst other substances, carbon monoxide (especially from petrol as opposed to diesel fuel), unburnt elements of fuel, and carbon dust. Carbon monoxide is toxic, and carbon dust can act as a carrier for carcinogenic (cancer producing) compounds. In conditions of sunlight, fumes can develop as eye and throat irritants.

In Britain, engine fumes do not yet rank as a major cause of atmospheric pollution, though they are certainly already contributive to smog. But it is scarcely open to question that fumes are now rendering urban streets extremely unpleasant, though once again, since it is a situation that most of us have grown up with, it needs a conscious effort to comprehend what has happened. This nuisance is now all-pervasive through towns, no street that carries traffic is free from it. It seems to be a widely held view that fumes gather only in canyon-like streets, but a walk across any of London's river bridges demonstrates the fallacy of this. Nor is there any freedom from fumes even for drivers and passengers inside vehicles, for they breathe air sucked in at 'fume level'. This is in contrast to noise, for it is a characteristic of most modern forms of transport that the passengers are largely unaware of the noise their conveyance is making, even though the din to outsiders may be unbearable.

The motor vehicle has been responsible for much else that affects our physical surroundings. There is its direct competition for space with environmental requirements, at its greatest in city centres where space is limited and traffic at its most dense. In very few towns is the record other than one of steady encroachment by the motor vehicle, often in small instalments, but cumulative in effect. There are the visual consequences of this intrusion of motor vehicles, the crowding out of every available square yard of space with vehicles, either moving or stationary, so that buildings seem to rise from a plinth of cars; the destruction of architectural and historical scenes; the intrusion into parks and squares; the garaging, servicing and maintenance of cars in residential streets which creates hazards for children, trapping the garbage and the litter and greatly hindering snow clearance; and the indirect effect of oilstains which render dark black the only suitable colour for surfaces, and which quickly foul all the odd corners and minor spaces round new buildings as motor-cycles and scooters take possession. There is the other kind of visual effect resulting from the equipment and works associated with the use of motor vehicles: the clutter of signs, signals, bollards, railings, and the rest of the paraphernalia which are deemed necessary to help traffic flow; the dreary, formless car parks, often absorbing large areas of towns, whose construction has involved the sacrifice of the closely-knit development which has contributed so much to the character of the inner areas of our towns; the severing effects of heavy traffic flows; and the modern highway works whose great widths are violently out of scale with the more modest dimensions of the towns through which they pass.

A Protest at Urban Environment
John Page

Reprinted with permission from John Page, 'A Protest at Urban Environment', *Political Quarterly*, Vol. 40, No. 4, 1969, pp. 436–46

The technology of city development is clearly facing a world-wide crisis in light of its environmental shortcomings. Interestingly, the technologists seem less worried than the citizens who make an important distinction between change and progress. The technologists at least achieve the satisfaction of seeing their ideas turn into urban hardware, even when it is environmentally misconceived. The owners and the occupiers of existing urban property, however, know only too well how easily the dreams of the planners, architects and organizers on urban progress turn into nightmares for individual citizens, who, more often than not, have to suffer severe environmental deprivation to make that urban change possible. The present urban technological system does not respect the environmental needs of the individual, whose protest is submerged to the point of ineffectiveness by the power of officialdom so easily bolstered by the simplified idea of acting on behalf of society, and yet not accepting society as a statistical assembly of individuals, each with their individual point of view. Basically, the urban system is out of environmental control as far as the individual is concerned.

It is hardly surprising that we find ourselves in a society where urban change is actively resisted by the majority of citizens close to the places of change, if they can find out soon enough. Naturally there is very great difficulty in finding out soon enough what is going on, for there are plenty of people with a vested interest in not letting others affected know what is happening. The conspiracy of silence is the best way of avoiding protest.

The well-based resistance to change which is usually for the worse, explains the obvious reticence of officialdom to release information, because the silent secret approach offers the greatest prospect of getting the obviously unacceptable accepted, if at all possible. Protest is stifled by providing no information on which to base an effective protest, or providing it too late; the Skeffington Report on 'People and Planning' exhorts a change, but does not demand it, in a situation where it is the vested interest of officialdom to keep the *status quo* of minimum public involvement. This leaves one doubtful as to whether the Skeffington proposals are workable on a voluntary basis. Even if an individual citizen manages to find out about adverse developments in time, the complications of the administrative machine baffle him, and he is faced with the choice of the escalation of personal costs involved in using lawyers or keeping quiet. For the most part, he grumbles on his way, keeping quiet, so joining that great band of citizens disaffected with the present planning machinery, which claims to represent his social interests, but so obviously in many ways does not. By organizing himself into a wider protest group, he gains some strength, but there are few developments other than airports that affect all citizens simultaneously at one time. Numerically, therefore, a particular protest is usually weakly supported, and officialdom is consequently confirmed in its belief it is serving the wider society. We each, however, tend to have our turn. So piecemeal, year by year, the environmental deterioration steadily proceeds. Many of those that can choose, opt out of the urban environment leaving the city socially deprived. This, in its turn, reduces the level of effective and informed protest, and so the standard deteriorates even more. The acceleration towards down-town status begins.

The Acceleration of Deterioration

Any reappraisal of the political problem of environmental deterioration must start with a discussion of the physical and social causes of such deterioration. Basically there are two main aspects of physical environmental deterioration to consider. One aspect is concerned with the physical operation of actually achieving a change of existing urban form, and the appreciable environmental deterioration so often encountered during the planning and construction phases, which may extend over a period of so many years as to become in effect a permanent deterioration for people living nearby.

The other aspect is concerned with the permanent environmental changes introduced once the new urban hardware is operational: increased noise, pollution and so on. The official machinery for handling environmental protest essentially gives some but limited weight to the second problem. The deterioration arising while waiting for reconstruction and during the actual construction, which may have a far more destructive environmental influence, is considered transitory and therefore of little importance, though it may sometimes last for ten years or more. The argument that it is going to be hell actually doing it is seldom accepted.

In fact a kind of utopian fallacy hangs over much of official planning practice and there still remains a vague belief that the city will one day be complete and all these transitory redevelopment problems will suddenly disappear. Given time, the well-planned city will be complete. In fact any policy of environmental control needs to be related to the dynamic of urban change which involves continuous reconstruction. This implies that we need not only to control what is done in the interests of society, but also how it is done. Unfortunately, our laws on how it is done remain for the most part weak and ineffective, if they exist at all.

The deterioration of the physical environment of our cities is primarily the consequence of changing patterns of the use of energy. In some ways, this changing pattern of energy is favourable. For example, the reduction of smoke from domestic premises which has resulted from vastly increased use of gas, electricity and oil. In other ways it is unfavourable. For example, the rising problem of pollution due to motor-vehicle exhausts which has already become a major menace in the USA and threatens to become an increasingly serious menace in the UK. I have recently made estimates which showed that urban pollution due to traffic fumes was likely to have increased (using existing technology) by a factor of at least 15 by the year AD 2000, compared to AD 1950, unless some effective steps are taken to lower pollution levels for individual vehicles. Furthermore, as urban density increases with increasing population pressure, the new urban forms generated will make it more difficult to disperse this pollution effectively to the atmosphere, as effective wind circulation is needed at street level to dilute the pollution with less contaminated air.

The amount of energy used per head is likely to increase by a factor of at least 10 by the year AD 2000 and a significant proportion of this energy will be used for transportation purposes. The aircraft transportation system has been growing at a rate of 15 per cent per annum on scheduled services, and 25 per cent or so on charter services, and aircraft are clearly going to become a much more important atmospheric pollution menace in future especially around airports.

Construction is being revolutionized by the application of vastly increased amounts of energy in equipment, like earth-moving equipment, graders, bulldozers, tower cranes, and so on. Familiar established menaces like pneumatic drills increase in number and are used with greater frequency.

Coming developments in the use of natural gas and electricity imply a total overhaul of our urban energy distribution systems, traditionally buried in our roads. Extrapolating forward on the data given in the Green Paper, 'The Task Ahead', it is easy to show the rate of digging up roads for energy services must increase by a factor of 3 or 4 by 1972, no doubt accompanied by vast amounts of noise from unmuffled pneumatic drills, and extreme traffic congestion with its fume problem.

At the same time, lowered energy costs combined with advances in chemical technology will throw up vast new chemical complexes involving huge problems of environmental pollution and its effective control.

On every hand there is mounting evidence that increased rates of deterioration of urban environment must come about if nothing is done. Any extrapolation of environmental factors into the future must therefore engender severe depression to all who are aware of our present *laissez-faire* attitude towards the physical environment, especially if one recognizes the low political prestige that seems to be attached to doing anything about it. Many local politicians seem to be aligned with their technical officers in a conspiracy of silence. It is so much easier that way.

Unfortunately one of the worst by-products of energy utilization is the associated noise-energy problem. Table 1 shows typical noise output in energy units for various sources of urban noise. It shows how adverse some of the recent developments are and, in particular, the magnitude of the noise sources thrown up by modern technology. The mobile society is the noisy society.

How much protection has the ordinary citizen got against noise and pollution? The answer is, in terms of accepted and legally enforceable standards, very little. Transportation technology has clearly failed to set acceptable social standards and planned developments like the London Motorway Box are going to produce severe environmental deprivation for large numbers of people and consequent financial loss. I remember recently driving in a bus along a residential area of Brussels threatened with a raised motorway down the centre of the road, where at least half the properties on either side were up for sale in a hopeless market. The principle of compensation for substantial environmental deterioration and loss of value has been strongly

Table 1. Approximate Equivalent Sound Power Radiated in Watts Emitted by Various Urban Noise Hazards

Noise Source	Approx. Sound Power Radiated in Watts	
Human being – soft whisper	0·000000001	
Human being – conversing	0·00005	
Human being – shouting	0·0007	
Luxury limousine at 30 m.p.h.	0·10	
4-tool diesel compressor	0·3	
Miniature passenger car at 30 m.p.h.	0·5	
180-H.P. angle dozer	3·0	
Sports car at 30 m.p.h.	3·0	
Miniature passenger car at 60 m.p.h.	4·0	
Motor-cycle 2-cylinder 4-stroke at 30 m.p.h.	5·0	
Unmuffled concrete breaker	7·0	
Diesel lorry at 30 m.p.h.	7·0	
75-piece orchestra	10·0	(Peak RMS levels over $\frac{1}{8}$ second)
Rubber-tyred tractor scraper	300·0	
S.R.N. 2 Hovercraft	630·0	
VC10 landing	1,600·0	(Under approach path $2\frac{1}{2}$ miles from airport)
Propeller aircraft take-off	10,000·0	
VC10 take-off	100,000·0	(Equivalent power in worst direction)
Supersonic aircraft take-off	500,000·0	(Equivalent power in worst direction)
	1,000,000·0?	

resisted by government and local authorities, because once acceded, it could open the door to an avalanche of claims in a society with no tradition of environmental standards. There has been some departure from this principle at London Heathrow, but otherwise the picture for any citizen affected is bleak. We have become, in fact, a nation of environmental gamblers, hoping that development goes the other way rather than our way.

The Inadequacy of Exhortation

The fundamental political question to be answered is what more effective action can be taken to bring our urban systems under environmental control. I am certain any voluntary action will prove quite ineffective in the face of the pressures that exist. There are several good reasons why exhortations directed towards social change cannot be really effective. First, environmental control involves spending more money – for example, on improved silencers, better dust-removing equipment, more land, and so on. Secondly, many individuals are psychologically disposed to enjoy any source of environmental pollution that gives them a sense of individual power. The problem of the adolescent and the motor-cycle or the sports car illustrates this principle too well. Many sports cars and motor-cycles are made deliberately noisier to sell better and afterwards silencers are further doctored to make them even noisier. It is a psychological fact that the noise one makes oneself is more acceptable than the noise others make. Making noise makes the insecure feel more secure.

The problem of resistance to environmental control is not confined to individual resistance. The resistance may be from a whole organization, even from a total local authority. This is particularly common where questions of livelihood are concerned. A good example has been provided by the resistance of the local mining communities to clean air legislation. This resistance is understandable but not always wise. The effects of pollution on health are well established: bronchitis in many parts of Europe is named 'The English Disease' in colloquial medical terms. The health records of the mining communities are bad, but many still resist strong pressure from central government for effective clean-air programmes. Air from one place moves to another, and parochial policies followed in one place may prejudice the more progressive policies followed in adjacent areas. Can we afford therefore to leave the establishment of environmental standards and policies to individual local authorities, or, acting in our mutual self-interest, do we not have to seek stronger powers at the centre?

As we have had such low standards in the past, many people have come to accept as inevitable the present state of affairs. A common criterion often used in official assessment is whether the new line of action is going to produce a further deterioration beyond the present level, regardless of the fact that the existing situation may be well below any acceptable standard based on consideration of health, well-being and amenity.

The recent political technique for attempting to deal with physical environmental problems seems to have been the establishment of a Royal Commission, Committee, or similar body to review the field on a wide basis and to make recommendations to the Government for further action. The report is then left on the shelf and no significant action results. The environment deteriorates further. Its recommendations are considered inappropriate as a consequence of the subsequent changes, and the report is condemned to oblivion as being out of date, and everybody concerned rightly feels they have wasted their time. So the decline goes on.

The Fate of Official Reports

It would perhaps be appropriate to trace the fate of some of the official environmental reports that have emerged over recent years. In my opinion by far the most successful report, as far as action is concerned, has been the Beaver Committee Report on Clean Air, because a number of the recommendations of the report have been actually adopted and real progress has been made, especially in places where there has been the will to take effective political action. The progress has essentially been towards smokeless air rather than clean air, and the problem of control of sulphur dioxide pollution is still far from an effective solution. Important gaps in legislation still remain.

A number of necessary conditions have had to be fulfilled to make such progress. The first and most basic requirement has been the drafting of the new legislation needed for effective support of the proposed action. The second requirement has been a national financial policy that has helped towards the conversion costs of individual householders so reducing the risk of serious opposition on grounds of individual financial hardship. The third requirement has been the existence of socially acceptable alternative methods of domestic heating that are economically viable, for example, smokeless fuels. As prosperity has increased, fuels of convenience like gas and electricity have replaced more and more traditional fuels, especially in more prosperous areas. Furthermore, the relative price of fuels of convenience has fallen in relation to the cost of traditional fuels like coal and coke. The problem of change has thus been very much eased by advances in technology.

It is interesting to note that in all cases where dramatic progress has been made, real political drive has had to be applied at the local authority level. The existence of the law in itself is not enough; it must be accompanied by the drive and determination to make full use of the new powers offered by the law, and of the administrative and financial aid offered by central government.

As environmental progress costs money, it is not surprising to note that, in general, most progress has been made in the more prosperous regions of the country which, in this respect at least, have had the least severe environmental problems, and slower progress has been made in the less prosperous, highly polluted regions, especially in areas linked with coal production. Many of these areas are desperately depressed environmentally, and need to improve their setting to attract new industry. Unfortunately they are the least well able to afford the extra investment, and the most likely to oppose such change on considerations of existing rather than future livelihood. They are also the areas most conditioned to accept low standards. Places like Sheffield form vigorous exceptions to this kind of statement, and in all such places the quality of the political leadership in environmental fields has been paramount to success.

Serious concern must be expressed about the exemption of statutory undertakings from so much of the legislation concerned with environmental control. The exempted statutory undertakings are bodies of substantial economic power in the wider community, often responsible directly to a Minister in Whitehall. Their actions can have a devastating effect on a local community. One might have hoped that nationalized industries, like the Coal Board, would have shown an exceptional degree of awareness of their general social responsibilities in the environmental field. Four years' experience on the Yorkshire and Humberside Planning Council has convinced me that just the opposite is true, and that the statutory undertakings have for the most part failed to accept their environmental responsibilities. Their record in this area of action demands reconsideration of their privileged status in relation to problems of environmental control at local level. It seems absurd that a Hospital Board can belch black smoke out of its hospital chimneys in defiance of a local authority's clean air legislation.

If one turns now to the numerous other official reports, the outlook seems bleak for environmental progress in the United Kingdom for government has ignored the reports, or, at least, the need to face up to the consequent legislation imperative for progress.

The problem of noise, for instance, was discussed in a clear and cogent way in the Report of the Wilson Committee on Noise, which covered the whole field of noise. Little effective action has so far followed despite an accelerating deterioration of the noise environment. In particular, little progress has so far been made towards establishing urban environmental noise standards, and the environment on and around roads, airports and building sites continues to deteriorate. The Wilson Committee, for example, recommended changes in the law relating to statutory undertakings which would remove altogether the present exemption of railway authorities from proceedings for noise nuisance. Suppose the environmental impact of the new proposed high-speed trains is unacceptable to particular local authorities. They are powerless to take any legislative action. As the noise energy produced by transport systems typically varies between the fourth and eighth power of the velocity of travel, how does society intend to deal with this kind of problem within the present law?

Failure to tackle the problem of airport noise is impeding the economic development of the aircraft industry, as the trials and tribulations of the Roskill Commission on the Third London Airport illustrate too well. The Edwards Committee treated the problem of aircraft noise as a trivial feature of their report, and the Roskill Committee in their report have made assumptions about a long-term fall in aircraft noise, but, unsupported by effective international legislation, what hope is there of achieving any reduction within the present international climate of aircraft development? Are sonic booms to be symbols of our economic prosperity and export potential, or is the need for environmental standards to be accepted and legislated for politically?

When is some effective action going to be taken about control of noise on building sites, before we are finally bush-hammered and bulldozed into a permanent acoustical daze? Are we to stay with concepts like 'the best means practicable' as a way of justifying the environmental *status quo*?

The Buchanan Report on Traffic in Towns covered another aspect of the environmental problem, but so far little progress has been made towards effectively implementing any of the recommendations. A few scattered pedestrian precincts have emerged, but for the most part the traffic continues in its unregulated growth, eating cancerously into the structure of our towns, destroying unchecked our environment. What effective means of protest has the individual against the traffic problem, for as a community we have never established any standards?

Health and the physical environment, too, are linked. Environmental deprivation promotes other problems of the kind discussed in the Seebohm Report. Ill-health of the heads of families and mothers particularly leads on to other social problems. Are we to continue to accept environments that promote the ill-health of their occupants?

The Need for Urgent Action

Basically, at least, politicians and local government officials seem to think the environmental problems of our technology are too difficult to grapple with, and that it is better to shelve them in the hope that something better will come along, thrown up by some technological benefactor who invents the noiseless plane or the pollution-free car. Effective legislation, in context, would force technological change in a more acceptable social direction.

All projective studies of the future point towards a rapidly accelerating decline of the urban environment, if we continue our present *laissez-faire* approach. There is a real need to take effective anticipatory measures now. This implies that great effort must be directed towards the problem of establishing the necessary standards for urban living, and that these standards must be based on concepts related to demographic and technological growth. There is an inherent danger in attempting to control the future on the standards of the past. Without action, the future is clearly going to be worse than the past. The necessary legislation needs to be drafted with urgency, followed by the adoption of new urban policies directed towards positive environmental improvement of cities. This will demand a determined attempt to upgrade the environmental education of architects, town planners, engineers and other officials in town halls. It will imply measures unpopular with pressure groups with vested interests in resisting progress in the control of noxious activities. Above all, it will require political vision to set up goals for the future, goals that are realistic and capable of economic achievement, but goals that are based on human standards and human needs, and not standards that emerge as the accidental by-products of the technology of a particular time.

My protest is therefore against our present political indifference to the future of our urban physical environment, the lack of political drive and foresight, the low priority allocated to environmental legislation, the exemption of statutory undertakings for so many of the provisions of the law concerned with environment. I add to my protest my deep concern about the secrecy of officialdom and lack of public discussion of the environmental consequences of planning decisions. Finally, I seek the creation of organizations to represent formally the environmental interests of the citizens, and to provide an effective channel of protest, compulsorily consulted. I reject the voluntary nature of the Skeffington proposals, and demand that the public have the right to be consulted on all planning decisions with environmental consequences. I object strongly to the lack of environmental control during the construction process and seek more effective laws to deal with disturbance during construction.

When planners decide what to do, it is often easier for them to forget the subtler consequences of their actions. Towns should be fine places in which to live. Our technology has made too many of them into places from which we try to escape. Rustication unfortunately has become easier for the individual than effective environmental protest, and men no longer live in cities in order that they may be civilized. This is not a necessary state of affairs, but a state we have come to accept through our environmental complacency.

Further Reading: Community

* R. FRANKENBERG: *Communities in Britain*, Penguin Books, 1966.
† R. WARREN (ed.): *Perspectives on the American Community*, Rand McNally, 1966.
  P. COLLISON: *The Cutteslowe Walls*, Faber & Faber, 1963.
* HMSO: *The Needs of New Communities*, 1967.
  B. JACKSON: *Working Class Community*, Routledge & Kegan Paul, 1968.
* J. JACOBS: *The Death and Life of Great American Cities*, Penguin Books, 1964.
  J. KLEIN: *Samples from English Cultures*, Routledge & Kegan Paul, 1965.
  G. D. MITCHELL AND OTHERS: *Neighbourhood and Community*, Liverpool University Press, 1954.

J. C. MITCHELL: *Social Networks in Urban Situations*, Manchester University Press, 1969.

J. M. MOGEY: *Family and Neighbourhood*, Oxford University Press, 1956.

* J. REX AND R. MOORE: *Race, Community and Conflict*, Oxford University Press, 1966.

C. VEREKER AND J. B. MAYS: *Urban Redevelopment and Social Change*, Liverpool University Press, 1961.

P. WILLMOTT: *The Evolution of a Community*, Routledge & Kegan Paul, 1963.

* Available in paperback
† Reference

3 Socialization

In general the term socialization is used to describe the ways
in which the individual learns the values, beliefs, and roles
which underwrite the social system in which he participates.
For the child living in Britain learns to be not only a performer
of roles which are applicable to his age and sex but also to
his position in the society to which he belongs. Crucial to
socialization is the idea of culture which may be defined as
learned behaviour which is socially transmitted. The idea of
culture involves 'a complete design for living'. From certain
points of view culture may be seen as a set of rules.

Since socialization is concerned with preparation for roles
in society it begins in the relationships which develop between
those with whom the child is in a position of subordination,
principally the parents, and those with whom he is in a position
of equality, principally in the early stages brothers and sisters.
By degrees the child takes over standards from the parents
and others with whom he is in contact. There are many
differences according to social class background in the way in
which this develops. These have been illustrated graphically
in the comparison between a group of children living in slums
and children going on to public schools in B. M. Spinley's
The Deprived and the Privileged. The differences in early
experience, she suggests, 'seem to be numerous, important and
fundamental'. Little overlapping was found in this study
between the groups in terms of their experiences. Two of the
most significant differences arose in the ways in which children
were brought up. In the case of the slum children there was
said to be no interference with the physiological satisfactions
of feeding or excretion in the first year but the period of
indulgence in this respect ceased at the birth of the next child
in the family. In the case of the children of higher social status
there was a consistent attempt to improve performance in all
respects, and this was also true in the second significant area
of difference, that of attitudes towards the future. The high
status child was taught to think consistently in terms of deferring

immediate gratifications whereas the slum child had no consistent set of values presented to him.

The middle-class model of socialization involves a great
concern by parents for the performance of their children and
training geared ideally to 'independence of action and a show
of initiative'. Competitive behaviour is rewarded and success
is acclaimed. For parents in many social groups the child is
typically the hope of the future and in particular where parents
have not themselves gone as far as they had hoped.

Some of these issues arise in the readings concerned with
relationships between parents and children to be found in
Chapter 1. Later other processes of socialization become
important. For a considerable period of time before maturity
the individual is socialized by the formal processes of the
educational system. Contacts with the peer groups to which
the individual belongs are also of considerable importance
particularly during the time when the 'youth culture' begins to
become more influential as the influence of the parents and
the school wanes. All three of the sources of socialization are
considered in the readings which follow.

Reference has already been made to the different patterns
of child-rearing in social groups in Chapter 1. The **Newsons**
have undertaken a sustained and intensive study of the
development of a large cohort of children, and their work in
this reading is largely concerned with differences in attitudes
towards child-rearing. Parental behaviour is seen to vary
considerably towards children. Among the underprivileged
its forms may compel the children to become independent and
turn from their parents to the peer group, and brings them to
distrust authority and, to some extent, hardens them emotionally. The *future-orientation* of middle-class children, their more
protected lives and the reciprocity built into their relationships
with their parents differs markedly from this. Growing
affluence is often assumed to lead to the adoption of specifically
middle-class attitudes and ideas but it does not follow from
the evidence presented here that there will be a rapid shift in
this direction.

The relationships between school and the wider society are
considered in the reading of **Bernstein**. He criticizes a term such
as 'compensatory education' with its implications that school
has to 'compensate' for something lacking in the family
whereas the children in question have not been offered an

acceptable educational environment. Labelling children as 'culturally deprived', referring to their 'linguistic deprivations', suggests that parents are inadequate and the consequences are lower expectations of children by their teachers. The focus needs to be upon the deficiencies of the school and, ultimately, the potential for change within the educational setting. The social experience of the child should be the starting-point and the validity and significance of this experience should be clear.

In the reading by **King**, access to education is explored in relation to the social class and sex of students. There is continuing evidence to suggest that rates of access for the middle class are greater than for the working class, and that this gap widens as the level of education rises. Theories that explain the class differentials are considered. As the author shows there is also a sex group in educational access, and a number of paradoxes arise from the application of theories to these facts. Finally, questions about the relationship between educational provision for girls and the increasing number of women in the labour force are posed.

Both the following readings are by American authors. In that by **Elder** the consequences for the life opportunity and personality of secondary-school children are considered. The main point which emerges is that those who develop low opinions of themselves as students tend to perform in accordance with their self-assessment. Streaming and the irrelevance of much of the subject matter in modern schools is also considered an element in producing the negative self-image of the products of that educational background. The importance of commercialized youth culture as having an influence on decisions to leave school early is also apparent. The question of youth culture is also raised in the article by Worsley in Chapter 7. **Gerstl and Perrucci** look at the mobility of the elite within a particular occupation and compare the situation in the United States and Britain. Trends in the recruitment to one occupation, that of engineering at a qualified level, are considered and the conclusion for both Britain and the United States is advanced that engineering is the best example of a career open to talent whatever the social background of its recruits.

The problems of children brought up in a situation where two cultures are present, one in the home and the other in the school and often the neighbourhood, are posed in the reading by **Butterworth.** Little systematic work has been done on the kinds of adaptation necessary for newcomers to British society, in particular those like the migrants from Asia who have to contend not only with problems of language but also of different cultural and religious traditions. These problems of socialization continue to arise for adults and it would be true to say that all members of a society continue to be socialized in response to new organizational arrangements and new values which arise with social change.

The segregation of roles between men and women in Muslim society, which is also true of Sikhs and Hindus to a slightly different extent, is a consequence of a particular social structure. Added to conflicts between generations which are a commonplace of life in a modern society are others which follow from these cultural differences. Attitudes towards people in authority, whether parents or teachers or others, may be modified in consequence of life in Britain, with long-term effects on the self-image and the capacity to identify with a particular group of the individual concerned.

The kind of education which is provided for particular groups within the population reflects in part the historical development of the system and the needs of society as these are perceived by the policy-makers. **Glass,** in the reading on 'Education and Social Change', looks at the different levels of provision and the assumptions which underlie them. In place of the view of a relatively static tradition he presents one which has experienced a considerable number of changes in consequence of new priorities being established but which remains in general strongly elitist in the distinctions made between middle classes and the rest in terms not only of potential but of educational opportunities.

The readings on teachers concentrate on three main themes. The first examines the changes in commitment to the school of boys entering a particular grammar school in a northern area over a period of time. Two examples are given by **Lacey** of boys whose careers, for reasons to do with the situation in the form, did not conform to the established relationship between social class and academic achievement.

The **Newsom** Report was concerned with those attending secondary modern schools. It makes the connection between the kinds of schools attended and educational success. One important influence, which the reading is selected to illustrate, is in the differential 'holding power' of schools in terms of the length of stay of their staffs in different kinds of neighbourhoods. The consequences, especially where this influence is one of a number of others including the mobility of the student population, the age of the school, its equipment and level of amenity, the attitudes of staff, and relations between home and school, are far-reaching.

The role of the teacher is obviously a crucial one, particularly when the school is not only an agency of social promotion but one of the few remaining agencies of social demotion. How he or she performs will reflect not only training but social attitudes and expectations. **Floud** considers the crisis in the teacher's role and in particular the bases of the moral authority of the teacher. Their traditional authority tends to be undermined by certain social pressures and it is also suggested that they are generally ill-equipped by their social and educational history to cope with the tasks confronting them.

Social relationships within the group form an increasingly important element in the process of socialization. **Downes** looks at the delinquent gang and how factors such as teenage culture and rehousing have undermined the traditional gang framework. He distinguishes clearly between adolescent peer groups, where young people can experience for the first time relationships embodying equality and democracy, and the gang, which tends to be hierarchical and tightly knit. This has consequences for the treatment of the seriously disturbed delinquent, and also how we view the types of adolescent protest. Spencer, in *Stress and Release in an Urban Estate*, about an area in Bristol, provides a contrasting view of the adolescent gang which sees it much more in terms of similar kinds of behaviour – in general outline though not in specific content – to that of young people in other countries from similar social backgrounds.

Most writing about socialization is concerned with the effects of the family on the orientations and attitudes of children; **Dowse and Hughes** are concerned in the reading taken from their work with the extent to which the political ideas and attitudes of parents are transmitted to their children. Their sample of children (from 11 to 17 years of age) and parents was drawn from Exeter. Earlier theorists stressed the primary importance of the family as an agency of political socialization, but, in a large proportion of the families studied, there appeared to be 'no strong politically communicative interaction between parents and their offspring'.

Changes in the Concept of Parenthood

J. and E. Newson

Reprinted with permission from *The Family and its Future*, J. A. Churchill, 1970, pp. 142–51

Whatever interpretive framework we choose to adopt it is fairly clear that, moving down the socio-economic scale, we are more likely to encounter a tradition-oriented, or 'old-fashioned', style of child upbringing. In the first place, sex roles between husband and wife are ever more rigidly differentiated as one moves away from the professional class, through the white-collar and skilled manual to the unskilled manual group. Work-roles in particular show this pattern; while most professional and white-collar occupations are open to women as well as men, and carry equal pay, there are a great many manual jobs which are exclusively reserved, by tradition, for men alone, and women at the manual level tend to be grossly undervalued. The degree of sex differentiation in the work-role tends to spill over into the division which is drawn at home between 'mother's role' and 'father's role'. Further down the scale, the father is less likely to take a share in feeding and tending the baby or in putting the toddler to bed. Perceived differences in maternal and paternal roles are also reflected in the ways boys and girls are differentially treated: parents' expectations of behaviour are more closely dependent upon the child's sex as one descends the class scale.

Other kinds of parental behaviour can similarly be seen as approximating more nearly to older traditions at the lower end of the scale. The father is more likely to be described by his wife as 'stricter' than herself, and accorded greater prestige as an authority figure. He is less likely to participate in story-telling, or to share an interest with the seven-year-old. Parents in the un-skilled manual class more often resort to smacking as a disciplinary technique, and rely heavily upon their inherent status as adults, exerting as such an inalienable right to respect and obedience, and thus deliberately creating a social distance between adults and children. In line with this, they also appear to suffer less anxiety over what methods to adopt in dealing with their children, and are less inclined than other parents to be self-critical with regard to their own attitudes and behaviour.

Although, in common with other investigators, we have found in this group a preference for non-verbal methods of controlling children, we have also shown that there is a simultaneous readiness to use a verbal technique of teasing or threatening the child, in ways which depend for their effectiveness upon his immaturity of understanding. In direct contrast to mothers at the other end of the social scale, who show an almost super-stitious respect for words as the agents of truth, lower-working-class mothers on the whole accept as normal the use of deliberate distortions of fact, often exploiting the child's natural fears and anxieties, in order to instil in him a salutary sense of their own power. It is perhaps significant how often such idle threats consist of a backing-up of the mother's own authority by some outside authority figure, which, being a more unknown quantity, to the child than the mother herself, is perhaps presumed to retain its effectiveness rather longer. Examples of idle threats and teases follow; they are representative.

'I say "A policeman will come and take you away, and you'll have no Mummy and no Daddy".'
'I often say "If I have to keep shouting at you, I'm going to the doctor's, and if I don't get any better I'll have to go away".'
'I tell her God will do something to her hand if she smacks me.'
'I've told him I'll have to put him in a home if he's naughty.'
'She picks her nose – I tell her it's dirty and her nose will fall off.'

The following account is an example of how a chance occurrence may be deliberately used both to tease the child and to tighten control; similar examples have been reported from other cultures.

After I got your letter, mester asked what it was for; so my girl, naturally enough (*sic*), she said to Freddie (aged 4), 'Oh, it's to take you away, a lady's coming to take you away'. He said 'I don't want to go away'; so I said 'Well, you'd better be a good lad, then – or else she will'. (Do you often say that sort of thing?) Yes.

On the whole, the parental attitudes and group trends that we have so far discussed are those which differentiate most sharply between different working-class groups at the lower end of the social scale; which, in fact, characterize the unskilled worker's family from those of other manual workers. They suggest a traditional pattern of child-rearing which would these days be condemned by most middle-class commentators and experts, and by a majority of parents generally, as at best uneducated and lacking in psychological insight, and at worst unkind and extremely undesirable. We must, however, remind ourselves that this style of parent-child relationships has a long history and deep cultural roots. The pattern would appear to share many features with patterns adopted by economically underprivileged parents in urban communities all round the world, and in societies which are, in many other respects, very different from our own. It has probably evolved in such a way that it allows parents and their children at least to survive and cope at a certain level; and whether or not this method will be successful in producing children who are reasonably well adapted to the kinds of conditions they are liable to face as young adults, at the least privileged end of the social spectrum in our decaying city centres, is still rather an open question. It could be argued, for instance, with some cynicism but also with some force, that a socialization pattern which compels children to independence; which turns them, at an early age, away from their parents and towards the peer group; which teaches them to distrust as unreliable all adults in positions of authority; and which, to some extent, hardens and desensitizes them emotionally, will continue to serve a function in making a hard life at least tolerable for the exceptionally underprivileged. It may also, of course, make them irreclaimable to such opportunities as exist.

However, it is necessary to emphasize that the pattern of child-rearing which we have been describing is nowadays only to be found, in its essential form, in a small minority of families in our sample. Nottingham is a prosperous city with a low unemployment rate and a vigorous policy of slum clearance and rehousing on new estates. The old densely-packed terraced housing in the central districts is steadily being eroded and replaced. For the majority of children, even within the working-class group, the socialization pattern has already changed. Father has come down from his erstwhile pedestal to be a friend to his children and a help to his wife. Relationships between parents and children have already become a good deal more egalitarian and democratic. And parents pinpoint the change by their pleasure at their children's willingness to talk to and share confidences with them with a freedom that they found so much more difficult, or even impossible, to attain with their own parents. In the context of a culture in which the major attitude changes over time have already affected all socio-economic groups except the lowest, much of our work has been to attempt a description of the skilled and semi-skilled working-class style of upbringing, and to show how it still differs in more subtle ways from middle-class modes of behaviour.

At this point, then, let us consider a whole variety of interlocking ways in which the experience of middle-class children differs from that of working-class children; in other words, we will switch our attention away from differences between groups at the bottom end of the social scale, and towards a consideration of differences between middle-class children and working-class children as a whole. It is convenient to do this in terms of a number of pro- positions which can be backed up by both qualitative and quantitative evidence drawn from the results of our study of seven-year-olds and their mothers. Briefly to define our terms, we take the middle class to comprise white-collar workers and upwards, and the working class to include all manual workers with the exception of foremen.

(1) Middle-class children are *future-oriented*. Their parents tend to marry somewhat later, on average, than those of working- class children, and this is often quite deliberately planned in order to allow the middle-class father to establish himself vocationally on some career which will have a rising income- curve through time. The middle-class child is thus born into a family which can look forward to considerably improved standards in the future – not because everyone in the country will gradually get richer, but because middle-class workers expect to benefit from a promotion system which brings them to their peak in middle age, whereas manual workers know that their earning power is likely to fade proportionally to their failing health and strength. This is what lies behind what Brian Jackson has succinctly described as 'the middle-class ethic of postponed pleasure'; and it is nowhere more strongly evident than in the way children in different social groups are taught to handle their pocket money. We have calculated, taking all

different sources of income into account, precisely how much pocket money is at the disposal of the seven-year-old child in the course of a week; oddly or significantly, depending on one's viewpoint, there is a perfect inverse correlation between this average figure and the social class affiliation of the child: that is to say, the lower down the class scale, the more money the child is given to spend each week. It must be remembered, of course, that the middle-class child is probably enjoying rather more luxurious living-standards, and may be receiving considerable benefits in kind such as plenty of fruit, drawing materials, outings etc.; however, the fact remains that the working-class child has more immediate spending power. His mother is also more likely to give him extra if she happens to have it, without making conditions as to its sensible use. What is more, once the money has been put into his hands (often in small daily amounts), there is considerable tolerance of his spending it at once, although there is a tradition of saving up as a holiday approaches; whereas middle-class children are generally expected *on principle* to save a proportion of their smaller sum.

(2) Middle-class children – particularly the boys, compared with working-class boys – appear to lead *more sheltered and protected lives* than their working-class counterparts. Sometimes this is the result of parents actively discouraging their children from 'playing out' in the neighbourhood or forbidding their wandering off beyond their own road into an area where the children might be less 'nice'; but in practice it is seldom necessary for the middle-class mother to make such blatant restrictions, since middle-class areas tend anyhow to be geographically distinct and insular. It is also broadly true that the catchment areas of the state primary schools tend to reflect such social divisions. When house-hunting, middle-class parents are often strongly influenced to choose a particular area because of the reputation of the local primary school; and, even when they live outside the normal catchment area of a favoured school, they will tend to exercise the right of parental choice (allowed for by the education act, but rather seldom invoked by working-class parents) so as to allow their child to attend a 'better' school some distance from their home. Alternatively, they may opt out of the state system altogether and send their children to private schools.

When we first began to look into the question of protection, our original intention was simply to obtain some measure of children's independence at the age of seven years. To this end, we endeavoured to form a scale based on answers given to a number of different specific questions, which could be rated and then summed to yield a composite index or independence score for each child. When, however, the separate questions were analysed as a function of social class, the results were not at all consistent from one question to the next. For instance, when we asked whether the child was permitted to go to the park or recreation ground alone, we found a clear class trend indicating that, as we move down the social class scale, more and more children are permitted to do this; when we asked about children going shopping alone, there was no consistent social class trend; and when we asked about travelling alone by bus, there was a significant trend showing that a greater proportion of middle-class children are expected to cope with this. Again, whereas more middle-class children are taken and collected to and from school, it is also true that fewer working-class children ever have the experience of staying away from home overnight, for pleasure, without their parents. Thinking in terms of some global concept such as 'independence training', these divergent results are not easy to reconcile. The evidence instead suggests that middle-class and working-class children are taught to be independent in somewhat different ways. Taking into account a good deal of additional evidence, one arrives at the conclusion that the working-class child is taught to be independent in the sense that he must learn to fend for himself *among other children* in a variety of situations where adult supervision is likely to be minimal. He is allowed to wander further, through very much more crowded streets, in order to reach a recreation ground where, again, he is likely to have to cope with large unsupervised groups of children; and he is expected to make his own way on foot to his local school. By contrast, the middle-class child is encouraged to be independent of his own parents by learning to rely on other *adults* for help and support. Parents expect some control over his choice of companions, by selecting both his school and the location of his play. Selection of school gives rise to problems of distance; these they solve either by ferrying or by teaching him to use public transport, an adult-supervised activity. He may stay a night away from home with a friend, but it is fully understood that the friend's mother is in charge. Thus the middle-class child is introduced to independence by degrees and in a highly protected context.

At first sight, this tendency on the part of middle-class parents to protect and supervise their children so closely might appear to restrict the range of experiences to which the middle-class child has access. It is true that the middle-class child grows up without much acquaintance with a busy street life, the hurly-burly of traffic, hostile and friendly adults and a mob of neighbourhood children. Adult memories of back-street childhoods evoke a richness of mingled delights and fears: the parents of back-street children often express considerable anxiety as to the unfortunate influences from which they are powerless to shield the child effectively. The middle-class child's experience is very different, but probably no less rich. Intellectually, his parents expect to provide opportunities for his own self-expression as well as for learning; socially, they provide the formal opportunity to play both guest and host. Outside the home, there is a deliberate widening of the child's experience, again under supervision. As one might expect, middle-class seven-year-olds are more likely than their working-class counterparts to be taken on visits to theatres, concerts, exhibitions, art galleries and historic buildings; but it is interesting that it is the middle-class children who also more often attend sporting events such as football matches with their parents, and also the cinema. A higher proportion of middle-class children also go to church with their parents, belong to Sunday School and are members of organized clubs or church groups.

(3) This leads to a further broad generalization: that middle-class children are expected to *learn communication skills* of many different kinds as early as possible. We ourselves have shown how, as early as four years old, the middle-class child is effectively rewarded for his skill in verbally stating his case for arbitration; and Bernstein has made an especially important contribution by his emphasis of the difference between an explicit and a context-bound use of language. The point at issue is whether the child is able to use language to communicate meaningfully, without recourse to gesture and pronominal indications of the context; such gestures in fact restrict him to communicating his thoughts only in contexts which his listener already shares. For example, the child who normally sees no need to be more explicit than 'You know him, out there, well he pushed her just here all like that' is entirely dependent for communication upon his listener's ability to watch his gestures and look out of the window to see to whom these gestures refer. He is more likely to have difficulty in putting

his thoughts across in situations where the context is not available than the child who has the habit of being explicit: 'That boy in next door's yard, he twisted his sister's arm right up behind her back.'

It is, of course, precisely this comparative lack of familiarity with the context-free use of language which makes it difficult for many working-class adults to use the telephone effectively. Conversely, the telephone for most middle-class people, in work and at play, is an indispensable tool of communication. In perhaps the majority of middle-class households, its possibilities are taken for granted; middle-class children need little encouragement to learn its use from an early age, in order to take messages for their parents, and quickly discover its advantages to further their own social enjoyment, and indeed to break through the geographical restrictions still imposed on them at the primary-school age. Every middle-class parent of reasonably sociable children becomes irritably aware of the telephone as a successful medium for children's conversations with their peers. The working-class child, however, even if his father's job atypically demands a telephone, finds that very few of his friends have access to one, and that therefore his own use of the facility is negligible. The situation is a good example of a technological innovation which offers a specific if unlooked-for training in a communication skill, and it is interesting that the use of telephones is now encouraged as a deliberate pedagogic technique in schools for underprivileged children.

This is, of course, not the only way in which middle-class children acquire more opportunity to learn and practise the skills of explicit language. They are also read to more often from story books, frequently full length books taken on a serial basis. They more often 'say their prayers' at bedtime. They are encouraged to communicate their private fantasy life to their mothers, who have more welcoming attitudes to fantasy and imagination than working-class mothers, and therefore reward the child by their interest and approval for describing to his mother what only he *can* describe. Middle-class children are also more likely to prefer imaginative, role-playing games to the play of the rough-and-tumble variety which is the first choice of more working-class children; while it is not altogether clear why this preference should exist (factors may be parental encouragement and greater privacy and space in the home), certainly imaginative play provides a much more powerful stimulus for the explicit use of language, whereas rough-and-tumble play is well enough served by purely implicit forms.

When we turn to other communication skills such as the child's developing ability in reading and writing, we of course find enormous social class differences in the extent to which parents expect such activities to spill over from the school setting into the child's home life. That parents look upon reading and writing as a normal part of *anyone's* life, not just something one learns at school, must inevitably determine in part the child's ability to use such skills as flexible tools rather than as some kind of trick unrelated to real life. The writing of letters by children, story writing for their own pleasure, membership of public libraries and ownership of books all correlate dramatically with social class. To state the obvious, the skills of literacy are virtually indispensable to adults in middle-class occupations; and it is largely through writing letters and memoranda to one another that the professional and managerial classes exert power and influence over events and hence earn their livelihoods. Inevitably, then, middle-class parents are hypersensitive to any difficulties their children may have in learning to read and write; what is more, a knowledge of this fact brings a subtle but strong and effective pressure to bear on all teachers in primary schools within middle-class catchment areas.

(4) Turning finally to the ways in which parents attempt to control their children, the differences between the two major class groups are not simple. When the children in our sample were only a year old, there was a substantial group in all social classes, albeit a minority group (38 per cent overall), who felt that it was totally inappropriate to smack a baby of that age for any reason; and there was also a clear difference between the professional/managerial class, for whom this was a majority opinion, and the rest. By the time the child had reached four, the situation had changed somewhat: four is an age when, in all sorts of ways, the child comes into conflict with his mother, while at the same time he is still highly egocentric and not particularly amenable to his mother's reasoning. At this age, smacking is rather widely seen as appropriate, even if an unfortunate necessity, and there is no class difference in approval or disapproval of its use, although the top and bottom classes smack significantly less and more often respectively. By the age of seven, rather more parents see smacking as inappropriate, and smacking has in fact

decreased over all classes; but class differences in frequency of smacking retain the same pattern.

There are also interesting divergences in the kinds of things for which smacking is thought to be a suitable punishment: for instance, at seven, middle-class parents are less likely to smack their children for untruthfulness and for rudeness; and in fact it is rather typical of these mothers that they do not like smacking for matters which they regard as serious. In our view, however, it is a mistake to place too much emphasis upon smacking as such. The discipline of the human child is accomplished primarily by means of language. Acts of physical punishment are not generally important in and of themselves; they act merely as punctuation marks in a continuing dialogue between the parent and the child. On their own admission, nearly all parents in our culture are at times driven to smacking their children; but smacks are almost invariably accompanied by a barrage of verbal pressure, and it is not without interest that in Nottingham it is this verbal 'telling-off', rather than the hitting, which goes by the name of 'chastisement'.

Is there, then, any essential difference between the social classes in their handling of discipline generally? We have shown elsewhere how the middle-class mother tries to use verbal reasoning methods in attempting to influence her child, and we have linked this preference for verbal control to her democratic intentions in her style of discipline. The ordering of family behaviour on a democratic system immediately involves a high degree of verbal interaction as disagreements are talked out and every voice is heard; whereas the authoritarian system preferred further down the scale has no need of more talk than a firm 'Do this!' Basically, the democratic ethic boils down to a *principle of reciprocity*, and this is the most important idea that middle-class parents try to teach their children: that they should have respect for the rights and wishes of other persons *as individuals*. In the end, this principle can only be taught by example, backed up by endless verbal persuasion and reiteration: 'Don't do that to me, I wouldn't do it to you'; 'I know you don't want to share your bike with Jane, but she's your visitor, and you'll be *her* visitor when you go to her house'; 'Answer Mrs Brown when she speaks to you, you wouldn't like it if someone didn't answer you'. Middle-class parents consciously want their children to realize how other people feel when they are at the receiving end of thoughtless behaviour; they expect their children to make an imaginative effort to put themselves in the place of others, and thereby to become sensitive to the impressions which they create. The whole process is a painfully slow one, dependent as it is upon the gradual growth of self-awareness and social empathy. It is a necessary part of this orientation towards an integrated rather than piecemeal socialization, that the child himself is valued as a person whose wishes and desires must be respected, and is accorded status in his own right.

With this in mind, it is worth looking at class differences in what we may call 'child-centredness'. From a number of different areas of interaction between the mother and the seven-year-old, it has been possible to draw certain indicators of a child-centred attitude, and to construct an index of child-centredness on this basis. Briefly, the responses were scored as positively child-centred, as follows: the child has a place to keep his own possessions, if only a cardboard box; his friends are allowed to play inside the house most weeks; his mother shows sympathy if he does not want to go to school (not necessarily to the extent of allowing his absence); she shows sympathy if, to escape school, he pretends he is not well; she takes complaints of school seriously, i.e. does not ignore them; she keeps or displays some of his drawings; she shares a special interest with the child; she does not punish but only rebukes or ignores rudeness to her; she is prepared to say 'sorry' sometimes when she has been cross with him; she lets him have some say in plans for holidays or outings. On this index, mothers who score 7+ out of a possible 10 are considered highly child-centred, while those who score 4 or less are rated as low on child-centredness. Class differences are in fact very marked: 51 per cent of middle-class, compared with 25 per cent of working-class, mothers rate as highly child-centred on this criterion, while 15 per cent of middle-class mothers and 40 per cent of working-class mothers score low. It is possibly of interest that working-class mothers are significantly more inclined to child-centredness where girls are concerned, while middle-class mothers reverse this trend, though not to significance level. Clearly, the overall results show that the middle-class mother, in contrast to her working-class counterpart, accepts her stated principle of reciprocity as a practical way of life.

We have attempted here to outline and illustrate just a few of the characteristic differences in attitudes towards child-rearing which sharply distinguish middle-class from working-class parents. We have argued in general terms that such divergences are to be expected because different social class groups have their own expectations and their own outlook on life, and these in turn lead them to attach importance to different qualities in the upbringing of their children. It is sometimes assumed that, as material living standards rise, people will instantaneously adopt specifically middle-class attitudes and ideas. Obviously working-class families want to share the good things which a modern technological society has to offer, and quickly acquire a taste for better clothes, more varied foodstuffs and consumer durables which were hitherto only available to a middle-class minority. It does not follow from this that we should expect a very rapid shift towards middle-class ideals and values generally.

Education Cannot Compensate for Society

B. Bernstein

Reprinted with permission from *New Society*, 26 February, 1970

I find the term, 'compensatory education', a curious one for a number of reasons. I do not understand how we can talk about offering compensatory education to children who in the first place have not, as yet, been offered an adequate educational environment. The Newsom report on secondary schools showed that 79 per cent of all secondary-modern schools in slum and problem areas were materially grossly inadequate, and that the holding power of these schools over the teachers was horrifyingly low. The same report also showed very clearly the depression in the reading scores of these children, compared with the reading scores of children who were at school in areas which were neither problem nor slum. This does not conflict with the findings that, on average, for the country as a whole, there has been an improvement in children's reading ability. The Plowden report on the primary schools was rather more coy about all the above points, but we have little reason to believe that the situation is very much better for primary schools in similar areas.

Thus we offer a large number of children, both at the primary and secondary levels, materially inadequate schools and a high turnover of teaching staff; and we further expect a small group of dedicated teachers to cope. The strain on these teachers inevitably produces fatigue and illness and it is not uncommon to find, in any week, teachers having to deal with doubled-up classes of 80 children. And we wonder why the children display very early in their educational life a range of learning difficulties.

At the same time, the organization of schools creates delicate overt and covert streaming arrangements which neatly lower the expectations and motivations of both teachers and taught. A vicious spiral is set up, with an all too determinate outcome. It would seem, then, that we have failed to provide, on the scale required, an *initial* satisfactory educational environment.

The concept, 'compensatory education', serves to direct attention away from the internal organization and the educational context of the school, and focus our attention on the families and children. 'Compensatory education' implies that something is lacking in the family, and so in the child. As a result, the children are unable to benefit from schools.

It follows, then, that the school has to 'compensate' for the something which is missing in the family, and the children are looked at as deficit systems. If only the parents were interested in the goodies we offer, if only they were like middle-class parents, then we could do our job. Once the problem is seen even implicitly in this way, then it becomes appropriate to coin the terms 'cultural deprivation', 'linguistic deprivation', and so on. And then these labels do their own sad work.

If children are labelled 'culturally deprived', then it follows that the parents are inadequate; the spontaneous realizations of their culture, its images and symbolic representations, are of reduced value and significance. Teachers will have lower expectations of the children, which the children will undoubtedly fulfil. All that informs the child, that gives meaning and purpose to him outside of the school, ceases to be valid or accorded significance and opportunity for enhancement within the school. He has to orient towards a different structure of meaning, whether it is in the form of reading books (*Janet and John*), in the form of language use and dialect, or in the patterns of social relationships.

Alternatively the meaning structure of the school is explained to the parents and imposed on, rather than integrated within, the form and content of their world. A wedge is progressively driven between the child as a member of a school. Either way the child is expected, and his parents as well, to drop their social identity, their way of life and its symbolic representations, at the school gate. For, by definition, their culture is deprived, and the parents are inadequate in both the moral and the skill orders they transmit.

I do not mean by this that in these circumstances no satis-factory home–school relations can take place or do not take place; I mean rather that the best thing is for the parents to be brought *within* the educational experience of the schoolchild by doing what they can do, and this with confidence. There are many ways in which parents can help the child in his learning, which are within the parents' spheres of competence. If this happens, then the parents can feel adequate and confident both in relation to the child and the school. This may mean that the contents of the learning in school should be drawn much more from the child's experience in his family and community.

So far I have criticized the use of the concept of 'compensatory education', because it distracts attention from the deficiencies in the school itself and focuses upon deficiencies within the community, family and child. We can add to these criticisms a third.

This concept points to the overwhelming significance of the early years of the child's life in the shaping of his later develop-ment. Clearly there is much evidence to support this view and to support its implication that we should create an extensive nursery-school system. However, it would be foolhardy indeed to write off the post-seven-years-of-age educational experience as having little influence.

Minimally, what is required *initially* is to consider the whole age period up to the conclusion of the primary stages as a unity. This would require considering our approach, at any *one* age, in the context of the whole of the primary stage. This implies a systematic, rather than a piecemeal, approach. I am arguing here for taking as the unit, not a particular period in the life of the child – for example, three to five years, or five to seven years – but taking as the unit a stage of education: the primary stage. We should see all we do in terms of the sequencing of learning, the development of sensitivities within the context of the primary stage. In order to accomplish this, the present social and edu-cational division between infant and junior stages must be weak-ened, as well as the insulation between primary and secondary stages. Otherwise gains at any one age, for the child, may well be vitiated by losses at a later age.

We should stop thinking in terms of 'compensatory education' but consider, instead, most seriously and systematically the conditions and contexts of the educational environment.

The very form our research takes tends to confirm the beliefs underlying the organization, transmission and evaluation of knowledge by the school. Research proceeds by assessing the criteria of attainment that schools hold, and then measures the competence of different social groups in reaching these criteria. We take one group of children, whom we know beforehand possess attributes favourable to school achievement; and a second group of children, whom we know beforehand lack these attributes. Then we evaluate one group in terms of what it *lacks* when compared with another. In this way research, unwittingly, underscores the notion of *deficit* and confirms the status quo of a given organization, transmission and, in particular, evaluation of knowledge. Research very rarely challenges or exposes the social assumptions underlying what counts as valid knowledge, or what counts as a valid realization of that knowledge. There are exceptions in the area of curriculum development; but, even here, the work often has no built-in attempt to evaluate the changes. This holds particularly for educational priority area 'feasibility' projects.

Finally, we do not face up to the basic question: What is the potential for change within educational institutions as they are presently constituted? A lot of activity does not necessarily mean *action*.

I have taken so much space discussing the new educational concepts and categories because, in a small way, the work I have been doing has inadvertently contributed towards their formulation. It might be, and has been, said that my research – through focusing upon the subculture and forms of family socialization – has also distracted attention from the conditions and contexts of learning in school. The focus on usage of language has sometimes led people to divorce the use of language from the substratum of cultural meanings which are initially responsible for the language use. The concept, 'restricted code', to describe working-class speech, has been equated with 'linguistic deprivation' or even with the 'non-verbal' child.

We can distinguish between uses of language which can be called 'context-bound' and uses of language which are less context-bound. Consider, for example, the two following stories which the linguist, Peter Hawkins, constructed as a result of his analysis of the speech of middle-class and working-class five-year-old children. The children were given a series of four pictures which told a story and they were invited to tell the story. The first picture shows some boys playing football; in the second the ball goes through the window of a house; the third shows a man making a threatening gesture; and in the fourth a woman looks out of a window and the children are moving away. Here are the two stories:

(1) Three boys are playing football and one boy kicks the ball and it goes through the window the ball breaks the window and the boys are looking at it and a man comes out and shouts at them because they've broken the window so they run away and then that lady looks out of her window and she tells the boys off. (No. of nouns: 13. No. of pronouns: 6.)

(2) They're playing football and he kicks it and it goes through there it breaks the window and they're looking at it and he comes out and shouts at them because they've broken it so they run away and then she looks out and she tells them off. (No. of nouns: 2. No. of pronouns: 14.)

With the first story, the reader does not have to have the four pictures which were used as the basis for the story, whereas in the case of the second story the reader would require the initial pictures in order to make sense of the story. The first story is free of the context which generated it, whereas the second story is much more closely tied to its context. As a result, the meanings of the second story are implicit, whereas the meanings of the first story are explicit.

It is not that the working-class children do not have, in their passive vocabulary, the vocabulary used by the middle-class children. Nor is it the case that the children differ in their tacit understanding of the linguistic rule system. Rather, what we have here are differences in the use of language arising out of a specific context. One child makes explicit the meanings which he is realizing through language for the person he is telling the story to, whereas the second child does not to the same extent.

The first child takes very little for granted, whereas the second child takes a great deal for granted. Thus, for the first child, the task was seen as a context in which his meanings were required to make explicit, whereas the task for the second child was not seen as a task which required such explication of meaning. It would not be difficult to imagine a context where the first child would produce speech rather like the second.

What we are dealing with here are differences between the children in the way they realize, in language use, what is apparently the same context. We could say that the speech of the first child generated universalistic meanings, in the sense that the meanings are freed from the context and so understandable by all; whereas the speech of the second child generated particularistic meanings, in the sense that the meanings are closely tied to the context and would be only fully understood by others if they had access to the context which originally generated the speech. Thus universalistic meanings are less bound to a given context, whereas particularistic meanings are severely context-bound.

Let us take another example. One mother, when she controls her child, places a great emphasis on language, because she wishes to make explicit, and to elaborate for the child, certain rules and reasons for the rules *and* their consequences. In this way the child has access through language to the relationships between his particular act which evoked the mother's control and certain general principles, reasons and consequences which serve to universalize the particular act.

Another mother places less emphasis on language when she controls her child and deals with only the particular act; she does not relate it to general principles and their reasoned basis and consequences.

Both children learn that there is something they are supposed, or not supposed, to do, but the first child has learned rather more than this. The grounds of the mother's acts have been made explicit and elaborated; whereas the grounds of the second mother's acts are implicit, they are unspoken.

Our research shows just this. The social classes differ in terms of the *contexts* which evoke certain linguistic realizations. Many mothers in the middle class (and it is important to add not all), relative to the working class (and again it is important to add not all by any means), place greater emphasis on the use of language in socializing the child into the moral order, in disciplining the child, in the communication and recognition of feeling. Here again we can say that the child is oriented towards universalistic meanings which transcend a given context, whereas the second child is oriented towards particularistic meanings which are closely tied to a given context and so do not transcend it. This does not mean that working-class mothers are non-verbal, only that they differ from the middle-class mothers in the *contexts* which evoke universalistic meanings. They are *not* linguistically deprived, neither are their children.

We can generalize from these two examples and say that certain groups of children, through the forms of their socialization, are oriented towards receiving and offering universalistic meanings in certain contexts, whereas other groups of children are oriented towards particularistic meanings. The linguistic realizations of universalistic orders of meaning are very different from the linguistic realizations of particularistic orders of meanings, and so are the forms of the social relation (for example, between mother and child) which generate these. We can say, then, that what is made available for learning, how it is made available, and the patterns of social relation, are also very different.

Now, when we consider the children in school, we can see that there is likely to be difficulty. For the school is necessarily concerned with the transmission and development of universalistic orders of meaning. The school is concerned with making explicit – and elaborating through language – principles and operations as these apply to objects (the science subjects) and persons (the arts subjects). One child, through his socialization, is already sensitive to the symbolic orders of the school, whereas the second child is much less sensitive to the universalistic orders of the school. The second child is oriented towards particularistic orders of meaning which are context-bound, in which principles and operations are implicit, and towards a form of language use through which such meanings are realized.

The school is necessarily trying to develop in the child orders of relevance and relation as these apply to persons and objects, which are not initially the ones he spontaneously moves towards. The problem of educability at one level, whether it is in Europe, the United States or newly developing societies, can be understood in terms of a confrontation between (1) the school's universalistic orders of meaning and the social relationships which generate them, and (2) the particularistic orders of meanings and the social relationships which generate them, which the child brings with him to the school. Orientations towards 'metalanguages' of control and innovation are not made available to these children as part of their initial socialization.

The school is attempting to transmit un-commonsense knowledge – i.e., public knowledge realized through various 'metalanguages'. This knowledge is what I have called universalistic.

However, both implicitly and explicitly, school transmits values and an attendant morality, which affect the contents and contexts of education. They do this by establishing criteria for acceptable pupil and staff conduct. These values and morals also affect the content of educational knowledge through the selection of books, texts and films, and through the examples and analogies used to assist access to public knowledge (universalistic meanings). Thus, the working-class child may be placed at a considerable disadvantage in relation to the *total* culture of the school. It is not made for him; he may not answer to it.

The universalistic functions of language – where meanings are less context-bound – point to an 'elaborated code'. The more particularistic functions point to a 'restricted code'. Because a code is restricted it does not mean that a child is non-verbal, nor is he in the technical sense linguistically deprived, for he possesses the same tacit understanding of the linguistic rule system as any child. It does not mean that the children cannot produce, at any time, elaborated speech variants in *particular* contexts.

It is critically important to distinguish between speech variants and a restricted code. A speech variant is a pattern of linguistic choices which is specific to a particular context – for example, when talking to children, a policeman giving evidence in a court, talking to friends whom one knows well, the rituals of cocktail parties, or train encounters. Because a code is restricted it does not mean that a speaker will not in some contexts, and under specific conditions, use a range of modifiers or subordinations, or whatever. But it does mean that where such choices are made they will be highly *context-specific*.

It is an accepted educational principle that we should work with what the child can offer; why don't we practise it? The introduction of the child to the universalistic meanings of public forms of thought is not 'compensatory education'; *it is education*. It is not making children middle class; how it is done, through the implicit values underlying the form and content of the educational environment, might.

We need to distinguish between the principles and operations that teachers transmit and develop in the children, and the contexts they create in order to do this. We should start knowing that the social experience the child already possesses is valid and significant, and that this social experience should be reflected back to him as being valid and significant. It can only be reflected back to him if it is part of the texture of the learning experience we create. If we spent as much time thinking through the implications of this as we do thinking about the implications of Piaget's development sequences, then it would be possible for schools to become exciting and challenging environments for parents, the children themselves and teachers.

We need to examine the social assumptions underlying the organization, distribution and evaluation of knowledge, for there is not one, and only one, answer. The power relationships created outside the school penetrate the organization, distribution and evaluation of knowledge through the social context. The definition of 'educability' is itself, at any one time, an attenuated consequence of these power relationships.

We must consider Robert Lynd's question: 'knowledge for what?' And the answer cannot be given only in terms of whether six-year-old children should be able to read, count and write. We do not know what a child is capable of, as we have as yet no theory which enables us to create sets of optimal learning environments; and even if such a theory existed, it is most unlikely that resources would be available to make it substantive on the scale required. It may well be that one of the tests of an educational system is that its outcomes are relatively unpredictable.

Unequal Access in Education – Sex and Social Class
Ronald King

Reprinted with permission from *Social and Economic Administration*, Vol. 5, No. 3, July 1971, pp. 167–74

The purpose of this paper is to explore the relationships between three variables; access to education, social class and sex. The study of class differences in education has been a major theme in the sociology of education; sex differences have received less attention, and some reasons for this neglect will be suggested later on. When the pattern of interaction between all three variables is examined, it becomes clear that the separate explanations suggested for class and sex differences in educational access require some modification.

Social Class and Access to Education

The relationship between social class and education is a well-established and familiar one. As Table 1 indicates, the pattern is one of higher rates of middle-class access compared with the working class at all levels of education, and a widening of the class gap as the level of education rises.

Table 1. The Class Gap – Percentage incidence of entering courses

| | Father's Occupation | | |
	Non-Manual	Manual	Ratio NM/M
'O' level or post-school course	79·0	45·5	1·74
'A' level or SLC	32·9	8·9	3·70
Full-time degree course	12·0	1·5	8·00

Derived from: *Higher Education* Appendix One: Section 2 Table 1 p. 38. 'Highest course of education: by father's occupation. G.B. Children born in 1940/41' HMSO, 1963.

The evidence suggests that the class gap has closed to some extent in the last 40 years, but has closed least at the University level.

Four broad explanations or theories have been proposed to explain the phenomenon of these class differentials.

The differential ability theory proposes that the class differences in educational attainment are explained by differences in academic ability. Leaving aside any psychological significance, it is generally accepted that an intelligence test, particularly of the verbal kind, forms the best *single* predictor of general academic success. It is also well-established that the mean score for intelligence tests is higher for children in the higher socio-economic groups. There is, therefore, some evidence for the theory, but its explanation is only a partial one. Several surveys have shown that the class gap exists at all ability levels. The gap, however, is smaller at the higher ability levels, and widens out, for all abilities, when the level of education rises. It should also be made clear that the variation in measured intelligence is greater within the classes than between them, and that numerically there are more able working-class children than middle-class, using any reasonable criterion of high ability and class.

Even accepting the partial explanation afforded by the differential ability theory, there remains the problem of explaining the class differences in measured intelligence, which immediately leads to the continuing hereditary/environment controversy. This is further complicated by the growing evidence that suggests that measured intelligence may be significantly changed as a result of the experience of the educational process.

The differential access theory is one that was popular in the period when public examinations were exclusive to certain types of school. It was widely believed that the abolition of fees in maintained grammar schools after the 1944 Education Act, would lead to an increased proportion of working-class pupils entering such schools. The belief has not been substantiated, and in some areas the proportion actually dropped.

There is no denying the class differential in access to private education, but it has yet to be clearly established that private schools do confer educational advantages on their pupils in terms of examination success. Douglas has shown that boys do equally well in maintained grammar schools and independent schools, when social class and measured intelligence are kept constant. There is also some evidence to suggest this may also be true for comparisons of pupils in maintained grammar and direct grant schools. However, if access to Oxford or Cambridge is considered an educational advantage over access to other universities, then it is still the case that public school pupils (virtually all middle class) have preferential entry.

The differential educational provision theory proposes that the social class differences in educational attainment exist because the middle class get a better education than the working class. Clearly this theory relates to the differential access theory when the private/public distinction is under discussion. The indices used to measure the value of educational provision have usually been economic and material. Accepting the value-judgements implied in the use of such criteria it is true to say that much evidence exists to show that the educational provision for middle-class children is better than that for working-class children. The predominantly middle-class pupils of the high status sector of private education do have more money spent on them than pupils in maintained schools, as shown in smaller pupil/staff ratios and material facilities. Within the maintained sector it is the primary schools and modern schools in the working-class areas which have the worst material provision.

However, despite the existence of a fairly clear class differential in material provision, there is little evidence to indicate a connection between material provision and educational attainment. This is not to deny that such a relationship may exist, or that good material provision cannot be valued for other reasons.

The *culture gap* or *cultural discontinuity theory* is one of the most commonly used in sociological studies of class chances in education. Briefly, the theory proposes that the principal function of education is that of cultural transmission, and that the culture transmitted by the educational system, in terms of knowledge, norms, values and beliefs, is mainly derived from the dominant group in society, which in modern Britain is identified as the loosely defined, middle class. Thus middle-class children are in better cultural continuity with the educational system, and show a more favourable adaptation to it, which is manifest in higher levels of attainment. This theory is wide in its scope and may actually subsume the differential access and differential provision theories, and provide an explanation for the social class differential in ability. It has been posed, implicitly and explicitly, in several different forms, including deferred gratification, the Protestant ethic and basic value-orientations. A documentation of its application becomes virtually a bibliography of the sociology of education.

It is difficult to estimate to what extent these theories exist in the general consciousness, and to what extent they relate to particular educational policies. The differential ability theory is undoubtedly implied in the American programmes of compensatory education. The differential access theory is implicit in the integration recommendations of the Public Schools Commission. The differential provision theory is implied in the Educational Priority Area programme, and in some way each of these policies may be related to the cultural discontinuity theory.

Certainly elements of all of these theories inform the principal political educational ideology of modern Britain, that of equality of opportunity, which is usually manifest in its meritocratic variant which proposes equal opportunities for those of equal ability. Specifically, the ideology is seen operationalized in the abolition of fees for grammar schools, the abolition of secondary selection and the comprehensive movement. The egalitarian variant of the equality ideology is less common. Its proposal that educational provision should lead to equal educational outcomes, that the culturally discontinuous working class should have more and better opportunities, is implied in the EPA schemes, but the scale of its financial provision represents a token of concern rather than a major programme of reform.

Sex and Access to Education

Paradoxes abound when the statuses of sex and social class as independent variables in the analysis of education are compared. Social class seldom appears in the official statistics; sex, frequently. Social class is the key variable in the sociological studies; sex is often naïvely ignored.

Table 2. The Sex Gap – Percentage incidence of entering courses

	Boys	Girls	Ratio B/G
'O' level or post-school course	63·8	40·7	1·57
'A' level or SLC	19·1	10·6	1·80
Full-time degree course	5·8	3·0	1·93

Derived from: *Higher Education* Appendix One: Section 2 Table 1 p. 38. 'Highest course of education: by father's occupation. G.B. Children born 1940/41' HMSO, 1963.

Table 2 shows that it is possible to refer to a sex gap in educational access. As with the class gap, it widens as the level of education is raised. Bearing in mind the differences in the conceptual status of sex and social class, and the relative crudity of the data, it may be seen, by referring to Tables 1 and 2, that at all levels of education the class gap is bigger than the sex gap, and that it widens more as the level rises.

Is it possible to account for the sex gap using similar theories to those used in connection with the class gap? A sex-differential ability theory would propose that girls are less academically able than boys. However, longitudinal studies of children have shown that girls tend to obtain slightly higher scores than boys in ability tests, especially in the early years of schooling. There is no clear evidence of a sex-differential in access to key institutions that would explain the phenomenon. At one level, there are slightly more girls in selective schools; at another, there are more places for men at Oxford and Cambridge. Similarly, there is no clear evidence for a sex-differential provision theory. Some evidence actually flies in the face of its basic proposition. The provision for science in girls' grammar schools is inferior to that in mixed grammar schools, but a larger proportion choose to specialize in science in the single sex schools.

A sex-cultural discontinuity theory to explain differences in access would propose the existence of a specifically masculine component in the transmitted culture. In terms of the knowledge transmitted and the legitimacy of the educational process this may be partly true, but in terms of personnel and social control the educational system is predominantly feminine, especially at the primary school level where 75 per cent of the teachers are women. Several surveys have shown that girls show a better adaptation to education than boys, particularly in the early stages. This may be explained in terms of feminine value-orientations, for example, the compliance with authority which may form a part of the more conservative political orientation of women.

A further paradox is that girls show the better adaptation to education than boys, but receive less education. Clearly it must be posed that adaptation to education is not necessarily related to its evaluation. What is left to propose as a theory is a sus-piciously functionalist one; that girls have a stronger orienta-tion towards marriage than towards occupations compared with boys.

A final paradox is that although sex differences, and not class differences, appear in the official statistics of education, the sex differences have seldom been related to social policy. There seems little popular concern about the sex gap, compared with that about the class gap.

Sex and Social Class in Access to Education

At each level of education the sex gap is bigger for the working class than the middle class, and the class gap is bigger for girls than for boys. As the level of education rises the sex gap widens for both classes, but widens more for the working class. The class gap also widens for both sexes, but more for girls than for boys.

It would be a very difficult exercise to explain these patterns in terms of any of the four types of theory discussed before. The difficulties arise from a lack of research in which both sex and social class have been used as independent variables. This may reflect the high proportion of men carrying out such research, and their motives for doing such research. Are they sometimes trying to explain their biographical selves, or are they reflecting the general societal orientation of little concern about sex-differentiation in education? What is clear is that the cultural discontinuity theory requires some modification in order to account for these sex differences. What is required is a theory that will not just explain class differences in education, but the different educational experiences of four basic pupil types; middle-class boys, middle-class girls, working-class boys and working-class girls.

At the level of the evaluation of education a tentative model based upon a distinction made by Havighurst may be proposed. The distinction is between the symbolic value of education, where it is valued as an indicator of social status, and the functional value, in which it is valued as a means to enter a desired occupation. Figure 1 shows the emergence of a four-fold typology based upon this distinction and a dichotomous high/low degree of evaluation.

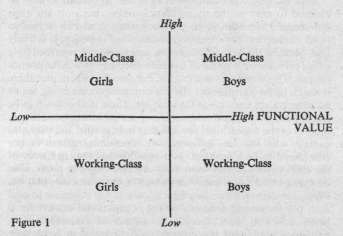

SYMBOLIC
VALUE

High

| Middle-Class | Middle-Class |
| Girls | Boys |

Low —————————————— *High* FUNCTIONAL
VALUE

| Working-Class | Working-Class |
| Girls | Boys |

Low

Figure 1

Middle-class boys show a high evaluation of education for both symbolic and functional purposes; they have to maintain status and gain entry to occupations through certification. Working-class boys do not have status that is confirmed by the receipt of education but many gain access to desired occupations through education; hence their low symbolic evaluation and possibly high functional evaluation. Middle-class girls have a high symbolic evaluation (status confirming), but a lower functional one, related to their stronger orientation to marriage. Working-class girls show a low evaluation of both the symbolic and functional; their orientation is towards early marriage, they have no status to confirm. This simple model could be elaborated by the inclusion of ability and adaptation variables.

Conclusions

This discussion of unequal access in education by sex and social class, has illuminated a number of important problems which concern the relationships between the social consciousness of inequalities, the attribution of problem-status to perceived inequalities, the operationalization of the solutions for inequalities as social policies, educational research, and the nature of the educational process.

Both sex and class differences in access to education may be claimed to exist in the social consciousness, but only the class differences have been given problem-status, and only solutions in its connection have been operationalized in policy. It is likely that because the sex differences in access are not regarded as a social problem little research has been directed towards the phenomenon. This neglect is regrettable, because it is likely that there is much to be learnt about the educational process using sex as an independent variable in the analysis. There is also much to be learnt about the origin and nature of sexual identity in society. Studies of the educational process may help in this, and may also explain why the sex difference in educational access is not considered to be a problem. Is it possible that the lag theory of the efficiency of British secondary education may be adapted as an explanation? A common argument in the fifties was that the divided system of secondary education was not adequate to deal with the increasing demands of the occupational market for a better educated work force. The growth of examinations in modern schools and the comprehensive movement have been explained and rationalized in these terms. Is there a lag between educational provision for girls and the increasing proportion of women in the labour force and the emergence of the two-phase career for women? Clearly, these problems, and those of sex and social class in education, represent a very rich research field. The puzzle is, why it has been neglected for so long?

Life Opportunity and Personality
G. H. Elder, Jnr

Reprinted with permission from 'Life Opportunity and Personality: Some Consequences of Stratified Secondary Education in Great Britain', *Sociology of Education*, Spring 1965, Vol. 38, No. 3, pp. 184–99

Presumably assignment to a low-status school or to a low academic stream within a school affects a British youth's public esteem which, in turn, affects his private self-esteem. Typically, youth who have a low opinion of themselves as students perform in accordance with their self-assessment. Since low self-esteem is associated with anxiety, defensiveness, low achievement, and low future aspirations, the consequences of eleven-plus failure and of allocation to streams within the grammar and modern school are likely to be substantial. The enduring consequences of being typed as a failure during childhood are revealed in the experience of the head of one comprehensive school in Western England: 'after extensive enquiries, I have not found any pupil who failed the eleven-plus who has overcome his sense of inferiority at this failure, irrespective of his performance even at university level.' In addition to the psychological harm produced by the eleven-plus, this selection procedure contributes little towards developing every youth's ability to the fullest capacity.

The extent to which student classification influences self-conception among impressionable youth is only partially known; presumably many youths maintain delinquent ways because they are labelled as delinquent and are expected to act accordingly; children placed in the slow stream in school may surpass all expectations in playing the role of 'dummy'; and children sent to modern schools as eleven-plus failures may perform splendidly as 'ordinary' students even though they may be capable of much greater effort and accomplishments. In discussing the social-psychological consequences of classification, Patricia Sexton makes the following observations:

> The teacher learns that he has a low IQ rating and puts him into a slow-moving group where he is not expected to do much or be given much attention. He is bright enough, however, to catch on very quickly to the fact that he is not considered very bright. He comes to accept this very unflattering appraisal because, after all, the school should know. He is in his pigeon-hole. He can't get out, and what is more, he doesn't try; he accepts his fate. His parents accept it, since after all, the schools should know. Intellectually, he is lost. He has accepted this low appraisal of himself; and both he and society must suffer the consequences.

The restriction of a youth's opportunities, coupled with the punishment associated with failing, tends to engender a negative self-image which, in turn, is apt to be associated with an under-utilization of mental abilities. Instead of coping with and exploring scholastic tasks, the student with a negative self-image is apt to avoid such demands.

In discussing the basic tensions of modern schools, Taylor concludes that the 'scholastic atmosphere of the modern school, its position in the educational and social structure, may tend to depress performance and aspirations, and its examination streams and advanced work may not be fully effective in countering this effect.' The available evidence supports this conclusion. Students who enter grammar school tend to increase in their test scores, whereas modern school students often decrease in their scores. Vernon tested a group of 800 boys at 11 years and 14 years and found that those who attended grammar school gained an average of seven points in their IQ score over those who entered non-selective schools. In the Douglas survey, a consistent decline in average ability scores was obtained for students entering modern schools, a finding which strikingly contrasts with an average increase by grammar school students in test scores. Decline in scores between ages 11 and 15 is common to middle- and working-class youth in each ability group who entered modern schools. Indeed, the image of modern schools in the minds of some grammar school students and their parents as a place 'where they play all day', suited 'for those who are good with their hands', 'where the lessons are easy', and which 'offers little in the way of opportunity' is fulfilled in the performance of capable modern students. Students in grammar school, in contrast, tended to increase their test scores substantially from age 11 to age 15, regardless of their social-class background.

The effects of streaming within primary schools on academic achievement are comparable to the consequences of being assigned to selective and non-selective secondary schools. Among students of equal measured ability in primary school, Douglas found that those of middle-class status were more likely than working-class students to be assigned to upper streams. Academic deterioration was characteristic of students in lower streams, especially those of working-class status. Relatively low-ability students seemed to benefit most academically between ages 8 and 11 if placed in upper streams, while brighter students suffered most in the lower streams. (From a probabilistic standpoint it should be noted that large gains are more possible for low-ability youth as are large losses for bright youth.) Jackson and Marsden, in a study of the educational careers of 88 working-class children in Marburton, observed that few of the working-class children in grammar school who were placed in ability groups below A lasted for the sixth form. 'Once declared "C" children, did they not begin to learn, play, act, think, and feel as "C" children? Precisely that.' The mobility aspirations of youth in different streams conforms in ordinal progression to their respective status levels in the school; 'A' stream youth are more upwardly mobile in their aspirations than 'B', 'C', or 'D' children. Persistence in Secondary School – variations in scholastic achievement by social class and secondary school – are paralleled by differences in student persistence in grammar and modern school.

The lack of meaningful courses for modern school youth who desire to remain beyond the age of 15 is an important condition producing this response on the part of able students in modern schools. Children of high ability in modern schools are commonly aware of the difficulty in obtaining adequate preparation for the GCE. In one or two years of extended courses, modern students are frequently faced with accomplishing what grammar school youth achieve over four or five years of schooling. In the words of one modern school student: 'It takes a long time at my school to get enough GCE subjects; you would need about twenty

years before you got enough.' Boredom, and complaints about
lethargic teachers were common themes among 200 students
from five modern schools in Sheffield. 'Many boys and girls
seemed to have spent a lot of their time at school in a state of
boredom and learning little. Occasionally they "had fun" –
notably when they managed "to get a teacher off the subject". To
achieve this was one of the satisfying accomplishments.' Some
of the more ambitious boys were highly resentful of the slow
pace; 'We didn't do enough work there,' said one boy. 'It was
terrible. Most of the teachers just said do something without
explaining it, and when you had finished it, instead of going on
to teach something more advanced, they just told you to get out
a book and read.' Many of them felt that 'they had reached a dead
end at school. They preferred to get out into the world and devote
their energies to something new, rather than vegetate at schools
or struggle against the odds to get on terms with grammar school
children. It was better, too, not to take an examination at all than
to take one and fail.' Although there are substantial variations
among modern schools, students from these schools are generally
less positive towards school and are aware of the low status of
the school in the community. Findings from the Gallup survey
are similar.

The seeming irrelevance of modern school for the life situations
of many enrolled youth has left a void in their lives which has
been filled in large measure by commercialized youth culture. This
culture and the seeming irrelevance of school are major pressures
encouraging modern school youth to leave school as soon as
possible. As a result, teachers in some modern schools are faced
with the frustrating task of teaching youth who could not care
less about their course work.

Educational Channels and Elite Mobility

J. Gerstl and R. Perrucci

Reprinted with permission from 'Educational Channels and Elite Mobility', *Sociology of Education*, 1965, Vol. 38, No. 2, pp. 226–32

As a contribution to the accumulation of case studies in comparative mobility, we are concerned with changes over time in the recruitment into one elite occupation in Great Britain and the United States. The specific occupation for which we have comparable information is that of the engineer – an elite by dint of professional standing, with similar prestige in the two countries.

The general framework for this comparison is necessarily the total mobility pattern for the two countries involved. Three separate indices of upward mobility in Britain and the US from Miller's analysis are shown in Table 1. The rates of intergenerational movement from manual to nonmanual categories are very similar for the two countries. However, consideration of movement into elite occupations from either the manual or middle-class level shows the two to have dissimilar patterns. Britain has much less mobility into elite occupations than does the United States.

Table 1. Upward Mobility Rates for Great Britain and the United States

	Manual into Nonmanual	Middle Classes into Elite I and II	Manual into Elite I and II
Great Britain	24·8	8·6	2·2
United States	28·8	19·8	7·8

Part of this difference is due to the relative size of the elite category and is thus not only a reflection of the amount of individual movement or pure mobility. In America, with larger elite strata, there is a structural push towards a higher rate of mobility into the elite. In addition, the mechanisms for gaining access to elite occupations are very different in the two societies. The contrast is that of contest and sponsored mobility, seen most dramatically in the proportions gaining access to higher education.

The more recent US engineers are increasingly the sons of professionals (21 per cent to 30 per cent). Younger British engineering graduates, on the other hand, are less likely to be the sons of professionals than are their older colleagues (52 per cent to 28 per cent). The increasing proportion of high-status sons moving into engineering in the US seems to have paralleled the upgrading of engineering as a profession. The increasing emphasis upon mathematics and the physical sciences as necessary for engineering has also enhanced its respectability. In addition, these prerequisites for engineering as a career are more likely to be a part of the high school curriculum of the high-status son than of the low-status son. A similar pattern of upgrading the engineering profession does not seem to have occurred in Great Britain, despite the continued concern regarding recruitment into the profession. This may account for the lack of attraction which engineering in Britain has for sons of professionals. The contrasting status of engineers in the two countries is indicated by the one-way flow of the 'brain drain', England constantly losing personnel to the US.

While there has been little change in recruitment patterns for American engineers in the two most recent time periods, the amount of upward mobility for the British has been steadily increasing. Interestingly, for the most recent engineers, the proportion coming from professional backgrounds is similar for the two countries. The total pattern that emerges with respect to changes over time is one of declining mobility in American recruitment as contrasted with increasing mobility in Britain.

It is, of course, possible that the relatively small shifts in recruitment that have occurred in the US sample (as compared to the British sample) may be due to changes in the proportion of the labour force in various occupational categories. Thus, the increasing proportion of engineers coming from professional origins would be due simply to an increasing proportion of the labour force who are professionals. An examination of the occupational structure over the last half-century in the US does not indicate that our changing patterns of recruitment are only reflections of the changing composition of the labour force.

Between 1910 and 1960 there has been a steady increase in the proportion of the labour force in professional occupations and in clerical and sales occupations. Our recruitment data show similar increases in the proportion of engineers having fathers of professional and clerical and sales occupations. However, census data also indicate that there has been a sizeable increase in the proportion of the labour force in skilled and semi-skilled occupations. Our recruitment data, on the other hand, indicate that the largest recruitment decline has occurred among sons of skilled and semi-skilled fathers. An additional consideration is that for this same time period of 1910–60 the number of engineering graduates coming out of the universities has gone from approximately 1,000 to 36,000. Thus, the marked growth in engineering enrolments has not come from any increased recruitment of manual working-class sons to this occupation.

We may hazard a few guesses as to the continuation of these recruitment trends for the two countries in question. The increasing proportion of recruitment from manual strata in Britain is likely to continue. The changes in British education beginning with the 1944 Education Act concerning secondary education, are only now affecting higher education as indicated in the Robbins report. On the other hand, the trend of increasing recruitment from high-status origins in the US will probably continue considering the apparent flow of high calibre students into engineering and science. It would appear that even the increased manpower needs for engineers, as suggested by several personnel projections, will not necessarily increase the recruitment of lower-class youth, since the increased needs will occur in management and basic research functions, while traditional engineering functions will remain stable. In this connection, we would suggest that it is the traditional engineering image that would most likely attract the mobile lower-class youth, while the basic research and managerial functions would require academic knowledge and social skills that are differentially distributed in the class structure. Thus, the lower-class youth in the US is disadvantaged both by the lack of social supports and inducements to undertake science oriented curricula, and by the absence of such programmes in the schools he is most likely to attend.

A refinement in the analysis of the degree of mobility attained may be introduced by considering the degree of success achieved in professional engineering careers. Clearly, not all engineers are of equal status. If success is independent of social origins, this would be an additional indicator of the openness of the social structure.

As access to the means for mobility (i.e. engineering training) becomes wider, differential rewards are more likely to be related to social origins. For access to training operates as a screening mechanism which, if highly rigorous, is more likely to result in equal treatment once the initial hurdle is passed. Since university entrance is much more selective in Britain than in the US, we would expect that this is the stage at which the crucial sorting out process takes place. Just as almost all British entrants to university survive through their final year while Americans do not, so the success of British graduates in the same field should be more independent of their social origins than it is in the US.

All British engineering graduates are seen to have good chances of success, whatever their origins. Although those of manual origins do somewhat less well, there is no difference between sons of professionals and those from middle-class backgrounds.

Our most general finding emerging from the comparison of one elite level occupation in two countries, both in terms of changing patterns of recruitment over time and in the relation of social origins to degree of success, suggests the degree of fluidity in Britain to be greater than in the US. This does not by itself refute the conclusion of the broad similarity of trends in industrialized countries. It may well be, for example, that the pattern for other occupations is very different and may off-set trends that apply in the case of engineers. However, the importance of engineering as indicative of patterns for elite occupations must not be underestimated. For, engineering is the single largest professional category in an industrial society (excluding teaching, of course, which is primarily female). Furthermore, it is likely that engineering is the one profession most open to entry, engineers tending to have lower-status origins than members of other professions. In addition, once entry to the engineering profession is realized, success should be more susceptible to intrinsic career criteria than in other professions. For example, in medicine and law, family influence, as manifest in contacts and financial aid in starting a practice, is much more relevant than it is in the organizational world of the engineer. It is in this respect that engineering is most exemplary of 'careers open to talent'. These considerations apply equally to engineers in Britain and in the US.

Two Cultures

Eric Butterworth

Reprinted with permission from D. Martin (Ed.), *A Sociological Yearbook of Religion in Britain* 2, London, SCM Press, 1969, pp. 151–4

There is much stronger emphasis within the Muslim family on the authority of its senior members and in particular of the father. In a society without social security and welfare the obligations of children to support parents are stressed. In the presence of parents the child must be docile and quiet, and a degree of formality develops in the relationships between fathers and sons as the sons get older. One aspect of this is the way in which fathers lay down what their children should do. In more permissive situations there is a conflict between what children from this background see as being the practice of their schoolfellows and what their parents expect of them at home. In addition there are great distinctions between the roles of men and women. Generalization is difficult because so much depends upon the personal circumstances of the individual, and women of a higher social group, especially if living in cities, may have more freedom than their rural counterparts. In Pakistan there is a discrepancy between the rights which women are accorded by the teachings of religion and their actual situation. Under Muslim law women have rights, for example, to inheritance and divorce, but there is a great discrepancy between what their situation is according to law and what it is in practice if they live in remote rural areas.

The activity of women is mainly confined to the domestic sphere. Men spend their leisure time with companions of their own sex and marriage is an alliance of families. Girls are protected, after puberty, from contact with men who are not related. When a girl marries she is expected to have had no contact with young men at all. One informant said, in contrasting British and Muslim practice:

It is really unfortunate that even some teachers approach Muslim parents to allow their daughters to adopt the English way of life, such as having boy friends, which is totally unacceptable to our culture.

The kind of problems which arise in practice in the school situation include girls sitting next to boys and talking to them. In a Muslim society they cease to mix at an early age. Girls adopt traditional female dress which covers the legs and they remain in a secluded world. Any hint of irregular behaviour on the part of the girl, such as conversing with boys, may affect not only her marriage prospects but also those of her relatives.

The difficulties of preserving this degree of separation, and the institution of 'purdah', by which women are protected from contact with males outside their family circle, are obvious in Britain. At first some women were taken to clinics by their husbands but conflicts arise between the need for husbands to be at work and to protect their wives. Modifications of practice are inevitable in many cases and have taken place. Often women look upon the visit to the clinic or shops as an excursion. If possible they go with another woman, who is usually related.

Preserving dietary practices may also be difficult. Quite large numbers of Muslim men appear to drink alcohol, and it is not always possible to check where the foodstuffs come from and in particular whether meat is being killed in the approved way. Children who stay for school meals may be particularly liable to eat food which is not prepared according to precept.

In the sphere of education the demands of parents, or the conflicts between the values of the family and the values of the school, cause tensions for the child. One practical issue is that the desire to teach the child about Muslim culture and religion may mean that children, often quite young, spend long hours at the weekend or after school or both, learning about their traditions. Though not all children attend the classes which are provided there are increasing constraints to do so. However, if parents become aware of the strains which this is imposing they may well question the importance of traditional studies of their religion and culture as compared with the subjects taught in the school situation. Those with a strong motivation for their children to do well and adapt themselves and obtain better jobs may be more resistant to this development.

The methods employed by the teachers at the schools set up by the communities or groups are far more formal and authoritarian than those in an English school. The reverence for learning which is inculcated stresses forms of rote learning and knowledge of 'facts' rather than power of analysis. Thus even for the child in a good school environment problems of adaptation frequently arise and the teaching models reveal considerable differences between the situation in which he learns about his background and that in which he learns to adapt himself to English society. There is also the problem of the 'helpful' parent, teaching in a way alien to the tradition in this country. Parents adopting an inflexible, authoritarian attitude may well dominate their children and, for example, keep them within the confines of the home quite effectively, but in a number of cases there may well be open discontent and the possibility of family breakdown. To specify the kinds of breakdown which could arise, and put a relative value on them, would be difficult at this stage of the settlements, but undoubtedly delinquency is one possible area of deviation. Others include relationships with people of the same age group of the opposite sex. The fears in this respect are almost always expressed on behalf of the girls rather than the boys.

The changes going on in patterns of life and consequent effects on religious beliefs and cultural practices seem to be anticipated hardly at all by the Muslim community in Britain. On the whole the attitude of the religious leadership is to ignore the kinds of consequences that are likely to arise from life in a more affluent, sophisticated and urban environment. Some informants suggested that parents were aware of some of the considerable problems but hoped that they would not arise in an acute form in their own lifetime. Those in a position to make a choice and who move to the edges of the areas may well accommodate themselves to some aspects of life in Britain and obtain far more benefits both for themselves and for their children. On the other hand these are people in the front line of integration, as it were, and the response to them will depend on the general character of race relations in the country. Accommodation that does take place will reflect the growing similarity of interests, at least in certain respects, between migrants and native-born.

With increasing affluence and the extent to which the society remains, or becomes, more 'open' in terms of opportunities linked to ability, changes are more likely to take place. One of the more significant developments in recent years has been the emergence of a definite class structure which, professional people apart, is not entirely based on the working class. There are two main groups of the upwardly mobile. One is of those professional people in medicine or law who provide services both for the minority group and for the host community. The other, a much larger section, is of people who have begun as workers but, by dint of saving, have acquired business and commercial interests. The form this takes is either through the ownership of property or the ownership of shops or businesses. Styles of life in some cases may begin to approximate more closely to those of the equivalent groups in the host community. Many similarities exist between those who have emerged from the working class and those who have stayed in it, but it is conceivable that, for some, class and social group interests may come to outweigh the ethnic loyalties which previously have prevailed.

Not all will be influenced, especially in a situation where there is a high density of settlement. It is possible that the greater the concentration in the ghetto situation the more the need for a siege mentality will develop. At the same time great changes are likely to come about in traditional structures of authority. How far the Muslim religion can retain its hold in a completely different situation and in a modern society which has few similarities with those in which the majority of Muslims live is an open question.

Education and Social Change
D. V. Glass

Reprinted with permission from M. Ginsberg (Ed.), *Law and Opinion in the Twentieth Century*, London, Stevens & Sons, 1959, pp. 322–7

In the late nineteenth century England was still educationally a very underdeveloped society. It would, of course, be both incorrect and unjust to minimize the part which religious and philanthropic bodies had already played in establishing schools. The incidence of illiteracy could not have been as high as it is in some underdeveloped countries today. Even so, a third of the men marrying in 1840 in England and Wales, and half of the women, signed the registers by a mark; the proportions in 1870 were still 20 per cent and 27 per cent. The rate of change in the provision of education since 1870 has been so rapid that it must be taken into account when considering present-day educational deficiencies.

It must be equally clear that the phrase 'the English tradition of education' not infrequently used in arguing against further rapid change in the character of secondary education, has a very limited validity. It can scarcely apply to the public system which, even during its brief history, has greatly altered in respect of objectives, structure and methods of selection. Nor, in the sense of a centuries-old persistence of character, is the term really applicable to the private sectors, whether secondary or university. It is true that, as an institution, the grammar school 'has a thousand years of history behind it'. But the present character of grammar schools derives from action taken during the nineteenth and twentieth centuries, action originally taken because, however deeply rooted the grammar school idea may have been, the schools themselves had ceased to be effective as educational institutions. In any case, most grammar schools today are not private. They are maintained by the local education authorities; they are thus part of the public system; and they have been exposed to powerful pressures for change in the curriculum, in the universe from which pupils are drawn, and in the qualifications of teachers. The public schools, too – the schools belonging to the Headmasters' Conference and the most firmly imbedded and 'traditionalist' part of the private system – bear little resemblance to their original form. They were, on the contrary, the first schools to be reconstructed in the nineteenth century. Indeed, it was the reforms introduced by Arnold and others which, as G. M. Young has said, 'reconciled the serious classes to the public school', and which encouraged the establishment of additional schools; fifty-one out of the present one hundred and sixteen independent public boarding schools were founded in the nineteenth century. The curriculum has also changed, though more slowly, and half the present public schools specialize in science and mathematics. The process of change has applied equally to the universities. The history of university reform is too well known to need documenting here. But it is evident that Trevelyan's description of Oxford and Cambridge in the days of decay as 'little more than comfortable monastic establishments for clerical sinecurists with a tinge of letters' would scarcely apply now. Moreover, the larger part of the university complex is itself the creation of the nineteenth century, and almost two-thirds of today's university students are studying in institutions established since the 1830s.

Much of the present educational system is thus not traditional.

Moreover, many of its characteristics are not particularly English. Even during the first half of the nineteenth century, once the memory of the French Revolution had become a little clouded, educational reformers in England drew markedly upon the experiments which were being conducted on the Continent. And this was just as well, for the new influences helped to replace the more specifically British contributions of Lancaster's mutual system and Bell's 'Madras' system, which appeared to require a school to be a combination of factory and of Bentham's Panopticon. Later in the century Matthew Arnold imported from France the term 'secondary education' and with it the objective of a reorganized and comprehensive system. Technical education, too, especially in its shifting emphasis from craftsmanship to general principles and their application, was influenced both by foreign competition and by foreign models. All this has clearly been to the good. But along with these innovations there has been one underlying continuity – the influence of the class structure on the images of education and its function. It is this continuity and its consequences which I should now like to discuss.

During the nineteenth century, educational developments reflected two fairly distinct sets of considerations, one relating to the mass of the population and the other to the middle classes. Public concern with elementary education was in large measure concern to meet certain minimum requirements in a changing society – the need to ensure discipline, and to obtain respect for private property and the social order, as well as to provide that kind of instruction which was indispensable in an expanding industrial and commercial nation. Though many individuals and groups showed a far broader vision, these minimal considerations are evident in the very limited objectives of the system which grew up at that time. In the earliest period, the Bible and the catechism were sufficient, Hannah More thought; she would 'allow no writing for the poor'. Later, the sights were set a little higher. Speaking of the working-class child, James Fraser, subsequently Bishop of Manchester, told the 1858 Newcastle Commission that: 'we must make up our minds to see the last of him, as far as the day school is concerned, at ten or eleven . . . and I venture to maintain that it is quite possible to teach a child soundly and thoroughly, in a way that he shall not forget it, all that is necessary for him to possess in the shape of intellectual attainment, by the time that he is ten years old'. The Commission accepted the fact that most children would go to work at the age of ten or eleven. A similar assumption underlies the 1870 Act. It is not surprising that H. G. Wells referred to it as 'an Act to educate the lower classes for employment on lower-class lines, and with specially trained, inferior teachers'.

To gentle the masses was another explicit purpose. 'A set of good schools civilizes a whole neighbourhood', said the Newcastle Commission; and Forster, when he introduced his 1870 bill in Parliament, spoke of 'removing that ignorance which we are all aware is pregnant with crime and misery, with misfortune to individuals and danger to the community'. And he continued, 'I am one of those who would not wait until the people were educated before I would trust them with political power. If we had thus waited we might have waited long for education; but now that we have given them political power, we must not wait any longer to give them education.' Some of these notions were changed when the 1902 Act provided a framework for both elementary and secondary education. But the civilization motive had a longer currency, and even in 1929 Sir Cyril Norwood argued that it was largely elementary education which had prevented 'Bolshevism, Communism, and theories of revolt and destruction from obtaining any real hold upon the people of this country'. 'I hope,' he added, 'that those who attribute the scarcity of domestic servants to the unreasonable institution of elementary education, by which they are made to pay for the teaching of other people's children, will lay in the other scale this other service, which has made of Bolshevism only a bogy which sits by their pillows and frightens them in the night.'

Concern with secondary education sprang from different motives. The effectiveness of the public schools and the endowed grammar schools as educational institutions for those groups who could afford to make use of them was the main issue. In the early part of the century an attempt had been made to compel the public schools to give the local poor the rights to entry provided by the founders' statutes. But the attempt failed, and the place of the public schools in the national system of secondary education was not again discussed by a Government committee until 1942. Instead, in 1861 a Royal Commission was appointed to study the quality of the education in what have ever since been known as the 'Clarendon schools' – nine schools with 2,815 pupils. And the Clarendon Commission was immediately followed by the Taunton Commission, which inquired into the education given in the endowed grammar schools. Though expressing some disquiet at existing class distinction in education, the Taunton Commission in the main accepted the situation as they found it, and their recommendations were drawn up for the benefit of the middle classes by whom the schools were being used. What is particularly interesting is the emergence at this stage of a fresh criterion of the effectiveness of secondary education, the criterion of providing an avenue to the universities; and there were unfavourable references to the fact that 550 grammar schools sent no boys to universities, in sharp contrast to the large numbers now going from the nine Clarendon schools and from some of the recently founded proprietary schools.

For university education, like secondary education, was coming to have a new meaning. The changing society needed individuals of greater educational maturity and tested qualifications. The old and the new middle classes needed avenues of employment which would provide both prestige and relatively high income for their sons. Considerations of both scientific and social status were causing the existing professions to raise their standards of entry, and additional professions, including the higher civil service, were beginning to develop, also demanding considerable educational attainments.

Institutions and Teachers

C. Lacey

Reprinted with permission from 'Schools and Academic Streaming', *British Journal of Sociology*, September 1966, Vol. XVII, No. 3, pp. 245–62

The Local Education Authority of Hightown sends about 15 per cent of its 11-year-olds to grammar schools each year. This clearly does not imply that 15 per cent of the pupils in *any* junior school in the town will find themselves in the same grammar school. There are six grammar schools in Hightown and these are specialized in a number of ways; there are two Roman Catholic grammar schools (one for boys and one for girls) which serve the separate RC education system in Hightown and the surrounding area; and four LEA grammar schools (two for girls and two for boys) which draw their pupils almost exclusively from Hightown. For non-Catholic, 11-year-old boys in Hightown there are then three possible grammar school avenues; entry to a direct grant school outside the town, Hightown Grammar School and Hightown Technical Grammar School. (A very small fraction attend public schools.)

The boys entering Hightown Grammar are selected from a large number of junior schools, and the selection test tends to scoop a few pupils from each school. Over half the boys come from schools that send six or less pupils. Evidence from a variety of sources (junior school reports, autobiographies and the statements of junior school teachers etc.) clearly shows that these contingents include the vast majority of top scholars, team leaders, school monitors, head boys and teachers' favourites. In short they are the 'best pupils'.

When the boys arrive at Hightown Grammar they are divided at random into four classes. The classes are also House Groups. The pupils in them remain together for prayers, school meals and registration as well as lessons.

A more comprehensive picture of the degree of isolation of the first-year boy, on his arrival at Hightown, must therefore take into account the effect of the school organization: 58 boys out of 118 questioned had no friend from the same junior school in their class. Thus almost half of the first-year intake spend the great majority of their time at school in a class in which they are isolated from their previous friends.

It can be seen from the foregoing analysis that any batch of new boys assembling at Hightown Grammar School are likely to make up a highly selected and homogeneous group. The annual intake being about 120, they repesent under 4 per cent of their age group in the community and all are boys who have ostensibly been selected on the basis of their sex, religion and academic achievement.

The homogeneity of the intake and the relative isolation of individual new boys from their junior school friends are both important factors affecting patterns of behaviour in the first-year classes. The first-year pupils show a high degree of commitment to the school. School uniform is rigidly adhered to; caps and blazers are proudly displayed, school functions and clubs are attended disproportionately by first-year boys. Their behaviour in the classroom is characterized by eagerness, cooperation with the teacher and a high degree of competition among themselves. 'Please sir, Willy Brown is copying my sums' is a remark that could only come from a first-year boy. I once tried to measure the response rate to a narrative and question-and-answer lesson given by a History teacher. So many responded to each question that I could not record them. As the tension mounted boys who did not know the answers looked around apprehensively at those who did. These were in a high state of excitement and they smiled triumphantly at those who did not know the answers; they stretched their arms and bodies to the utmost as they eagerly called, 'Sir', 'Sir', 'Sir', every time the master glanced in their direction. When the master said 'All right Green, you tell us', there were quiet sighs and groans as those who had not been called upon subsided into their seats. The whole performance was repeated as soon as the next question was asked.

During such spells the desire to participate was so great that some boys would put up their hands and strain for notice, even though they had no idea of the answer. And, if asked to give the answer, they would either make a gesture suggesting that they had suddenly forgotten, or else subside with an embarrassed and confused look, to the jeers and groans of the rest of the class who would then redouble their efforts to attract attention.

The type of enthusiasm characteristic of a first-year class was occasionally found in second- or third-year forms but there were a number of observable differences. The second and third forms were more likely to 'play dead' and to allow five or six people to 'do all the work'; and, even if the master succeeded in getting a larger proportion to participate, there was always a residue of boys who hardly participated or who only did so by giving obviously wrong or funny answers. Finally there was the possibility that the form would use any excitement of this kind to sabotage the lesson or to play the fool. For example, a boy will stretch so hard that he falls out of his desk, another will accidentally punch the boy in front as he puts up his hand and the form's 'funny man' will display his wit in response to an ambiguous question – sometimes isolating the teacher from the class by referring to a private class joke.

On one occasion, for example, a master asked three boys to stay behind after the lesson to help him with a task calling for a sense of responsibility and cooperation, the master called 'Williams, Maun and Sherring'. The class burst into spontaneous laughter, and there were unbelieving cries of 'What, Sherring?' The master corrected himself. 'No, not Sherring, Shadwell.' From the context of the incident, it was clear that Sherring's

reputation was already inconsistent with the qualities expected
of a monitor. On another occasion, Priestley was asked to read
and the whole class groaned and laughed. Priestley, a fat boy, had
been kept down from the previous year because of ill health
(catarrh and asthma) and poor work. He grinned apprehensively,
wiped his face with a huge white handkerchief and started to read
very nervously. For a few moments the class was absolutely
quiet, then one boy tittered, Priestley made a silly mistake, partly
because he was looking up to smile at the boy who was giggling,
and the whole class burst into laughter. Priestley blew his nose
loudly and smiled nervously at the class. The teacher quietened
the class and Priestley continued to read. Three lines later a
marked mispronunciation started the whole class laughing again.
This performance continued with Priestley getting more and
more nervous, mopping his brow and blowing his nose. Finally,
the master with obvious annoyance snapped, 'All right, Priestley,
that's enough!'

This short incident, one of several during the day, served to
remind Priestley of his structural position within the class and to
confirm the opinions and expectations of the class and the teacher
towards him. Priestley's behaviour was consistent with his
performance in the examinations at the end of the Autumn Term
when he was ranked twenty-ninth out of thirty-three.

During this period of observation I also noticed the significance
of the behaviour of another boy, Cready. Cready first attracted
my attention because, although his form position was similar to
Priestley's (twenty-sixth) he habitually associated with a strikingly
different group. He behaved very differently in class, and had a
markedly different reputation.

A sociogram for the class showed an apparent inconsistency.
In class Priestley was frequently in the middle of a group of
mischievous boys. If there was trouble Priestley was in it. I
expected him to be fairly popular with some of the boys who led
him into trouble, but none of them picked him as a friend. He
chose five boys as his friends but the only boy to reciprocate was
the other Jewish boy in the class.

The other boys used Priestley to create diversions and pass
messages, and because he was so isolated he was only too pleased
to oblige. He could never resist the temptation to act as if he were
'one of the boys'. However, when he was caught out they deserted
him and laughed at him rather than with him. He was truly the
butt of the class.

These incidents, seen in the context of the structure of the class, show how Priestley had fallen foul of the system. He was not in control of his own situation, and anything he tried to do to improve his position only made it worse. His attempts to answer questions provoked laughter and ridicule from his classmates. His attempt to minimize the distress this caused, a nervous smile round the class, a shrug of the shoulders; pretending either that he had caused the disturbance on purpose or that he did not care, served to worsen his position with the teacher.

He compensated for his failure in class and lack of academic success by learning the stocks and shares table of the *Financial Times* every week. This enabled him to develop a reputation in a field outside the sphere in which the school was competent to judge. He would emphasize the *real* importance of this in his future career and thus minimize the effect of his scholastic failure. Even this did not improve his standing in the school, especially with the staff. It served only to explain his laziness, his bad behaviour and lack of concern with school work.

It is interesting to note the family background of these two boys. Priestley is Jewish, second in a family of three and lives in an area of expensive detached houses. His father is a clearance stock buyer. Cready on the other hand lives on a council estate, is fourth out of six in the family and his father is a quality inspector in an abrasives factory.

Cready and Priestley do not, therefore, conform with the established correlation between academic achievement and social class. Cready, a working-class boy from a large family on a council estate, is making good, while Priestley, an upper-middle-class boy from a smaller family, is failing academically. However, this negative case highlights the point I want to make; there was a measure of autonomy in the system of social relations of the classroom. The positions of Cready and Priestley are only explicable in the light of an analysis of the system of social relations *inside* the classroom. This system is open to manipulation by those who are sensitive to its details. Hence Cready, who had all the major external factors stacked against him, was able to use the system of social relations to sustain and buoy himself up, while Priestley, despite all the advantages that he brought to the situation, had fallen foul of the system and was not only failing but also speedily losing any motivation to succeed in the sphere in which the school was competent to judge him.

I reiterate that this is not an attempt to disprove the general established trend but to highlight the fact that there are detailed social mechanisms and processes responsible for bringing it about, which are not completely determined by external factors. By studying these mechanisms it will be possible to add a dimension to our understanding of the general processes of education in our schools.

The Staffing Problem
The Newsom Report

Reprinted with permission from *Half Our Future*, A report of the Central Advisory Council for Education (England), London, Her Majesty's Stationery Office, 1963, pp. 245–9

'Are you going to stay with us, Sir?' was the question which greeted the hero of a recent novel about a modern school as he got to know the boys in his form. They had had a long experience of transient teachers and had not enjoyed it. Were they particularly unfortunate, or is this what must be expected? The schools in our sample were asked to report their staff changes since September, 1958, so that we might know how many comings and goings of teachers the Browns, Jones and Robinsons of our report had known in their secondary modern schools.

There must, of course, always be changes in school staffs. Experienced teachers reach retiring age, promising men and women get promotion and young men and women are appointed to fill their places. This is a natural and a healthy process. In addition the years covered by our enquiry have been years of increasing numbers of pupils in secondary schools and extra teachers have been appointed to meet the bulge. There were 14 per cent more men and 11 per cent more women teachers in the schools in our sample in 1961 than in 1958.

There is no precise way of deciding from the information in our possession what a normal and healthy turnover would be, but it is necessary to have some kind of yardstick by which to judge the present position. Probably few heads of schools would wish to appoint a man or woman to the staff who would not stay at least three years with them. Heads of training colleges and university departments of education would probably advise their students to stay three years in their first post. Allowance must be made for young teachers who run into difficulties in their first school and are well advised to move to another school where they can avoid the mistakes they have made. Older men and women may find promotion unexpectedly come their way within three years of joining a school staff. It seems reasonable to suppose that somewhere between 10 per cent and 15 per cent of new appointments may rightly move on within three years for one or other of these reasons. The period under review in our survey was one of three years. We know for each school how many men and women were appointed to the staff after September, 1958, up to and including September, 1961. If the argument of this paragraph is sound, we should hope that the schools would still have on their staffs somewhere between 85 and 90 per cent of those appointed during this period. A school with a holding power of this order is in a healthy condition.

An index of 'holding power' was calculated for all schools. Holding power was defined as the proportion of teachers appointed to the staff after September, 1958, who were still in post in September, 1961. On this basis the overall holding power of schools where men teachers are concerned was 65 per cent and for women teachers 58 per cent. Even if our estimate of a healthy situation in the last paragraph proves somewhat too exacting, the contrast between it and these figures indicates an unhealthy state of affairs in modern schools generally.

To some extent this is clearly a national problem – one consequence of the general shortage and wastage of teachers and the greater opportunity of promotion to graded posts since 1956. The difference between the holding power index for men and women teachers is no doubt associated with the early wastage of married women teachers. In the conditions which prevailed in the 1930s both generally and among teachers, the holding power of the schools was almost certainly greater.

But excessive turnover is not only a national problem. The differences in holding power between schools are more than can be explained by sampling fluctuations. Some variation is in any event to be expected just as it is when twenty coins are each tossed ten times. But undue variation – and what is undue in this context can be evaluated mathematically – would be evidence of something odd in the coins themselves. So here the variation is more than would arise accidentally, and is evidence of real differences in holding power not only between categories of schools but between schools in the same category.

The distinction between various kinds of neighbourhood has often been useful in interpreting the data from our survey. The school staffing situation is no exception. Thus, while the average holding power index for men in modern schools is 65 per cent, in socially mixed neighbourhoods it is 70 per cent and in rural schools 76 per cent. In the special group of slum schools it is only 34 per cent. The full picture by neighbourhoods is given in Table 1.

Table 1. Index of Staff Holding Power by Neighbourhoods

	Rural	Mixed	Council	Mining	Problem Areas
Men	76%	70%	67%	58%	55%
Women	69%	57%	58%	60%	56%

These differences are not unexpected and they are certainly important, but perhaps even more important is the fact that these groups are far from homogeneous. The differences between schools in the same type of neighbourhood are often greater than can be explained by chance in the sense in which we have used it. It is reasonable from our data to infer that the quality of the school as a community can on occasion increase or lower its holding power, proving stronger than the effects of the neighbourhood in which its work is done. Some schools at least can help themselves.

Teaching in the Affluent Society

Jean Floud

Reprinted with permission from 'Teaching in the Affluent Society', *British Journal of Sociology*, September 1962, pp. 301–6, 307–8

The prestige of the teacher's office and the social and intellectual characteristics of the profession are closely bound up each with the other and with the opportunities for teachers to develop the personal influence over their pupils implied in the notion of 'leadership', which depend on the state of the relations in the wider society between the generations and between family and school. The point about the affluent society is that by its influence in all these interrelated matters it presents formidable obstacles to the successful exercise of institutionalized leadership in teaching; indeed, it precipitates a crisis in the teacher's role which is a familiar feature of the American scene and in this country incipient and potentially severest in the secondary schools. I want briefly to review the familiar social factors at work before turning to the teachers – incumbents of a social role which they are both predisposed and taught to conceive in traditional missionary terms, but which must be performed in the affluent society under conditions which all but transform it.

'The Affluent Society' is a fancy name for an advanced industrial society in which pre-Keynesian economics of scarcity are giving way to post-Keynesian economics of plenty as the results of the twentieth-century technological revolution are assimilated and its dynamic imposes itself, bringing about an unprecedented rate of all-embracing social change. The revolutionary consequences of these developments for education are being explored by economists and sociologists. I do not want to dwell on them here, but merely to recall that they involve, firstly, a great extension and prolongation of formal schooling as education is recognized as a crucial investment for the exploitation of the new technology and as it rises ever higher in the order of public preferences for consumption goods; and secondly, the imposition of new tasks on the schools in connection with the process of social selection.

The pace of social change set by technological developments is ably described in the Crowther Report; its implications for the teacher are more obvious in America where these developments are much farther advanced than in this country; they are vividly rendered by Margaret Mead. Speaking of 'the fantastic rate of change of the world in which we live', she says:

> ... children of five have already incorporated into their everyday thinking ideas that most of the elders will never fully assimilate ... Teachers who had never heard a radio until they were grown up have to cope with children who have never known a world without television. Teachers who struggled in their childhood with a buttonhook find it difficult to describe a buttonhook to a child bred up among zippers, to whom fastnesses are to be breached by zipping them open, rather than fumblingly feeling for mysterious buttons. From the most all-embracing world image to the smallest detail of daily life the world has changed at a rate which makes the five-year-old generations farther apart than world generations or even scores of generations were in our recent past, then people whom we bear and rear and teach are not only unknown to us and unlike any children there have been in the world before, but also their degree of unlikeness itself alters from year to year.

To this we must add that just at the time when the social and spiritual gulf between the generations is widening in this manner to chasm-like proportions the biological gap between them is narrowing as adolescents mature earlier and adults marry younger.

In these circumstances, on what can the teacher's moral authority rest? Certainly not on the old pretensions – not on the superiority of his culture and experience, the value of which is no longer at all self-evident. And as his moral authority dwindles, so that of the peer group waxes, and pedagogical devices to establish his personal authority over his pupils are rendered both more necessary and more difficult to carry into effect as his institutional position weakens.

On the other hand, however, the affluent society endows teachers, if not with moral and intellectual authority, then at least with a new power over their pupils. Under conditions where the bond between occupation and schooling is very tight – where vocational qualifications are the modern 'means of production'

(Geiger) and in scarce supply, the school becomes an important agency for the distribution of 'life-chances'. What has long been commonplace among parents is now being recognized by teachers – that the school is not only an agency of social promotion but also, in the Welfare State, one of the few remaining agencies of social demotion. So that, so far as parents are concerned, it is less a trusted collaborator in the task of educating their young according to their ability and aptitude than a resented bureaucratic or 'Official' arbiter of their children's social fate.

However, this extraneous power over pupils which is thrust on to the teacher in the affluent society is no simple substitute for his eroded moral authority. In so far as parents and pupils acknowledge and defer to this power (and this, as one knows, is very much a matter of social background) it tends to induce a utilitarian, more or less cynical attitude towards what the teacher has to offer – an unflattering preoccupation with his more commonplace intellectual capital of knowledge and skills, an emphasis on instruction and know-how and an unwillingness to be educated. Alternatively, pupils may react to the pressures of the new situation by withdrawal and flight into indifference to learning or into the active anti-intellectualism of the adolescent sub-culture. This is a phenomenon with which we are all familiar and which Professor Parsons touches on in his essay 'The School Class as a Social System'. It underlies the disturbing picture painted by Riesman of the lengths to which the deterioration in the teacher's traditional authority can go. He shows him entirely dependent for success in the classroom on a tenuous status with his pupils as 'opinion leader', under cloak of which he must manipulate and persuade them to the best of his ability in the light of personal values which are increasingly secular, neutral and imprecisely defined.

How far, we may ask, are we in this country along the road to this particular perdition? The same general social pressures are certainly to be felt over here; but in a radically different social and educational setting and at a lower level of affluence their impact has been more restrained. Thus, the progressive movement in education which deliberately underplays, even when it does not actually deny, the element of authority in the teacher's relationship with his pupils, and is thus both kin and accomplice of the processes we have been describing, cannot be said to have played itself out with us to the point of becoming positively dysfunctional in the way that Riesman most plausibly suggests that it has in America. It still stands here for progress in the class-room – for a more humane and technically more skilful pedagogy and for the elimination of some of the occupational hazards to teachers' personalities. Its beneficial effects are most in evidence in our primary schools. But that there is an incipient crisis in the secondary teacher's role cannot be doubted.

Apart from the well-known fact that they are inadequately paid and consequently in very short supply, the striking fact about teachers – at least secondary teachers – is that they are, speaking generally, ill-equipped by their social and educational history to cope with the tasks confronting them in the schools. The majority of our secondary teachers are college-trained non-graduates, successors of the nineteenth-century teacher-missionaries with whom they retain close affinities. A small proportion of secondary teachers, serving mainly in the selective schools, descend from a different tradition – a tradition of being, not social missionaries, but guardians at the gateway into higher education and initiators into the national heritage of learning and culture. Neither group of teachers can be said, for different reasons in each case, to be adequately equipped to man the new national system of secondary schools, the absence of which in this country makes one wonder why we persist in using the term 'affluent society' so freely. If I may generalize wildly, I should say that at a time when all secondary schools must aim to provide for pupils likely to proceed to higher education, the college-trained non-graduate teacher is ill-prepared intellectually, having snatched his personal education from a crowded course of professional train-ing; whilst the graduate teacher, trained or untrained, is ill-equipped to understand the social dimensions of his work even in the selective schools in which he mainly serves. Social factors play an increasingly important part in the work of these schools. They have an intake of pupils which is increasingly representative of the population at large and, like the non-selective ('modern') schools, are undergoing a subtle change of social function.

It seems that the college-trained secondary teacher needs to be more of an intellectual and the graduate teacher more of a social worker. The fact is that the intellectual qualifications for teaching are bound both to rise and to become more uniform throughout the profession in the affluent society, and I think that this should be encouraged.

The teacher-missionary in the nineteenth century needed less education than character, less of the trained intellect than of stamina nourished on firm religious (or sometimes, as in the case of France, secular philosophical) beliefs and principles. In the early history of the normal schools and colleges in which they received their education and training the authorities had frequently to rebuff candidates of superior ability or social standing who could not be expected to remain in the profession once they had received a little education; or to lower the academic quality of the college course in order to narrow the difference between the level of education acquired by teachers in training and the more modest equipment needed on the job in the schools. Fortunately, as we know, they were fighting a rear-guard action against the educational upthrust of the working class – an upthrust which is by no means yet spent – so that the teachers have always had among them a substantial number of able individuals of humble origin out to get an education otherwise inaccessible to them. Nevertheless, the effect of this social and educational history has been to cut the main body of secondary teachers off from the older professions based on the universities.

It is ironic that the Welfare State, in the ante-chamber of the affluent society so to speak, should have introduced measures of educational and social reform which, by democratizing secondary and higher education and widening the occupational horizons of school-leavers, have changed the social basis of recruitment to teaching and threatened its intellectual quality by removing the traditional supply at a discount of able working-class candidates just at the point when the universities were brought to a gesture of recognition (through the institutes of education) of their responsibilities for the education and training of teachers. It is even more ironic, however, to consider that the likely effect of the sluggish expansion of higher education in the next decade will be to drive back into the training colleges large numbers of able working-class boys and girls who will be unable to find places in universities under conditions of intense competition. They will get a better educational bargain than they might have hoped for with the introduction of the three-year course in the colleges, which through the Institutes of Education are in constitutional relationship with universities. But they will emerge nevertheless unnecessarily poorly prepared for the tasks they will confront in the schools.

The problems facing teachers in the affluent society, whether they work in the suburbs or in the slums, are formidable. We have seen how their traditional authority is undermined by social pressures over which neither they nor we can have much control, and how if they are to achieve the indispensable moral ascendancy over their pupils without which they cannot teach, they need to understand, in a way that has perhaps never before been necessary, the social dimensions of their work – the social determinants of the educability of their pupils, the hidden social tensions of the learning situation in contemporary schools, especially in secondary schools.

The case for reshaping the prevailing patterns of recruitment and education for teaching in the light of these considerations seems to me to be overwhelming. Riesman feels 'forced to take for granted the vested interests – the very vested existence – of the schools, and the prevailing patterns of career choice out of which teachers and scholars arise' and is accordingly pessimistic for the future social role of teachers in the United States. Our situation is more flexible and I think we should seize the modest chance offered by our position on the threshold of a period of expansion and reconstruction in higher education to bring the recruitment and education of our teachers into line with the complex demands of the social situation in which they now have to work.

Peer Groups

D. Downes

Reprinted with permission from 'The Gang Myth', *The Listener*, 14 April, 1966

What research has been done in Britain implies a radically different group framework for delinquency to that portrayed in the American literature, though it is true that British work is limited to the mid-nineteen-fifties and after. In the most systematic study so far, Dr Peter Scott, a psychiatrist at the Maudsley Hospital, interviewed 151 boys who were known to have committed group offences. The results were published in 1956 – which was, after all, about the heyday of the teddy-boy movement, which was supposed to have been, according to T. R. Fyvel's vivid study, a gang phenomenon. Scott found that only 12 per cent of the boys could be described as members of 'gangs proper', and these were generally in the youngest age-group – between eight and thirteen. He defined the gang as a group with a leader, definite membership, persistence over time, and definitely delinquent purposes; and he showed that far from supplying the bulk, or even the hard core, of his subjects, gangs barely figured at all as a significant factor on the delinquency scene. Yet the boys he interviewed were in a remand home, and generally this means that they were fairly serious offenders. The majority of them – 86 per cent – had offended in what Scott termed diffuse, or loosely structured, groups, whose usual activities were not delinquent, and which did not attempt to coerce any member into delinquent activity – a feature which is inconceivable in the 'gang proper'.

Nevertheless, delinquent gangs were probably much commoner in this country up to and even after the Second World War than they are now. In his widely reported New Society article, 'Beat Killed the Gang', Colin Fletcher argued, on the basis of personal experience, that gangs were prevalent in Liverpool until the mid-nineteen-fifties. Then the growth of teenage culture and the great increase in adolescents' spending power diverted the energies and aspirations of 'the boys' into the legitimate fields of youth culture and away from the street-corner gang.

Fletcher's analysis makes sense in more ways than one: the gang seems to be very much a phenomenon of the urban slum, which collects together the most deprived and exploited members of society at a great social distance from the more respectable areas and strata. The effect of teenage culture, and rehousing, was simultaneously to break down the parochial focus of slum adolescents' horizons and to disperse them geographically. And both factors served to undermine the traditional gang framework. There is perhaps an even more fundamental reason why this should be so. The adolescent peer group is, in most societies, a normal and necessary framework for youth. It occupies the stage between childhood dependence on parents and the social responsibilities of adulthood. With their peers – that is, people of the same age, sex, and status – adolescents really experience for the first time relationships embodying equality and democracy.

The gang is a relatively authoritarian form of peer group, so that unless there are powerful reasons why they should take the gang form, adolescent peer groups are most likely to be fluid, democratic and egalitarian, rather than hierarchical and tightly knit. Hence, we often mistake 'peer groups' for 'gang', and infer a 'structure' and 'hierarchy' which their members would themselves regard as ludicrous simply because of barriers to communication between them and us when the groups are both working-class and occasionally delinquent.

Yet the gang myth survives, and it is resurrected at appropriate intervals. The mods' and rockers' riots, for instance, were reported as 'gang delinquency'. An earlier example was the Finchley affray, the incident in which a boy was stabbed in a Finchley youth club after being sought out for some insult said to have been inflicted on a member of the 'Mussies', a couple of dozen boys from Muswell Hill in London. This case was heralded as 'gang warfare' by the bench and the press alike.

The only exception was the *Observer* reporter, Christopher Brasher, who took the trouble to visit the cafés where the boys hung out, and critically examined the gang stereotype. He wrote:

The fight was reported as a 'gang feud' between the 'Mussies' and the 'Finchley mob' . . . The judge said: 'All of you have behaved in a way that would bring discredit on a pack of wolves . . . This gang warfare has to be stamped out.' Yet in north London, as the police will tell you, the 'gangs' are no more than social gatherings in dance-halls and cafés of bored youths from the same area. They have no organization, no accepted leader, and no real name – they are just referred to as 'the mob from Highbury' or 'the mob from the Angel'. They seldom get out of hand, and their fights are usually restricted to a bash on the nose to settle an argument. But the danger is that anyone like Ron Fletcher (the leader of the 'Mussies', who was imprisoned for five years, and who was two or three years older than the rest) anyone like him can quickly whip up a gang to 'turn over' any individual or group which has 'offended' him. Then the iron bars and the knives appear like magic.

From Brasher's account, it is clear that the 'Mussies' constituted a 'gang' for the duration of the offence only; they were assembled virtually overnight by Fletcher from sheer acquaintances; and they would probably have dispersed anyway even if the police had not intervened so successfully. The crucial distinction to be drawn here is that between the 'gang' and what an American sociologist, Lewis Yablonsky, has called the 'near-group'. The 'near-group' lacks persistence over time, and any consensus on membership; it is activated by a hard core of as few as two or three usually seriously disturbed boys, who manipulate a large periphery of short-term members; and it acts through spontaneous mobilization for a single 'flare up' rather than through protracted organization for gang conflict. Obviously, the Finchley affray, and the mods' and rockers' riots, are much closer to the 'near-group' conflict than the 'gang' warfare model.

This distinction may seem trifling if you are worried by delinquency but not by the niceties of how it happens. Given the fact of a messy conflict, who cares whether 'gangs' or 'near-groups' are involved.

In this country gangs are virtually non-existent, but mobilization of 'near-groups' is possible in extreme situations. In a study in Exeter, M. R. Farrant located just this pattern, of 'five groups (of a few members each) which were in fact leadership nuclei of larger "quasi-groups" '; and these quasi-groups were mobilized and fused into a gang-like solidarity only on very rare occasions of extreme stress.

If we accept Colin Fletcher's view that the disappearance of the gang framework has left the seriously disturbed delinquent isolated, it follows that sporadic outbreaks of 'near-group' conflict will be highlighted much more than in the past – for the seriously disturbed individual was then assimilated into the relative normality of the traditional gang. This means that if we want to prevent delinquency we should concentrate on locating these seriously disturbed adolescents and attempt to get them referred for social psychiatric treatment, rather than adopt social group work techniques and try to resocialize the 'near-group' as a unity through its so-called 'leader'. Obviously, this type of leader has emerged in a situation of conflict. If we divert the group's energies as a group into more conventional field, we undermine his leadership and render his position even more desperate. To my mind, the most valuable function of the so-called 'detached workers' is not so much to organize delinquent groups and channel their energies as to find out what is going on and document the reality – to act, in fact, as a communication link.

But once we have disentangled the occasional 'near-group' outbreak from the delinquency pattern as a whole, we are left with the rather unspectacular reality of thousands of small cliques who are from time to time engaged in often quite serious forms of delinquency; but this is essentially a phase they will outgrow, and they do not appear to contain any more psychiatric abnormality than you would find in the normal population. These tend to be what Brasher called 'social gatherings . . . of bored youths'. But how does the gang myth help to distort our understanding of these adolescents, and why is it perpetuated in the face of all the evidence to the contrary?

First, the gang myth makes adolescents' occasional delinquencies appear much more purposeful and systematic than they in fact are, so that when we try to understand them we stress their differences from the more conventional members of society, almost to the point of abnormality, and we tend to overlook their similarities, in values, tastes, and aspirations. This means that we cannot accept that they drift into delinquency; rather we see them as being marauders, committed to law-breaking as a 'way of life'. Secondly, this conveniently deflects us from our real task, which is to tackle the roots of their fatalism; these lie in the poor job opportunities, the run-down slum schools, the social hypocrisy they sense when the rhetoric of equality in our society clashes blatantly with their sole experience of inequality.

On one point I would like to develop Fletcher's thesis a little further. If 'beat' has killed the gang (or at least delivered the final blow of a slow, long-term dissolution) it certainly has not killed delinquency. Perhaps this is because those adolescents who are most conspicuously successful in the world of teenage culture are not builders' labourers and van-boys, but those who would have been socially mobile and relatively successful anyway, ex-art-students, for example. If one adopts David Matza's idea that there are essentially three types of adolescent protest – delinquency, bohemianism, and radicalism – then the effect of teenage culture seems to have been an increase in bohemianism at the expense of radicalism, but not at the expense of delinquency. So it is nonsense to suggest that the values of teenage culture are intrinsically delinquent – or even 'delinquescent' – that is, potentially delinquent. They are no more delinquent in themselves than the values of an Oxford high table or a board room meeting.

But teenage culture does generate goals and aspirations, and the divergences between these unreal goals and the drabness of real life could periodically erupt into a search for 'kicks' – and lead to supposedly 'motiveless' delinquency. But bohemianism is just as likely a response, especially among middle-class adolescents. The two are far too often confused in adult minds – 'beatniks' and 'mods and rockers' are not equally anti-social. But both are protest roles which are only intermittently played out by their incumbents, who most of the time act conventionally.

In conclusion, teenage culture provides yet another area of discontinuity in the experience of the lower-working-class boy; and it may have increased delinquency by creating a new hierarchy of success in leisure in which he is, as in work and education, at the 'bottom of the heap'. But we would not expect the gang to re-emerge as a result of these pressures. This would probably happen only if new slums are created for, in particular, the immigrant communities; or if mass unemployment returns to the adolescent job market. Instead, we would expect an intensification of delinquency, but in intermittent and mundane forms, with the occasional 'near-group' outbreak. By perpetuating the gang myth, we fail to see the direction in which delinquency is moving; and as a result we fail to see the lessons it can teach us about the quality and faults of our society as a whole.

The Family, the School and the Political Socialization Process

Robert E. Dowse and John Hughes

Reprinted with permission from *Sociology*, Vol. 5, No. 1, January, 1971

A major enterprise of political socialization studies is to assess the relative influence of the various socializing agencies with which the young come into contact. An early claim was that the institution most crucial in shaping the basic political orientations of each new generation was the family. Hyman, in his survey of work in the area of political socialization, recognized the importance of other institutions, but concluded that, 'Foremost among agencies of socialization into politics is the family'. This view was consistent with ideas developed in social psychology and sociology which stressed both the direct and indirect roles of the family in forming the basic general social orientations of its members. Accordingly, it seemed reasonable to infer that the family would also be critical in forming a sub-set of these general orientations, namely, orientations to politics. It was recognized, of course, that the formative influences at work within the family context were various and complex and might have only an indirect connection with political life as usually understood. Apart from any direct transmission of values which might take place between parents and their children, other important processes might include those shaping basic personality which, in turn, could conceivably play a part in determining the content and style of political beliefs and behaviour. But, whatever the processes at work, earlier theorizing stressed the primacy of the family as an agency of political socialization.

Closer to traditional political science, studies of adult political behaviour provided evidence which, on the face of it, was consistent with the thesis of family dominance. It had been noted with certain variables, especially party choice, that there were high levels of agreement between parents and their children. To quote the conclusion of one such study, Campbell and his associates claimed that '... an orientation to political affairs typically begins before the individual attains voting age and ... this orientation strongly reflects his immediate social milieu, in particular his family'.

Unfortunately, from the point of view of providing evidence relevant to the thesis of family primacy in the political socialization process, such studies suffer from a number of difficulties. First, they ignore parent-child similarities on political attitudes other than party choice; this is the characteristic most firmly fixed in adults and hence a poor guide to the levels of inter-generational agreement to be found on other, perhaps less stable, attitudes. A second difficulty is the reliance of these studies on retrospective reports by adults of their parents' beliefs and attitudes. It is not known to what extent the respondents' recall is accurate. Thirdly, allowing accurate recall, similarity on such variables as party preference between a group of adults and their parents is not, by itself, evidence that it is the family which causes the similarity. For example, where parents and their offspring are exposed to similar occupational milieux this could lead to similar views of the social order which might be reflected in similarities on more specific characteristics such as partisan loyalties. But to acknowledge the possibility of intergenerational similarities as a product of extra-familial agencies entails the possibility that family socialization may be only temporary and subject to modification by experiences intervening between child and adult statuses. Schools, mass media, occupation, may all expose the individual to attitudes and values other than those experienced within the family context.

Thus the assessment of family influence on the political socialization process cannot be undertaken by relying on adult samples. More recent data based on studies of children provide stronger evidence to build an assessment of family influences on the developing political orientations of pre-adults. Hess and Torney, in a study of American school children provide evidence which questions the thesis of the family's overriding importance. They conclude that family efficacy in transmitting political attitudes and values may have been overstressed in previous research and that only certain kinds of political attitudes may be the result of specifically family socialization. These were party preference, an early attachment to country and government, and general attitudes towards 'authority, rules and compliance'. In a later American study by Kent Jennings and Richard Niemi, this time on a systematic parent-child comparison, it was found that apart from party preferences the associations between parents and their children on a series of political attitudes were low. On the basis of this evidence the authors conclude that 'any model of socialization which rests on the assumptions of pervasive currents of parent-child value transmissions is in serious need of modification'.

Apart from the family, one possible institution which might have some marked impact on the political orientations of the new political generation (since it is an institution in which the pre-adult is involved for a considerable period of his life) is, of course, the school. A conclusion of Hess and Torney's study is that in the United States the 'public school appears to be the most important and effective instrument of political socialization . . .'

In Britain the connection between education and social class has been observed and recognized for many years. Numerous studies have shown the strong relationship that social class bears to educational selection and the relationship of such selection to social mobility and occupational status. This selection plays a large part in determining adult occupation and, consequently, social class position. Grammar school children, regardless of their social origins, are much more likely to obtain non-manual employment of some kind than those children who have attended secondary modern schools. Given the strong relationship between social class and differential party support to be found in Britain the effects of social mobility are likely to be politically consequential.

It becomes obvious, then, that the process of political socialization is complex and one which, in industrial societies, cannot be attributed to one prime agency, whether the family or the school, or whatever. The main purpose of this paper is to assess the relative weight of the family and the school in shaping some attitudes and the political knowledge of a group of English school children. We do this with a matched parent-child sample, a technique which has not hitherto been employed at all in studies of socialization in Britain and has only been utilized in a very few cases in the USA.

The Data

The data are taken from a study of a sample of school children between the ages of 11 and 17 plus years from Exeter, Britain. The sample was drawn from a girls' grammar school ($n=148$), a boys' grammar school ($n=146$), two girls' secondary modern schools ($n=193$), and a boys' secondary modern school ($n=140$). The number of children in each school sampled represents a randomly selected 20 per cent of all children in each school. This sample constitutes a good cross-section of the state secondary education sector of the town. Each child in the sample was asked to complete a paper and pencil questionnaire under the supervision of one of the investigators. After completion of the questionnaire, each child was asked to take home to his parents an envelope containing a further questionnaire to be completed by the child's father. The completed parent questionnaire was to be returned in a sealed envelope to the school within a few days. In this way we obtained questionnaires from 627 children and from 327 parents.

The technique of gathering and matching information from both children and parents has a clear advantage over techniques which place reliance on recall by asking either children or adults to report parental attachments and attitudes without any independent check on the accuracy of such reporting. In our study this advantage was only partially realized. First, incomplete return of the parent questionnaires meant that a systematic parent-child comparison could only be undertaken with 52 per cent of the sample. Within both grammar and secondary modern schools the pattern of parental response/non-response was more strongly associated with parental class than with any other factor; but the relationship is not a significant one. Even less significant were the observed differences on other variables, such as political knowledge, political efficacy, frequency of political discussion with parents and so on. Hence, we do not feel that the low parental response vitiates our results, but it is a factor to be borne in mind. Secondly, although the children had been told most specifically that we wished their fathers (where available) to complete the parent questionnaire, we found, nevertheless, that in some cases wives rather than husbands had completed the questionnaire. We have, nonetheless, used the responses in an undifferentiated manner taking them simply as 'parent responses'. To what extent we can assume in this sample similarity between husbands and wives on political attitudes is unknown. At any rate, it is undeniable that it does introduce a possible margin of error.

The Direct Transmission of Attitudes from Parents to Children

In this section of the paper we shall examine our evidence relevant to the proposition that there is a *direct* transmission of politically relevant values and attitudes from parents to children. If the thesis is correct, then one would expect strong similarities in attitudes and values between parents and children.

Party Identification

As mentioned earlier one of the main arguments produced to support the thesis that the family transmits political values was the coincidence of intergenerational partisan preferences. Party preference is perhaps *the* variable that might be expected to be transmitted by parents to children since it is probably the known political characteristic most firmly fixed in adults. Also, for a majority of adults, voting for a party is their most salient political act. Accordingly, if children are aware of any of their parents' political attitudes or beliefs, it is likely to be party preference. Furthermore, if parents are the major political role models available for their children to 'imitate', then one might expect high levels of intergenerational similarity on party preference.

In the questionnaire each child was asked to state whether he or she 'supported' a political party and, if so, to name that party. In addition, each child was also asked to state which party his or her father voted for in the last general election, that of 1966. This meant that we could measure the extent to which the childs' preference, if any, corresponded to their perception of parents' preference. The difficulty here is the possibility of a spuriously high level of intergenerational agreement due to the child interpreting the parents' party preference in terms of its own. So, as a check on the accuracy of the children's perceptions of parents' vote, the parent questionnaire contained an item asking for which party, if any, the parent voted in the last three General Elections, including that of 1966. As far as the political socialization process is concerned, this question of accuracy is important in interpreting the link between parents and children. For, if the perceptions of the parents' party preferences are accurate, this is reasonable evidence to suggest that some political facts, at least, are a feature of parent-child interaction. If, on the other hand the children's perceptions are inaccurate this would not only cast doubt on the use of offspring's report as an indicator of parental party preference – a characteristic technique of many adult studies – but would also suggest a fairly low level of direct political communication within the family.

As will be seen, the picture is complex. In Table 1 the biggest category (30 per cent) are those children who state neither a parent nor a personal party preference. Of those children stating *both* a parent and a personal party preference, the majority preferred the party which they report for their parents (see Table 2). But perhaps the most interesting cases are the 39 per cent of the children who state either a self preference or a parent preference, but not both (Table 1 rows C and D). Although in fact fuller knowledge of these cases may reveal higher levels of actual agreement than is shown by these data, the interest about these children is what is represented by the one-sided reporting. Though they state either a self preference or a parental preference, they do not see their parents' preferences as underpinning or determining their own party choice.

Similarity of party preference between parents and children was not strongly associated with sex, social class, or education. Boys were slightly less likely than girls to give the same party preference as their parents, as also were grammar school children as compared with modern school children. On social class there was no significant difference at all.

For those children reporting a parental preference, the accuracy of their perceptions was fairly high, as shown in Table 3. Although this is a high level of accurate reporting, it must be remembered that fully 47 per cent (Table 1, rows D and E) of the

Table 1. Child's Preference and Perceived Parent's Vote

			Totals
Children whose own party preference and their perception of their parents' party preference is identical	A	25%	159
Children whose own party preference is different to their perception of their parents' party preference	B	6%	38
Children who report a parent party preference but state no self preference	C	22%	138
Children who state no parent party preference but who state a self preference	D	17%	104
Children who state neither a parent nor a self party preference	E	30%	188
		100%	627

Table 2. Relationship Between Children's Party Preference and Perception of Parents' Vote in 1966 General Election*

Children's Party Preference

Children's Perceptions of Parents' Vote	Labour	Conservative	Liberal	Any Other Party	Totals
Labour	75%	15%	8%	2%	100% (95)
Conservative	4%	90%	6%	0%	100% (82)
Liberal	5%	15%	70%	10%	100% (20)
Total	(75)	(91)	(27)	(14)	197

gamma $=0.79$ $\chi^2 p < 0.01$

* This table is taken from a total sample of children who both perceived a parent vote and stated a self party preference. The equivalent gamma association for the group of children whose parents had not returned questionnaires was 0.78; $\chi^2 p < 0.01$.

total children sampled did not know what their parents' vote was in the relevant election nor did they guess. This suggests that for a large proportion of the families, political discussion is not a marked feature of family interaction. This is supported by the finding that where there *is* interaction in terms of fairly 'frequent' political discussion between parents and children, these children are more likely to perceive a parental party preference and to perceive it accurately, *although the associations are small*.

Table 3. Accuracy of Children's Perceptions of their Parents' Vote in 1966 General Election

Parents' Vote in 1966 General Election

Children's Perception of Parents Vote in 1966	Labour	Conservative	Liberal	Total
Labour	86%	10%	4%	100 (81)
Conservative	18%	67%	15%	100 (55)
Liberal	22%	33%	45%	100 (9)
DK/NA	42%	58%	0%	100 (89)
Totals	(119)	(100)	(15)	$N=234$

The gamma association, excluding those parents whose vote was not known was, $0.83 \chi^2 p < 0.01$.

The figure of 53 per cent (Table 1, rows A, B, and C) of the sample of children who could report a parental party preference puts the British family (on the basis of this study, at least) on a point mid-way between the American and the French family as an agent of political communication. Converse and Dupeux report that less than 30 per cent of French adults were able to report what their parents' party preferences were when they were children. In the United States, on the other hand, between 75 per cent and 80 per cent of children have been found able to report their parents' party preferences.

It might be expected that the accuracy of the child's attribution of parental vote would improve with the child's age, but in fact this was not the case. It might also be thought that the coincidence of child and parental preference would increase with child's age, and to a marginal extent this was so. The association was, however, a weak one (gamma $= 0.13$, $\chi^2 p > 0.10$). Nor was it the case that older children were more likely than youngsters to state a party preference of their own (gamma $= 0.037$, $\chi^2 p > 0.10$). Finally, younger children were only slightly less likely to state a parental preference than were older children (gamma $= 0.11$, $\chi^2 p > 0.05$). Hence, it seems that the level of parental transmission is *not* materially affected by developmental factors within our age range.

The lack of any overwhelming similarity between parents and children on party preference is not necessarily inconsistent with adult studies showing much higher levels of intergenerational agreement. It may be that a greater correspondence between parents and children occurs later in life when such experience as work and the playing of a more direct, adult political role can shape more meaningful political orientations. But these later experiences have little direct connection with family transmission of political preferences as such.

Clearly these findings are not definitive. For one thing there is missing in this study a more direct measure of party identification than a vote for a party. Vote, the measure of party identification used here, is by no means an adequate indication of the meaning of party identification to the respondent. The problem is compounded when it is realized that the election of 1966 showed a strong swing to the Labour Party, and it may be that during this election a number of people may have changed their vote, thus displaying only weak partisan attachments.

There is a further problem to which attention must be paid if one is to interpret these findings fully. Although only a minority of the children report a party preference similar to that which they report for their parents, this association does not conclusively establish that it is the child's perception of parents' party preference which determines its party preference. Such a level of intergenerational agreement might be that expected from any group matched for relevant socio-economic characteristics. Accordingly, we tried to assess the relative influence of variables such as parents' social class, child's education, and sex to see whether they were as strongly associated with the child's party preference as was the child's perception of his parents' preference. The association between the perceived parents' party preference and the child's self preference was 0.79. On social class the association ranged from a maximum – that between manual social class and Labour preference – of 0·58 to a minimum – between manual social class and a Liberal preference – of 0·02. On education the associations ranged from a maximum 0·50 for grammar education and a Labour preference to a minimum of 0·24 for grammar education and a Conservative preference. On sex there was no perceptible association on party preferences. In all cases, none gave an association stronger than that given by the child's perception of parental preference.

So, on the basis of this evidence, it would seem that if the child states a party preference and also has some perception of his parents' party preference then this perception is likely to shape his own party preference, and certainly has more effect than social class, education, or sex. But for a large proportion of the families there would seem to be no strong politically communicative interaction between parents and their offspring.

Social Class and Politics

The strongest of all findings in voting studies is the correlation between social class position and voting for a particular political party. And, according to Alford, Britain, of all Anglo-Western democracies, shows the highest index of class voting. But, it is not known to what extent this link between class and voting preferences is a function of family socialization. In other words, do children, prior to any occupational experience, develop an awareness of the political dimension of social class, and is it parentally transmitted?

Parents and children were asked whether they thought that Britain was divided into classes. Parents were much more likely to respond affirmatively than were their children. Eighty-eight per cent of the parents claimed that Britain was divided into classes contrasted with 58 per cent of the children. There was no significant association between parents and their children's responses (gamma=0·01, $\chi^2 p > 0·10$). But slightly more of the children (18 per cent to six per cent of the parents) gave a 'don't know' response to this item. Among the children 29 per cent of those attending secondary modern school gave a 'don't know' response compared with 8 per cent of the grammar school children. This suggests that the responses to this item were likely to be cognitive. (The association between grammar school and a 'yes' response to the question was gamma=0·59, $\chi^2 p > 0·01$.) Only 19 per cent of the children replied positively to a question asking them whether they thought that class was important. In other words, though a majority of the children 'knew' about social class very few felt it was important.

Although the children's awareness of social class is relatively limited and seems to have little direct bearing on parental transmission of ideas about social class, nonetheless the children showed some knowledge of how social class related to electoral politics. In response to a question asking which party they thought people who held certain jobs would probably vote for, the children were, overall, well able to make accurate discriminations at the top and the bottom of the social scale. The children claimed, for example, that Company Directors, and Doctors mainly supported the Conservative Party and Lorry Drivers and Bricklayers mostly supported the Labour Party. There was less firmness in the responses to the less easily graded occupations such as School Teacher, Clergymen, Farmers (see Table 4).

There is evidence here that a good proportion of the children see aspects of the political world as involved in some way with the notion of social class. Specifically, that occupational position implies certain partisan preferences; that the occupants of 'high' social class positions tend to be Conservative while 'low' class positions tend to Labour preferences. We are unable to offer any substantial evidence concerning the rationale children would use to explain this link, but in view of other evidence mentioned earlier it is more than likely that the perceived connection between social class and political preference is little more than a cognitive framework not really associated with strong feelings about the importance of the link. Perhaps what we are seeing in these children is a trend noted by other writers who have pointed to the declining importance of social class in British politics. Continuing increases in the standard of living, the growing similarity between classes in terms of life style could mean a gradual erosion of the class basis of political choice. This might suggest that the parents, brought up in a political context where class and politics had some crucial social meaning, communicate class perspectives which have less meaning to their children. Certainly, few of the children's attitudes to class could be traced to similar feelings on the part of their parents. Another possible explanation lies in the particular political culture of this part of Britain. Exeter is a non-industrial, relatively small town, and it is possible that class feelings are not supported by socio-economic structures. Alternatively, it may be that whatever the attitudes

Table 4. Children's Responses to Predominant Voting Preference of Particular Occupations

Political Parties

Occupations	Labour	Conservative	Liberal	Vary	DK/NA	Totals
Company Director	23	45	6	17	9	100% (627)
Clergyman	13	20	15	35	18	100% (627)
Doctor	21	32	11	22	14	100% (627)
School Teacher	23	25	10	29	13	100% (627)
Policeman	23	18	9	32	18	100% (627)
Lorry Driver	50	14	7	17	12	100% (627)
Bricklayer	50	12	8	17	13	100% (627)
Shopkeeper	28	23	12	26	14	100% (627)
Roadmender	47	13	8	19	12	100% (627)
Garage Mechanic	39	15	8	24	15	100% (627)
Farmer	23	22	16	22	16	100% (627)

of the parents concerning class, such topics are never or rarely part of parent-child interaction.

At this stage, then, the burden of the evidence provided by our data is that, apart from party preference, there seems to be little similarity between political values of parents and their children. Even party preference, overall at any rate, is not strongly transmitted to the children, although, among the children who do report a party preference, their perception of their parents' preference is more strongly associated with the children's self-preference than either social class or education.

Why is it, then, in spite of the fact that parents are believed to have a crucial role in the general socialization process, there should be this lack of transmission of political values from parents to children? The first and perhaps the most obvious reason is the generally low salience of politics as a focus of parent-child interaction. Only 16 per cent of the parents in the sample reported that they were 'very interested' in politics, whereas 29 per cent claimed that they were 'not very interested'. It is quite likely that this latter figure underestimates the lack of interest since a number would on an item like this tend to overrate their real level of political interest, especially since the questionnaire was so clearly about politics. Also, the possibility is that it was the less interested parents who failed to fill out the questionnaire, further underestimating the low level of political interest. So given this generally low level of political interest it is not surprising that little political communication takes place between parents and children. Only 7 per cent of the parents reported that they 'often' discussed politics with their children. Forty-two per cent said that children should be encouraged by their parents to take an interest in politics, yet other evidence suggests that this, by and large, was merely verbal acquiescence to the norm and had few behavioural consequences. In any event, the fact that non-manual parents and parents of high education were more likely to affirm that children should be encouraged to take an interest in politics suggests that the earlier response is indicative of a general tendency of this group to encourage a broad social awareness in their children rather than a focused attempt to awaken any specifically *political* interest.

The second reason why there are few resemblances between parents and children is that there are developmental factors which influence the form and the content of the child's ideas about politics (and, of course, the world generally). Greenstein, Hess and Torney, Easton, and Dennis in their studies of American children all show the developmental pattern of children's ideas and thinking concerning the political world. Such studies suggest that young children more than adults tend to take a benevolent and trusting view of political figures. Certainly the children in our sample took a rather uncritical view of aspects of the political system. For example they tended to see the party system as satisfactory, only 27 per cent saying that the country would be better off without political parties. There is also evidence to suggest that such an uncritical perspective tends to decrease with age. The affirmative responses to a question, 'Do you think good men go into politics?' did so. Of the 11–12 years old, 57 per cent said 'yes' to the question, while only 38 per cent said 'yes' among the 15 year olds and over.

Both the foregoing arguments may go some way to explaining

the relatively low attitudinal similarity between parents and children. A third possible reason is concerned with the fact that children are in contact with other potential political socializing agencies, especially the school, which may modify any effects of parental influence, such as they are. In other words, to reiterate a point made earlier, familial influence, whether direct or indirect, is not likely to operate in isolation from other possible socializing influences. And compared with very young children, this is truer of the children of the age-group studied here whose contact and interaction with other potential socializing agencies is much broader.

Conclusions

Although the secondary modern children are cognitively at a lower level of political awareness than are children in grammar schools, it is not the case that they differ very significantly in their evaluations of political life. For example, on a question asking about the effect of politics on everyday life, grammar school pupils were only marginally more likely to say it had a 'great effect' (72 per cent against 67 per cent). Again, on the 'cynicism towards politicians' questions, secondary modern pupils were not much more likely to be cynical (57 per cent cynical as against 49 per cent). On a question which asked respondents to choose between the sons of a clerk, a duke, a managing director, and a scientist as potential P.M.'s, the secondary modern children chose the Duke's son (38 per cent) rather more than did grammar school children (27 per cent) but in the spread of choices there were no really significant variations. About the same order of difference also emerged in the answers, divided by school, on the political efficacy scale. We have shown above that children in both grammar and secondary modern schools were quite accurate in assessing voting potentials of various occupations, but only a small minority regarded class as 'important'. Perhaps a few more examples will clinch the point: 29 per cent of grammar school children thought the country would be 'better off' without political parties whilst 35 per cent of secondary modern pupils agreed. Both groups agreed that for the opposition to win the next general election would not be a 'disaster for the country'. Finally, 62 per cent of grammar school children thought 'good men go into politics' and 67 per cent of secondary modern children thought the same.

Table 5. Child's Political Knowledge as a Function of Child's Education, Parents' Education and Class

Row	Parents' Education (H) High (L) Low	Parents' Social Class (H) High (L) Low	Child's Education (H) High (L) Low	Child's Rank on Political Knowledge based on Percentage high scorers	Percentage High Political Knowledge scorers	Totals
A	H	H	H	1	87% (42)	48
B	L	H	H	2	69% (27)	39
C	H	L	H	3	63% (10)	16
D	L	L	H	4	59% (30)	51
E	L	H	L	5	18% (7)	38
F	H	L	L	6	13% (1)	8
G	H	H	L	7	12% (2)	17
H	L	L	L	8	7% (6)	91
					$N=$	308

It was only on knowledge and interest that very clear and significant differences emerged – both are items structurally supported in the grammar school – and it is probably the case that these constitute the crucial differences between the two groups. Such differences are significant in the sense that they may well account for, or at least underpin, the known differential rates of political involvement amongst adults. However, if the differences are important the affective resemblances are quite clearly crucial, assuming that our data are generalizable for the UK, since they tap important elements of the political culture. There appears to be general satisfaction and support of the political regime, the community and the authorities. The support is clearly not a very participatory one, especially amongst secondary modern pupils; it seems, indeed, one of general acquiescence in the system. But it should be remembered that in the grammar schools the foundations of potential involvement are laid.

Marginal but consistent differences emerged between the two groups on the affective level; grammar school children consistently appeared less cynical, more potentially participatory in the sense of believing that power and influence are relatively widely distributed in the political system and of attaching more importance to policies than leaders. But it should be stressed that the differences *are* marginal and despite the academic differences between the two school types they do not lead to, or obviously support, very different political sub-cultures.

Our findings indicate, in a context other than the American, that the process of political socialization amongst children can be looked at as complex interaction between many agencies but especially school and home. We have explored a number of dimensions of this interaction in order to demonstrate that the 'traditional' emphasis on the home is misplaced. Our study strongly suggests that the school is the more significant agency, although it does not work in isolation from the home. This points to the need for further exploration of the relationship between these and other institutions in the formation of children's political attitudes and values.

Further Reading: Socialization

H. GERTH AND C. WRIGHT MILLS: *Character and Social Structure*, Routledge & Kegan Paul, 1956.

*† A. H. HALSEY, J. FLOUD AND C. ARNOLD ANDERSON (Eds.): *Education Economy and Society*, A Reader in the Sociology of Education, The Free Press, and Collier-Macmillan Ltd, 1961 (and 1965 paperback).

* D. RIESMAN ET AL: *The Lonely Crowd*, Doubleday Anchor, 1953.

* M. CARTER: *Into Work*, Penguin Books, 1966.

* J. W. B. DOUGLAS: *The Home and the School*, MacGibbon & Kee, 1964 (and Panther Books, 1967).

D. H. HARGREAVES: *Social Relations in a Secondary School*, Routledge & Kegan Paul, 1967.

J. B. MAYS: *Growing Up in the City*, Liverpool University Press, 2nd edn., 1964.

M. D. SHIPMAN: *The Sociology of the School*, Longmans, 1968.

* M. D. SHIPMAN: *Childhood. A Sociological Perspective*, National Foundation for Educational Research, 1972.

J. SPENCER: *Stress and Release in an Urban Estate*, Tavistock, 1964.

W. TAYLOR: *The Secondary Modern School*, Faber & Faber, 1963.

* Available in paperback
† Reference

4 Work

When we want to describe someone, we characteristically do it in terms of his occupation. Words like 'miner', 'chemist', 'shopkeeper', and so on are more than convenient labels; they indicate and illustrate aspects of a whole way of life. This is true, perhaps even more so in the negative, for when we describe someone as 'out-of-work', 'retired', 'under age', and so on, we indicate that the person so described is in some way out of the mainstream of social life. Just as these shorthand descriptions of a person illustrate the way 'jobs' are deeply woven into the language we use to interpret everyday social events, so occupational roles have significance for the whole social structure.

There are many different ways of studying the phenomenon of work in contemporary society, and *Men and Work in Modern Britain*, a companion book to this one, examines some of these in more detail. What we have tried to do in this chapter is to pay particular attention to the subjective experience of work and to the significance of work for the individuals who are directly involved in it. But i tis obviously important also not to lose sight of the institutional framework within which work takes place. Moreover, it is necessary to bear in mind the specific historical experience of a particular industry or occupation in attempting to interpret and explain behaviour at the present time.

Eccles's analysis of the relations between management and men on the Liverpool Docks shows how the pattern of industrial relations in a particular industry depends very much on historical factors. The fluctuations in the flow of work were used by management to justify a casual system of labour in which there would normally tend to be a pool of idle men available for any unexpected need, for instance, to load a ship which wished to take advantage of a favourable tide. But the dockers themselves derived some benefits from the casual system because it preserved their independence and permitted them to organize their work to some extent to suit themselves. But the Second World War and the imposition of regulations governing employment and organization on the docks indicated that regularity of employment had several advantages. The creation of the National Dock Labour Board likewise made substantial progress towards rationalizing a situation in which there was a multiplicity of employers, some of them very small. But although rationally and objectively the stage was set for a more harmonious future, this did not occur. Eccles shows how the legacy of past confrontations, as well as errors of judgement and timing, served to vitiate the possibilities of steady progress towards decasualization and the continued prosperity of the Liverpool docks.

The research on which the paper by **Goldthorpe** was based was carried out in Luton between 1962 and 1965 as part of a study of affluent workers. A more complete account is available in the book by Goldthorpe, Lockwood, Bechhofer and Platt referred to in the list of Further Reading. To quote the authors, 'The main objective of this study was to test empirically the widely accepted thesis of working-class embourgeoisement: the thesis that, as manual workers and their families achieve relatively high incomes and living standards, they assume a way of life which is more characteristically "middle class" and become in fact progressively assimilated into middle-class society.' They interviewed over two hundred 'affluent' car assemblers, machinists, setters, chemical process workers, and maintenance men. They show that these social meanings given to work, based on previous experience, can largely determine the *content* of experience within the factory itself, and play a more important role in developing work-place attitudes and behaviour than the organization of work or technological imperatives. In other words 'assembly-line man' may be largely a fiction, which obscures the extent to which the labour force attracted to and entering a specific field of employment may be 'pre-selected'.

This approach emphasizes the importance of subjective experience in 'creating' a work environment, within certain limits set by the production technology, and the administrative structure of the organization through which the work activities of individual participants are controlled.

Lupton indicates the relevance of this approach to the problem of 'restriction of output'. He shows that what appears at first glance to be 'irrational' behaviour in economic terms on the part of workers, in fact makes good sense when con-

sidered as part of rational strategies of action developed to
cope with *real* conflicts of interest between management and
workers. Focusing on the problem of controls exercised by
workers on output and earnings, he lists the various factors,
some 'internal', some 'external' to the structure of the firm,
which may be associated with differences in the behaviour of
workers on the shop floor. This study compares two firms, one
('Wye's') in the rubber-proofed garment industry, the other
('Jay's') an electrical components manufacturer. Lupton did
not use survey methods, but gathered his material by the
intensive method of 'open participant observation', which
involved his working in the two firms for a considerable
period.

Lockwood analyses the work situation of the clerk, as it
has developed from the nineteenth-century 'counting-house'
to a more rationalized, large-scale type of office. Relying
mainly on documentary and historical materials he traces the
increase in 'rationalization' and the growth in the average
size of the office, during this period in this country. The
ratio of non-manual to manual workers in manufacturing
industries has increased, as has the proportion of workers
in 'white-collar' industries generally. But the physical concentration of large numbers of 'black-coated workers' has been
counterbalanced by an increase in specialization so that the
actual working group remains rather small in size.

Lockwood discusses the forms of organization and conditions of work which are conducive to the development of
class-consciousness. He argues that the chain of command
between 'management' and 'clerical staff' is rooted in personal
contact, which leads to cooperative social relationships and a
tendency to perceive the aims and ends of management and
clerks as essentially similar, so that no fundamental conflicts
of interest are felt to be present.

But the pace of change in industry means that even office
staff and systems are subject to the impart of procedures and
techniques which radically affect the nature of the work itself.
Many of these changes are conveniently summarized under the
shorthand term – 'automation', the chief agent of which has
been the high speed digital electronic computer. **Mumford and
Ward's** article was written in 1965, but its predictions about
the extent and scope of the automated revolution have proved
remarkably far-reaching and accurate. They indicate that even

the manager's position is liable to radical change as the result of the introduction of the computer.

The work situation of the coalminer described by **Dennis, Henriques and Slaughter** is different from that of the clerk in many ways, but in two which have particular relevance. While the clerk is in the mainstream of society, working in acceptable conditions, and only rarely involved in shift-working or any major disruption of conventional working routine, the miner is a representative of an 'extreme' occupation. He works under conditions of unpleasantness and physical danger, and is isolated from society by the nature of the work he is engaged in and the social relations of the community he lives in. Moreover, he may typically perceive relations between management and workers in terms of a conflict of interest, rooted in the economic wage-nexus and reinforced by the historical experience of depression and deprivation. Here again, as in Lupton's study, participant observation was the major research method and two of the three research workers lived in the small Yorkshire town that was the subject of the study, for some time.

While the precise details of the organization of work have changed since Dennis, Henriques and Slaughter undertook their study, the confrontation between management and workers is still endemic in the social relations of mining. In this field as in much of sociology, a good deal of research has been undertaken into aspects of social behaviour which, taken in isolation, may appear to be unusual, abnormal, or irrational. However, analysis of the context in which such behaviour takes place, and of the typical explanations and justifications advanced for it, can enable us to interpret the apparently 'irrational' by elucidating its 'subjective rationality' in terms of the norms and values of the appropriate social groups, and its 'objective rationality' in terms of the networks of relationships which being a member of such a group involves.

Thus Tunstall in *The Fisherman* explains the apparent irrational resentment felt by deck-hands on a deep-sea trawler for the radio operator, which makes him a scapegoat for the crew, although he provides an essential function and role in the fish-catching team.

The radio operator 'is isolated from the deck-hands by the nature and place of his work, by social origin and style of life, and by his closeness to the skipper'. Moreover, 'he does not

do a physically demanding job', which conflicts with the
deck-hands' conception of fishing as a job requiring a good
deal of strength, toughness and physicality. A scapegoat is
required to absorb the tensions produced by the demanding
conditions of the job. 'Being an object for their combined
hostility the sparks helps to cement the unity of the deckmen.'
Hollowell's book examines the sub-culture of another group
whose working conditions tend to isolate its members from
'conventional' society.

Another theme of general relevance is that caused by the
need to set boundaries to analysis and explanation of aspects
of social behaviour. Both Goldthorpe and Lupton stress the
importance of features of the social situation 'external' to the
work place for understanding behaviour that occurs *within* it.
Dennis, Henriques, and Slaughter place their analysis of the
work-place relations of coalminers in the context of the
historical experience of the social class of wage-earners, who
sell their labour power to owners of capital in return for the
opportunity of utilizing the facilities of employment to earn a
wage.

That the confrontational style of industrial relations
described by Eccles, and again by Dennis, Henriques and
Slaughter is not restricted to dock work or coalmining is
emphasized by **Beynon's** study of motor-car manufacturing.
The instability of the industry and its susceptibility to short-run
fluctuations of the market have combined to produce a history
of insecurity for the workers. Periods of boom, with a high
demand for cars that could only be met by systematic overtime
were typically followed by a recession in which short-time
working was the norm. But wherever the management pointed
to external factors beyond their direct control as the cause of
the fluctuations in employment, the workers tended to point
the finger at the failure of management to predict market
demand and thus to plan in advance for continuity of employment.

Beynon's study builds on Lupton's analysis when he points
out that the market *directly* affects relationships in the plant.
As Beynon points out 'in a situation ridden with latent
conflicts, the decision to lay men off can be likened to a
declaration of war, and it is not only the workers who attempt
to exact reprisals against the other side in this situation'.

Within this broad context, there are important links between work and the family and community. The particular occupational group may largely determine patterns of leisure also. Thus **Parker** distinguishes between three types of occupational groups. Among miners and fishermen leisure is sharply demarcated from work and is seen as providing both physical recuperation and compensation for the rigours of a dangerous way of life to which their attitude is generally hostile. Social workers on the other hand, and many other professional workers who are more involved in their work, may regard leisure as largely an extension of activities in which individuals pursue 'special interests' and projects as a means to the development of personality. Parker found that bank employees fell into neither of these two groups, but tended to adopt a more 'passive' attitude towards leisure which is associated with an 'indifferent' attitude to work.

Sport, and betting on it, plays a big part in the life of the British. **Gosling** looks at the appeal and origins of greyhound racing in ways which convey an immediate feeling for the 'night at the dogs' and also the satisfactions it provides and of the reasons for its place in working-class life. The changes which are taking place in what is still the second most popular sport in the country are indicated, and in particular the consequences of legalizing the betting-shop which have led to much more betting but less customers attending and a hundred dog-tracks closed. For these and other reasons it has become a 'rather respectable pleasure'.

Dock Work

A. J. Eccles

This extract was especially written for this volume and has not previously been published in this form.

Work in the docks can only be understood in the context of its history. Attitudes and behaviour have been defined by earlier experiences – particularly by the casual nature of dock work. Only in 1967 did British dockers become permanently employed and many traces remain of the earlier days.

The Early Days

It was to be expected that cargo handling would start off as casual work. Villagers would turn out to unload a ship which laid up on their beach and then return to their fields or fishing boats. The advent of docks created embryo ports but the handling of cargoes was still temporary work for men who would often have other jobs. As the disciplines of factories grew, other industries developed a continuity of employment, but dock work was still open to anyone who wished to take part in it.

When industrial work was slack, unemployed men would pour down to the docks prepared to work for a minimal wage, and the habitual dockers' chance of obtaining work was thereby reduced. Consequently, dock workers, like all casual workers, were a depressed and demoralized class, and a constant reproach to the prosperity of Victorian Britain.

In 1893 Charles Booth's investigation into the trades of East London showed that casual labour was 'a gigantic system of outdoor relief'. The dock-worker communities were characterized by 'quixotic generosity', 'jealousy of their leaders' authority', 'conservatism' and 'close-knit loyalty'. The solidarity of shared hazards made them stand by one another when faced with external threat (though they would fight each other for a job regardless of the rights or wrongs of the immediate issue). In a casual-labour system sticking together to face their employers was their only source of strength.

The casual system endured because employers were afraid that if they did not have a pool of idle men they would not be able to cope with fluctuations in the amount of work. Ships' arrivals were erratic and regularity of work seemed to be a mirage. The men prized their independence; preferring to work long spells day and night, followed by a few days' idleness. Even the union leaders could not agree that non-casual labour was feasible on the docks and, whilst agreeing that more regular work would improve dockers' lives, felt that permanent employment would 'crush the men out'. The men clearly enjoyed being their own masters, although their families bore the hardships of irregular earnings.

Nevertheless, some attempts were made to improve matters. In Liverpool, the dockers' leader, Jimmy Sexton, tried to establish a clearing house in 1911. Registering all dock workers would have been the first step to decasualization by excluding the part-time workers who moved in and out of the docks when they felt like it. But the dockers' independence overcame this attempt, with objections to men 'being numbered like cattle'. They resisted the scheme so fiercely that Sexton had to seek police protection. It was a striking example of the conflict between security and opportunity, which made it difficult for union leaders to take the men in any agreed direction.

The employers were similarly disorganized. It was open to any person to hire dock labour – all that one needed to do was to express a wish to undertake work on the docks. An employer did not have to work on the docks permanently. He could do a particular job and then vanish from the scene for months. Having no loyalty to the industry the casual employer would simply seek to make the best of the particular job he had obtained, no matter how expedient and shortsighted his employment policies might be. It was nearly impossible for the more regular and permanent employers to devise any coherent employment strategy.

The Shaw Commission of 1920 did agree that some way had to be found to tear up the casual-labour system by the roots, but merely proposed that another body be set up to study the problem. Led by Ernest Bevin, the fragmented trade unions finally amalgamated into a national body for transport and port workers in 1922 – the Transport and General Workers Union. However, any desire to change the situation was overwhelmed by the economic problems of the inter-war period.

The outbreak of the Second World War brought with it methods of labour organization which would have been unacceptable to employers and men alike in peacetime. Labour was directed to jobs and all dockers were registered and provided with permanent employment under the Defence Emergency Regulations. In spite of some shortcomings, this scheme worked well and at the end of the war the union leaders were adamant that a return to pre-war conditions of casual labour would be intolerable. Through experience the men had found that regular employment was attractive rather than restrictive.

A National Dock Labour Board was set up with local boards in each major port. No casual workers were to be allowed in normal times and all the registered dockers would be guaranteed a 'fall-back' wage even if no work was available. The local boards hired out men to employers to carry out a particular job, say loading or unloading a ship. When the job was finished the men were returned to the board from the employer and were available for re-hire by another employer. At long last the men, although not permanently employed by a particular employer, were assured of a regular minimum weekly wage. But the new scheme had its oddities. Casual employers were still allowed, the fall-back rate was low and dockers could not go and find outside work in slack times without losing their registration.

Although these boards were regarded by the men as protecting them indirectly from the employers, their attitude towards the board was nevertheless ambiguous. This was scarcely surprising, since their own union representatives on the board were required to sit in judgement upon them if a disciplinary charge arose.

However, the creation of the board was a sincere attempt to provide secure employment in a notoriously unstable industry.

Work and Attitudes

Three kinds of dock worker made up the 10–20 man 'gangs' which were the working units on the docks.

First, the 'perms' or permanent employees who sought to be taken on to the books of a particular employer as weekly workers – never returning to the board for re-hire. Failing the attainment of this objective, these men would attach themselves to a particular foreman and develop a working relationship with him so that he would always hire them in preference to other workers. These permanent gang workers were highly security conscious and also enjoyed higher than average earnings due to their continuous employment. The T&GWU always resisted the extension of this category beyond 10 per cent of all workers, fearing that an elite would be created which would threaten the dockers' security.

The hiring system for dockers was particularly repugnant to the security conscious men. It involved men being locked in a large shed or 'pen' so that latecomers could not get in and people inside could not escape if poor jobs were available. The hiring foremen would then appear and take the registration books from the men they wished to hire. The dock's grapevine is effective and the hundreds of men in the pen would know which foreman had good jobs and which bad ones. Accordingly, men would either fight one another to get a particular foreman or fight to get away from another. It was a degrading spectacle in which foremen would be chasing men round the pen trying to hire them for poor jobs. The would-be 'perms' used to be hired first by clustering in a spot to which they knew their foreman would come.

The remaining men split into two roughly equal groups. The 'floaters' actively chased the good jobs and believed themselves to be the highest paid dockers. They valued independence, individual enterprise and variety more highly than security. Their belief about earnings was often erroneous in that they tended to remember only the good times and to forget their low earning patches. In fact, the continuously employed 'perms' usually averaged a higher wage than the 'floaters'.

The final group of men were the 'drifters'. Sometimes weak, old or timid, these men could be floaters who were past their prime. This was the depressed class of dockers, always at the back of the queue and with low average earnings. Yet, either because of timidity or because of their previous history as floaters, they accepted the situation in which they always had the rough end of any deal.

The dockers' solidarity; their ambivalence towards security and opportunity; their unease about the role of their union officials – these were not the only features of the dockers' work situation.

In Liverpool there existed a working practice which gave them extensive amounts of leisure during working hours. It was known as 'the welt'. A similar practice existed at Glasgow, where it was known as 'spelling'.

Basically, the welt operated by having half the gang of dockers working at any given time whilst the other half disappeared to whatever leisure activity they wished. It was partly a feature of over-manning, partly of varying work-load which caused the low labour utilization, partly a response to long working hours. More importantly, it was a rational economic response on the dockers' part to the design of the wage payment system. Unlike London, Liverpool was not traditionally a piecework orientated port. Output incentives were a modest part of the wage bill. Even in 1967, when the weekly wage averaged £20 the piecework element was about £3. However, overtime payments at Liverpool were never less than double the basic hourly rate and on Sunday these could rise to quadruple the basic rate.

Hence, to maximize the wage in relation to the number of hours worked it paid the men to practise the welt and to spin out work to gain lucrative overtime pay. The alternative of all remaining on the job and working hard to maximize the bonus payment was not nearly so appealing. The welt was not used where the bonus rate was attractive for a particular type of cargo, or where one's mates would be struggling if one left them.

Nevertheless, it was widespread, and the typical working day would start with everyone booking on with the timekeeper at 8 a.m. Half the holdsmen and quayside porters would disappear (it was less easy for crane drivers and deckhands) whilst the others worked until 10 a.m. The missing workers would then return and relieve their mates until noon. After lunch everyone would book on at 1 p.m., half would disappear until 4 p.m., when they returned to work until 7 p.m., leaving the others free to go home. Thus, out of a ten-hour long day each man would work for five hours. Standard finishing time was 5 p.m. but two hours overtime was a regular feature Monday to Thursday, though not on the Friday pay day. Hence the hours from 5 p.m. to 7 p.m. were overtime paid at double time, and so a man would receive twelve hours basic pay for ten hours notional attendance and five hours actual work.

Neither the employers nor the union liked the welt. The employers found it an affront to notions of discipline and it cut down the output per gang hour by about 20 per cent. The union found the welt difficult to defend on moral grounds and it was embarrassing for an official to argue with an employer when half the men had disappeared from the job. The men, however, had extensive leisure time during the day and a wage which was both maximized absolutely and also in terms of wage per hour worked. Their actions were economically rational, if morally uncertain.

There were less than 20 union officials at Liverpool for over 10,000 men spread over several miles of docks. The men were allocated to areas, usually an adjacent pair of docks, in units of 500 to 2,000 men each. In the small areas the relevant union official would just about keep pace with problems but in the big areas there could be delays in servicing the union members. Although not long by factory standards – a matter of hours usually – they were crucial in the fast-changing cargo situation in the hold of a ship.

The most notable queries concerned abnormal conditions for which one could get 'dirty cargo' or 'impedance' awards. Perhaps the cargo was infested with weevils or the sacks were splitting and difficult to handle. Access to the cargo might be difficult, depending on the design of the ship. The result was that gangs would frequently stop work when a claim was pending – partly to avoid working their way through the evidence and partly to speed up consideration of their claim. Such short-lived stoppages were frequent but would rarely spread beyond the ship which was affected.

Bigger issues would cause strikes to spread rapidly. Solidarity was unstinting and immediate. Should a call come from another ship, work would stop without debate as to the issue involved. It was enough that one's mates were in trouble. Considering the issue would follow the action, not precede it.

Dockers and Unions

The men's ambiguity towards the union had led to the sporadic creation of ginger groups amongst dockers who felt that the T&GWU was not militant enough in trying to improve wages and conditions, an impression not reduced by the fact that the union officials, once elected, were no longer accountable to the membership for re-election.

One ginger group was a rival union – The National Association of Stevedores and Dockers. 'National' was something of a misnomer. Traditionally it operated solely in London's enclosed docks where, alongside the T&GWU, it had negotiating rights. In the mid-1950s it started recruiting dockers dissatisfied with the T&GWU in both Hull and Liverpool. After protracted disputes with the TUC over this violation of the 'Bridlington Agreement' (which governs inter-Union membership poaching) it was expelled from the TUC having failed to win negotiating rights anywhere outside London. Nevertheless it still had members in Liverpool and, not surprisingly, this was deeply resented by the T&GWU. However, the dockers themselves were indifferent to its existence and T&GWU attempts to dislodge the Blue Union were regarded with disinterest which could grow into antipathy if the T&GWU pressed their case against the 'Blues'. Such action violated the men's solidarity, for all were dockers, and attempts by the T&GWU to oust the Blue Union were failures.

This left the Blue Union free to provide a focus for discontent and its policies were almost always more militant than the T&GWU. Despite this it failed to make more serious inroads into the T&GWU membership because the militants were themselves divided. Some joined the Blue Union in the hope of replacing the T&GWU, some joined to force the T&GWU to become more adventurous, others remained in the T&GWU on the grounds that advances could be made only by working within the union which did have negotiating rights.

Management Systems

Management-worker relations were poor by industrial standards. The Dock Labour Boards interposed themselves between men and employers and made normal relationships impossible. The casual-labour system meant that the employer had few permanent employees. Port-wide working agreements made it difficult to vary work and conditions to build up a loyal workforce.

There was a further crucial deficiency. Neither management nor workers had an effective middle-management structure. There were no shop stewards to bargain over local matters, just the few overworked union officials. How could you have shop stewards in a casual system? Who would be their constituents and where would be their constituencies?

The employers were lacking in man/management skills. Most of them were from the shipping industry with its necessary accent on discipline aboard ship. Their Dock Superintendents were ex-Merchant Navy Officers whose careers had been in this hierarchical industry, far removed from the subtleties of factory life and its attendant consultation procedures. The gap between employer and shop floor was enormous. Against this background major changes were brewing. Casual work was becoming less acceptable and, by 1960, there was concern that the erratic conduct of the port transport industry was hampering the growth of Britain's international trade. The industry was fragmented with little vertical integration between hauliers, dock employers, shipowners and the shippers of goods. Furthermore, each port operated as a separate entity, competing with others for trade and each investing in facilities without adequate regard for general over-provision of port facilities. Dockers, too, found inter-port cooperation to be difficult. The solidarity was within the community and rarely extended to other communities of dockers unless there was a mutual benefit to be obtained.

The problems of fragmentation and distaste for the casual system combined to create a demand for nationalization of the docks, supported by some managers on efficiency grounds as well as by the Labour Party, which adopted it as official policy.

Other methods of rationalization were in the offing. The technology was beginning to change rapidly as containerization of cargoes gained pace. This capital-intensive development itself accelerated the vertical integration of segments of the industry by offering a door-to-door service for goods.

Thus there existed a labour hiring system quite inappropriate for effective utilization, an ineffective wage payment system, rapid technological change, few management skills, a gulf between worker and employer, a fragmented industry and political commitment to change both the employment system and ownership of the assets. These pressures were present in an industry which had shown high levels of resistance to change. The auguries were depressing.

In 1961 there was a national attempt to decasualize the docks. It failed because there was too little decasualization and too much concern with abolishing working restrictions.

The 'new deal' at Liverpool envisaged four categories of docker with varying degrees of job security. It was a complete flop, since it failed to give equality of treatment for all and so violated the dockers' solidarity.

A national enquiry was set up under Lord Devlin, which reported finally in 1965. His Committee's White Paper (Cmnd. 2734) is an industrial thriller and is recommended reading for anyone interested in the docks industry. The main proposals were that every worker should be decasualized on the same terms and allotted to a small number of permanent employers. Negotiations about restrictive practices were to follow separately. Devlin recognized the dockers' suspicion of change and was insistent that, to avoid rejection through fear of confusion, any deal would have to be both attractive and simple.

The basic deal comprised a 16 per cent wage rise in exchange for an estimated 6 per cent rise in productivity arising from the stopping of the casual hiring system. It was an attractive package, particularly in ports like Hull where the proposed £16 per week fall-back pay appealed to dockers who were signing on because of lack of work. There were a few frictions over the implementing of Devlin but no problem of great substance emerged – except in Liverpool.

Here, the employers – now down to 21 members, compared with 114 three years earlier – ignored Devlin's injunction to keep the deal simple. They decided to stop the welt on the D-Day of decasualization. The T&GWU accepted this and neither party felt the need to negotiate a *quid pro quo* for this change in working practice. The men, however, could see the results of the welt's disappearance only too clearly. They would have to work a full eight hour day and then, each gang having turned out 20 per cent more than when welting, there would be little chance of lucrative overtime. Given the unattractiveness of the incentive scheme, there would be little overall compensation in the wage packet. Faced with the prospect of working longer hours for no more money they struck for six weeks – led jointly by the Blue Union and the newly created T&GWU shop stewards who had been selected for the coming of permanent employment.

The strike was ended only when a Court of Inquiry recommended a revision of the wage structure and the immediate payment of a 10p per hour guaranteed bonus. The men returned to work but found that the employers could not enforce the end of the welt and that, since the guaranteed bonus was higher than they could earn by piecework effort, there was no incentive to high performance. Productivity slumped, massive overtime reappeared and the backlog of strike-bound ships remained whilst earnings rose 45 per cent to nearly £30 per week.

Nor were the shop stewards inactive. In order to prove their worth to the men they had to demonstrate their skill in negotiating quayside issues. Pressure intensified for bigger dirty cargo payments which jumped from shillings to pounds. The T&GWU

shop stewards took over negotiations from the union officials. A new pay scheme bought out the dirty cargo awards and reduced the overtime rate to time-and-a-half.

The stewards promptly turned their attention to increasing the impedance awards, and these rose quickly. On both this and the earlier dirty cargo question the stewards had been able to press their case for two main reasons. First they could depend on the solidarity of the men, particularly when they were obtaining quick and easy results. Secondly, by localizing the issues they were able to out-manoeuvre the employers who responded by amalgamating several managements under the aegis of the Port Authority, itself an employer of dockers. Shopfloor pressures had given Liverpool a reputation for unreliability through unpredictable strikes. Ships had been diverted to more tranquil (not necessarily cheaper) ports; charges for both ships and cargoes had been raised repeatedly to try to recoup the cost of earlier financial mismanagement, thus driving more ships away and so requiring yet further increases in rates. A vicious circle was created which culminated in the financial collapse of the Port Authority in late 1970.

Containerization was spreading quickly and all major ports were providing these labour-saving facilities. Dockers, faced with an erosion of their work, tried to extend their working rights into inland container depots.

London's Tilbury container terminal lay idle for months whilst the arguments raged. No such problem occurred at Liverpool where the new container docks opened without fuss in 1972 and the dockers later agreed a new wages system ranging from between £26 per week for day work and £36 for night work with an intermediate evening shift at £29, all with bonus additions – thus giving the port 22 hours per day cover.

Despite the shorter hours embodied in these agreements, the threat of redundancy continued to grow as containerization bit into the traditional manning scales. Employers in London began to return their unwanted dockers to the Dock Labour Board which halved their earnings. Successive increases in severance pay failed to solve the problem and a Committee was set up to take a speedy look at dock job opportunities. The problem came to a head with the pressure over inland container work which led to the jailing of the 'Pentonville Five'. A national dock strike began immediately as 26,000 dockers walked off the job in protest.

The committee proposed that any elderly or unfit dockers who wished to leave the industry should receive up to £4,000 from a government severance scheme – even in ports where there was no shortage of dockers. It had little to say about new job opportunities, but proposed to disperse unallocated dockers to all existing employers. The report was accepted.

The number of unfit dockers shot up. Two thousand men applied to leave in Liverpool, which had no labour surplus. The scheme cost nearer £30 million than the £7½ million which had been forecast. A shortage of dockers developed.

By early 1973 the Liverpool employers were demanding more productivity and the union was demanding more recruitment – which the National Dock Labour Board declined.

Many things had changed. The country's dock labour force had dropped in a few years from 65,000 to less than 40,000. Most employers had departed. Port authorities were taking on more and more the complete running of their ports. The over-investment in container facilities had largely been absorbed by short-falls in predicted productivity. The shop steward movement had gathered all workforce bargaining power down at the grass roots. Wage structures had been simplified. But the men's solidarity, militancy and short-time horizon left Britain's ports as a vulnerable pressure point in the economy. It is not just a British phenomenon. In many cultures dock work is an incident-prone industry. In few industries have historical experiences proved so enduring.

Attitudes and Behaviour of Car Assembly Workers
John H. Goldthorpe

Reprinted with permission from 'Attitudes and Behaviour of Car Assembly Workers: A Deviant Case and a Theoretical Critique', *British Journal of Sociology*, Vol. XVII, No. 3, September 1966, pp. 227–40

In the literature of industrial sociology since the Second World War studies of workers in car assembly plants have almost certainly outnumbered those of any comparable industrial or occupational group. The essentials of the characterization are by now familiar. The car assembly line is 'the classic symbol of the subjection of man to the machine in our industrial age'; the assembler 'approaches the classic model of the self-estranged worker'; he is 'the blue-collar prototype of "the mass men in mass society"' and, often, he is 'the prototype of the militant worker as well'.

In this paper, our first aim is to present results obtained from a study of workers, in a British car assembly plant; results which, in certain respects, differ fairly clearly from the pattern which has emerged from previous investigations. The nature and extent of the differences are not such that they would lead us to challenge in any comprehensive way the 'image' of the car assembler which is generally accepted. However, the 'deviant' aspects of our findings do indicate certain *theoretical* weaknesses in the sociology of the assembly-line workers as this has so far progressed: specifically, they suggest that (a) too great a weight has been given to technology as a determinant of attitudes and behaviour in the work situation; and that (b) too little attention has been paid to the prior orientations which workers have towards employment, and which in turn influence their choice of job, the meaning they give to work and *their definition of* the work situation. The second objective of this paper is, thus, to substantiate this argument and to point to the theoretical developments which would appear to be necessary.

The study on which we report was based chiefly on interviews with workers in six assembly departments of the Luton plant of Vauxhall Motors Ltd. Our sample was a random one of men in these departments who were: (i) Grade I assemblers; (ii) between the ages of 21 and 46; (iii) married; and (iv) resident in the town of Luton itself. The number in the original sample was 127; and of these exactly 100 (79 per cent) agreed to be interviewed at work. In connection with the wider purposes of our research project, 86 of these men were then re-interviewed in their homes and together with their wives. The data from this study which we wish to consider here can be advanced under the following three heads: (1) the assembler and his job; (2) the assembler and the shop-floor group; (3) the assembler and the firm.

The Assembler and his Job

In this respect, our findings were closely comparable with those produced by earlier inquiries.

(1) Assemblers appeared to derive little intrinsic satisfaction from their jobs; rather, in performing their work-tasks they tended to experience various forms of deprivation: Primarily monotony (reported by 69 per cent), and to a lesser degree physical tiredness (48 per cent) and having to work at too fast a pace (30 per cent).

(2) These deprivations were directly related to characteristic features of assembly-line jobs: the minute sub-division of tasks, repetitiveness, low skill requirements, predetermination of tools and techniques, and mechanically controlled rhythms and speeds of work. Of the men in our sample 63 per cent said that they would prefer some other shop-floor job to their present one; and of these men, 87 per cent said they would have liked to move off the 'track' altogether, chiefly into jobs such as inspection, maintenance, rectification and testing. Moreover, among the reasons given for favouring such a move, those relating to the content of work were paramount. Jobs off the 'track' were seen as offering more opportunity to exercise skill and responsibility, greater variety and challenge, and more freedom and autonomy.

(3) Consequently, the workers we studied were for the most part attached to their present employment chiefly through the extrinsic economic rewards which it afforded them. Thirty-one per cent stated that the level of pay was the *only* reason why they remained in their present work, and, in all, 74 per cent gave pay either as the sole reason for this or along with others. The reason next most frequently mentioned was that of 'security' (25 per cent), and this, it was clear, was thought of far more in relation to long-run income maximization than to the minimum requirement of having a job of some kind. On the other hand, in contrast to this emphasis on economic considerations, only 6 per cent of the sample said that they stayed with their present employer because they liked the actual work they performed. In other words, then, our assemblers defined their work in an essentially *instrumental* way; work was for them primarily a means to ends external to the work situation. More specifically, one could say that work was seen as a generally unsatisfying and stressful expenditure of time and effort which was necessary in order to achieve a valued standard and style of living in which work itself had no positive part.

These findings are, we repeat, in all respects markedly similar to those of other studies of car assembly workers. To this extent, thus, our results tend to confirm the idea that the responses of men to the work-tasks and roles of the car assembly line are likely to vary little more, from plant to plant, than does the technology itself.

However, to our last point above – concerning the assembler's instrumental view of work – we would wish to give an emphasis which differs rather significantly from that of most previous writers. Generally, the 'devaluation' of work which is implied here has been taken as perhaps the clearest symptom of the car assembler's alienated condition. For Blauner, for instance, this concentration on the purely extrinsic rewards of work is 'the essential meaning of self-estrangement'; and in Chinoy's view, the alienation of the auto worker basically results from the fact that this work has become, in the words of Marx, 'not the satisfaction of a need but only the means to satisfy the needs outside it'. It is not our aim here to dispute this interpretation. But, at the same time, we would wish to stress the following point: that, at least in the case of our sample, the predominantly instrumental orientation to work was not simply or even primarily a *consequence* of these men being car assemblers; rather, one could say that most had become car assemblers *because of* a desire, and an eventual decision, on their part to give priority to high-level economic returns from work at the expense, if necessary, of satisfactions of an intrinsic kind. In other words, their instrumental orientation had led to their present employment, rather than *vice versa*.

These data would suggest, then, that the workers we studied had for the most part been impelled, by their desire for higher incomes, into taking work which was in fact better paid than most other forms of employment available to them largely to compensate for its inherent strains and deprivations. If, therefore, these workers are to be considered as 'alienated', the roots of their alienation must be sought not merely in the technological character of the plants in which they are now employed but, more fundamentally, in those aspects of the wider society which generate their tremendous drive for economic advancement and their disregard for the costs of this through the impoverishment of their working lives.

Furthermore, it also follows that in seeking to explain the industrial attitudes and behaviour of these workers generally, one must always be prepared to treat their essentially instrumental orientation towards their employment as an *independent* variable relative to the work situation, rather than regarding this simply as a product of this situation.

The Assembler and the Shop-Floor Group

In most previous studies of car assembly workers, attention has been given to the way in which assembly-line technology inhibits the formation of cohesive work groups. Although the majority of men work in fairly close proximity to others, the fact that they tend to be strung out along the length of the 'track' means that the development of specifically *group* relations is usually impeded; that is to say, workers are prevented from sharing in *common* networks of social relationships, set off from others by more or less distinct boundaries.

Findings of this kind have, without exception, been interpreted as evidence of yet further deprivation in the working life of the car assembler.

The results of our study which relate to the shop-floor situation at Vauxhall go contrary to the findings, and perhaps still more to the interpretation, of previous studies of car assemblers in two main respects.

It was apparent from observation in the assembly departments that the nature of technical organization did in fact largely rule out the possibility of the formation of cohesive work groups. Most workers were close enough to others to be able to exchange words fairly easily: 59 per cent of the men we interviewed said that they talked to their workmates 'a good deal', and 29 per cent 'now and then', as against 11 per cent saying 'hardly at all'. But there was little to indicate that shop-floor relations amounted to more than a generally superficial camaraderie. Thus far, our findings conformed entirely to the established pattern.

However, not only did we find no evidence of a high degree of group formation within the assembly department, but we were equally unable to find evidence that the majority of men in our sample were actually *concerned* with 'group-belongingness' in work, or felt deprived because this was not to be had. Rather, our data pointed to the opposite conclusion. For example, we asked our respondents: 'How would you feel if you were moved to another job in the factory more or less like the one you do now but away from the men who work near you? Would you feel very upset, fairly upset, not much bothered, not bothered at all?' The result was that only 4 per cent answered 'very upset' and 25 per cent 'fairly upset'. The remainder were almost equally divided between 'not much bothered' (34 per cent) and 'not bothered at all' (36 per cent). And those men who talked to their mates 'a good deal' were as likely to fall into the latter two categories as were the others. Moreover the further comments which respondents typically made on this question confirmed the obvious implication of these data: that maintaining stable relationships with workmates was not generally regarded as a very important aspect of the work situation.

Moreover, this interpretation is corroborated by further data we have on the extent to which, among the workers we studied, work relations formed the basis of friendships outside the plant. Like an earlier investigator of the Vauxhall labour force, we found that for most men, work and non-work were largely separate areas of their social life. When asked: 'How many of the men who work near to you would you call close friends?' 63 per cent of the sample did in fact claim at least one such friend. But the answers to further questions revealed that only in a small minority of cases (18 per cent of the total sample) were these workmate friends actually seen outside the factory in other than a more or less casual way; and that in fact 40 per cent of those claiming 'close friends' among their mates saw these men outside the factory either not at all or only by pure chance. These findings were subsequently confirmed by data from our 'home' interviews which showed that workmates made up only a relatively small proportion of the persons with whom our respondents spent most of their leisure time and whom they entertained in their homes.

Most studies so far made have in fact revealed that assemblers express a relatively high degree of dissatisfaction with their firms and tend to show hostility towards their policies and management. Furthermore, it is clear from statistical evidence that in Great Britain and the United States, at least, the car industry is among the most strike-prone of all and suffers in particular from a high rate of 'unofficial' disputes.

In choosing Vauxhall as the basis of our study, we virtually ensured that, so far as workers' relations with their firm were concerned, our findings would in some degree diverge from those that have come to be regarded as characteristic of car assembly plants. For, as is well known, Vauxhall is conspicuous among major car manufacturing firms in Great Britain for its success in maintaining an almost strike-free record. However, our findings would in fact indicate that Vauxhall's atypicality goes some way beyond this low incidence of overt conflict, and in ways which again give rise to significant theoretical issues.

Our data point, in fact, to the possibility that, given a prior orientation to work of a largely instrumental nature, car assemblers may well see their relationship with their firm in a generally positive way; that is, as centring on a bargain that provides, better than most others available to them, the high-level economic returns which, for the present at least, they wish to derive from their work. Thus, in spite of the deprivations which their jobs on the line may entail, these men will be disposed to maintain their relationship with their firm, and to define this more as one of reciprocity and interdependence rather than, say, as one of coercion and exploitation. And furthermore, if among these workers' wants and expectations from their employment such 'social' satisfactions as 'belongingness' and 'togetherness' do not have high priority, then the impersonality and anonymity of the car assembly plant are no longer likely to give rise to discontent and resentment of a generalized kind. In conclusion, then, the several specific criticisms which we have levelled at the theoretical basis of earlier studies of car assemblers may be summed up in a single more general argument. Most previous writers, we would suggest, have tended to oversimplify the problem of workers' response to the stresses and constraints of assembly-line technology (and have tended to assume greater uniformity in this respect than proves to be the case) because they have left out of account an important *variable*; that is, the orientations which men *bring* to their employment and which *mediate between* the objective features of the work situation and workers' actual experience of, and reaction to, this situation.

The approach which we have found necessary, in order to make intelligible the attitudes and behaviour of our Vauxhall assemblers, entails a 'social action' perspective. The starting point is not with assembly-line technology, but rather with the ordering of wants and expectations relative to work, and with the meaning thus given to work, which result in men taking up and retaining assembly-line jobs. And the key explanatory notion to which we have then referred is not that of the enterprise as a production system, but that of the definition of work and of the work situation, dominant among the assemblers we studied; that is, as we have shown, a definition of work as an essentially instrumental activity – as a means to ends external to the work situation, which is not itself regarded as a milieu in which any worthwhile satisfactions of an immediate kind are likely to be experienced. In this approach, therefore, technology and formal organization are treated not as the direct determinants of shop-floor attitudes and behaviour but rather as constituting a set of limiting factors, the psychological and social implications of which will vary with the significance which workers attach to them. In brief, we reject the idea that workers respond or react in any automatic way to features of their work situation, object-ively considered; and we emphasize the extent to which the 'realities' of work are in fact created through workers' own subjective interpretations.

On the Shopfloor
T. Lupton

Reprinted with permission from T. Lupton, *On the Shop Floor*, Oxford, Pergamon Press, 1963, pp. 187–8, 195–9

The expression 'restriction of output' is commonly used to describe the behaviour of workers who set standards of output below those which management considers that it can reasonably expect from them. The question 'why do workers restrict out-put?' has produced various answers. The most widely accepted of these is that which stresses the incompatibility of the rationally contrived controls over workers' behaviour which are imposed by management, and the controls which are to be found in the spontaneous social relationships which workers enter into at work. According to this interpretation, management formulates an expected level of output which is based upon considerations of technical efficiency. The behaviour of workers is then directed towards the achievement of this level of output. The social groupings in the workshops, which are based upon sentiments of friendship and sociability, and which adhere to values which are traditionalistic rather than rational, develop their own norms of what constitutes a 'proper' level of output and impose their own controls upon behaviour. The workshop norm may be well below what management expects. This interpretation of 'restriction of output' is attractive because it does not imply laziness, malice, or deliberate planning by workers to defeat the purposes of management. Its widespread acceptance is due largely to the influence of the work of Elton Mayo and his followers. It suggests that workers do not restrict output deliberately so as to safeguard themselves from exploitation, but to protect what they believe to be their best interests.

There are at least three questionable assumptions implicit in this interpretation of 'restriction of output' which I have thus summarized. The first of these is that there exist methods, which allow of accurate prediction for assessing the expected performance of productive units. Secondly it is assumed that the main impediment to the fulfilment of management expectations lies in informal relationships in the workshops. It is not admitted that expectations may not be fulfilled because of lack of ability by management to translate plans into actual output. Thirdly, the possibility is ruled out that there may exist real conflicts of interest and viewpoint between managers and workers. If such conflicts could be shown to exist, then it would be entirely reasonable to explain fears of rate-cutting and the like in terms of a rational and realistic appraisal of their interests by the workers.

There is no doubt that the market for electrical transformers is much more stable, and that there are no severe seasonal depressions. It is also clear that competition between the firms in the industry is not intense: indeed there is a good deal of cartelization, and there are many collusive marketing arrangements. The firms are very much larger and certainly the amount of capital required to enter the industry would not encourage any workers to expect to become an owner.

Thus there is, in the electrical components industry, more stability and less downward pressure on wage rates. One does not hear from managers at Jay's the kind of remark we heard from a sales manager in the rubber-proofed garment industry: 'A halfpenny on the price might mean the difference between getting an order and losing it.' Neither does one hear in the garment industry the kind of remark heard from workers at Jay's: 'When you are sitting around waiting for work the firm just passes the cost on to the customer, and the consumer pays through the nose for the special jobs we do, so why should the firm worry.'

Trade unionism is highly developed in heavy electrical

engineering and its organization is highly effective at workshop level. Thus at the same time as the structure and the economics of the industry create the 'elbow room' for manipulation, the existence of Trade Union power in the workshops provides workers with one of the means to control their situation. Since management is not pressed by competition continually to seek to 'trim' piecework prices they can accept 'fiddling' as a reasonable way of adjusting their relationships with the workers and their unions. And this is further made possible because labour cost is a much lower proportion of the total cost of the product than it is in the garment industry, 8–10 per cent as against 13–15 per cent. Thus, if market conditions are adverse, savings can more easily be effected elsewhere. It would seem that the hypothesis suggested by me in an article based upon the Wye study emphasizing the importance of 'external' factors is consistent with the material from Jay's.

The difference in behaviour which I observed between the two workshops would seem to be explained if it can be shown that both management and workers made a realistic appraisal of their situation, and then acted according to their interests as they saw them. The material suggests that they did this. This is not to say that everyone always behaved rationally in the light of his or her interests. Much of the behaviour we observed can be interpreted in terms of 'Mayoism'. But a great deal of the field material ceases to make sense unless one admits of a realistic appraisal of interests, and of discrepancy – even conflict – between the goals of workers and managers in many situations.

I do not claim of course, that all the workers in the workshops I studied were aware in detail of all the factors which affected their interests. Obviously they were not, although I was often struck by the extent and accuracy of their knowledge. Sometimes their behaviour appeared to be directed against their own best interests. But lack of knowledge does not necessarily imply lack of realism. One acts on the knowledge one has. This applies to management too. For all the techniques of modern management it is not possible to predict production targets exactly, or so I found. Nor are the controls which management exercises perfect in their application. And this is because management also acts on incomplete knowledge. Although partly one of communications, the problem is greater than that. Knowledge which is in the nature of things incomplete, is communicated, and upon this knowledge people must act. It is in this area of incomplete knowledge and understanding that the social adjustments which I have described are made. I conclude that in Jay's, where there was security, and 'elbow room' to make adjustments, the 'fiddle' was a quite stable adjustment of the discrepant goals and interests of management and workers. In Wye, 'looking after No. 1' seemed a logical sensible policy in the circumstances.

I have checked my findings with previous work in the field, and I have enquired about the state of affairs in other parts of the electrical components industry. In Roy's work, which describes a 'fiddle' closely resembling that at Jay's, there is not much reference to what we have called 'external' factors. His study was carried out in the steel industry, and it is reasonable to suppose that the complex of external factors closely resembles that which I found at Jay's. Enquiries made at a large electrical firm in the same area as Jay's making a similar product, and with a similar wages structure, revealed that an almost exactly similar 'fiddle' operates. A manager there told us that this firm had lately taken on some foreign labour. The story is now being told in the firm that the first English phrase that the newcomers learned was 'one hundred per cent'.

My analysis has taken me some way towards a definition of the conditions under which restrictive and non-restrictive behaviour may be found. It is now possible to list the factors I have been discussing under the headings 'external' and 'internal' with the object of discerning whether any particular combination, or clustering of factors seems to be associated with certain kinds of worker behaviour in relation to controls over output and earnings.

When one compares the situation at Wye and at Jay's, it is seen that with regard to all the factors listed there are significant differences. And these differences are associated in each case with differences in the pattern of shopfloor behaviour. Thus we may define the situation in each workshop in terms of a 'cluster' of the characteristics listed in Table 1, and state the hypothesis that when the cluster of characteristics in column A is found one will find behaviour in the workshops which resembles the behaviour which I found in the workshop at Wye, and that when the Jay's type of cluster is found, one would expect to find Jay's type behaviour. I would also suggest that these two kinds of cluster are those which would be most commonly found. For example, it is in industries with small firms and intense competition that one would probably find lack of mechanization, high labour cost.

Table 1. 'External' and 'Internal' Factors

	A Situation at Wye	B Situation at Jay's
External		
Market:		
(a) Stability	Unstable	Stable
(b) Size	Small Differentiated	Large, Undifferentiated
Competition	Intense, lack of collusive arrangements	Weak, Collusion and pricing arrangements
Scale of Industry	Small with small firms predominating	Large, small numbers of large firms
Location of Industry	Concentrated in one area	Widely dispersed
Trade Unions	Local, weak in workshops, poorly developed Shop Steward system	Nationally organized Powerful. Strong in workshops. Well developed Shop Steward system
Cost Ratio	High labour cost	Relatively low labour cost
Product	Consumer goods	Capital goods
Internal		
Method of Wage Payment	Straight piecework Simple	Bonus system Complicated
Productive system	Minute breakdown of operations. Batch Production. Individual as unit in work flow Short time span	No minute breakdown Batch Production Section as unit in work flow. Long time span
Sex of Workers	Women predominate	Men predominate
Workshop Social Structure	Sociable grouping not co-extensive with productive groupings	Sociable groupings are also productive groupings. Collective attitude to output and earnings. 'Comfortable.'
Management-Worker	Economic interests tend to converge. Personal relationship, but values divergent. Worker control has no part in adjustment.	Stable. Worker control plays part in adjustment. Economic interests diverge but large area of value convergence.

women workers and weak Trade Union workshop organization. In an industry with large firms and little competition one would probably find mechanization, low labour cost, men workers and strong Trade Union workshop organization. But these are obviously not the only possible clusters. For example, one might find an industry which is composed of a large number of small firms which are not locally concentrated but widely scattered, but with Trade Unions that are strong at workshop level in such an industry. Or one may find that Trade Unions are strong in the industry in one area and weak in another. Or one might find a competititive industry of small firms which is highly mechanized. It is also true that some items in any 'cluster' may be very influential in relation to other items in the cluster and to shop-floor behaviour. I have myself suggested already in the Wye and Jay's cases, that some items seem to have more weight than others.

On the whole I consider that the Wye and Jay type of cluster will be commonly found, and one could consider them as lying at either end of a continuum, with all sorts of combinations making up the clusters in between, but with similar clusters themselves clustering at each end of the continuum. Those clusters at either end are in a sense definitions on the one hand of situations where there is much collective worker control over output and earnings, and on the other of those where there is little control of this kind.

The Blackcoated Worker

D. Lockwood

Reprinted with permission from D. Lockwood, *The Black-Coated Worker*, London, Allen & Unwin, 1958, pp. 89–95

In all these ways – physical distribution, organization of work-groups, occupational differentiation and status difference formally and informally established within the hierarchy of the office – the work situation of clerical labour forms a social context in which office workers tend to be separated from each other on the one hand and closely identified, as individuals, with the managerial and supervisory cadres of industry on the other. Some of these factors, of course, are also to be found in the work situation of factory labour, but it may safely be asserted that they operate more powerfully in the environment of the clerk than in that of the bench-hand.

The converse of the working cooperation of clerks and management is the social isolation of the office worker from the manual worker. The completeness of the separation of these two groups of workers is perhaps the most outstanding feature of industrial organization. Because of the rigid division between the 'office' and the 'works' it is no exaggeration to say that 'management', from the point of view of the manual worker, ends with the lowest grade of routine clerk. The office worker is associated with managerial authority, although he does not usually stand in an authoritarian relationship to the manual worker, the order governing the labour force being transmitted from management through the foreman rather than through the clerical staff. Naturally there are degrees of isolation and contact between clerks and manual workers. Groups such as warehouse, railway, docking and colliery clerks are obviously more likely to be brought into contact with manual workers than are banking, insurance and civil service clerks. Finally, the administrative separation of the office worker from the operative, which is based primarily on the conception of the secret and confidential nature of office work, is completed by the separation of the works canteen from the staff dining-room.

Labour Market Bureaucracy

Above and beyond these features of office organization, however, there is another dimension of the work situation of the office worker which may be interpreted as a further influence making for his social isolation. This has to do with the nature of clerical work itself, and the degree to which it is peculiar to the individual enterprise.

There is a sense in which the 'market situation' of clerical labour is not really a market situation at all; at least for many clerks. The prime social characteristic of a labour market is its impersonal nature. Insofar as a labour market exists, there is a tendency for skills and remuneration to be standardized. In this way, we can speak of a 'class' of operatives, such as fitters or turners. Labour power is thereby made homogeneous and comparable, and is divorced from the setting of a particular firm.

A fitter means much the same thing in firm A as in firm B; he is a worker with recognizable skills and standard remuneration. Manual workers have thus been identified with one another through the emergence of a market for their labour and the concomitant growth of such common standards of skill and payment.

Well into the present century, and over wide areas of commercial employment, the typical clerk was not really in the market at all in this sense. His initial engagement was secured through the personal contact of relative, schoolmaster or friend. It contained the implication that he would stay with his employer and perhaps become a partner himself, or at least a chief clerk, in due course. Moreover, the highly individual nature of business methods introduced him to a routine peculiar to the firm in which he started his career. He definitely acquired skills, but it was difficult to say exactly what they were, or to compare them with those of other clerks. His maturing experience would be peculiar to his own firm, often highly valuable to his particular employer, but relatively worthless outside. Promotion was given and responsibility added, not by virtue of his progressive certification, but in accordance with his employer's estimation of his merit and worth – in other words, by the value of a particular clerk to a particular employer in a particular business routine. Needless to add, all this could, and often did, rebound to the clerk's disadvantage.

How far a real market for clerical labour is emerging at the present time is difficult to estimate. But there can be little doubt that hitherto the lack of universally acknowledged standards of grading office work has weakened common identification and solidarity among commercial and industrial clerks. This deficiency has been frequently noted by the Union concerned with their organization.

Insofar as common standards are not instituted in office work, then the clerical work force is not only physically scattered, but, also socially separated into isolated units, between which there is little comparability in terms of work, skill and remuneration.

In fields other than industry and commerce, notably in the civil service, in railways, banking and to a lesser extent in local government, large-scale organizations have emerged in which many thousands of clerks are employed. In such administrative units, the rationalization of the work situation has been achieved other than by the creation of a labour market for clerical work. Through the introduction of uniform scales of remuneration, through the rigid classification of jobs, through the establishment of explicit criteria of merit, through the articulation of the individual career with prescribed examinations and certificates, through the facilitation of mobility within the organization – in short, through bureaucratization – the equivalent of a market situation has been brought about. The market and the bureaucracy are alternative modes by which the labour relationship may be rationalized. But in both cases, the ensuing relationship has the same basic character; the individual worker is related to his fellows through uniform and impersonal standards.

Such a work situation possesses features which differ substantially from those to be found in less rationalized structures of administration. In a bureaucracy positions are defined as clearly as possible, and the amount of skill, responsibility, income, status and authority going with them is made transparent. Competition for advancement between clerks is regulated in an orderly fashion through seniority and merit systems which are explicit and do not admit of exceptions to the rules. Such a situation may be contrasted with that in which the job is tailored to fit the man, in which promotion is left to the discretion of the supervisor, in which office titles are proliferated indiscriminately to satisfy prestige cravings. Both types of system encourage individualism; but the one through impersonal, the other through personal, criteria.

These differences, to be sure, are relative. Some large industrial and commercial undertakings may be highly bureaucratic in their staff organization; on the other hand even the most formally established bureaucracy never works according to blueprint. Between the small-scale paternalistic administration of a private firm and the large-scale 'civil service' bureaucracy of a public organization come admixtures of both types. A quasi-bureaucratic form is to be found in banking for instance. The various large banking concerns form a system in which there is a high degree of comparability of administration as between one bank and another, but not complete identity. Strong loyalties on the part of the staffs of the rival houses are encouraged deliberately, and clerks are not allowed to move from one bank to another in the wider system. Within the banks, such features as incomplete grading of jobs and secret reports on office staffs cause their internal administration to fall short of the pure bureaucratic form. The practical result is to create a working environment in which the common identification of bank clerks, both between banks and inside banks, is less than it would be were their mobility unhindered and their position unambiguously defined.

The degree to which administrative relations take on a purely bureaucratic form, therefore, is a crucial factor in the work situation of the blackcoated worker. In principle there is no difference between the impersonal and standardized relationships of the bureaucracy and those of the factory. But in most areas of private industry the small size of the office work force relative to the total number of employees, and the very diversity of competitively related firms, set narrow limits on the establishment of highly bureaucratic forms of administration. It is in the public or quasi-public organization whose labour force is predominantly clerical that bureaucratic administration flourishes, and is indeed imperative.

Mechanization

Mechanization is a process affecting clerical work that is distinct from rationalization, although the two often go together. Thus machinery was first introduced to meet the rapidly growing demands that were being made on office staffs, and then extended with the aim of reducing the cost of clerical work. It is, however, fallacious to argue, as is so often done, that the mere introduction of 'machinery' into offices reduces the status of the clerk to that of a factory operative. The meaning of mechanization, the different types of office machinery, the relation between the organization of machinery and the administrative division of labour, and the actual extent of office mechanization – all have to be examined before we can determine the degree to which the work status of clerical employment has been affected by the introduction of office machinery.

One of the main changes in the division of labour has been the appearance of the specialized, semi-skilled office employee who is responsible for the 'processing' of data. The actual division of tasks very often preceded mechanization, but machinery has speeded up the trend by which a small group of executives, who make decisions about the selection and analysis of data, are separated from a mass of subordinates whose functions less and less justify their classification as brain workers. 'The nature of the work tends to isolate the machine worker, and affords little opportunity for her to gain a general knowledge of the undertaking in which she is employed, which might lead to promotion into other grades of work. Continuous employment over a period of years on one process tends to create a rigidity of outlook which militates against the assuming of responsibility. This is true of all monotonous employment but the additional danger as far as machine workers are concerned is the fact that their work isolates them and creates of them a class apart.' 'Office workers, therefore, are now divided into classes. The managerial staff is being more and more sharply distinguished from the subordinates, and the standardization of duties and the fixing of salaries within narrow limits have placed the latter category in a position similar to that of factory workers. Before mechanization, on the contrary, duties were not so exactly defined, and the level of earnings was not subject to any uniform scale; consequently office workers, whatever their duties, did not feel a sharp distinction from one another.' To the extent that mechanization of this kind has taken place in large undertakings, the sense of separation from management through the impersonal relations of the work situation, which as we have seen is one of the main factors in the growth of working-class consciousness, is reproduced in the work situation of the office worker. 'Another psychological consequence of new organization methods in offices is that the division of labour and specialization have meant the loss of the power to satisfy what *de Man* has called the instinctive desire for importance. In the old-fashioned office, even the office boy felt that he was somebody, simply by belonging to the undertaking; but the invoice clerk who now works a bookkeeping machine all day is nothing but an impersonal unit. In workshop and yard there has always been a considerable number of nameless hands; but these are undoubtedly a new feature of office work.' Further, 'the development of methods of selection has undoubtedly contributed towards the present feeling of inferiority among subordinate staff. One of the reasons why the office boy of the old days thought himself an important person was the fact that no impassable barrier separated the lower from the higher grades, and many cases of a rise from one to the other did occur. But in selecting staff by modern methods for well-defined mechanical duties, the employer runs the risk of eliminating those who have not the physical qualifications for the use of certain machines, but have on the other hand the gifts of intelligence and character which would permit them to reach the higher rungs of the ladder. The inverse is equally true: owing to such methods, the employee employed as a machine operator receives a strong impression that he is meant exclusively for this unimportant function and must remain his whole life in an inferior post.'

Such a division of labour affects also the age and sex composition of office staffs. 'Visits to big mechanized undertakings will suffice to show that young persons of either sex between sixteen and twenty-five are very commonly used to work and supervise machines.' In the civil service, the introduction of machinery was accompanied by a large increase in the proportion of women in the machine-operating grade. The same was true of banking and railway office staffs during the inter-war years. Since the war, this development has speeded up, so that the machine-operating grades are almost exclusively filled by young girls.

When the mechanization and rationalization of office work has proceeded to the extent that relatively large groups of semi-skilled employees are concentrated together, separated from managerial and supervisory staffs, performing continuous, routinized and disciplined work, often rewarded in accordance with physical output, with little chance of promotion – then clerical work becomes, in terms of social and physical environment, extremely like that of the factory operative. The sense of isolation, impersonality, the machine-dominated tempo of work, the destruction of the unitary nature of the product, are all reproduced in varying degrees.

Conclusion

Although the above account by no means exhausts the topic, it may safely be asserted that the rationalizing tendencies of modern office administration have by no means completely swept away the personal and particular relationships of the counting-house work environment. The following appear to be the main reasons why this is so.

(1) In most fields of blackcoated work the average size of the unit of administration, and the resulting physical concentration of clerical workers, is still small relative to the unit of production.

(2) The division of labour inside the office normally tends to

separate office workers from each other by department, job grade and status, and to distribute them in small working groups where they are in personal and cooperative contact with management.

(3) There is a relative lack of universally accepted criteria for the standardization of clerical skills and qualifications. In other words, the rationalizing influence of a labour market for clerical work has been but weakly developed, though in the case of certain large-scale organizations an alternative rationalization of the work situation has been produced, in varying degrees, by the growth of bureaucratic administration.

(4) The intensive mechanization of clerical tasks, though comparable in its most advanced form to factory mechanization, has not played a particularly important role in the rationalization of the work situation because its application has so far been narrowly limited by the size of the administrative unit and the nature of clerical work itself.

Managers and Computers
E. Mumford and T. Ward

Reprinted with permission from 'How the Computer Changes Management', *New Society*, 23 September, 1965

At present the effects of computer installations are discussed almost wholly in terms of their impact on lower grade staff. We are told of vast armies of clerical workers about to be thrown out of employment while the work they do now is carried out by some fast, quasi-intelligent machine.

Whether this will happen we simply do not know. It depends on many factors such as the speed of introduction and the extent of office automation, together with the rate of expansion of the economy as a whole. In 1965 there were less than 1,000 computer installations in this country and few have caused any significant release of labour. But only the most progressive and expanding companies are as yet using computers and these are the most easily able to absorb labour displaced from computerized departments.

In fact, it seems likely that computers will have a more immediate effect on one unexpected area of organization, that of management structure and power.

Managerial Power

All these organizational changes must affect the firms' power structure. Some managers will gain power, others will lose it. Inevitably, while the organization is in a fluid state there will be struggles for power as different groups strive to strengthen or retain their position.

At the top, it is now possible for a small elite of senior managers, supplied with the necessary information by the computer, to be responsible for most major decision making. This presents its own problems; senior management now has an increased work load, a very heavy responsibility and a new communications language to master. (Data is presented by the computer in mathematical terms and not in written reports.)

In addition, senior management may be forced to take decisions in an area where it, as yet, has little experience or expertise. For example, the initial decisions on whether to install a computer, on which model to get, and on the use of the equipment must come from the very top of the management hierarchy. Senior management is here at the mercy of the new breeds of expert, the systems analysts, programmers and computer technologists generally.

Of course, some managers will gain from an extension of computer technology, and find that by being freed from many routine procedures they are able to pay more attention to the really fundamental parts of their jobs. The American shoe company finds that 'the trend is to take away statistical and record-keeping work from people in middle management jobs, and to leave them with what is really the essence of their management task. They used to spend a lot of time in record keeping and supervision of large clerical staffs, but that part of the job has disappeared.'

However, many managers will see themselves as losing both function and status from these developments, particularly when their subordinates are greatly reduced in number. Inevitably they will strive to preserve the status quo. But their fight to retain power will be hindered by their lack of understanding of the new business techniques and by the unwillingness of the new computer specialists to take much account of their opinions.

The future role of many managers is likely to be directed much more at looking after the personal needs of their staff and sorting out human relations problems than on business procedure as such.

Perhaps the most interesting product of the use of computers is the group associated with their operation – the systems analysts, programmers and so on. These new groups often have great power – a withdrawal of their labour, for example, would bring a highly computerized firm to a halt – yet little responsibility. They are there to provide information without which the business cannot operate, but have no responsibility for the economic goals of the organization, and are remote from such things as profit and loss accounts. Their casual attitude to spending vast sums on equipment would frighten managers brought up in the old school.

As a group they show interesting and unusual characteristics. They are technical specialists identified with computer technology rather than with the aims of the business. This means that their reference group will be systems analysts and programmers in other firms, not their firm's management group. They are often physically separated from the day-to-day operation of the business. Computers are frequently in separate buildings situated some distance from the firm itself. Compared with the rest of the clerical staff, their surroundings may be luxurious. Because they are associated with a machine which needs space, air conditioning and temperature control, they are often provided with a better physical environment than other officer workers. To their colleagues outside the computer centre they represent a new privileged elite.

Rolling Stones

For this technical group William Whyte's concept of 'organization man' has little or no meaning. They are likely to be transients, staying with a firm during the interesting phase of introducing a new system, then moving on when the system is in operation and the work routine. Many business firms using computers can only give their computer personnel a job, not a career. To progress they must move on for there is little chance of promotion within the walls of the computer centre and – as educated today – they may not be suitable material for management. An American computer manufacturer has said that 'there is nearly always a problem of communications between the manager of the computer installation and his own senior management'.

At present computer specialists are narrow in approach and, compared with other technical groups, relatively uneducated. Many systems analysts and programmers acquire their skills on the job with little or no formal training. Whereas the engineering apprentice will spend five years learning his trade, the systems analyst or programmer – who has far more power and influence – is not yet required to produce any certificates and diplomas to show his competence, yet will be engaged on work which can dramatically change the structure of the enterprise.

Management Succession

This organizational rearrangement and new distribution of power brings with it a number of difficult internal problems. One of these is management succession.

The weakening of the middle management function raises serious problems for the recruitment of top management. Traditionally experience gained in the various levels of management is regarded in business as a necessary preliminary to a higher management responsibility. The concentration of power at the top and in the new computer centre groups will reduce the possibility of internal training for top management in a situation where it is increasingly difficult to recruit from outside.

It might be argued that, in the future, top management should be recruited from computer technologists as it is these men who have the knowledge of modern business operation. But the direction of a firm requires breadth of vision, insight, sociological understanding and an ability to devise imaginative goals and policies. Computer specialists are not, at present, usually these kind of people.

Other problems stem from the importance one or two key personnel now assume in the firm – if the computer manager or senior programmer leaves, the business may be in trouble – and from the lack of flexibility of a computer system – once in operation it is extremely expensive to alter. If the computer breaks down the work of the firm may be seriously disrupted as there is no possibility of carrying on manually for a temporary period. A computer application implies an extremely tight system; in any traditional business operation there is normally some 'slack' in the organization of work. If there are delays these can be made up by working longer or more quickly. Once a computer is introduced office workers have to meet 'deadlines', work must go on to the computer at a certain time and there is no allowance for crises or holdups.

There are also major problems of communication and coordination, some of which have already been referred to. The development of integrated data processing implies the growth of other specialist groups besides computer staff. There will also be O. & M. specialists, operational research groups and statistical forecasters. All of these technologists bring with them new skills and techniques, and use the language of mathematics. If they are to be fully integrated into the organization, it is important to have some mechanism for coordinating their activities. The creation of centralized management service departments is one solution to this problem. The skills and knowledge of these new specialists can then be directed in a controlled way to the fulfilment of the organization's goals.

Finally these organizational changes bring with them broad ethical problems. Is industry taking us to a future of productive and satisfying work for the majority or to prosperity and idleness? A number of American writers have suggested that industry is moving away from narrow economic self-interest and becoming much more aware of its group and community responsibilities.

Whyte has said that the old protestant ethic of individual striving for success is being replaced by a new 'social ethic' which pays attention to the group rather than the individual.

Built-in Ethic

Now the question is whether the new technology is diverting us from these ethical goals, without our realizing it. It seems that computer technology has its own built-in ethic, that of striving for a totally rational and efficient business system. The new power groups who control electronic data processing techniques are motivated by technical perfection and have no responsibility for, or understanding of, wider human needs. Senior management, which has a responsibility both for commercial success and for looking after employee interests, does not yet seem aware that the new techniques, in accomplishing the former, may sacrifice the latter.

Management and society must together solve the problems we have been discussing. At the moment neither group seems aware how imminent they are.

Social Relations in the Mining Industry
N. Dennis, F. Henriques, C. Slaughter

Reprinted with permission from N. Dennis, F. Henriques and C. Slaughter, *Coal Is Our Life*, London, Eyre & Spottiswoode, 1956, pp. 38, 44–5, 73–4, 76–7, 79–80

Although older miners insist on the increasingly easier nature of the collier's work today, it is invariably said by miners that pitwork can never be other than an unpleasant, dirty, dangerous, and difficult job. A description of the different types of work in the mines will be useful in a discussion of attitudes to work, and the relation between work and life; if broad differences emerge between the work today and past conditions, then we will expect these to be reflected in the lives and attitudes of the different generations of workers.

Mineworking in Ashton itself is fairly typical of British mining, the degree of mechanization not being exceptional in any way. Approximately 53 per cent of all underground mineworkers in Britain are 'contract-workers', i.e. they are engaged on piece-work. This percentage includes all those working at the coal-face, and men engaged on development work, which is usually either the making of roads, i.e. tunnels in the rock, or the opening out of new coal-faces. Those at the coal-face consist of 'colliers' (the term varies for different parts of the country – hewers, fillers, etc.) 'machine-men', 'drawers-off', 'rippers', 'pan-turners' (or panners), and a few others.

A very common phenomenon is for men to stick together through many different contracts for years on end, sometimes for a score of years and even a working lifetime. A whole team often moves from a worked-out face to a new one, and with a few changes may last as a team for a dozen years. There tends to be a core around which the team is built, some of the additions staying on, others drifting to a new team, being rejected, or finding employment at another colliery. The strongest and most permanent alliances are between pairs of men, though sometimes three men will stick together for long periods. These groupings affect the day-to-day work. Friends will work next to each other, help each other out in filling and timbering, in certain conditions even work their stints jointly. There are occasions when the team for a new coal-face is made up of, say, two groups of three who are unacquainted one with the other, with a few single additions to make up the team; whether or not a harmonious combination is built out of such elements depends on the extent to which the smaller groups are closed and on the personalities of the individuals concerned as much as on their skill. As a rule a good workman is accepted by the rest of the team, but if he does not also fit in socially it is doubtful if he will stay long in the team; he must be a good miner, and his workmates must feel they can trust him. In teams of colliers containing two or three different nuclei of close friends there exists either good-natured rivalry and chaffing ('kidding') between the groups or just tolerance so long as efficiency is maintained. Colliers cannot afford to allow such differences to develop into antagonisms.

The miner does a job in conditions which are still worse than those in any other British industry, though he can see that improvements are rapidly being made. Higher wages were the first step, and the miner sees this as a sign of his emergence from the lowest ranks of society. In addition, he is proud, as he ever was, that he does a difficult, arduous, and dangerous job which deserves greater appreciation than it ever gets. Miners constantly say that no non-miner can appreciate the nature of pitwork and few would challenge them. When they hear complaints of miners' high wages, they confidently offer an exchange of jobs, and this is enough for most public-house politicians. In the pit itself, among his workmates, the miner is proud of doing his job as a good man should, and to a great extent a man becomes identified with his particular job. Recognition that one job belongs to one man is recognition of that man's fitness and his control of that job. Men in Ashton will half-jokingly say when they have spent a shift deputizing for another man, 'I've been Joe Hill (or whoever it is) today.' On the morning after the retirement of a 65-year-old deputy, W. H., two men greeted his successor (whom they knew well), 'Is tha' Bill H. today then?'

Pride in work is a very important part of the miner's life. Old men delight in stories of their strength and skill in youth. A publican or a bookmaker will often joke about the number of tons 'filled off' each day in his establishment by the old men. Older men in the pit who go on to light work will confide that they can still 'go as well as the young 'uns' but they think they deserve a rest. Men of over sixty still working heavy contracts are visibly proud of themselves and resent any preferential treatment. Another influence may be discerned in this pride of miners in their work. For long, and they know this, mineworking has been looked down on; this is felt strongly, and a man's assertion of pride in being a miner is often partly an attempted self-assurance that he does not care what non-miners think of him.

The identification of a man with his work is reinforced, and reaches a higher level of social significance, by the impact of class relations on the carrying out of work. It has been remarked that one of the tactics of which the employers were suspected by the miners in earlier days was an attempt to provoke competition between workers as a safeguard against the growing of their solidarity and strength. This suspicion is by no means dead, and it recurs in situations where a workman is sent to replace another, or to do any job which is not his own. Before a market-man proceeds to his allotted task for the shift he will ask, 'Am I being sent to do somebody else's work?' He wonders whether there will be too many men on the job to ensure a good rate for the regular contractors, or he may suspect that the fact of a face not being filled-off is the result of a dispute, so that in effect he would be blacklegging. These suspicions lend strength to the identification of a man with work commensurate with his skill and status.

It is clear then that the work a miner does and the wage he receives both express concretely his status as a man and as a member of his profession.

Many years of hard toil and social conflict had given rise to a social structure and an ideology in mining which were fraught with dissensions, contradictions, and suspicions. The ideology of the days of private ownership, the days of depression, unemployment and bitter social strife, certainly is operative in everyday social relations in mining. It is more difficult to say whether those relations themselves have changed, and this problem cannot be fully treated until some analysis of trade unionism is put forward.

In his everyday work the miner has seen great improvement in the physical conditions of labour; the reward for his labour has been comparatively great since 1939; mining offers complete security of employment in the West Yorkshire and most other coalfields. Nationalization, a long-standing aim of the miners, has been achieved. The prestige of the miner in the working class is higher than it has ever been, and the miner knows this. Does all this mean that the miner has experienced a basic change in his status and in the society, a change which goes with a transformation of the relations between the miner and his work? In fact no such basic change has occurred. In the first place the actual changes have been absorbed into the miners' traditional ideology rather than transformed it. Secondly, changes within the mining industry, and the quantitative improvement of the miners' position in relation to other workers, have been unaccompanied by any profound modifications in the general economic framework of which mining is a part, or of the social structure within which miners exist. Most miners know, for example, that the first charge on the industry's profits is compensation to the old colliery companies. They know that representatives of those companies were among the many non-workers appointed to the executive and administrative staff of the nationalized industry. They saw no change in the local management of the mines when nationalization took place. In all these ways they see themselves opposed to the same forces as before nationalization. When they are told not to strike because of impeding the national effort, when they hear of economy drives and efficiency teams, they see no reason why they should regard such admonitions any differently from the pre-nationalization period.

The fact of common residence is naturally of more significance in a town of Ashton's size than for larger industrial communities. A man's workmates are known to him in a manifold series of activities and contracts, and often have shared the same upbringing.

The effect of a common set of persisting social relations, shared over a life-time by men working in the same industry and in the same collieries, is a very powerful one. In the main, this factor is responsible for the reinforcement and reaffirmation of those social bonds which have been shown to be a characteristic of present-day mineworking. Solidarity, despite the division into interest groups among the miners in a given pit, is a very strongly developed characteristic of social relations in mining; it is a characteristic engendered by the nature and organization of coalmining: it is a characteristic that has been given added strength as a result of the high degree of integration in mining villages. A miner's first loyalty is to his 'mates'. To break this code can have serious consequences in any industry, but for a miner his whole life, not only his work, can be affected by the actions and words of his fellows. The 'blackleg' miner must be made a social outcast in every way, and not only at work. This is possible in any situation where the workers in an enterprise are living together in one community and form the majority of that community; naturally it does not apply only to coalminers.

Insecurity and Struggle in the Car Industry
Huw Beynon

Reprinted with permission from, *Working For Ford*, Penguin Education, 1973, pp. 153–9

In spite of publicity to the contrary, and talk of easy times on the dole, the life of a working man without work is often desperate. What most working men want of a job is that it offers them some security. Married men with children value a regular wage above all else in their work. Such men dominated the labour force at Halewood, and their stewards, we remember, consistently mentioned security as the most important aspect of a job.

The significance attached to job security becomes all the more important when placed alongside the fact that the production of motor cars has been characterized, almost above all else, by instability. The interdependence of the car plants, the proliferation of small, independent suppliers and market fluctuations have synthesized in the lay-off and short-time working. All of the Halewood workers I talked to had experienced a period of lay-off in the time that they had been employed in the PTA, and eight of the stewards and fifteen of the members mentioned instability of wages as a major drawback to working in a car plant. The Ford Motor Company in its move to Halewood attempted to handle fluctuations in the demand for cars through regulating the hours worked by a stable labour force, rather than by seasonal recruitment and lay-off. As a personnel officer put it: 'this has been a hire and fire industry for too long. What we have tried to do in this plant is to keep a stable labour force. Not to kick them out at the drop of a hat, but to try to give continuous production. That's the way to build up a loyalty to the Company.' Ford's operation of this policy made overtime for the workers on the line almost obligatory during periods of peak demand. The shop steward organization grudgingly accepted this, provided that 'proper notice' was given. However, the policy was no safeguard against the market. Market recession brought with it short-time working.

In the summer of 1965 for example, the Company introduced a period of short-time working in which the hourly paid employees in all its British plants were put on a four-day week. The joint steward committee of the three Halewood plants met to consider the situation and produced a three-page leaflet on short-time working which was distributed throughout the trade union movement. In this they explicitly attack the meaninglessness of 'continuity of employment' at Ford's – a concept which had been one of the keystones of management's negotiating position within the Halewood plants. To quote from the leaflet at length:

The trade unions agree to commit their members to a policy of a high amount of overtime during the peak spring and summer periods when schedules are running high, as opposed to the hiring of extra labour who would be fired when schedules drop. They also agree to 'mobility of labour', whereby men are constantly redeployed to maintain efficiency of plant operations, often with great inconvenience to the men concerned. Both these measures are patiently endured, and much cooperation is given. The reward for this is labelled 'continuity of employment', virtually a guaranteed five-day week, and yet the Ford Motor Company, the only company to have secured such agreements, is the first of the motor car manufacturers to cast its employees on to short-time working and imperil their livelihood with redundancy tactics.

The trade unions are also angry at the complete lack of prior consultation and ultimate refusal of negotiation. This, despite the case that can be made by ourselves for the non-necessity for the Ford Motor Company to resort to the drastic measure of introducing short-time working. Had the desire been great enough, here was a splendid opportunity for the Ford Motor

Company to make a magnanimous gesture to its workpeople and at the same time reap tremendous benefits for its Halewood plant. This plant, so stricken of late with quality problems of the highest magnitude, from a multiplicity of sources, also in the throes of a mighty expansion programme, could have set its house in order and benefited immensely by merely cutting back its production schedules, at an estimated negligible cost to this wealthy company of some £300,000. This measure could have presented the Company with valuable time and an excess of labour which could have been utilized to successfully clear the back-log of defective vehicles in the selling line area, which at the time of writing, number a daily growing congestion of approximately 1300 cars. The workers in this plant are aware that schedules not intended for production until the October, November period, have already rolled off the production lines, the reason being that for some fifteen weeks prior to the annual summer shutdown, this plant had obviously greatly over-produced. During this period men were actually disciplined for failing to comply with excessive fifteen hours per week overtime demands, in addition to Saturday, which in the main were readily adhered to. Now we are callously confronted with 'short time'. After impressing upon us for months the importance of building 'quality' into the job, which responsibility we have readily accepted as it is our 'bread and butter' at stake, the Company now choose to ignore our suggestions to improve the situation. We are now facetiously informed that it is not Ford's intention to attempt to build Rolls-Royces thus indicating that once again it is the sole prerogative of the Ford Motor Company, to the exclusion of the trade unions, to determine the future of Halewood and its workers.

It has long been our contention that any move taken by this devious Company, backed by the money, brains and resources it commands, has at least a double-edged benefit for itself in the outcome. In light of the above facts, therefore, we are more than suspicious that one of these benefits could be the new models or 'facelifts' as they are termed. Unlike its competitors, it is not the practice of the Ford Motor Company to stockpile unsold vehicles. The cutback in production effected by the reduction in the working week would therefore alleviate the problem of producing vehicles which would shortly become obsolete with the advent of the new models at the Motor Show. Instead of using a cutback then to rectify the atrocious quality of jobs currently produced and at the same time give value to the consumer, the Company choose the 'new model' benefit, to the detriment of its employees.

The committee then was severely critical of management's failure to enter into consultation with them before arranging the short-time working. In this, and in their treatment of quality and overproduction, the stewards raise the questions of market forces and managerial prerogatives. This strikes at the heart of power and politics within a car plant; and the history of the Halewood stewards' committee, and of motor car production generally, is played upon themes such as these. Again and again they occur. During the last six months of 1967 the production was halted in the PTA plant on two occasions and the workers were laid off and sent home. One of these lay-offs occurred in the middle of the night, the other at a more civilized hour. This one occurred at 2.30 on a Wednesday afternoon and lasted until the following Monday. During the previous weeks the number of cars in the storage parks around the estate had been increasing gradually. The plant was overproducing. The cars that were being produced weren't being sold and so on the Wednesday production was brought to a halt and five thousand men were laid off.

On that day I was in one of the material handling sections talking to the steward and a few of his members. After the dinner break several of the men reported a rumour that the plant was to shut down. The steward asked me if I had heard anything about a potential lay-off. I told him that I had been in the Personnel Department that morning and had talked with the convener during the dinner break but had heard no mention of a lay-off. By two o'clock the rumour was confirmed by the section supervisor and by half past two production was halted and the plant was empty and silent.

The men in the material handling section were angry about being laid off. They considered it to be wrong and unjustifiable that they should lose half their wages for the week.

It's always us. We *make* the fucking cars, we chase around here all day like fucking morons and as soon as anything goes wrong it's us who get the shit. They'll be all right up there in the office. They'll get their wages. It's always the same, we take the knocks for their stupidities. We've got kids and mortgages as well. They don't seem to consider that.

They didn't consider the lay-off to be unavoidable or a logical consequence of large-scale production. Rather that it was the fault of management. The management had made faulty predictions and had planned badly, but it was *they* (the workers) who suffered. Furthermore it was felt that once management had created the situation by way of their own errors, or inconsideration, they then proceeded to manipulate the situation to their own advantage.

All you've got to do is to watch the car park. You watch the car park and you'll get a pretty good idea of what will be going on inside this plant. When the park starts filling up a bit they start to push a bit. Little things like, but you haven't got to be a genius to work out what's happening. Whenever we have a strike here we have it when it suits Ford's. Never when it suits us.

The market then affects relationships in the plant. Economic fluctuations reveal themselves in the balance of power on the sections. Given this the actual decision to shut the plant becomes one of a number of strategies in the power game, and the game isn't over once the decision has been made. The men's biggest complaint was that they weren't given more than half an hour's notice of the lay-off.

They take a terrible attitude to the men on the shop floor here. I don't know how they behave as they do. They tell you nothing. Look, we've been laid off this afternoon and we haven't even been told that officially. They tell you nothing. All your pay can be stopped and they tell you nothing. That's typical of this firm.

Members of the Personnel Department explained the shortness of the notice by the fact that the decision didn't become inevitable until after the dinner break, and that right up to that time it was hoped that a lay-off could be avoided. Even if there is some truth in this explanation – even if the Halewood management were hoping for a reprieve from Warley – it doesn't adequately explain why the possibility of the lay-off was kept as such a closely guarded secret. The reason given for this secrecy by the stewards and several of the members I talked to, was simply that management was afraid of the consequences.

They see it like this see: they're going to shut the plant down at 2.30 and by that time they'll have produced so many cars. Then they'll know how many cars they'll have to get rid of, they'll be able to work their numbers out. So what they're afraid of is what the blokes will do once they know that the plant is stopping. Nobody trusts anybody in this place. What they're afraid of is the lads saying 'sod you' and either going home or doing bad jobs. It happens you know. When there's trouble like this you often get lads going down the lines with pennies or knives, scraping the paint off the cars.

In a situation ridden with latent conflicts, the decision to lay men off can be likened to a declaration of war, and it is not only the workers who attempt to exact reprisals against the other side in this situation. Often a depressed demand for cars encourages a supervisor to settle some old scores with his steward or with men on his section who have given him trouble. On the material handling section, for example, a skeleton crew was to remain in the plant during the shutdown. The decision on the manning of the crew was left in the hands of the supervisor who announced that he intended to 'draw up a list'. The shop steward and several of the men on the section opposed this violently. One of them remarked that 'that bastard wants to fill the place with his "blue eyes".' A group of the men wanted to crowd into the supervisor's office and 'have it out with him'. Jeff the steward persuaded them against this, arguing that it would be playing straight into his hands. Instead he went to see the supervisor and after a long furious argument it was agreed that the names of the skeleton crew would be picked out of a hat. Jeff said:

That's what we've got to put up with here see. Big Joe wants to run this section his way all the time. He'd have us saluting if he could. We've managed to get it through to him that we're not having it, that we want some say in what goes on here, by standing up to him. But it only takes something like this for him to think he can start waving the whip again.

The men objected strongly to being laid off; they had children, hire purchase debts and mortgage repayments to make, and to lay them off with half an hour's notice wasn't right. The lay-off can be seen to produce a heightening of the critical attitudes that these men held towards the company. Turner (Turner, Clack and

Roberts, 1967, p. 331) in fact attributes the industry's strike record and the militant demands of its workers to the fact that men who possess a low moral commitment to their employer and who tend to be more like 'economic men' than other workers experience a very considerable instability of earnings. This example clearly reveals how the lay-off is structured into the world of the assembler, how the elements of instability, monotony and conflict over the wage-work bargain all cohere to produce situations of heightening conflict.

There seems to be some evidence that members of management in the motor industry are aware of the significance of insecurity of earnings. To quote Bob Ramsey, The Ford Motor Company's Director of Labour Relations:

Men have been too easily bounced out of this industry in the past. We have been much too inclined to lay people off. We don't lay people off now unless it's absolutely necessary. You've got to draw the line at some point. But we don't do it if we can help it. We feel that the track shouldn't be stopped by either side. If we keep laying people off they are quite right to say 'why should I worry about production?' We want to get away from all that.

It seems likely that statements such as these, if carried into practice, would have a considerable effect upon work relationships. Nevertheless, it is important to remember that it is not so much the lay-off *in itself* that has given rise to conflict in car plants, but the coherence of other elements in the work situation around the insecurity of employment. Furthermore it should also be remembered, as Ramsey indicates, that the market sets very definite limits upon the extent to which any motor car company in Britain can guarantee security of employment to its workers. Given the instability of motor car production and the severe dependency of the assembly plants upon the supply of components, it seems likely that even where fall-back rates have been negotiated, the assembly-line worker will continue to experience insecurity of earnings during the seventies.

This leads to a second, more general point. Apart from administering the selection of skeleton crews on sections where such crews are required the shop steward is virtually helpless in the face of a lay-off. Job insecurity brings home very clearly the fact that while a degree of job control may be established by workers through the shop stewards' committee, to work in a factory means to work, to a very large extent, on management's terms. While a shop steward may well find himself in a situation where he has to challenge management's authority on the shop floor, he is more often in situations where he is forced to play the game management's way. Another senior executive of the company saw it like this:

It's difficult to say what type of steward does best for his members. A militant may well force a few concessions, but we'll always be waiting to get them back or to make life a bit difficult for him. While a quiet, more reasonable bloke may be less dramatic he'll probably get more for his members because if he's in any trouble we'll help him out. We make concessions to him that we wouldn't make to the other bloke.

In the face of a powerful, prestigious adversary, the soft-sell is often the best form of attack and self-defence. This is particularly the case if you're meeting him on his home ground. It takes a lot of courage, conviction and confidence to stick out a confrontation with a manager in a posh office, desk, carpet, good suit. And you in your overalls. It's even more difficult if he flatters you and appears reasonable. Many stewards rarely get over this. For most of the time they play negotiations management's way. They learn the limits of the game and in the routine of their lives in the plant tend not to step outside them: 'You can't fight a battle every day.'

But sometimes they've got to. And this is what makes nonsense of most public debate on industrial relations. Too often it is assumed that if only the shop steward and his members had the 'right attitude', strikes and industrial conflict generally would be tremendously reduced. The only attitude that would ensure this is one of subservience and stupidity. For what the pundits fail to recognize, or choose to ignore, is that we live in a world dominated by capital and a capitalist rationality. In this world decisions are understood as 'investments', what makes a thing good or bad is the 'return' on it. Not it in itself. A good becomes a commodity valued not for what it can do, so much as the price it can be exchanged for. People too become commodities for the commodity world has men's labour at its centre. Spun round by capital and transformed into charts on office walls. 'Labour costs' – that sums it up. Production based upon the sale of labour power. By men, putting themselves at the disposal of other men for over half their lives. In order to live they preserve capital and their bondage. It is not perversity that makes assembly-line workers claim that they are treated like numbers. In the production of motor cars they *are* numbers. Numbers to be manipulated by people who are trained and paid to do just that. To cut costs, increase output. And lay men off. As a commodity, so is their power to labour treated. This is not to say that managers are necessarily inhumane people. Many managers, and employers, deeply regret the need to lay men off, to make them redundant. But they recognize that it is a need, a necessity dictated by market forces, for this necessity applies to them as well.

There are real lines of conflict within a car plant. A conflict that will be more obvious at one time than another. But it can never be assumed away, for it runs deeper than the 'cooperativeness' or otherwise of the assembly-line workers and their union representatives. It is underpinned by the very existence of wage labour and the market. While a shop steward may well attempt to play the game management's way, in many circumstances this attempt will be fraught with severe tensions.

Work and Leisure

S. R. Parker

Reprinted with permission from 'Work and Non-Work in Three Occupations', *Sociological Review*, March 1965, pp. 65, 70–5

There is a growing literature tracing the ways in which the kind of work men do influences their pattern of life. Studies of leisure which have hitherto focused on social class differences are now developing the theme that there are occupational differences within class and status groupings which play a large part in determining the style of leisure, family behaviour, political orientations, as well as more general values. The investigation reported below is of people in three occupations at broadly the same class/status level, but who differ substantially in the kind of work they do and the conditions under which they do it. An attempt is made to analyse some of the specific components of these varying work situations, to determine the role which work plays in the lives of the people concerned, and to see whether they have typical ways of relating work and leisure spheres. The findings on the last point are likely to be useful in dealing with the social problem of the use of increasing leisure time which the growth of automation is likely to bring.

In the summer of 1963 a pilot study was carried out consisting of interviews with two hundred men and women in ten occupations, half business and half service (mainly social work). The main hypothesis at this stage was that people in different occupations would vary not only in their degree of commitment to their present jobs, but also in the part that work plays in their lives as measured by the encroachment of work on leisure time, the function of leisure, the extent of colleague friendships, and the preferred life sphere (work, family or leisure) of involvement. Of the occupations studied, bank employees were found to be one of the least work-involved; for example, they tended significantly more often than the people in service occupations to experience lack of scope in their jobs, to see their jobs mainly as a means of earning a living, and to prefer to do another kind of work if financially free. At the other end of the scale, child care officers showed a highly work-oriented pattern, and these two occupations, together with a third group of youth employment officers, were chosen for more intensive study.

The Following Patterns Emerge

(1) The bank employees characteristically enjoy leisure because it is completely different from work, do not have much of their free time taken up by things connected with their work, and have their central life interest in the family sphere, with leisure second.

(2) The child care and youth employment officers characteristically enjoy leisure because it is satisfying in a different way from their work, have a lot or a little of their free time taken up by things connected with their work, and have their central life interest in the family sphere with work second.

Certain differences also emerged in the type of people who tended to be work or non-work oriented. One in two of the single women in the youth employment and child care samples appeared to have work as a central life interest compared with one in four married men in those occupations. However, the fact that only one in ten of the single women in banking had work as a central life interest shows that sex and marital status are not decisive but contributory factors. The propensity to have work as a central life interest was found to be related (at better than the two per cent level of significance) to: wishing to continue present job or do something similar as opposed to wishing to do something different; being subject to a way of dealing with changes or difficult problems other than superiors deciding without consultation; and to believing that people get ahead in that kind of work by working and studying hard. Even reasons for enjoying leisure – because it is completely different from work or because it is satisfying in a different way from work – are related respectively to wishing to do something different if financially free and wishing to continue present job or do something similar. In all of these ways, the significance of work in the life pattern and the role of leisure can be shown to be deeply influenced by the way people work, and in particular by the social conditions under which they work.

From these particular survey results, and from the pilot interviews, it appears that people in such occupations as youth employment and child care tend to have a way of relating their work to their leisure which may be called extension: their leisure activities are often similar in content to their working activities, they make no sharp demarcation between work and leisure, they are 'work-involved', and the main function of leisure to them is to develop their personality. By contrast, people like miners and distant-water fishermen have been shown to have a pattern of opposition between work and leisure: their way of spending leisure is typically contrasted with the way they work, they sharply distinguish between what is work and what is leisure, their work is done chiefly to earn a living, and leisure functions for them as compensation for dangerous and damaging work.

The bank employees who took part in the survey reported here do not appear to fall into either of these categories, and may well be representative of a third pattern which could be called complementarity: as with the 'opposition' pattern, leisure activities are different from work and a demarcation is made between them – both, perhaps, to a lesser extent. But these people are neither so engrossed in their work that they want to carry it over into their spare time, nor so damaged by it that they become hostile or develop a love-hate relation to it – they are largely just indifferent to it and unmarked by it in their leisure hours. Similarly they are led neither towards 'spillover' leisure nor compensatory leisure, but rather towards a middling pattern of relaxation. Their comparatively high preference for agriculture as alternative work may partly reflect their need for complementing the mechanized paper world of banking with a quieter, more basically productive life on the land.

These three hypothetical modes of relating work to leisure may be summarized as follows:

Table 1

	Spheres	*Demarcation*	*Attitude to work*	*Main function of leisure*
Extension	Similar	Little	Involved	Development of personality
Complementarity	Somewhat different	Some	Indifferent	Relaxation
Opposition	Very different	A lot	Ambivalent or hostile	Recuperation

The probability of an individual approximating to any one of these patterns will vary with type of occupation and with work situation or work values held in that occupation. In the present study, type of work was the main variable, but the work-leisure pattern may discriminate among individuals within occupations. Thus research carried out at the Regent Street Polytechnic on scientists in industry suggests that scientists oriented to progress within the employing organization have an instrumental attachment to their jobs and a non-work central life interest which are equivalent to the pattern of complementarity outlined above; while scientists oriented to the values of science have an expressive attachment to their jobs and have work as their central life interest, which can be equated with 'extension'.

On the basis of studies carried out so far, it seems clear that the work-leisure relationship is more than a personal preference; it is conditioned by various factors associated with the way people work. Further research needs to be undertaken to test the validity of these three possible patterns and the types of work situation in which they typically apply. In particular, an attempt should be made to explore more fully the opposition pattern which some of the bank employees responding to the questionnaire showed to some extent, and which is probably more typical of occupations which have not so far been investigated specifically for this purpose.

A Night at the Dogs
Ray Gosling

Reprinted with permission from *The Listener*, Vol. 89, No. 2292, March 1973

When I hear the Leeds Police Choir sing, their massive voices raised in harmony praising the Lord Messiah, I think what a wonderful country we live in for half-hidden pleasures. Who edits the Wayside Pulpit? And think of all the people who win prize cups and medallions for dahlias, darts, or chihuahuas. There are more people about than we think taking part in pleasures that never hit the headlines but are immensely popular, like choir practice, darts and dogs. The second most popular sport in the country is dog-racing. I met this fanatic who said to me: 'Do you know that the greyhound's the only dog mentioned by name in Holy Scripture, in the Book of Solomon, and it's on Egyptian coins – the greyhound is as old as Tutenkhamun.'

Certainly in England since cock-fighting stopped and mill chimneys were built, the working class have bred and kept greyhounds and whippets. Whippets are half-castes, a cross between a pure greyhound and a terrier. They don't have whippets at proper dog-tracks. But miners and others have used them for donkey's years to race and go rabbiting with, and no matter what the law of the land has said, people have held race-meetings with whippets and greyhounds, and someone has kept a book in which people can bet. That's the point of it: at the dogs there is no pomp and camp, no royal patronage – you cannot pretend you're there only to watch the pure joy of an animal racing, its muscles moving. If there wasn't betting there wouldn't be dog-tracks.

Twice as many people in Britain watch dogs race as watch horses: its a proletarian sport. If you thought it had all died out with Music Hall it hasn't. There are more dog-tracks in England than casinos, and that's just counting official ones.

In the summer I went to a New Town just outside Liverpool. The proud local council had laid on an annual show: a gymkhana, an exhibition of prize-winning jam and beetroot, and a fair. Half-way through the day, on one edge of the big school field, a man in a flat cap appeared. Cool, swift and silent, he stretched out some wire a few hundred yards long, to which he attached a flapping handkerchief rag and an apparatus, and rigged it all to a car battery. Then from nowhere, with nothing spoken, ten or twenty folk appear, with muzzles in hands, wire cages to put over a dog's head, and little jackets with numbers on. And then there's a hundred more watching. And men open books. Pound notes and fivers change hands almost in silence, as if performing an ancient religious rite, with no laughter, no advertisement. Some dogs line up and the owners hold them back, but how they yap. The flat-cap man puts a wire to the car battery, and the rag speeds, nervously flapping, up the field, the dogs yapping and straining. Their owners let them go. Bawling and shouting from the crowd, from everybody, and one dog wins. In seconds it's over. Money changes hands. And then they do it again, and again: different dogs, same dogs, I couldn't tell. Was a vet present? I doubt it. It lasted for a couple of hours, and then the crowd evaporated, just as if nothing had happened. It was unbelievable. I watched as the flat-cap man put the battery into a car boot, and the rag that had done for a hare in his pocket. He wrapped the wire up, put it into a box, and off he went. I followed him through the Morris dancing as far as the flower-arrangement tent where I lost him among the potted cacti.

The Chinese bet on two flies crawling up a wall, or don't they do that now? Some Englishmen still bet on which dog will kill a live hare over a course. But that's uncertain for the promoter and for the punter. What put the big time into hounds was electricity: a substitute for a hare on electric wire. They did it first at the back of the Welsh Harp pub in North London in 1876, and it didn't catch on. Then a man called O. P. Smith got it organized in the United States, and a Canadian, Brigadier Critchley, brought it back to England in 1926, the year of the General Strike, when he opened a greyhound-racing track at Belle Vue, Manchester. Seventeen hundred people went to his first meeting, and a few weeks later the crowd was more than ten thousand. Between 1927 and 1932 scores of tracks opened everywhere. It boomed like Ten Pin Bowling has – no, more like Bingo in our time. Overnight the dogs rivalled soccer, and in some towns there'd be a bigger crowd at the dog-track than the soccer field. Local newspapers ran weekly Dog Supplements, and a whole legend grew, made up of apocryphal stories of mythical dogs: 'Feed it on gin to get its spirits up and then it'll win,' 'Feed it on meat pies to bring its handicap down,' and 'Did you hear the one about the dog that ran so fast it caught the hare and got electrocuted?' All that legend is unrecorded. I can't find a short-story writer from the dog-track.

The success was because in those days, and up to 1961, there were no betting-shops. The law of the land said you could only bet at a racecourse. Horse race-meetings happened only now and then, and generally only in the daytime and in the country. The bookie's runner was illegal and unreliable, so the dogs provided a bet for the working classes. In your town, every town, a course for racing dogs at night, in your own free time, two or three times a week, and not Mrs Grundy or the police could stop you from having your bet. In the beginning the promoters tried to get people like colonels onto the board, aping horse-racing, but they failed: it was never to be a sport of kings.

They then realized that if you'd got enough ordinary people it didn't matter that you hadn't the patronage of those who supposedly matter. Admission charges were always kept low, as in the Bingo boom of a quarter of a century later. The small punter was encouraged. In its heyday, in the thirties, there were 220 tracks in Britain: today there are only 118. Since the coming of the betting-shop there's been a rationalization. But still eight million people went to watch the dogs last year: twice the number who go to watch horses race. They went to small flapper tracks – that's where the rag flaps – in Scottish mining villages, the North-East, the West Riding, South Wales and the Asian town of Southall. But the big tracks are in the big cities, and they thrive.

On the swamp behind the gasworks, I went to a matinee meeting at Hackney Wick: clean and professional, almost dull it was. They don't proselytise at the dogs, and at a big track the owner of a dog doesn't keep it at home, and the dog isn't even English. Sixty per cent of them are born in Ireland, trained there for the first 15 months of life and then bought by the stadium who re-sell to an owner, your dentist or publican, a business man, a musician or an independent lady. I wonder if they could do that with football-players? Anyway, the owner of the dog pays the track, the stadium, about £3 a week to feed and groom it. And when it wins, the owner picks up the prize: £10, £15 – it's not a lot, surprisingly. The dog never leaves the stadium until, after two and a half years, its racing life is over. No dog can race more than once at any meeting, and no more than three times in a fortnight. There's a vet to see the dog's fit and undoped, and they're stricter about that than they are with horses today. A little tannoy fanfare sounds, and out come six competitors, never more than six to a race, led by kennel lads. At some places they have girls, but at Hackney it's lads. It's a full-time job and nobody who works on the kennel staff can bet. The six are paraded before the spectators: they put their little paws up and take a last pee and the spectators make knowledgeable remarks. The dogs are then led to the traps and their tails wag. They look surprisingly happy: Makokis, Sleeping Judy, Crediton Flash, Be Virile. The background music stops. 'Your last chance to place a bet. Your last chance to place a bet.' The bookmakers go mad. There's waving elbows and fingers – it's a tic-tac. The bells are rung and the bookies' bags are shut, shutters on tote windows, and all eyes then turn to the track. A hush fills the stadium. Then the electric whir like a train rushing into a tunnel, and a bright-coloured electric toy hare on a rail rushes past the stand at amazing speed and the dogs are off. Everyone shouting: 'Come on number six!'

It would be very boring to watch dogs go round an oval track, except that it happens so fast. It's over in seconds. More bells are rung. In fact, all that afternoon bells rang and people came and went like it was school or a Scottish bar. The race pattern is repeated eight times at a Hackney matinee, and it's all on the flat – no hurdles. Fifteen minutes between each race, and the bars are open all afternoon. The crowd was quite small because the point of a Hackney matinee is to provide a betting service for the afternoon punter in 75 per cent of Britain's betting-shops. On a cold and frosty afternoon when horse-racing's abandoned, the dogs can save the bookie's bacon – and my God, how fat the bookies have got! Since 1961, 15,000 betting-shops have opened and a hundred dog-tracks closed. Since 1961, attendance at dog meetings has gone down by 4·5 per cent a year, and last year by 10 per cent. But last year was exceptional. It was ironic, because the miners were on strike, so the power was cut: no floodlights, and no electric hare.

Since the betting-shop has been legalized, attendance at horse race-meetings has also declined. But the horse-race people get compensation through a levy on bets placed in all betting-shops. But the dogs get nothing. They've got no George Wigg. The dogs' heyday was when they were the only place a working man could regularly legally bet. Now they're still the number two sport and more money goes on dogs than football pools. On the actual courses, £100 million is bet a year. But the stadiums are having to advertise themselves and chic themselves up – cricket is having to, too.

On the Friday after Christmas, I looked in the London midday paper, still half as much of it devoted to dogs as horses, and I went to Wimbledon. They advertise themselves as the South London Excitement Centre and they've doubled up so that when the dogs aren't there they've got stocks and super-stox, hot-rod cars and speedway.

It was an evening meeting, and where you'd expect it: on the watery side of town, beside the River Wandle and behind the sewage farm. But inside, Wimbledon is as smart as the Palais, with coloured lights and beer: a fountain plays by a Christmas tree in the centre of the track, Tom Jones sings muzak, closed-circuit television has replaced the blower, and nearly all the accommodation was under cover. Working-class, yes, but the working class have money, and the immigrants, Chinese, Negroes, Sikhs and Jews, are as smart at the cheap end of eight bobs as at the posh end at 70p. Well-shod folk: I looked at the shirt cuffs and the stocking heels – not many of them had holes. It's a different world. It was like a commercial to prove there's nothing wrong with a little flutter if you can afford it, and obviously people at Wimbledon could. Air-conditioning took cigar smoke to heaven. A winner bought a bottle of champagne and a glass for the barmaid – 'for you, my lovely'. The young, and there were lots of them, weren't at all like soccer spectators. They were quiet and well-behaved, more like Billy Graham converts.

It was almost as if the dogs were an incidental break in a night out. A moment of silence and concentration when the lights are dimmed, then the roar of the crowd as the flash of the colour is seen behind the plate-glass. Then the lights go up and it's back to social intercourse. There was a dog disqualified for fighting, Gypsey Myross. Well, I never saw it. There was as much commotion over the winner of the ladies' lucky number on the programme. Everybody jolly: friends and regulars, 4,500 of them, enthusing, hobby-type people, carefree – a lot of laughter and free spending on their thing. Few loners – and the absence of the poor puzzled me. Where had they gone: the nail-biting, shirt-losing, lonely, marriage-broken men, the dirty-haired and baggy-eyed, cheating the devil. They weren't at Wimbledon and they weren't at the Hackney matinee meeting. Nor at that sturdy do in the Liverpool New Town. Have they died? No, I don't think so. We've hidden them. We've taken them off the tracks by putting a betting-shop on every council house estate. That's where they are.

As horse-racing has become like the theatre, and gets a subsidy, the dogs have become like cinema – and when was the last greasy mackintosh you saw in yours? Poverty is out of fashion: pushed into the corner bookie's is the dirt and the debt and despair. And the dog-tracks? They stand to become cliquey, a bit beery, most enthusiastic, a little in-grown, but a rather respectable pleasure.

Further Reading: Work

* w. BALDAMUS: *Efficiency and Effort*, Tavistock, 1961.
*† T. BURNS: *Industrial Man*, Penguin Books, 1969.
*† T. CAPLOW: *The Sociology of Work*, McGraw Hill, 1964.
* w. A. FAUNCE: *Readings in Industrial Sociology*, Appleton-Century-Crofts, 1967.
* R. FRASER: *Work*, Pelican, 1968.
  JOHN H. GOLDTHORPE, D. LOCKWOOD, F. BECHHOFER AND J. PLATT: *The Affluent Worker, 1. Industrial Attitudes and Behaviour*, Cambridge University Press, 1968.
  P. HOLLOWELL: *The Lorry Driver*, Routledge & Kegan Paul, 1968.
* M. MANN: *Workers on the Move*, Cambridge University Press, 1973.
* s. MARCSON: *Automation, Alienation and Anomie*, Harper & Row, 1970.
  W. A. T. NICHOLS: *Ownership, Control and Ideology*, Allen & Unwin, 1969.
*† S. B. PARKER, R. K. BROWN, J. CHILD AND M. A. SMITH: *The Sociology of Industry*, Allen & Unwin, 1968.
  M. WARNER: *The Sociology of the Workplace*, Allen & Unwin, 1973.
* D. WEDDERBURN: *White Collar Redundancy: A Case Study*, Cambridge University Press, 1964.
*† D. T. H. WEIR: *Men and Work in Modern Britain*, Fontana, 1973.

* Available in paperback
† Reference

5 Class

Almost all societies are stratified in some way, divided that is into strata, for instance, 'castes', 'estates', 'classes', 'status groups', the members of which possess certain characteristics in common, which serve also to mark them off from members of other strata.

However, a stratification system is not an inevitable and unalterable feature of all societies, but is associated with the historical development of particular societies, and not therefore with underlying 'natural' or biological characteristics of the members of the strata. In fact a good deal of sociological research has been devoted to analysing the lack of concordance between distinctions of 'ability' or 'fitness' and the divisions of rank and reward which form part of the structure of society.

Thus while stratification of some sort is a nearly universal feature of all societies, its particular forms vary from one society to another, and do not, therefore, guarantee any 'natural' or 'proper' division into ranks.

For Marx, social classes were rooted in the system of production, by the fact that different groups stood in different relations to the means of production, and had different interests in it. Thus economic factors were paramount in determining class membership and class interest. The two most clearly distinguished classes were the bourgeoisie and the proletariat. The former both owned and controlled the means of production, and had the opportunity to accumulate surplus wealth; the latter had only their labour power to sell.

Weber further distinguished stratification by social status, honour, and prestige, and treated political power as an independent influence on stratification, rather than as a mere product of the class system. But the core of Weber's reformulation was to widen the notion of the economic basis of class formation, to include any situation where a market for scarce resources operated. **Dahrendorf** points to the emergence of other bases of social conflict, in particular the distribution of authority within 'imperatively coordinated associations'.

Within this broad framework a number of major themes have engaged the attention of sociologists.

Marx predicted that the class system would tend to polarize and the relative gap between bourgeoisie and proletariat would grow, leading to an exacerbation of class conflict and eventually to a revolutionary situation in which the ruling class would be overthrown. However, the last hundred years has seen the growth of many intermediate groups of salaried and professional workers, bureaucrats, managers, technicians, and office workers for instance, who are neither clearly bourgeois nor clearly proletarian, but represent a sort of 'new middle class'. Some of the possible consequences of this are examined by C. W. Mills in *White Collar*.

Again, although the wage levels and standards of living of manual workers have risen a good deal in absolute terms during this century, there is a good deal of doubt about how much of a redistribution of wealth from rich to poor there has been. A clear and succinct account of this debate is given by R. Blackburn, in the paper recommended for further reading.

The diffusion of property ownership, through shareholding, and the growth in size of many economic enterprises have provoked rethinking about the nature of the link between ownership and control. Burnham argued that the managers were destined to become a new ruling class because of their control of the means of production and their crucial position in governmental administrative organizations, but this notion is radically questioned by others who examine the interlinkages between shareholding and managerial power. The thesis that the 'logic of industrialism' inevitably produced a 'convergence' between the class structures of Communist and non-Communist societies at a similar stage of development is examined critically by Goldthorpe.

However, empirical analyses of the class structure depend on the availability of data relating for instance to the distribution of wealth or income. Rex indicates the kinds of questions which sociologists require to be able to ask of this sort of statistical data before it can begin to make sense. Although this reading is extracted from a review of a book published several years ago, the criticisms are still very relevant.

Goldthorpe and Lockwood examine the consequences of the idea that the general improvements in the standard of living of

manual workers, greater economic security and the underpinning provided by the Welfare State may have tended to
produce an 'embourgeoisement' of the working class. The
suggested consequences of this are for instance that 'affluent
manual workers' would aspire to middle-class status, and
become assimilated to it, would adopt middle-class patterns of
consumption and recreation, and would tend to vote Conservative rather than Labour. The authors distinguish between
the 'economic', 'normative' and 'relational' levels of stratification, and indicate that it is fallacious to argue a point at one
level with data drawn from another level. Their overall conclusion is that 'middle-class' and 'working-class' patterns of
life are clearly distinguishable and it is thus premature, if not
simply inaccurate, to talk of Britain being a 'middle-class' or
'one-class' society, or to argue that class is no longer a useful
category for the sociological analysis of an affluent capitalist
society.

The Marxist tradition of class analysis has always emphasized the distinction between classes as mere interest
groupings (or 'class-in-itself') and classes as coherent groups
which are coordinated and united for class action and conflict
(or 'class-for-itself'). In order for differences of interest over
the distribution of the surplus value created in the system of
production to be transmitted into class action two conditions
have to be met. The group concerned had to generate a political
structure which would transcend particular grievances and
agitation and it had to achieve an understanding of its historical destiny and of its position in the class struggle as a
whole. This consciousness of class becomes the basis of an
ideology which supports and sustains the group.

Class consciousness implies a common awareness of exploitation among individuals who occupy a similar position in
respect of the systems of control and distribution, of solid
resources, and in particular of industrial property.

But this analysis has not always proved easy to interpret, in
particular in relation to those who occupy intermediate positions in the industrial hierarchy, and especially clerks and
other 'blackcoated workers'. Some sociologists have classified
clerks as members of the propertied class, while others have
argued that their interests are more akin to those of the
proletariat, the group who neither own nor control societal
resources.

Weir's paper examines the social perspectives of clerical workers employed in private industry in an attempt to identify whether these perspectives conform to the 'middle-class stereotype' described by Goldthorpe and others.

It may be helpful also in this context to refer to Bernstein's work reprinted in Chapter 3, in order to consider the way in which class factors actually work in concrete social situations. By conditioning and modifying the style of language which children develop and use, whole modes of apprehension of the external world and ways of relating to it are in fact determined. Thus a working-class child, brought up in what Bernstein calls a 'public language' style, may have a much more limited range of possibilities of relating to social situations and other people, than a middle-class child, who is equally fluent in a language style which encourages abstractness, symbolization and analysis, rather than description and personalization. Thus Bernstein draws attention to the importance of language in the process of the definition of social situations, and as the medium for the maintenance of distinctive class cultures.

Social mobility is often seen as an important feature of industrialized societies, and particularly of capitalist ones (although downward social mobility is only rarely studied). However, the majority of people at any point in time in contemporary British society remain throughout their careers in their class of origin. But changes in the occupational structure, involving the expansion of professional, managerial and white-collar work, and the decline of many traditional manual occupations have led to an increase in the number of people in non-manual jobs, many of whom have parents who were themselves manual workers.

Increasingly the crucial nexus in the process of social mobility is the educational system, and **Turner** shows in a comparative study of the USA and Britain, how differences in the definition of the 'organizing norms' concerning the way in which upward social mobility should take place, are related to other features of society, and may predetermine which categories of the population are 'eligible' for mobility.

It is often argued that the conditions of modern industrial organization, the growth in size of the enterprises, and the necessity for aspiring executives to move from place to place to obtain promotion, have produced a class of managers who are highly mobile in geographical and social terms. This has consequences for social affairs as the 'spiralists' tend to withdraw from the local community, and to leave local leadership to the shopkeepers and small business men and others described by Watson as 'burgesses'.

Payne looks critically at some of these typologies, comparing Watson's burgesses and spiralists with Gouldner's 'locals and cosmopolitans' and Stacey's traditionalists and immigrants.

The operation of a traditional social structure relatively unaffected by industrialization is traced by **Williams** through his illuminating account of the terms and descriptions used by members of the social groupings in the Cumbrian village of Gosforth about themselves and each other.

Pahl examines the impact on a village in the rural-urban 'fringe' where a local community way of life had previously been established, of an influx of 'spiralists' of the kind described by Watson. The newcomers effectively introduce a two-class system, and cannot become assimilated to the 'rural way of life' because they have no means of suffering the deprivations which gave the village community its sense of isolation, and promoted strong internal bonds of social cohesion between the villagers.

Finally, **Littlejohn** illustrates from a study of a rural parish in the south of Scotland, how the factors of economic class, language style, and opportunities for social power, operate in a concrete situation to produce a local class and status system. Although this system has several 'objective' features it remains flexible and open to definition in different ways by its members, so that no single value is seen as predominant, or fundamental.

A social class is neither a mere category arbitrarily defined by myself on the basis of one or two 'characteristics' such as property ownership, nor is it a group in the strict sense of the term as implying clear cut boundaries and a constitution laying down a limited set of relationships among its members. A class is rather, for its members, one of the major horizons of all social experience – an area within which most experience is defined (Littlejohn, p. 242).

The Authority Structure of the Industrial Enterprise

R. Dahrendorf

Reprinted with permission from *Class and Class Conflict in Industrial Society*, Routledge & Kegan Paul, 1959

One social institution to which Marx devoted a great deal of attention has survived capitalist society: the industrial enterprise. Trivial as this statement may sound, there is no reason to avoid it. There can be no doubt that many changes have occurred in the century between 1850 and 1950 both outside and inside the industrial enterprise. It may appear meaningless to identify the small factory of a capitalist entrepreneur in 1850 with the large corporation of 1950 in terms of productive capacity and number of employees, technical perfection and spatial extension, complexity of organization and conditions of work. However, although these changes are by no means irrelevant for conflict analysis, we have to start with a more fundamental relation which remains, or has remained so far, unchanged. In capitalist as in post-capitalist society, in the Soviet Union as in the United States, the industrial enterprise is an imperatively coordinated association. Everywhere it displays those conditions of social structure which give rise to social conflict in terms of class theory. Wherever there are industrial enterprises, there are authority relations, latent interests, quasi-groups, and (industrial) classes.

In dealing with the formal organization of the enterprise, a distinction is usually made between the 'functional' aspect of the division of labour and the 'scalar' aspect of super- and subordination. Both are functionally necessary; they are complementary aspects of industrial organization. One of the secrets of the increase of productivity by mechanized factory production lies in the subdivision of the total process of production into co-operative detail processes. Every one of these is equally indispensable for the accomplishment of the total process. From a strict functional point of view, the unskilled labourer, the foreman, and the executive stand on one level; the enterprise cannot function if one of these positions remains vacant. However, for purposes of the organization, coordination, and leadership of such subdivided detail processes a principle other than the division of labour is needed. A system of super- and subordination guarantees the frictionless operation of the total process of production – a system, in other words, which establishes authority relations between the various positions. The incumbents of certain positions are endowed with the right to make decisions as to who does what, when, and how; the incumbents of other positions have to submit to these decisions. Nor are the commands given and obeyed in the industrial enterprise confined to technical work tasks: hiring and firing, the fixing of wage rates and piecework systems, introduction and control of disciplinary regulations, and other modes of behaviour are part of the role expectations of the incumbents of authority positions in the enterprise and give rise, therefore, to its scalar or authority structure. For the industrial worker, the labour contract implies acceptance of a role which is, *inter alia*, defined by the obligation to comply with the commands of given persons. Industrial authority does not, of course, involve the subordination of total persons under other persons; it is restricted to persons as incumbents of given, limited roles; but it is therefore no less authority, i.e., a 'probability that a command with a given specific content will be obeyed by a given group of persons'. Although, in other words, the foreman cannot legitimately command his workers to collect stamps in their leisure time, there exist in the industrial enterprise, within a definable range, authority relations in the strict sense of class theory.

Since the industrial enterprise has an authority structure and is therefore an imperatively coordinated association, we are entitled to assume that the incumbents of positions of domination and subjection within it are united in two conflicting quasi-groups with certain latent interests. This inference follows from the model of class formation. If the theory of group conflict proves useful, its validity is as universal as the imperative character of the enterprise itself. Wherever there are industrial enterprises, there is a quasi-group of the incumbents of roles of domination, the latent interests of which are in conflict with those of a corresponding quasi-group of incumbents of roles of subjection.

In disputes between trade unions and employers, an argument is often put forward by the employers which has found its way into sociological literature also. Employers like to assert that they represent the interests of the total enterprise whereas the unions merely stand for partial interests. It might appear that there is no convincing refutation of this argument. However, in the light of the theory of group conflict it becomes apparent what the basis of this argument is and why it is ideological, i.e., demonstrably false – a fact which is of considerable significance for class analysis. We have seen earlier that the interests of a ruling group assume, as ruling interests, the character of accepted values in a unit of social structure. They are a reflection of the real structure, the existing conditions, although these are upheld and guaranteed by the rule of but one class. They might therefore appear as binding for all elements of a unit of social structure. Yet the theory of class exposes the fact that the existing conditions are themselves in a sense merely 'partial', that they exist by virtue of the authority of one part, or class. As the prime minister is both representative of the whole nation and exponent of the majority party, the entrepreneur is both 'the enterprise' and one partial interest in the conflicts generated by its structure – depending on the image of society underlying our analysis. In this sense, 'conservation' and 'modification' of a *status quo* are, from the coercion point of view, strictly equivalent 'partial' interests the conflict of which can be conceived as one of the determinants of the dynamics of social structure.

Two objections are frequently raised these days against the universal reality of conflicting latent interests in industry. They are easily disposed of, yet it may further clarify the issue to discuss them briefly. The first of these objections is based on the thesis that what is often called the 'bourgeoisification of the proletariat', i.e., the improvement of the economic situation of industrial workers, makes the assumption of continuing conflict unreasonable and, indeed, nonsensical. If, it is argued, the workers are no longer proletarians, if they do not live in poverty and suppression, they no longer have reason to revolt against their employers. The public of post-capitalist societies realizes, with baffled surprise, the continued reality of strikes and yet insists, at the same time, on the theory that industrial conflict has lost its causes and issues where the standard of living is high. This paradox testifies to a remarkable consistency of conviction, if not to insight. The theory of group conflict does not postulate any connection between class conflict and economic conditions. For the emergence of social conflicts the standard of living of their participants is in principle irrelevant, for conflicts are ultimately generated by relations of authority, i.e., by the differentiation of dominating and subjected groups. Even if every worker owns a car, a house, and whatever other comforts of civilization there are, the root of industrial class conflict is not only not eliminated, but hardly touched. The fact that economic demands may provide the substance (a substance situationally specific and in that sense incidental) of manifest interests must not give rise to the erroneous notion that satisfaction of these demands eliminates the causes of conflict. Social conflict is as universal as the relations of authority and imperatively co-ordinated associations, for it is the distribution of authority that provides the basis and cause of its occurrence.

A second objection against the assumption of the persistence of a latent conflict of interest consists in the thesis that the replacement of capitalists by managers has removed the basis of industrial class conflict. Upon closer inspection, this thesis, too, proves untenable. As we have seen, latent interests can be conceived of as quasi-objective role expectations. They are held not by persons, but by positions, or by persons only insofar as they occupy certain positions. If a person occupies a position of domination in an enterprise, it is irrelevant in principle whether his authority is based on property, election by a board of directors, or appointment by a government agency. For the latent interests of the incumbents of positions of authority, their incumbency of these positions is the sole significant factor. Although, therefore, their modes of recruitment and bases of legitimacy make for significant differences between capitalist and manager in other contexts, their authority positions in the enterprise are alike, and their places in conflicts of interest identical. For the explanation of group conflict, the factual relations of authority are the crucial factor. To this extent I agree with Burnham's thesis and with Marx's and Renner's analysis of joint-stock companies; the replacement of functioning owners or capitalists by propertyless functionaries or managers does not abolish class conflict, but merely changes its empirical patterns. Independent of the particular personnel of positions of authority, industrial enterprises remain imperatively coordinated associations the structures of which generate quasi-groups and conflicting latent interests.

The National Class Structure

J. Rex

Reprinted with permission from *The Yorkshire Bulletin of Economic and Social Research*, Vol. II, No. 1, 1959

Originally published as part of a review of *A Survey of Social Conditions in England and Wales as illustrated by Statistics*, A. M. Carr-Saunders, D. Caradog Jones and C. A. Moser, Clarendon Press, Oxford University Press, 1958

Sociologists often exasperate their colleagues by their apparent concentration on theoretical speculation, and their failure to undertake what, to common sense, would appear to be the first task for a science of society, namely the accurate description and classification of contemporary societies. It has been pointed out with some justice that British sociologists know more about Trobriand or Andamanese society than they do about modern Britain. Yet there are better reasons for this state of affairs than the critics of sociology will allow. The methods of the anthropologist are not really relevant to the investigation of the larger social structures of an industrial society, and it is usually necessary to glean what information one can about them *by inference* from the available statistics. These statistics, however, will not have been collected necessarily with a view to describing society. For the most part, they are gathered in order to throw light on some administrative problem, or with a view to promoting social reform by throwing light on the inequalities of opportunity currently existing. If they are to be sociologically useful, then it is essential that the sociologist should confront each new compilation with the question which theoretical considerations suggest are of importance in the description of industrial societies.

There are four important sets of questions which must be answered if a useful description of contemporary British or any other industrial society is to be given. Each set may be grouped under a general question as follows:

(1) What are the social relations which exist between the various roles in industrial production, and between the dependants of those who participate, as a result of their participation?

(2) What are the processes whereby individuals are recruited, selected and trained for the fulfilment of key roles in the industrial system?

(3) In what ways do members of the society behave in their leisure time?

(4) What is the extent and the manner of deviance from the social norms assumed in the answers to questions 1, 2 and 3?

Our first question may now be broken down into six questions as follows:

(1) What is the size of the labour force and what proportion of the total, the male and female, single and married population does it represent?

(2) How is this labour force divided between industries and occupations?

(3) What status differences exist between different occupational roles, and what is the size of the various status groups?

(4) What income differences exist between different occupational and status groupings?

(5) What are the differences in property ownership between the participants in the industrial systems and, in particular, who owns and controls the means of production?

(6) What is the size of the various groups in industry, classified according to their relationship to the means of production?

When we pass beyond classification of the population by industry to classification by occupation and status, the significance of the statistics becomes less clear. In the census classification of the population by occupation, for example, the largest group consists of those in manufacturing occupations, but the use of another heading 'administrators, directors, managers, not elsewhere specified' indicates that there is some doubt as to whether the category headed 'manufacturing' is not really an 'industrial' rather than an 'occupational' one. In fact, it probably falls between the two. Perhaps, however, it can be agreed that the percentage of the population in manufacturing occupations remains the largest single group. Much clearer is the continued growth in the percentage of workers in clerical occupations. Less than 1 per cent in 1850, their percentage rose to 6·8 per cent by 1931 and no less than 10·5 per cent by 1951.

The significance of such a growth in size of the clerical population clearly lies in its impact upon the status and class situation in industry. But the attempts of the Registrar-general to distinguish the various status groups in industry still seem unsatisfactory. Three separate classifications are quoted by Carr-Saunders and his colleagues. These we may state summarily as follows:

Table 1.

I. Industrial Status

	%
Employers	2·1
Managers	3·7
Operatives	86·9
Own account	5·3
Unemployed	2·0

II. Type of Income

		%
Salaries		22
Managerial	7	
Technical & Professional	6	
Clerical	9	
Wages		78
Industrial	65	
Non-industrial	8	
Agricultural	5	

III. Social Class

	%
Professional, Administrative, etc.	3
Intermediate	15
Skilled occupations	53
Partly skilled	16
Unskilled	13

It is figures like this which drive the theoretically oriented sociologist to something like despair. Is the classification of the population into status groups meant solely as a statistical exercise, or are these classifications meant to refer to groups who might act as groups, or who might be thought of by their fellows as sharing a common way of life and meriting a characteristic degree of esteem? Clearly there does seem to be some claim that these represent real groups rather than statistical classifications. The third table above is said to be a classification according to 'social class'. But the implications of this term are left open to be filled in by the reader according to his own ideological pre-conceptions. Surely it would be more valuable if statisticians, who continually claim to be using sociological concepts, were to find out what groupings were of real sociological importance and then seek to describe these, rather than the groupings which are of little importance, but which happen to be easily measurable.

One of the facts which we should like to know about a status group or a social class (terms which are carefully distinguished from each other by the major sociological theorists like Weber and Tönnies) is what the 'life-chances' (to use Weber's term) of its members are. In particular, we should like to know what their income level was. Unfortunately the statistics of income which we have are mainly collected for other purposes, and are, for the most part, classified in terms of arbitrary statistical levels. The one potentially useful table from the point of view of a sociologist is that which shows the distribution of income according to income type. Both pre-tax and post-tax income tables show 'rent, dividends and interest' to have lost ground to salaries and wages. Curiously, salaries appear to have improved their position since the war, but this is largely due to the definition of the salarist so as to include the salaries and even some fees of directors as well as the salaries of top management.

Comparison of the spread of incomes pre-war with those of 1956 suggests a considerable degree of equalization. After adjusting the groupings to take account of the changed value of money, the bottom group has shrunk from 88 per cent in 1938 to 65–70 per cent in 1956, while the top group has shrunk from about 0·5 per cent to 0·25 per cent. But there is one omission from these figures. They take no account of either expense allowances or capital gains. We do not know how large a difference incomes from this source would make, but we may reasonably conclude that if account were taken of them, the income figures would show a lesser degree of redistribution away from the highest group (if not, as many people believe on the basis of their own observations of continuing conspicuous consumption, showing them to be actually maintaining or improving their position), and a greater relative share of the burden falling on the middle income groups and on the lower orders among the salariat. It is perhaps unfortunate that the possible effect of these factors is not mentioned, for students might easily jump to too glib conclusions about the extent of equalization which has gone on in our society.

That the figures given for the distribution of incomes may be misleading can readily be seen by looking at personal property. Before the war, 1 per cent of the population owned 56 per cent of total property. In the period 1946–50, 1½ per cent owned 54 per cent. At the other end of the scale, pre-war 75 per cent owned 5 per cent, post-war 62 per cent owned 3 per cent. This does not suggest a society in which there has been a dramatic and revolutionary change in property ownership. It shows that the property-owning classes have exhibited a remarkable resilience in the face of the egalitarian atmosphere of the post-war world.

The mere facts of unequal property distribution, however, do not tell the whole story, or provide the answer to significant sociological questions. The sociologist is interested not merely in who owns property in an economic sense. He wants to know what kind of property different groups hold, because one kind of property puts its owner into a different social setting from that which another does. At the bottom of the scale, estates consisted mainly of money savings, furniture and houses (one in five households owned their house, outright or with a mortgage), while industrial shares counted for nothing. In the £2,000–£3,000 range, shares still only accounted for 4 per cent of estates, but in the £100,000–£500,000 they accounted for 50 per cent. Land also became an increasingly important type of property among the highest groups.

These are the only figures which are given about the ownership of industrial property, and from a sociological point of view, the failure to analyse the nature of groups owning and controlling industry represents an unfortunate omission.

What I am appealing for here is the presentation of statistics of the industrial population in a new form. We should spend less time in trying to make classifications according to some highly elusive criterion of status and direct our attention to the description and measurement of those social groups who, because of the distinctive way in which their motivations are bound into the industrial system, do tend to behave, and to be regarded as groups.

Affluence and the British Class Structure

J. H. Goldthorpe and D. Lockwood

Reprinted with permission from 'Affluence and the British Class Structure'
Sociological Review, Vol. 11, No. 2 New Series, July 1963, pp. 133–63

Until relatively recently, most discussion of change in the British class structure has been carried on in terms of (1) shifts in the occupational distribution of the population, (2) the reduction of extreme economic inequalities and (3) the amount and rate of intergenerational social mobility.

(1) Writers such as Cole, for example, have documented the process whereby technological advance and economic growth have greatly increased the importance of clerical, administrative, managerial and professional employments, and it has often been noted how in this way the overall shape of the British class structure underwent significant modification from the mid-nineteenth century onwards. A broad range of 'intermediate' strata emerged to bridge the gap between the 'two nations', perceived alike by Engels and Disraeli, of the manual wage workers and the major property owning groups.

(2) It has been shown how also from the mid-nineteenth century, and again largely in consequence of continuing material progress, the national distribution of income and wealth slowly became somewhat less skewed; and how, eventually, with the aid of developing social welfare services, the problem of mass poverty was overcome. In this way then, it may be said, the span of social stratification in Great Britain was reduced; in other words, the range of differentiation, in basic economic terms at least, became less extended.

(3) It has been frequently pointed out that as a result of the growing diversification of the occupational structure, the educational system, rather than kinship or 'connection', has come to act as the key agency in allocating individuals to their occupational roles; and further, that if for no other reason than the need to utilize talent more efficiently, educational opportunity, in a formal sense at any rate, has been made less unequal. Consequently, the degree of intergenerational social mobility, in

particular, has tended to increase and in this way the stability of social strata has been in some degree diminished.

On these lines, then, a picture has been built up – and it is one which would be generally accepted – of a system of stratification becoming increasingly fine in its gradations and at the same time somewhat less extreme and less rigid.

The chief sociological implications of the argument that the more prosperous of the country's manual wage workers are being assimilated into the middle class would appear to be as follows:

(1) That these workers and their families are acquiring a standard of living, in terms of income and material possessions, which puts them on a level with at least the lower strata within the middle class. Here one refers to certain of the specifically economic aspects of class stratification.

(2) That these same workers are also acquiring new social perspectives and new norms of behaviour which are more characteristic of middle-class than of working-class groups. Here one refers to what may be termed the normative aspect of class.

(3) That being essentially similar to many middle-class persons in their economic position and their normative orientation, these manual workers are being accepted by the former on terms of social equality in both formal and informal social interaction. Here one refers to what may be called the relational aspect of class.

One would have thought it obvious that in any discussion of the thesis of embourgeoisement distinctions on these lines would have been regarded as indispensable. What is necessary, in our view, is that the economic, normative and relational aspects of the matter should each be studied as rigorously as possible, and that any conclusions concerning embourgeoisement should be formed on the basis of research specifically focused on the problem in this way, rather than being merely ad hoc generalizations drawn from a shapeless mass of data.

So far as income levels and the ownership of consumer durables are concerned, comparisons can be made with a fair degree of reliability between the more prosperous section of the working-class and middle-class groups. Such comparisons have in fact shown that in these respects many manual workers and their families have achieved economic parity, at least, with many members of the lower strata within the middle class. However, the point that we would stress here is that incomes and consumption patterns do not constitute the whole of the economic aspect of class stratification. Such factors as security and prospects for advancement are also relevant; and in this connection the evidence at present available indicates that broad differences remain between manual and non-manual employments. In relation to security, for example, the manual worker is still generally more liable than the non-manual worker to be dismissed at short notice; he is also less likely than the latter to enjoy various occupational fringe benefits, such as sickness pay and pension schemes. In relation to advancement, not only are the non-manual worker's chances of upward occupational mobility significantly greater than those of the manual worker, but in any case the former can often expect his income to rise by calculable increments throughout his working life, whereas the income of the latter is likely to rise very little once he reaches adulthood – save, of course, as a result of general improvements in wage rates gained through collective bargaining.

So far as promotion is concerned, the chances of the rank-and-file worker rising above supervisory level are, on all the evidence, clearly declining in modern industry. For those who leave non-selective secondary schools at the age of sixteen for a manual occupation, this kind of work is becoming more than ever before a life sentence. The same factors that are making for greater intergenerational mobility – technological progress, increasing specialization and the growing importance of education in occupational placement – are also operating to reduce the possibility of 'working up from the bottom' in industry, and are thus indirectly re-emphasizing the staff-worker dichotomy.

The treatment of the economic aspect of class in the thesis of embourgeoisement is then unconvincing because it is incomplete. In regard to what we have called the relational aspect of the problem, however, the neglect is more or less total. A variety of studies carried out in different parts of Britain over the last ten years or so have pointed to a marked degree of status segregation in housing, in informal neighbourhood relations, in friendship groups, in the membership of local clubs, societies and organizations and so on. And in all cases the division between manual and non-manual workers and their families has proved to be one of the most salient. It may, of course, be held that very recently and in certain particular contexts – say the New Towns or the suburban areas of newly developed industrial regions – the extent of this segregation has begun to decline. But the point is that so far no evidence of this has been brought forward and, further, that the basic importance of such evidence to the argument concerning embourgeoisement has not, apparently, been recognized.

In fact, apart from the statistical data on incomes and consumption, it is on evidence of changes of an attitudinal and normative character that the thesis of working-class embourgeoisement largely rests. This evidence, which we must now examine, is of two main kinds: (1) evidence provided by enquiries – some of them field studies – into the changing patterns of the family and community life of manual workers; and (2) evidence provided by attitude and opinion surveys of manual workers, in particular those dealing with individuals' own estimations of their class position. We may say at the outset that in our view the arguments put forward on this basis are again generally unsatisfactory ones. The material in question, we believe, has been treated in a far too uncritical manner and does not adequately sustain many of the interpretations that have been placed upon it.

It is our view, then, that if questions of class identification and class norms are to be at all usefully investigated through interview techniques, the pollster's overriding concern with easily obtainable and easily quantifiable results must be abandoned and an effort made to do justice to the complexity of the issues involved. Research has in fact already been carried out which gives a promising lead in this respect. In particular, one would cite here the studies of Popitz in Germany, of Willener in Switzerland and of Bott in England, which, although conducted entirely independently of each other, are essentially comparable both in their approach and their findings. In each case it was in effect recognized that the problem of the 'meaning' of respondents' statements on class and cognate questions could only be overcome by interpreting these statements in relation to respondents' overall perception, or image, of their society. Thus, in all three studies the elucidation of these images became a central focus of interest. It was generally found that as an idea was built up of the way in which a respondent saw his society, and especially its class structure, the more clearly the rationale of his answers to particular questions would appear. One was dealing, in other words, with a Gestalt, not with a series of separate and unconnected responses. A close interrelationship was seen to prevail between the individuals' perception of his society, his general value system and (insofar as these were investigated) the attitudes he took towards more specific social issues. Further- more, it was in each case revealed that among groups of indi- viduals occupying comparable positions within the social hier- archy, a broadly similar 'social imagery' tended to occur, to- gether with a more or less distinctive normative orientation.

In the findings of these studies we have in fact probably the clearest indications that are available of the basic differences in the social perspectives of working- and middle-class persons and, thus, an important guide to the core distinctions which would be relevant to any discussion of their respective life-styles. For this reason it may be useful to set out here – if only in a very simplified way – certain of the major conclusions which were arrived at in all three investigations.

(1) The majority of people have a more or less clearly defined image of their society as being stratified in some way or other; that is to say, they are aware of inequalities in the distribution of wealth, prestige and power.

(2) One 'polar' type of image is that of society as being sharply divided into two contending sections, or classes, differentiated primarily in terms of the possession or non-possession of power (the 'dichotomous' or 'power' model). Contrasting with this is an image of society as comprising an extended hierarchy of relatively 'open' strata differentiated primarily in terms of prestige (the 'hierarchical' or 'prestige' model).

(3) The 'power' model is that most frequently approximated in the images of working-class persons – that is, wage-earning, manual workers. The 'prestige model' on the other hand, is that most frequently approximated in the images of middle-class persons – that is, salaried or independent non-manual workers.

(4) Those images, at least, which approach at all closely to one or other of the two polar types serve as the focus of distinctive complexes of social values and attitudes.

(5) The distinction between these two complexes is chiefly that between two basic themes which may be called the collectivistic and the individualistic (these being understood not as political ideologies, but rather as the raw materials of social consciousness which political ideologies may articulate).

The rationale of this linking of collectivistic and individualistic orientations to 'power' and 'prestige' models respectively is not difficult to appreciate. On the basis of the research in question, and of earlier studies of class values and attitudes, it may be illustrated in the schematic and, we would stress, ideal-typical manner shown on p. 317.

One has here, thus, two sharply contrasting social perspectives, each of which comprises a set of internally consistent beliefs, values and attitudes. Whether the same degree of logic would be found in the case of any particular individual may well be doubted: so too may any exact correspondence between 'collectivism' and manual workers and 'individualism' and non-manual workers, especially in regard to occupational groups on the manual/non-manual frontier. However, in the light of the evidence available, it would seem likely that approximations to one or other of the ideal-type perspectives outlined do regularly occur among social groups with less ambiguous class and status positions.

In conclusion, we may attempt to pull together the threads of our argument by using the discussion of this paper as a basis for the following, necessarily tentative, views, concerning the probable effects so far of working-class affluence on the British class structure.

(1) The change which would seem most probable is one which may be best understood as a process of normative convergence between certain sections of the working and middle classes; the focus of the convergence being on what we have termed 'instrumental collectivism' and 'family centredness'. There is as yet, at least, little basis for the more ambitious thesis of embourgeoisement in the sense of the large-scale assimilation of manual workers and their families to middle-class life-styles and middle-class society in general. In particular, there is no firm evidence either that manual workers are consciously aspiring to middle-class society, or that this is becoming any more open to them.

(2) The groups which appear involved in normative convergence cannot be distinguished in terms of economic factors alone. Certainly, on the working-class side, affluence is not to be regarded as sufficient in itself to bring about the attenuation of solidaristic collectivism. The process of convergence must rather be seen as closely linked to changes in the structure of social relationships in industrial, community and family life, which are in turn related not only to growing prosperity but also to advances in industrial organization and technology, to the process of urban development, to demographic trends, and to the evolution of mass communications and 'mass culture'.

	Working-class perspective	Middle-class perspective
General beliefs	The social order is divided into 'us' and 'them': those who do not have authority and those who do. The division between 'us' and 'them' is virtually fixed, at least from the point of view of one man's life chances. What happens to you depends a lot on luck; otherwise you have to learn to put up with things.	The social order is a hierarchy of differentially rewarded positions: a ladder containing many rungs. It is possible for individuals to move from one level of the hierarchy to another. Those who have ability and initiative can overcome obstacles and create their own opportunities. Where a man ends up depends on what he makes of himself.
General values	'We' ought to stick together and get what we can as a group. You may as well enjoy yourself while you can instead of trying to make yourself 'a cut above the rest'.	Every man ought to make the most of his own capabilities and be responsible for his own welfare. You cannot expect to get anywhere in the world if you squander your time and money. 'Getting on' means making sacrifices.
Attitudes on more specific issues	*(on the best job for a son)* 'A trade in his hands'. 'A good steady job'.	'As good a start as you can give him'. 'A job that leads somewhere'.
	(towards people needing social assistance) 'They have been unlucky'. 'They never had a chance'. 'It could happen to any of us'.	'Many of them had the same opportunities as others who have managed well enough'. 'They are a burden on those who are trying to help themselves'.
	(on Trade Unions) 'Trade unions are the only means workers have of protecting themselves and of improving their standard of living'.	'Trade unions have too much power in the country'. 'The unions put the interests of a section before the interests of the nation as a whole'.

(3) Even among the 'new' working-class groups in which instrumental collectivism and family centredness are manifested, status goals seem much less in evidence than economic goals: in other words, the privatized worker would appear far more typical than the socially aspiring worker. The conditions under which status aspirations are generated may be regarded as still more special than those which are conducive to a more individualistic outlook. Thus, we return to the point that normative convergence has to be understood as implying as yet only a rather limited modification of the class frontier.

(4) Finally, it is consistent with the above views to believe further that the political consequences of working-class influence are so far, at least, indeterminate.

Class Consciousness among Clerical Workers
D. T. H. Weir

This extract has been specially prepared for this volume and has not previously been published in this form

The position of intermediate groups such as the clerks, draughtsmen and white-collar technicians in the class structure has been a topic of recurring concern for sociologists. Some, like C. Wright Mills, have argued that changes in the division of labour would inevitably throw the white-collar workers into the arms of the working class.

Mills argued that differentials of income between manual and non-manual workers have tended to narrow and that rationalization has lowered the levels of skill required for office work. Thus, offices have become more like factories. Moreover, the spread of education to the manual working class has tended to erode the white-collar workers' special claim to status.

While in the short term a 'status panic' might ensue in which white-collar workers would fight to protect their residual privileges, in the long run the result would be a proletarianization of office work.

Lockwood's analysis is rooted in a similar appreciation of the impact of mechanization and rationalization on the clerical work situation. But he is more cautious than Mills about the inevitability of proletarianization, because of the absence of a national labour market for clerical work.

The post-war period has seen an expansion in white-collar trade unionism and an apparent increase in union militancy among these occupational groups who were previously regarded as too respectable to become involved in collective action. It has been argued that this too is a consequence of changes in the work situation which have induced a collectivization of working conditions. In its turn, this has provoked a determination to seek the redress of grievance about pay, security and conditions, in collective action, by means such as trade unionism, which have been conventionally regarded as characteristic of organizations representing the interests of manual workers.

This analysis has not been uncriticized however. Recently, Bain in particular has challenged the belief that white-collar unionism is an inevitable consequence of changes in the white-collar work situation.

The well-known study of affluent manual workers conducted in Luton by Lockwood, Goldthorpe, Bechhofer and Platt, has cast doubt on the theory of the embourgeoisement of the working class. In their report, the authors cautiously suggest that 'it is important that the thesis of the white-collar worker becoming "proletarian" should be regarded as critically as that of the manual worker becoming middle class'.

In this debate a good deal of attention has been paid to the social perspectives of the various groups involved. Goldthorpe and Lockwood have identified a 'working-class' and a 'middle-class' perspective. The white-collar groups sit uneasily between these two major stereotypical perspectives. It is clearly premature to attempt to unambiguously identify the class situation of such groups as clerical workers as 'really' middle class or 'really' working class. But the examination of the social perspective of clerical workers is an important part of the task of understanding their position of the class structure as a whole.

The analysis which follows is based on a study of white-collar workers undertaken in the Hull area between 1963 and 1968. In all, over 1,400 white-collar workers were interviewed. But the analysis of this paper is based on a group of 98 married male clerks aged between 22 and 49, and all employed in large private sector firms. All those interviewed held 'staff' status and had relatively secure jobs but did not have direct management responsibility.

Although the interviews covered the most important aspects of the work situation, we only refer briefly here to some of the most significant findings, as our chief concern is with the perspectives on the class system held by these clerical workers. But there are some unusual divergencies from the stereotypical views described above.

(1) The level of identification and involvement with the employing organization was rather lower than had been anticipated.

(2) The clerks did not seem to be especially disposed to rate their own firm any better than others.

(3) The clerks in private industry were less confident than were those in the public sector organizations of obtaining promotion to management level.

(4) Under a third of the sample identified positively with management.

(5) The promotion structure of the firms tended to be regarded in a somewhat cynical and opportunistic way with luck and chance seen as important elements.

(6) Attitudes to unions were not uniformly negative but were tempered by the belief that unions were unlikely to be successful in *practical* terms in obtaining better salaries and working conditions than could be got from individual negotiation.

His recognition of points of differentiation and his unwillingness to identify strongly with the focal concerns of either management or workers are indications not of an irrational drive to maximize the meaningless distinctions of status, but of a rational recognition of his objective position in the organization, which is superior to that of the routine manual workers, but inferior to that of the manager. The clerk's perception of the distinctiveness of his position is underlined by his unwillingness to consider undertaking tasks for which his training and experience have not equipped him. This unwillingness is associated with an attitude towards clerical work that seems rather akin to that of the stereotypical 'craftsman', whose pride in the capacity to undertake the tasks of the job constituted a major source of job satisfaction. This 'craftsmanlike' concern is also associated with a characteristic perception of the supervisory role.

Instead of seeing the supervisor as a 'junior manager' or as an expert in human relations, the clerk tends to regard the good supervisor as an experienced and competent 'senior man' whose capacity to exercise control over the work group depends on his

superior performance, derived from long experience of the tasks
of the job.

These facets of the clerical worker's attitude towards his job
and to inter-personal relations at the workplace are likely to be
associated with his social perspectives in general and in particular with his perceptions of the class structure as a whole and
of barriers to individual and collective mobility, as well as to his
identification with fellow workers on the basis of class interest.

Fundamental to the view of class which sees society in hierarchical terms is the belief in the possibility of changing one's class
position by one's own efforts. This not merely represents an individual achievement, but also reflects the openness of the opportunity
structure, so that upward mobility becomes the norm.

We would predict, then, that to the extent that the white-
collar worker either sees himself as being a member, or identifies
in an anticipatory way with the norms and values of the middle
class, he will tend to perceive the social structure in an 'open'
way, even if he sees it as constituting a hierarchical structure.

Accordingly, having discussed with respondents their basic
ideas and perceptions of the social structure as a whole, we asked,
'Is it possible to change from one class to another – how easy or
difficult is it?' Only 16 per cent of the clerks were prepared to say
that it *was* possible without any qualification whatever, and a
further 5 per cent thought that while movement between some
classes was possible it was impossible to move into the upper
class. The largest single group adopted a position of cautious
optimism, saying that it was, in principle, possible, but with
some reservations. An almost equally large group adopted the
corresponding posture of 'cautious pessimism' and implied that,
on balance, it was rather difficult. The sample was thus fairly
evenly divided between those who thought mobility to be possible
and those who did not. It thus seems difficult to see in these
answers a strong perception of the class system as a relatively
open one in general.

But it may be objected that the mere statement of a belief about
the possibility of someone, somewhere, changing class is altogether *too* general and this question was therefore followed by a
more precise one which asked, 'Do many people change from one
class to another?' The answers to this question had even more
pessimistic implications, for 62 per cent reported that 'few or
none did *in fact* change class'. It seems that although there is
some agreement that mobility is, in principle, possible, the

Table 1. Perceptions of Class Barriers

Percentage replying to the question 'Is it possible to change from one class to another?'

	Clerks in Private Firms	
Yes	16	
Qualified Yes*	36	
Yes, but not into the upper class	5	
All positive answers		57
Qualified No†	31	
No	12	
All negative answers		43
	100	100

* e.g. 'It used to be impossible, but now it is getting easier', 'it is fairly easy', 'you have to change your friends', 'outwardly you can change, but inwardly you don't', 'you may not be accepted'.

† e.g. 'It is fairly difficult', 'it is only possible for your children; it takes more than one generation', 'it is easier to go down than up', 'it used to be possible, now it is getting more difficult.'

Table 2. Perceptions of Barriers to Inter-Class Mobility

Percentage replying to the question 'Do many people change from one class to another?'

	Clerks in Private Firms	
A lot do	27	
It can be done, it depends	10	
All positive		37
A lot try, a few make it	6	
Very few do	50	
None do	6	
All negative		62
Don't know	2	
	101	99

chances of its occurrence are not given much weight in realistic terms.

It may be objected again that this is quite compatible with the individualistic ethic. To one who is convinced of his own ability and fitness to move up the class structure, the chances and opportunities available to *others* may be irrelevant. So the issue was narrowed down once more, to be crystallized in the direct question, 'What chance would you say you had of changing to the class immediately above you?' Although this question is more particularized it is also more limited, for the respondent is not asked to refer to the chances of mobility within the system as a whole. Instead of having to evaluate the openness of the structure with reference to the chances of attaining the very top, he needs to consider only moves across one boundary, the next one above him. In the event, the degree of optimism was even weaker than those which related to the more general situation, and 57 per cent gave rather negative answers. Only 4 per cent, moreover, claimed that they 'didn't want to' and this is consistent with replies to other questions which indicated a fairly universal desire to obtain supervisory positions and move upwards in the hierarchy.

Table 3. Perception of Barriers to Inter-Class Mobility for the Individual

Percentage replying to the question 'What chance would you say you had of changing to the class immediately above you?'

	Clerks in Private Firms	
Very good	9	
Fairly good	13	
All positive		22
Fifty-fifty	15	
Not much chance	33	
None at all	24	
All negative		57
Not going to try	4	
Don't want to		
Don't know	4	
	102	79

The replies to these three questions taken together indicate a pattern that seems incompatible with the perception of the class structure as 'an open one, affording opportunities to all who possess the appropriate motivation to move upwards'. While there is some scepticism about the openness of the structure in general terms, *the scepticism hardens the nearer home the question is pressed*. While somebody *may* get to the top the odds are quite high that the individual himself is rather pessimistic about his own chances.

However, the motivation to move upwards (to judge from the answers to other questions about the desirability of promotion), is nonetheless fairly widespread. So it is difficult, though not impossible, to see in this pattern of responses much evidence of one particular type of deviation from the middle-class stereotype 'the lower middle-class "ritualist" . . . who has drawn in his horizons and has in effect rejected the obligation to continue to strive for material success', as Goldthorpe and Lockwood put it.

In any case, given our interpretation of the clerical worker's involvement in his organization as being rather low on normative elements, it is arguable that 'continuing to strive for material success' is not necessarily construed by the typical clerk as a moral obligation for him particularly, *any more than it is for anybody else in a society in which achievement tends to be evaluated in material terms.* Thus, we need not accept that clerks, in perceiving the class structure in this kind of way, are attempting to consciously register a rejection of the mandates of some moral imperative which is not equally pressing on members of other social groups. For, just as in the case of the social perspectives generated by the white-collar worker's participation in the industrial system, we may question whether these beliefs add up to a comprehensive 'anti-perspective' in which the class system is perceived as lacking legitimacy.

Moreover, the perceived lack of openness in the structure of opportunities does not seem to deprive the class system of all legitimacy because a large majority of respondents claimed that it would not be possible to conceive of a classless society, while 21 per cent of respondents said there didn't have to be classes. It is difficult to see here a widespread expectation, or indeed any positive enthusiasm for a classless society. But neither is this kind of response indicative of an attitude which rejects class and prefers not to talk about it. The clerk may fall

Table 4. Perception of the Inevitability of Class

Percentage replying to the question 'Do you think there have to be classes?'

	Clerks in Private Industry
Yes	72
Qualified Yes	7
Qualified No	10
No	11
	100

some way short of a wholesale embracing of the class structure and the principles underlying it, but he accepts it as a *fact* of his everyday life and does not see any imminent prospect of classlessness as being a possibility worth entertaining.

Although class is perceived as having a good deal of mileage left in it, this is not to imply that no alterations are possible, for when asked whether changes were expected and if so, what form they would take, only a quarter said categorically that there would be 'no change'. The predominant expectation was one which, without much distortion, could be labelled 'convergence'.

21 per cent thought that classes tend to become more alike, and a further 9 per cent saw the convergence as coming about because of the rise of the working class. Only 2 per cent thought that there would be an increase in individual mobility between classes. Another 25 per cent thought that there would be changes but did not specify in what direction these might operate or what form they might take.

Some respondents, indeed, elaborated on the mechanisms and processes by which change in the class structure may be expected to occur. Of those who made more explicit comments, the largest single group referred to changes in earning and income levels. The others referred to developments in industry, especially caused by an increase in automation, or to changes in the educational system. Few mentioned factors which affected individuals as such, rather than as members of groups, and spoke in terms of increased opportunities for individuals to 'get on' or said things like 'change comes about through an individual's personal efforts'.

Here is, however, a pointer to the underlying theme which these answers reveal. So far from depicting a view of the class structure merely as a *milieu* for the operation of the processes of individual mobility and career advance, there is a clear perception of classes as collectivities – as units with an existence and a membership which may be fluctuating but nonetheless possesses certain common characteristics. 'Mobility' is perceived *intrinsically* as a collective rather than an individual matter.

Their perspective is not unambiguously 'radical' by any means because they see the inequalities represented by the class structure as inevitable *in fact*, without necessarily making judgements on the moral value of class stratification as a matter of principle. The consonance between this perspective on the class structure generally and the attitudes and perceptions which emerge from the work-place interviews does not need labouring. It is pragmatic, cautious, and conditional, but one which over all nonetheless ascribes legitimacy to the system as it is perceived as being, rather than with reference to an idealization of what it might be expected or desired to be.

Class is very clearly perceived as an important feature of contemporary society and of their own situation. If this is the case, what sense would there be in answering in terms of the quite hypothetical possibility that some other kind of society could exist in which class was absent? At this point the clerk's distaste for high theory and the consideration of alternative futures also became relevant. In other words, in saying 'Yes, there have to be classes', the clerk is not making a conscious choice between a 'right wing' and a 'left wing' view of society; he is reporting on what *is* there, and what it looks like. These affirmations about the factual order of society need not necessarily be related to any firm belief in the *correctness* of such institutions in terms of moral values. The clerks' 'class consciousness' is related to a cognitive and rational understanding of how Western society works, rather than being based on a set of values which underpins and guarantees that kind of ordering of society in a moral sense.

When we were discussing the future and how things might change, we found that the sample was fairly equally divided between three groups. A third of respondents felt that there would be no, or very limited, changes, another third thought there would be changes, while the remainder tended to crystallize this expectation of change in the direction of a decline in class, or a convergence between classes. In other words, while the long-term implication of 'classlessness' contained in the question, 'do there *have* to be classes?' was rejected as rather meaningless, the short term changes could be visualized and conceptualized with the pragmatic and realistic one-step-at-a-time philosophy (or anti-philosophy) of these respondents. That the envisaged changes were *class* rather than *status* changes was implied by the tendency to relate the changes that were envisaged, to large-scale *collective* trends, rather than to changes in the personal situations of particular *individuals*.

However, although changes in *earnings* and income levels are given some prominence by our respondents, this does not indicate that their consciousness is of the 'pecuniary' type identified by Lockwood, as likely to be held by lower-grade clerical workers. Wealth, income, and total earnings are certainly significant, but these variables are almost always used as *descriptive* terms to characterize the attributes of groups who are identified in terms of occupation, style of life, patterns of inter-action and so on. We believe that there is sufficient evidence of a self identification in class terms, of perception of barriers to mobility of a *class* type, and of an underlying philosophical position supporting an analysis of social institutions in *class* terms, to justify our conclusions that this is considerably more than a merely pecuniary consciousness.

In conclusion, then, we would argue that the social perspectives of clerical workers do not conform directly to the 'middle-class' or to the 'working-class' stereotypes.

It is not clear that the view of society held by white-collar workers is any more 'hierarchical' than that held by members of the working class. In particular, if the implication of 'hier-archical' is that only *individual* mobility is possible between the various stages or grades of the hierarchy, this seems question-able. The chances of upward mobility for any individual are, in fact, regarded as rather small, although lip service may still be paid to a rhetoric of individual achievement and mobility motivation which is regarded as being 'appropriate'.

Several elements of the social perspective of the clerical workers may be summarized according to the typology sug-gested by Landecker:

(1) *Class-interest-consciousness:* these respondents conceive of classes in terms of the different interests of different groups. They

see themselves as possessing a distinctive pattern of interests.

(2) *Class-barrier-consciousness:* these distinctive interests are sufficient to mark them off from the other groups. The existence of barriers – discontinuities which modify and constrain the life and career chances of people like themselves on a collective basis – is clearly recognized, in both an upward and a downward direction.

(3) *Class-conflict-consciousness:* these barriers are perceived as impermeable to individual action, except on a *random* basis. They can only be broken down therefore by collective action which may bring their group into conflict with other groups whose interests in the situation are different.

(4) *Class ideology:* the relation of these interests to the possibility of action on a class basis by institutions representing class interests is restricted by a consciousness which is pragmatic, to some extent defensive and *conditional* on the institutions obtaining recognition and thus being able to act on their behalf. They accord legitimacy to trade unions and similar institutions on the basis of their practical utility, rather than on a basis of general 'values' of an individualist or collective kind.

These specific features of the white-collar social perspective allow us to modify the paradigm of 'middle-class' values and attitudes proposed by Goldthorpe. The perception of the social order as 'hierarchical' does not have unambiguous implications in terms of individual mobility which are based on the moral obligation to accept responsibility for one's own welfare and to strive to 'get ahead'. The wants and expectations of the white-collar worker are typically of a rather short-term nature, and are not structured necessarily around the notion of *career advance* because the employee's 'expectations' are not 'unlimited' nor are his wants 'capable of continuous enlargement'. Thus the 'deferred gratification' pattern, so central to the middle-class paradigm, is not especially appropriate to the situation of the white-collar worker. But we see no reason for regarding this lack of the expected orientation towards the future to be associated with 'ritualism' of the kind described by Merton. These white-collar respondents had not 'drawn in their horizons and rejected the obligation to continue to strive for material success'. For this 'obligation' does not exist for the clerk any more or any more *typically* than for other workers except as an inescapable part of

contemporary life in industrial society. The clerk's horizons are
adapted to the expectations of success he can realistically hold.
The clerk's 'social perspectives' thus have a good deal of internal
coherence and are, moreover, well adapted to the class situation in
which he is located.

Sponsored and Contest Mobility

R. H. Turner

Reprinted with permission from 'Modes of Social Ascent Through Education: Sponsored and Contest Mobility and the School System', *American
Sociological Review*, Vol. XXV, 1960, No. 5, pp. 855–67

The object of this paper is to suggest a framework for relating
certain differences between American and English systems of
education to the prevailing norms of upward mobility in each
country. Others have noted the tendency for educational systems
to support prevailing schemes of stratification, but this statement
will dwell specifically on the manner in which the *accepted mode
of upward mobility* shapes the school system directly and indirectly through its effects on the values that implement social
control. The task will be carried out by describing two ideal-
typical normative patterns of upward mobility and suggesting
their logical ramifications in the general character of stratification
and social control. In addition to showing relationships among a
number of differences between American and English schooling,
the ideal-types have broader implications than those developed in
this paper. First, they suggest a major dimension of stratification,
which might profitably be incorporated into a variety of studies
on social class. Second, they can be readily applied in further
comparisons, between countries other than the United States
and England.

The Nature of Organizing Norms

Many investigators have concerned themselves with rates of
upward mobility in specific countries or internationally, and
with the manner in which school systems facilitate or impede
such mobility. Preoccupation with *extent* of mobility has pre-

cluded equal attention to the predominant *mode* of mobility in each country. The central assumption underlying this paper is that within a formally open class system providing mass education the organizing folk norm that defines the accepted mode of upward mobility is a crucial factor in shaping the school system, and may be even more crucial than is the extent of upward mobility. In England and the United States there appear to be different organizing folk norms, which may be labelled *sponsored mobility* and *contest mobility* respectively. *Contest* mobility is a system in which elite status is the prize in an open contest and is taken by the aspirants' own efforts. While the 'contest' is governed by some rules of fair play, the contestants have wide latitude in the strategies they may employ. Since the 'prize' of successful upward mobility is not in the hands of the established elite to give out, the latter are not in a position to determine who shall attain it and who shall not. Under *sponsored* mobility, elite recruits are chosen by the established elite or their agents, and elite status is *given* on the basis of some criterion of supposed merit and cannot be *taken* by any amount of effort or strategy. Upward mobility is like entry into a private club, where each candidate must be 'sponsored' by one or more of the members. Ultimately, the members grant or deny upward mobility on the basis of whether they judge the candidate to have the qualities that they wish to see in fellow members.

Contest mobility is like a sporting event in which many compete for a few recognized prizes. The contest is judged to be fair only if all the players compete on an equal footing. Victory must be won solely by one's own efforts. The most satisfactory outcome is not necessarily a victory of the most able, but of the most deserving.

Sponsored mobility, on the other hand, rejects the pattern of the contest and substitutes a controlled selection process. In this process the elite or their agents, who are best qualified to judge merit, *call* those individuals to elite status who have the appropriate qualities. Individuals do not win or seize elite status, but mobility is rather a process of sponsored induction into the elite following selection.

The governing objective of contest mobility is to give elite status to those who earn it, while the goal of sponsored mobility is to make the best use of the talents in society by sorting each person into his proper niche. In different societies the conditions of competitive struggle may reward quite different attributes, and sponsored mobility may select on the basis of such diverse qualities as intelligence or visionary capability, but the difference in principle remains the same.

Under the contest system, society at large establishes and interprets the criteria of elite status. If one wishes to have his high status recognized he must display certain credentials that identify his class to those about him. The credentials must be highly visible and require no special skill for their assessment, since credentials are presented to the masses. Material possession and mass popularity are perfect credentials in this respect, and any special skill that produces a tangible product easily assessed by the untrained will do. The nature of sponsored mobility precludes this type of operation but assigns to credentials instead the function of identifying the elite to one another. Accordingly, the ideal credentials are special skills requiring the trained discrimination of the elite for their recognition. Intellectual, literary, or artistic excellences, which can only be appraised by those trained to appreciate them, are perfect credentials in this respect. Concentration on such skills lessens the likelihood that an interloper will succeed in claiming the right to elite membership on grounds of the popular evaluation of his competence.

Contest mobility tends to delay the final award as long as practicable, to permit a fair race; sponsored mobility tends to place the selection point as early in life as practicable, to insure control over selection and training.

A system of sponsored mobility develops most readily in a society with but a single elite or with a recognized elite hierarchy. When multiple elites compete among themselves, the mobility process tends to take the contest pattern, since no group is able to command control of recruitment. Sponsored mobility further depends upon a societal structure fostering monopoly of elite credentials. Lack of such monopoly undercuts sponsorship and control of the recruitment process. Monopoly of elite credentials is in turn typically a product of a society with a well-entrenched traditional aristocracy, employing such intrinsically monopolizable credentials as family line and bestowable title, or of a society organized along large-scale bureaucratic lines, permitting centralized control of movement up the hierarchy of success.

English society has been described as the juxtaposition of two systems of stratification, the urban-industrial class system and the surviving aristocratic system. While the sponsored-mobility pattern reflects the logic of the latter, our impression is that it pervades popular thinking rather than merely coexisting with the logic of industrial stratification. Students of cultural change note that patterns imported into an established culture tend to be re-shaped into coherence with the established culture as they are assimilated. Thus, it may be that the changes in stratification attendant upon industrialization have led to many alterations in the rates, the specific means, and the rules of mobility, but that these changes have taken place within the unchallenged organizing norm of sponsored mobility.

The most obvious application of the distinction between sponsored and contest mobility norms is to afford a partial explanation for the different policies of student selection in the English and American secondary schools. Although American high-school students take different courses of study and some-times even attend specialized high schools, a major preoccupa-tion has been to avoid any sharp social separation between the superior and inferior students and to keep the channels of move-ment between courses of study as open as possible. Even recent criticisms of the way in which superior students may be thereby held back in their development usually are qualified by insistence that these students must not, however, be withdrawn from the mainstream of student life. Any such segregation offends the sense of fairness implicit in the contest norm and also arouses the fear that the elite and future elite will lose their sense of fellow-feeling with the masses. Perhaps the most important point, how-ever, is that schooling is presented as an opportunity, and the principal burden of making use of the opportunity depends on the student's own initiative and enterprise.

The English system has undergone a succession of liberalizing changes during this century, but all of them have remained within the pattern of attempting early in the educational pro-gramme to sort out the promising from the unpromising, so that the former may be segregated and given a special form of training to fit them for higher standing in their adult years. Under the Education Act of 1944, a minority of students have been selected each year by means of a battery of examinations popularly known as 'eleven-plus', supplemented to varying degrees by grade-school record and personal interview impressions, for admission to grammar schools. The remaining students attend secondary modern or technical schools, in which the opportunities to pre-pare for college or train for the better occupations are minimal. The grammar schools supply what, by comparative standards, is a high quality of college preparatory education. Such a scheme embodies well the logic of sponsorship, with early selection of those destined for middle-class and better occupations, and specialized training to suit each group for the class in which they are destined to hold membership. The plan facilitates considerable mobility, and recent research reveals surprisingly little bias against the child from a manual-labouring family in the selection for grammar school, when related to measured intelligence. It is altogether possible that adequate comparative research would show a closer correlation of school success with measured intelligence and a lesser correlation between school success and family background in England than in the United States. While selection of superior students for mobility opportunity is probably more efficient under such a system, the obstacles to a person not so selected 'making the grade' on the basis of his own initiative or enterprise are probably correspondingly greater.

In the foregoing statement, two ideal-typical organizing norms concerning the manner in which mobility should properly take place have been outlined. On the one hand, mobility may be viewed as most appropriately a *contest* in which many contestants strive, by whatever combinations of strategy, enterprise, perseverance, and ability they can marshal, restricted only by a minimum set of rules defining fair play and minimizing special advantage to those who get ahead early in the game, to take possession of a limited number of prizes. On the other hand, it may be thought best that the upwardly mobile person be *sponsored*, like one who joins a private club upon invitation of the membership, selected because the club members feel that he has qualities desirable in a club member, and then subjected to careful training and initiation into the guiding ethic and lore of the club before being accorded full membership.

Upward mobility actually takes place to a considerable degree by both the contest pattern and the sponsorship pattern in every society. But it has been suggested that in England the sponsorship norm is ascendant and has been so for a century or more, and that in the United States the contest norm has been ascendant for a comparable period. A norm is ascendant in the sense that there is a constant 'strain' to bring the relevant features of the class system, the pattern of social control, and the educational system into consistency with the norm, and that patterns consistent with the ascendant norm seem more 'natural' and 'right' to the articulate segments of the population.

Typologies of Middle-Class Mobility
Geoff Payne

Reprinted with permission from *Sociology*, Vol. 7, No. 3, September 1973

Our ideas about the mobility process are drawn from a number of studies but here I wish to deal with three of the most important: the work of Merton on locals and cosmopolitans, the work of Mrs. Stacey on traditionalists and non-traditionalists, and Watson on burgesses and spiralists. Each of these widely-accepted dichotomous typologies has been treated as expressing established laws of social behaviour, and together they have formed the basis and inspiration for several recent works. But very little has been done to demonstrate exactly what are the intrinsic strengths of these similar dichotomous typologies which explain their acceptance as sociological common-places.

For example, Bell enthusiastically adopts Watson's concepts as

the most important advance in stratification theory since Lockwood's concept of work situation.

Although he later suggests three new sub-types of spiralist (depending on expectations of future mobility and whether they work for bureaucratic organizations) there is no discussion of the basic processes involved, and the sub-types are not used in the rest of the book to explain other data. But more important, Bell confuses three sets of terminology: spiralist/burgess, cosmopolitan/local, and non-local/local. For instance he says on page 47 that his respondents 'can be spiralists and burgesses, or in Merton's (1957) terminology cosmopolitans or locals', a confusion he repeats on pages 6 and 19. Subsequently in 'Community Studies', he and Newby compound the error by equating Stacey and Merton in at least two places (a mistake first made by Frankenberg).

More recently Edgell has been equally uncritical, quoting Bell's high regard for Watson's advance in stratification theory, defining spiralism, and then using it with no further discussion.

While he is concerned to relate spiralism to family life, so extending the idea of spiralism by looking at its consequences, he nowhere considers whether the spiralist/burgess dichotomy is the most useful typology in the first place.

Even Pahl, who has been the major contributor in recent studies of mobility, has added to the confusion in an article which first appeared in 1966 and has since been reprinted. Indeed, in much of his work, there seem to be two implicit assumptions; not only are spiralists real people (not just types) but their behaviour in local milieux can be typified as clearly as their career behaviour. However, this typification is not a simple one. Around London, the spiralists from outside the South East 'find these outer metropolitan estates convenient transit camps' and therefore live insulated from their locality. But in a Hertfordshire New Town, while both husbands and wives of the mobile 'new radical middle class' favour part-time voluntary or paid work for the wife, and meetings and entertaining are popular activities, some other middle-class newcomers are isolated and lonely, and still others (more Conservative) have already migrated to nearby villages. In the villages the spiralists are 'joiners' – 'the village is defined in terms of the quality of its social life'; the spiralists 'have defined for themselves a village-in-the-mind'.

So there are a number of different typical spiralist adaptations to local social milieux which are not only unexplained by the type 'spiralist', but which must also raise the question of how far spiralism can be used to refer to anything more than specifically *career* behaviour. Certainly, when Pahl has to explain aspects of behaviour in local milieux by saying that some spiralists are localistic cosmopolitans, the time has come to reconsider the basic terms of the typologies.

This is not to say that typologies in general have no uses in sociology. But as Pahl has argued in 'Managers and Their Wives', knowledge about patterns can easily become a substitute for understanding the processes which give rise to those patterns. Unfortunately he does not go on from there to reconsider the basic mobility typologies in the light of his understanding of the dynamics of managerial careers and local behaviour. It is in an attempt to shift the focus from the currently-used (and abused) typologies to these underlying processes, that this paper considers the work of Merton, Stacey and Watson. In each case, the comments below seek to emphasize certain aspects which have been since overlooked, thereby showing that none of the studies should be treated uncritically as suitable bases for generalization.

Locals and Cosmopolitans

Merton was concerned with 'influentials', a term which refers specifically to a mode of inter-personal communications behaviour and has nothing to do with power, status, or structure. His data were collected from the American Small Town culture tradition as it existed 30 years ago. The sample was very small, and Merton himself makes few claims about his data. In two footnotes he reminds the reader

> Although figures summarizing our case study are cited from time to time, these are merely heuristic, not demonstrative in character. They serve to indicate the sources of interpretive hypotheses which await detailed, systematic enquiry.

Merton himself is quite clear that his is only a pilot-study, but it is a pilot-study which has in fact not led to the detailed, systematic enquiry which is needed.

Therefore the wide-spread acceptance of Merton's concepts is not based on any rigorous empirical groundings. This is not to argue that his concepts are totally wrong: even without solid research behind them or flowing from them for that matter, it could be the case that as ideal-typical constructs, they serve a useful function in conceptual mapping for other sociologists. But in fact Merton's dichotomy has limitations at this level as well, as a brief consideration of his work will show.

The two types can best be described by the ways in which they differ. For instance the cosmopolitan discussed international affairs (that is to say the War) at an international level, while the local talked about the repercussions international affairs would have on the local community. The local was more likely to be interested in Rovere people, to be involved in local politics, and to read the local newspaper. The cosmopolitan was more concerned with friends at a distance, with social services rather than politics, and was more likely to subscribe to several national periodicals. There is considerable variation within types, but a contrast between the ideal-typical cosmopolitan and local shows that the former is younger, significantly more educated, and is a 'newcomer' who has lived in a number of communities, unlike the local influential.

Here he is relying too heavily on his 'heuristic' figures. What he misses is that the career patterns of the two groups are different, and that the cosmopolitan has a wider and more varied life experience outside the town and fits less well into the community because of his recent arrival, as Merton's own data show. It can be argued that because of more extensive ties (of kinship and friendship) outside of the community, he is *held back* from joining: because he is alien, he is *pushed back* by the community.

If Merton's data are treated from this point of view, different patterns of previous experience are seen to explain modes of influence, not *vice versa*. In the same way, differences in associational membership are explained not by community orientation, but by the previous experience. It follows that immigrants need not necessarily be cosmopolitans, as this depends on the range of their life experience and the extent to which they can integrate into the community.

The popularity of the local/cosmopolitan typology does not lie in its empirical strength, nor in its heuristic utility. Indeed it could be argued that it does not lie in Merton's original work at all. Rather it arises out of Gouldner's manipulation of the concepts. Gouldner applied the local/cosmopolitan dichotomy to academics in a small liberal arts college, and not surprisingly, the sociological profession was quick to appreciate its narcissistic potential. Among others, Glaser and Kornhauser explained the position of the highly-educated professional in the bureaucracy, in terms of these orientations. But while this usage may be valid to describe a narrow category of professionals and their occupational values, this is not the same as a blanket application to the rest of the middle class and their *community* behaviour. With a slight modification of terminology, it is this blanket usage which has been accepted into current urban sociology.

Traditionalists and Non-Traditionalists

One of the principal sources of ideas about mobility and orientation to local social milieux in Britain is Margaret Stacey's study of Banbury, 'Tradition and Change'. Like Rovere, Banbury twenty years ago was a small town isolated in a rural area, and not typical of the operation of local milieux generally. Few areas suffer such abrupt and massive invasions by outsiders, and few are so isolated and established in the first place. It might be reasonable to generalize from Banbury to other settlements which are experiencing similar influxes such as the development of new towns around cores of older villages. But it would be less plausible to generalize from Banbury to all new estates, and less so to individual families moving house. In these cases, which are far more common social phenomena, the ratio of newcomer to established resident is less likely to be disturbed, and the balance remains much more heavily weighted towards the established residents.

Nevertheless it might be argued that 'Tradition and Change' does provide a suitable theoretical starting point for a general typology. Unfortunately, this is not so, because there has been a confusion of three separate concepts; previous life experience (immigrant and non-immigrant), value orientation (traditionalist or non-traditionalist), and social class.

Stacey rejects actor-based estimates of what a 'Banburian' is, because 'estimates depend on the individual, upon his age, his occupation, his politics, his attitude to life, and his readiness to conform to and accept the ways of the town' and apparently, despite the later dichotomous picture, no clear pattern was perceptible. Instead four categories were used, depending on place of birth and residence to the age of 7. These migration categories are constructed in a way which ignores the fact that social relationships accumulate over life times.

In dealing with the second component of the typology, the traditionalist/non-traditionalist concept, it is easier to quote Stacey:

traditionalists: those who are part of the traditional social structure and who live by the traditional values and customs of old Banbury. There are others, the non-traditionalists who do not belong to the traditional social structure and do not accept its values and customs; they do not share any common social system or system of values and customs for they are composed of many different and sometimes opposed groups; they include those who have come in with quite other systems of values and customs and those who are developing new ways to meet the changed circumstances of their life and work.

Thus the non-traditionalists appear to include those who refuse to accept the local society and those who *do* accept it, and are attempting to integrate into it or compromise with it: two very different things. Stacey does discuss

> people who have come into the town from similar social backgrounds to follow traditional occupations, or who have accepted enough of Banbury's traditions to fit into it or to make their life in the locality with Banbury as their principal frame of reference. They, as much as the Banbury-born traditionalists, rely on the local papers as essential sources of information about the fortunes and misfortunes of local people and families or of the clubs and societies.

But is this further category as traditional as other Banburians, lacking informal gossip networks and local kinship networks, particularly as

> traditional society is made up of a network of face-to-face groups based on family, neighbours, occupations, associations, and status?

Even if the traditionalist/non-traditionalist and Banburian/immigrant definitions can be clarified, their application leads to a complex typology, in which there are 24 possible cells if we include 3 social classes. While some of these combinations are less common than others, all are logically possible. Stacey concentrates on examples for 11 of the 24 types, principally non-migrants who are traditionalists, and immigrants who are non-traditionalists. She says at one point 'Perhaps the majority of non-traditionalists are immigrants', in other words, at best a large minority of non-traditionalists are *not* immigrants, but throughout 'Tradition and Change' the respondents are discussed as if the traditionalist/immigrant attributes can be coalesced into a dichotomy for each social class. On Stacey's own evidence, this is not true at an empirical level, and there is certainly no heuristic value in such a confusion. As she has since pointed out, her perspective at the time was to extend the idea of traditional and non-traditional *systems* to traditional and non-traditional *individuals*. It is not surprising that no clear picture emerges from the data, beyond a basic polarization.

It is impossible to tell how far this class polarization would continue to be more important than migration and orientation, had these last two been kept separate in the analytical framework. Integration into a local social milieu is not just a matter of attitude and length of residence, as both can vary independently. Of course we have here concerned ourselves with only one aspect of the Banbury study, not with the study as a whole. But for our narrow purpose, it has neither the empirical groundings nor the analytical framework on which to build and support the generalizations about middle-class mobility which have been hung upon it.

Burgesses and Spiralists

Our third major source of ideas is Watson's work which is explicitly concerned with the generation of theories. In the case of his concepts of 'burgess' and 'spiralist', there is little to be said about the methodology as he himself says very little. Once again the original study was carried out around 1950; it concerned a small coal-mining community on the East Coast of Scotland.

In contrast to Merton and Stacey, Watson's concepts concentrate on the career structures of the middle class. The 'spiralist' works for national or international organizations, moving within and between them, from place to place and from job to job, in the course of his career. The 'burgess' remains anchored in one place, and therefore his identification with the local social milieu is different and more complete. As settlements become increasingly emmeshed in national economic and social organizations, so the presence of spiralists becomes more important.

Watson makes a number of distinctions between spiralists according to education, occupation, stage of career, and policy of employer, but he suggests that there is a common ethic of spiralism which largely depends on the experience of university education. While

the product of Eton and Oxford is a different social person from the product of Grammar School and Redbrick, (they both) share the general spiralist culture acquired through their higher education and prolonged training,

a culture which is different from that of each local community. Thus to Watson, education and training are important, rather than the subsequent events of interaction with the local system or the particular wider perspective acquired through a mobile career. Here Watson is treating both career and education as being broadly homogeneous for all the spiralists, but this does not explain his other concept of the blocked spiralist, a spiralist who decides to 'go local', stops spiralling, and settles into a local community. Only if we consider the modifying influence of successive residential periods (or changes in family cycle, or career values and so on) can Watson be adapted to explain the 'spiralist dropout'. Cumulative career experience is worth more attention than Watson gives it, for it is the degree to which successive local milieux succeeded or failed to meet his changing social needs that helps to shape the spiralist's consequent actions.

His second sub-category is based on the potential mobility of the particular job that the spiralist does. He points out that the difference between fee-paid and salary-paid professionals is that the former have been less integrated into modern bureaucratic systems and so are less open to mobility. Predominantly salary-paid professions depend on large scale units of production, expensive capital plant, bureaucratic hierarchies administering centralized directives, and large numbers of people. Fee-paid professionals are either an occupational elite (consultants to an industry as a whole, a relatively new hybrid) or individuals who are self-employed in small units of production needing relatively smaller populations to provide the cases which require the application of their skills.

A corollary to this which Watson does not develop is that those in the last category have different relationships in the local social system. The local inhabitants are largely irrelevant to the spiralist as far as his job goes: but the general practitioner, the family solicitor, the private tutor, the priest, the small shopkeeper, the social worker, and to a slightly lesser extent the bank manager and the estate agent, whatever their occupational contract with national organizations, all depend much more on the goodwill of the local residents. The local inhabitants are highly relevant to the non-spiralist *and* to the typical fee-paid professional in the very nature of their jobs. The essence of being a GP is not the practising of medicine, but the practising of medicine on the local inhabitants.

Similarly while clergymen do have a 'flat' occupational spiral, it entails a different integration into the local milieu than most other spiralist professions. In these others, the spiralist is selling his skills indirectly to the community (and through the organization, on a national scale) rather than to the local residents. Thus the case of the priest, bank manager, and to some extent the teacher, fall between the pure burgess and the pure spiralist; the personnel officer may have closer links with the local system than the research physicist, and line managers have closer links than staff managers.

Another ill-fitting category is the 'pseudo-local'. On the one hand he may be Pahl's spiralist (or immigrant), who has the village-in-the-mind and who is therefore committed to the social life of the locality: his rootlessness generates a 'Need for Place', apparently at a psychological level. He is unlikely to be accepted as a local by his own local class equivalents. Alternatively he may be a blocked spiralist who is adjusting his orientation. A third possibility are the wives of spiralists who use up their spare time in community activities out of commitment or out of boredom, pending their husbands' next move. In 'democratic' households, the husband is likely to be involved as an adjunct to his wife's self-presentation.

Watson also raises the issue of company policy. Some employers encourage mobility with removal grants, furnishing allowances, explicit training policies and so on. Others, such as ICI, combine this with entertainment grants to staff personnel for the first two years of residence in a new area, precisely to increase social intercourse with neighbours and presumably in the hope that new contacts dispel loneliness and improve morale among employees and their families, and are a good form of public relations with local residents. This modifies the social relations which arise out of the nature of occupations themselves. Conversely, other firms discourage local involvements so that personnel have no ties which hinder the efficient mobilization of all available talent at the time and place the company decides (the army barracks are an extreme form of this). Finally some firms encourage mobility within the organization, while others do not make this an explicit policy.

Conclusions

This review of the three core studies shows that while all relate migration to integration in local social milieux, they cannot be subsumed as one conceptual unit. Frankenberg, Edgell, Pahl, and Bell and Newby all treat these studies in an over-simplified way, without first considering the status of the basic concepts that they employ inter-changeably. There is nothing wrong in using mobility as a starting point in the analysis of local social behaviour, but in doing so there are better strategies on which to base research than typologies, as a more flexible social action approach indicates.

Thus if typologies, or twin-poled continua, are rejected, the way is open to study underlying processes: this will include the actor's experience before he arrives, and his subsequent reactions, both within the social milieu under study, and beyond it. As this widens the range of investigation, the next step must be to start to codify the factors involved.

Thus the response of the migrant is a function of his own previous experience of occupational and family life, and the features of the local milieux he enters. On his part, there is the dislocation, the severing of past ties and the search for new ones, the forgetting of inappropriate old values and customs, and the acquisition of new ones. There is also the needs which his family situation creates. Most studies of mobility have not given sufficient attention to family life-cycle. Children raise problems of care and education which can determine place of residence and interactions in that place. At the same time, dual career families have different problems from those where only the husband works.

It follows that migration and local orientation are complex subjects, covering a variety of processes. Rather than imposing a typological order, it is more useful to consider the clusters of related variables involved. The 14 areas for investigation listed below are a starting point in an attempt to conceptualize the process by which the mobile middle class take up their role and identity in local social milieux.

(1) *Orientation to the Local Milieu:* The migrant (or young local) may treat the local milieu as a 'staging post' and thus have no desire to integrate, or he may be eager to enter into the social life of the area. Previous life experience is particularly important here in explaining values and attitudes. It may be useful to know how the migrant integrated in his previous place of residence.

(2) *Orientation to Other Communities:* As well as retaining external reference groups in status terms, the migrant may well be 'held back' from joining his new social milieu because of previously acquired social relationships, particularly kinship ties. The adolescent period is important in this connection, as is social mobility in the conventional sense.

(3) *Orientation to the Occupation:* The individual may have a commitment to his local occupational organization, or to his profession in general, or something in between. Alternatively, he may value his occupation to such an extent that he isolates himself from the local milieu because of the time he gives to his occupation.

(4) *Occupational Need of the Local Milieu:* Some occupations relate directly to local residents like clergyman, head teacher, doctor, or even personnel officer. Other jobs, like research scientists (or sociologists?), are not intrinsically involved with local residents. This involvement may be informal, or at an institutional level such as social security, employment exchanges, other forms, welfare services, etc.

(5) *Need to use the Local Milieu as a (Status) Reference Group:* Individuals define themselves in terms of other people: thus house, garden, furnishings, etc., are seen as appropriate to a certain status. This may work by limiting social interaction (a big house removed but visible from the road) or by interaction (entertaining at home, conspicuous 'pseudo-local' use of a public house, etc.). Such a need for a status referent is an acute problem for the migrant, who is by definition isolated, especially at first. To some extent the answer is to use a non-located community: geographically distant professional colleagues, friends from previous places of residence, etc.

(6) *Need to Join the Local Social Milieu:* Whatever the migrant's orientation or need for a reference group, he and his family are to some extent forced to interact with other residents as an answer to routine problems like baby-sitting and shopping, and emergencies such as illness, child-birth and accidents, which can only be solved by cooperation with others or with formal (often voluntary) agencies. Stage in family life-cycle is most important here.

(7) *Skills in Joining Local Milieu:* Experience of mobility makes the migrant familiar with the techniques of adaptation and the problems that must be overcome if he is to participate fully in the local milieu.

(8) *Extent of Change:* The migrant's values and attitudes may be more or less inappropriate, depending on his previous experience. He may be exchanging a commuter village for another commuter village, or a village for an inner suburb; the degree of dislocation will vary.

(9) *The Recency of the Migration:* It is necessary to know not

only how long the migrant has been resident but also how his orientation and needs have changed since his move. Changes in the local social milieu must also be allowed for, in order to obtain a complete picture.

The remaining factors are not so much of the migrant, rather they are more conditions of the local milieu in which he finds himself.

(10) *Availability of Occupational Facilities:* An individual may be able to achieve promotion or change his employer without moving house if there are suitable occupational opportunities perceived as being within range. Alternatively he will have to move (as ultimately his children will probably need to do). When the wife also has a career, this is an acute problem, for the two careers are seldom in harmony, and priorities have to be assigned, usually to the husband's career.

(11) *Availability of Commercial Facilities:* The highly educated and affluent migrant demands a special range of shopping and public entertainment which may not be available locally. Wide experience allows comparison, and acquired tastes for the consumer styles of 'colour supplement life' may be the cause of considerable discontent, particularly in the case of wives. A sub-category of this is the availability of suitable housing (in a status sense) which helps to determine the geographical location of the migrant, with consequences because of the friction of space for his local activity. It is thus necessary to know something of the migrant's expectations and his perception of the locality, as well as the actual availability of these facilities.

(12) *Availability of Social Facilities:* The move will leave the migrant with relatively fewer kinship and friendship ties in the locality. If there are no personnel with whom to cooperate (as in (6) above) and no associations (or lack of numbers to support such associations which provide for the specialist interests of the migrant) then integration is harder as the voluntary association is an important mechanism of integration for the migrant. This is not to assume anything about the migrant's *need* to integrate; at this point the concern is the solution of any such need.

(13) *Availability of Transitional Roles:* The local sub-culture may include the role of recent immigrant and mechanisms to integrate him, or his arrival may be resented and resisted. The overall balance between locals and immigrants will probably influence this.

(14) *Extent of Cohesion in the Local Social Milieu:* At the start

of this article attention was drawn to the range of social relationships which can comprise a social milieu. In some highly integrated and visible milieux, joining one association or making one friendship labels the migrant as a particular 'type' for the residents, and so restricts his further interactions. In other milieux the migrant can remain invisible: compared with the ideal-typical village the city provides a greater resource of groups with which to associate – each of which is independent of the other groups.

With minor changes of syntax, the same areas of interest apply to the non-migrant, or 'native'. By using this term and the word 'migrant' attention can be focused on a single attribute of any person under study, his geographical mobility; it is then possible to discuss his orientations and needs separately, and also to see the relative effect of dislocation due to mobility as opposed to lack of integration due to orientation and needs. At the same time, an understanding of particular milieux can be obtained. This is something which the studies above have failed to achieve.

The reason for discussing these ideas about middle-class migration was not merely the migrants' intrinsic interest or significance within modern capitalist society, although that is important. Rather, they can throw light on the operation of local milieux, a problem which in its various disguises has dominated urban sociology. The list of areas for investigation not only deals with the migrant, it forms a provisional framework with which to investigate the behaviour of any middle-class resident in any area, as part of a general social action approach to the analysis of local social milieux.

Class in the Village

W. M. Williams

Reprinted with permission from W. M. Williams, *The Sociology of an English Village*, Routledge & Kegan Paul, 1956, pp. 86–9, 103, 104–5, 107–20

It was soon obvious from the behaviour and conversation of the people of Gosforth that, apart from personal likes and dislikes, their attitudes towards certain parishioners, both as individuals and groups, tend to vary along well-defined lines. In a chance encounter – on the village street, or at an auction sale – the behaviour of any two or more people will depend largely on whether they think themselves members of the same group or not; in the latter case it will depend further on what is locally regarded as the 'correct' relationship between the specific groups involved. This division of the parish into groups of people became more apparent with time. There were men who were 'a different type from the village' and others were 'people who won't acknowledge you'. There were 'better class folk who make you feel awkward' and 'people who are different because of the way they carry on'. These groups or classes are also believed to possess qualities which make them 'better' or 'higher' than another class. Gosforth has its 'Upper Ten' or 'Top Class' and there are 'people you look up to' and 'people you look down on'.

Since the same people were always mentioned in connection with a particular class, and never as belonging to another class, it became possible to divide the parish up into a number of classes, each with a comparatively fixed membership, and arranged in a graded series. Two methods were used to determine the nature and membership of each class and the results showed that the people of Gosforth believed themselves to be split up into seven social classes.

Each class is thought by members of other classes to have special attributes and modes of behaviour. The seven classes will be described in turn, as more or less separate entities. Although this is in keeping with the local belief that a class has definite limits and a social reality of its own, it must however be borne in mind throughout this chapter that each class has position only in relation to other classes, and that the characteristics of any one class become meaningless when divorced from the total system.

The fact that everyone is expected to act according to a prescribed code of social behaviour, dependent on individual rank, is of enormous importance as a controlling factor in everyday life. On occasions far too numerous to count, a person's actions in a specific situation were explained as having taken place because 'He (she) was afraid people would think he (she) was a snob'.

When a person fails to behave 'properly' and ignores the comments and criticisms of neighbours, then he or she ceases to be regarded as a living member of Gosforth society to all intents and purposes. There were several people in the village, surrounded on all sides by neighbours, who had 'no friends or visitors'.

When the socially maladjusted person is a stranger the isolation is even more marked. The family with no kinship ties coming to live in the parish for the first time is soon assigned a position in the class system, and is thereafter expected to live in the same way as other families of equal rank. When this does not happen, the newcomers find themselves living in a social vacuum. There are three such families in the parish who have lived there, two, five and seven years respectively. The first of these is known by name to most people in Gosforth, but no one admitted to knowing the family personally or could think of anyone who did. The names of the other two families were known only to their immediate neighbours, and people living less than half a mile away from them stated that they had never heard of them. This was often demonstrably untrue, but it was undeniable that as a social fact their existence was, and would probably remain, unrecognized.

It will be clear from what has been written in this section that since the 'social perspective' varies from class to class (compare, for example, the respective attitudes of the 'Upper Ten' and the lower class to a stranger) each class will have its own conception of the other classes and behave towards them accordingly. Since there are seven classes, even representative attitudes cannot be considered fully, let alone deviations from the norms; but some conception of the more important differences may be gained from the following 'class perspectives'.

(i)	*Upper-Upper class:*	
	Upper-Upper class	'Our social level.' 'Better class.'
	Lower-Upper class	'Social climbers.' 'Not quite our class.' 'He *tries* to behave like a gentleman, but . . .'
	Intermediate	'Neither here nor there. More intelligent than the normal run of people around here.' 'Quite well educated and very handy when you have about a dozen village organizations to see to.'
	Upper-Medial	'Social climbers in the village.'
	Medial and Lower Medial	'Villagers and farmers.' 'Decent lower class people.' 'The country people.'
	Lower class	'The immoral element in the village.' 'The worst kind of countryman.' 'The worst of the lower orders.'

(ii)   *Lower-Upper class:*

Upper-Upper	'The Upper Ten.' 'The people who have more breeding than sense.' 'They have no money, but because they talk like a BBC announcer and their great-grandfather was a tuppeny-ha'penny baronet, they think they own the place.'
Lower-Upper	'Ambitious people.' 'Go-ahead people.'
Intermediate	'In between.'
Upper-Medial	'The village aristocracy. They try their best to get ahead, but everything is against them.'
Medial	'Farmers and small professionals.' 'Farmers and village tradesmen.'
Lower-Medial	'The village.'
Lower class	'Dirty people. I can't understand them. Some of them are quite well off, but you'd never think it to look at them.'

(iii) *Intermediate class:*

Upper-Upper	'The Nibs.' 'The usual well-off people you find in the countryside these days. Mostly retired people; very few of them are old established.'
Lower-Upper	'The money-maker class. They have ambitions of climbing, but they don't seem to have much luck.'
Intermediate	'We are in a class of our own.' 'Our position is not a very easy one to understand.'
Upper-Medial	'The kind of people who don't mix with their neighbours. Usually they are social climbers.'
Medial	'The majority of ordinary people with good jobs – including farmers, of course.'
Lower-Medial	'The average villager.'
Lower class	'An unfortunate minority. You can tell them by the way they live. Most of them are dirty.'

(iv) *Upper-Medial class:*

Upper-Upper	'The sort of people you can really look up to.' 'The proper gentry.' 'The better class people.'
Lower-Upper	'They are not Upper Ten but they like to think they are. They are not all that different from us, except for their money.'
Intermediate	'School teachers and that sort.' 'I think folks make far too much fuss about them.'

(iv)   *Upper-Medial class [contd.]*

Upper-Medial	'People who keep themselves to themselves.' 'Decent people who try to get on.' 'The sort of people who try to improve themselves a bit.'
Medial	'Farmers and such.'
Lower-Medial	'Village people.' 'The ordinary working-class people.'
Lower class	'People who don't try to lift themselves.' 'Dirty people who have no self-respect.'

(v)   *Medial and Lower Medial:*

Upper-Upper	'People who are higher class than we are.'
Lower-Upper	'Folks like X who have plenty of money and plenty of cheek. They want to get on in t'world.'
Intermediate	'In-between because of education.'
Upper-Medial	'Snobs.' 'Stuck-up folk.'
Medial and Lower-Medial	'Ordinary Gosfer' folk.'
Lower class	'Folk who don't care what they look like.'

(vi)   *Lower class:*

Upper-Upper	'Them posh folks living in the big houses.' 'They won't acknowledge you and the way some of them behaves you'd think you was some mak o' animal.'
Lower-Upper	'The folk with brass who acts like they was big nobs.' 'Bloody snobs.'
Intermediate	'Don't know much about them. A lot o' bloody barrack room lawyers if tha ask me.'
Upper-Medial	'A lot o' **** **** **** snobs.'
Medial and Lower-Medial	'Village folk like us, but some on 'em is very high and mighty.'
Lower class	'Decent folk.' 'Folks that like to do what they wants to.'

Some mention must also be made of the concept of 'the old standards' in relation to the social classes. The people to whom 'the old standards' are ascribed are generally those whose families have lived in Gosforth for generations, even centuries. While they are not confined to one social level, they are to be found mainly in the Medial and Lower-Medial classes, and never in the Lower-Upper class. Being of the 'old standards' implies high rank within a class, but at the same time there is a strong suggestion that these families are in some way outside the normal working of the class system. People would often remark that 'Such and such a family isn't in the same class (as "A", "B", etc.) but they are the real old standards you know' or 'That mak o' folk is different from the rest of us.'

In the same way, life-long bachelorhood and marriage of first cousins both of which are more typical of families belonging to the 'old standards' than of others, are considered 'natural' to the former and very abnormal otherwise.

Life in the village is greatly influenced by two important facts. Firstly, that the people live close together, and secondly, in part as a result of this, that they see much more of each other and of strangers. Consequently there is ample scope for the development of devices to increase personal status, the maintenance of which occupies much of the villager's time and energy. As one villager remarked, 'You can't blow your nose in Gosfer' without ivverybody knows about it; and half on 'em knows about it afore you does it.'

The Two-Class Village

R. E. Pahl

Reprinted with permission from 'The Two-Class Village', *New Society*, 27 February, 1964

I have been concerned in an examination of the post-war social changes in three contrasting villages in Hertfordshire. 'Dormersdell', which I have chosen to describe here, is admittedly a rather extreme example, but served to highlight some of the problems in which I was interested. I wanted to know, for example, more of the reasons people give for living in the country and the way the newcomers react on the established village community. To what extent does the more mobile, cosmopolitan middle-class manager and his wife make any sort of contact with the villagers and how do village organizations change or respond to the new situation?

Dormersdell has a population of just over 1,000 and a 50 per cent household sample was taken in the spring of 1961. Of the

144 households interviewed, 90 of the heads of households were classified as middle class, on a scale derived from the Registrar General's Classification of Occupations (1960). The remainder were classified as working class, apart from twelve heads engaged in agriculture, who were exempt from this stage of the analysis, and a further five for whom no information was obtainable. About 60 per cent of the middle-class group is concentrated in an area of woodland about a mile from the centre of the village. This area, known simply as the Wood, became synonymous with both the middle class and newcomers.

Some 29 per cent of all chief earners work in London or the Greater London conurbation and 53 per cent work in the surrounding Hertfordshire towns; only 18 per cent work in the parish or the neighbouring parish. However, it was not so much the place of work which seemed to be important but rather the class, as defined by occupation and the place of residence in the parish, the two going together. The community was not only polarized spatially but also socially. The two worlds of the working class (the old established villagers) and the middle class (the immigrant professional and managerial people) could hardly have been further apart.

Commuters and Joiners

Many middle-class people move out to a village in order to be a member of a 'real' community, which, in practice, means joining things. It might be thought, however, that the length of the journey to work would make it difficult for commuters to get home in time to participate in local organizations in the evening and that the women might be housebound on account of their children during the day. Discussion has often centred on the lack of participation in local activities by middle-class commuters, while it has long been widely known that it is not part of the working-class culture to join formal social organizations. The working-class men may be members of the local darts team or football club but their wives would not be expected to join a dramatic society or discussion group.

In fact Dormersdell is renowned for the wealth of activities which flourish there. The joiners and organizers of most village activities are middle-class commuters' wives. It is true, of course, that the middle class considerably outnumber the working class, but it appears that in the working class it is only some of the wives of commuters who take any part in village activities. It is interesting that among the middle class there is some indication that commuting is not a disincentive for some of the men to take active part in local organizations, and the proportion of the joiners who work in London is about the same as of those who work locally in nearby towns. When considering office holders, the contrast between the classes is striking. As well as taking a large part in running the village, the middle-class men are also very likely to hold office in organizations meeting outside the village. This is further evidence of the urban, mobile and outward-looking middle class living in a wider, regional sphere of action.

Although it first appeared that middle-class people are well integrated into village social organizations and indeed appear to run most of them, this is in fact a rather false picture of middle-class dominance, although one the working class seem happy to hold. Certainly this is the case in the Women's Institute, which has, as already described, been taken over by the middle class. The Badminton Club is also entirely run for and by young middle-class men and women. However, this is no great loss to the working-class villagers: the younger ones monopolize the Youth Club and the Football Club and have good representation in the Cricket Club: the old-age pensioners go to the Greenleaves Club (that is the women do – the men go to the pub) and a few older middle-class people in fact enjoy to go and serve tea or act as treasurer without the indignity of becoming a member! Perhaps the only club where the village and the Wood meet on anything like equal terms is the Village Horticultural Society.

Sport is, of course, also a potential mediator between the classes but there are few young people in their teens and twenties living in the Wood since most of the immigrant newcomers arrive in their thirties. The Church also provides some common meeting ground for the two worlds. Here the respectable, conservative working class is matched with a similar proportion of middle-class people. To summarize the interaction of the middle and working class in the social sphere, it would appear that by and large the working-class people are not deprived of any activity by the middle-class immigrants (if we accept the Young Wives' Club as a substitute for the Women's Institute), despite many activities taking place in which they are not represented. Because of this lack of contact each group accuses the other unfairly.

S.M.B.   M

The wider, national class divisions in society are here played out in the local scene in Dormersdell. The contact between the classes becomes less, since however much the newcomers may try to be a middle-class squirearchy, the radical working class resent it, and the conservative working class find it no real substitute for the Gentry. How much the change is due to physical contact with the outside world in surrounding towns and how much it is due to the influence of the new middle class is difficult to say. My own view is that change in the village community has not taken place as rapidly as might be expected. To give an example, there are two pubs in the village. One is almost entirely devoted to the middle class, developing the atmosphere of a private party at which most people know each other. The other pub has tried to follow suit and certainly in the saloon bar has achieved some success. However, the public bar of the pub nearest to the village contains little sophistication. Talk centres around local events, neighbouring villages, football or cricket.

Generally the villagers were not effusive about Dormersdell. 'It's quite nice in summer but a bit dreary in winter' summed up many people's feelings.

The whole working-class situation was a highly complex structure of definite roles, relationships and behaviour, far too delicate to be able to generalize about. The broad distinctions between the middle and working class were so enormous that quite crude methods could be used to portray them. But within the classes much greater study in depth is required than was possible with a sample of this size. Not only has there been little contact between the worlds but the main way of breaking down these barriers – by the children of the two groups going to the same schools – seems less likely to take place.

A Process of Polarization

The different patterns of life which have been described are based on two main differences. The middle class have greater mobility owing to the use of private transport, particularly by the wives, often driving a second car. The changeover from the hierarchical social structure, which was functionally suited to the village as a community, to the polarized two-class division may be the chief cause of the working-class people's resentment. The more traditional working-class element is resentful, partly because it has lost its clear position in the hierarchy and the reflected status of the gentry for whom it worked, and partly because it now finds itself lumped with what it would feel to be the less respecfable working class. This traditional group would like to be given respect and position in society, but gets neither. The non-traditional working class see the segregated middle-class world as a symptom of the inequalities in society, and condemn all middle-class people as snobs and *nouveaux riches* without basing this on individual knowledge and experience.

The middle-class people come into rural areas in search of a meaningful community and by their presence help to destroy whatever community was there. Part of the basis of the local village community was the sharing of the deprivations due to the isolation of country life and the sharing of the limited world of the families within the village. The middle-class people try to get the cosiness of village life, without suffering any of the deprivations, and while maintaining a whole range of contacts outside.

New middle-class people are unprepared for what they find. Determined to move out of suburbia and influenced by the pastoral vision portrayed by everything from the Scott Report to the popular novel, many do expect to become the squire's successor. Indeed many of the women have the sense of service to others, sometimes found in the squire's wife. On the other hand, to the working class they might just as well not be there. The main exception to this is the advantage which many working-class women gain in the way of untaxed extra income from those middle-class housewives who employ them to clean their homes. This is probably the most direct form of social contact. Some firm friendships between Wood and Village exist at this level, but this does not extend to a more normal social relationship. National class divisions come into sharper focus in the local setting of such metropolitan villages as Dormersdell.

Local Class Structure

J. Littlejohn

Reprinted with permission from J. Littlejohn: *Westrigg, The Sociology of a Cheviot Parish*, Routledge & Kegan Paul, 1963, pp, 1, 2, 7-9, 81-4, 90, 111-12, 117-21, 223-9

Westrigg is an upland parish in a mainly rural county in the south of Scotland.

Settlement is of the dispersed type. There is no village in the parish, no shops or pubs; dwellings and the few public buildings are scattered along the valley floors with here and there a small cluster, the two most compact being forestry settlements. The two nearest towns are fifteen and seventeen miles away. Near the junction in the parish of the two roads from these towns are a post office, school and smiddy. This, the centre of communication, is thought of by parishioners as the centre of the parish, though the geographical centre is two miles north from it. By common agreement a Public Hall was erected at the geographical centre in 1922.

The scattered settlement pattern is partly due to the requirements of large-scale sheep farming. Almost every cottage is tied, i.e., is part of the property of a farm (or the Forestry Commission now) and can be rented only if one is employed by the farmer (or Forestry Commission).

However, the settlement pattern cannot be explained simply by reference to the environment and the requirements of sheep farming. The present pattern took shape under an organization of the farm in which the farm worker and his family belonged to the farm in a more strict sense than is the case now.

In everyday conversation parishioners categorize each other into three classes by using the terms 'gentleman farmer', 'working farmer' and 'working folk'. There are differences in the frequencies with which persons of these categories employ the terms; those designated 'working farmers' and 'working folk' use all three terms much oftener than those designated 'gentleman farmer'. The 'gentleman farmers' rarely use the term to refer to themselves, and do not often speak of 'working farmers' either, preferring the term 'small farmer'.

The local terms, gentlemen and working farmers, and working folk, obviously imply a classification of the agricultural population and of forestry labourers.

That the classes are viewed as superior and inferior to each other is soon apparent in conversation. When identifying a third party for me informants would say, e.g., 'he's not a working farmer, he's *only* a working man' or 'he's not a gentleman farmer, just a working farmer'. An upper-middle-class man once remarked of agricultural labourers 'of course some of these people are hardly better than animals in intelligence and way of living'. Sometimes irritation at one provokes sweeping condemnation of the class as when a farmer exclaimed *à propos* some minor lapse on the part of a shepherd, 'they're all alike these people, they just can't think'. A lower-middle-class woman remarked of a working-class neighbour, 'you can see the lower element coming out even in her'. A view of the working class widely held among both the middle classes is that they are 'childish'. Direct remarks like these are not very common: more common is the indirect and quite unmalicious reference like this by a farmer, 'This morning a stranger passed by the field where I was working and said "good morning" to me as if I were just a labourer. I was quite pleased, in fact a lifelong ambition of mine has been to be treated as if I were nobody.'

Employers of labour obviously wield power in the sense of being in the position to hire and fire, and in addition a farmer's power of influencing a workman's chances of employment in a district are by no means negligible. Farmers in any one district are in an informal compact as over against workmen, shown in this farmer's description of hiring. 'You advertise in the papers and wait and hope someone will answer. Then when you get an answer you ring up his employer and ask "are you finished with this man?" – "yes" – "is he any good?" – "wouldn't touch him with a barge pole" – "all right, thank you". Eventually you meet a man and tell him the conditions he'll work under . . .' When a workman leaves a job he is given a written testimonial containing no adverse judgements, which he knows to be worthless. A shepherd said, 'You only ask for the testimonial because if you don't get one your neighbours would think there was something far wrong. But the bosses talk about you on the telephone to each other. That's where they have you.' Several workmen cited cases of alleged victimization, in which a farmer prevented an employee he had sacked from finding another job.

The sociological problem of determining how class status is allocated cannot be solved solely by pointing to so many factors, all of which are already known, or by an arbitrary decision that one or other is 'fundamental'. What is important is that at different points in the system different factors become of crucial importance in the allocation of status. This again was clear from comments of informants while making class placements. An area where there was much hesitation in judgement (among informants of all classes) was the distinction between craftsmen and the smaller working farmers. A craftsman may own no more property than a bag of tools and a motor car, yet his income can be as sizeable as a small farmer's. A craftsman may be in a position of authority over an apprentice or may hire a young assistant, and though in such a relationship the teacher/pupil note will often sound, the craftsman has ultimate sanctions at his disposal not greatly different from those a small farmer has *vis-à-vis* an employee. In this area too it is often difficult to make a distinction between craftsman and farmer on the basis of 'standard of living' or style of life. Yet all informants eventually did draw a distinction solely on the basis of the sheer fact of land ownership (it being understood that 'land' meant a holding large enough to be an independent business enterprise). 'After all,' they would say, 'he does own a farm, and (X the craftsman) doesn't.'

Higher up the system neither the sheer fact of property ownership nor its amount distinguishes between one class and another, the professional people having none and several upper-middle-class farmers having holdings as small as those of lower-middle-class farmers. The point in land-values where factors other than size of farm come into play (in this community) seems to be at about 2,000 acres. Above this size farmers are all of the upper-middle class, and sheer size is an important qualification; of one farmer a class peer remarked 'he gets in (to our class) of course just because his farm's so big'. Below this size the farmer may be of either class. The other factors brought to bear on status judgements at this point with regard to both farmers and professionals are education and 'background', 'style of life' and estimate of relative income. Though I call these 'factors' as if they were four clearly distinguishable variables, informants did not in fact separately specify them as such. None used the actual term 'style of life', though women informants obviously meant this when they stressed the importance of good manners, eating customs and size of house as determinants of status.

It is implicit in the data presented above that the class system of the parish cannot be represented as three distinct groups sharply demarcated one from another so that boundaries are clearly apparent between adjoining classes. There is obviously a certain indefiniteness about it – a feature of class systems in industrial society which has often been commented upon. The area of indefiniteness in the system calls for some explanation but first it must be described. Briefly, the position is that while the upper-middle class is sharply distinguished from the lower-middle class there is not the same clarity of boundary between the latter and the working class. Taking the criterion of association this means that while members of the upper-middle class do not associate with members of the other two classes, some members of the lower-middle sometimes associate with some members of the working class.

This feature of the system is closely connected with another already discussed, namely that the class status of a person or a family is not necessarily determined by reference to one single value; and since the values used in allocating status are hardly commensurable on a single scale, in the area described status can be allocated or claimed on the basis of several values.

All informants agreed that speech and accent were the most trustworthy symbols in placing a stranger, with clothes and manners a fairly reliable second. That all these function as symbols of status is clearly seen in the treatment meted out to persons who attempt to display one of these traits as it is displayed by a class higher than the one they are known to belong to. They are ridiculed in a way which shows that they are held to be trying to claim a class status they are not entitled to. For example, recently some working youths bought a suit of clothing of the expensive sort worn in the upper-middle class. They were jeered at by their class peers and each given a nickname showing he was regarded as claiming illegitimate status – 'Lord Westrigg', 'Sir X', and so on. Similarly there is one working-class family whose speech is more like the middle classes than like the rest of the working class. The lower-middle class regarded this family with approval saying they did not speak so 'Scotch' as the others and were not 'rough' in manner, etc. To the rest of the working class the family is 'affected', accused of 'putting on airs' and 'thinking itself above us'.

The culture of the higher classes is officially defined as better than that of the lower. In the local school the language and manners taught are those of the middle classes. Though the majority of the children are of the working class they are discouraged from using their own normal speech. During one lesson, for example, the children were asked to name various sorts of buildings shown to them in pictures, of which one was a kennel. Asked to name it one of the boys replied correctly in dialect 'a dughoose'. He was somewhat chagrined to be told he was 'wrong'. In short the children are being trained to believe that their normal way of speaking is wrong and to imitate the dialect of the middle classes. The same applies to manners; the children are taught to address and refer to adults as 'Mr' and 'Mrs', to use handkerchiefs and to be circumspect in interaction with others. These are middle-class customs. Working-class men in particular demand of each other an immediate solidarity in interaction which seems to render middle-class manners superfluous.

This brief sketch of class culture I hope justifies the use of the term 'social milieu' to describe the nature of social class. A social class is neither a mere category arbitrarily defined by myself on the basis of one or two 'characteristics' such as property ownership, nor is it a group in the strict sense of the term as implying clear cut boundaries and a constitution laying down a limited set of relationships among its members. A class is rather, for its members, one of the major horizons of all social experience, an area within which most experience is defined. Encompassing so much, it is rarely conceptualized.

This does not mean that the concept of a local class system is a sociologist's myth; it only means that individuals, when asked about it, answer in terms of their own experience of it. That there is a system is I think shown by the fact that no informant placed him or herself wrongly, no one claimed a status higher or lower than that accorded by the majority of fellow parishioners. Each person knows his or her place in the system, can place accurately other people he has the requisite information about, but has no need to turn his experience of the system into a conceptual scheme.

The classes differ in the range and frequency of their association outside the parish. The norm here is that the higher a class the wider and more frequent are its contacts outside the parish;

or to adopt the network image, the higher the class the more dispersed is the network of relationships in which it is involved, the lower the class the more contained is its network. The basis of the difference in scale is the former's relative freedom from having to work to a routine timetable, and ownership of private means of transport and communication, as opposed to the latter's being tied to a daily job and dependent on public transport.

At this point it may be asked whether in fact the middle classes have lost power in the parish over the last fifty years. The data suggest that the more frequent contacts, both formal and informal, of the upper-middle class outside the parish serve to maintain their position of dominance within the parish.

It is the family and not the individual that is the unit of social class. By family in this context I mean those members of a family living together in the same household. It is necessary to state this because an individual can alter his class status in his own lifetime; the child can come to occupy a different status from his parents, the sibling from the sibling. In such cases persons of different status do not live together as members of the same household. That the family, in this sense, is the unit was clear both from informants, class placements and their comments while making them.

Since a family begins with a marriage, and since a class system restricts association among the population stratified, a full account of the connections between family and class must deal with the process known as assortative mating. Social barriers of any sort limit the possibilities of random contact among people, and tend to foster marriages between persons with similar social characteristics. Social class barriers are among the most important in this process. Where a class system prevails there are three possible combinations of class status of the spouses. The two can be of equal status, the man higher than the woman or the woman higher than the man. The first combination is the normal one; of all marriages in the parish only eight were not of this sort. The second combination is much more frequent than the third, the ratio here being seven to one.

It may be asked why any sort of marriage across class lines is relatively rare. Numerous reasons can be adduced which, however, are merely implicit in the class system itself.

These 'reasons' are, however, only aspects of the class system itself. Perhaps a more cogent explanation is to be found in the incompatibility between kinship norms and those governing relations between classes. There is a warm and friendly relationship between grandparents and children, and between parents' siblings and siblings' children. In cross-class marriage the children are in a different class from the parents and siblings of one of the spouses. People of different classes do not associate in warm and friendly relations. It seems likely that if marriage between members of different classes became general either the kinship system or the class system would have to alter very much from their present form. While I have no data to prove this, it is clear that in the community there is incompatibility between the two sets of norms and that where they conflict class norms take precedence. Relations with kinsfolk of a lower class are either severed or become characterized by a certain reserve. In either case accusations of snobbery are made by the lower against the higher. For example, one lower-middle-class man has an uncle in the parish who is a farm worker, but the two never associate. The former and his wife regard the latter as a tiresome old man, though he is highly respected among the working class. The uncle and members of his household sometimes express resentment against the nephew and his household.

That too frequent marriage across class lines might destroy the present class system is suggested by the fact that marriage of a woman of higher status to a man of lower is very much rarer than the opposite. It is regarded as a more serious breach of the norm. Association outside of work relationships is not merely a sociologist's index of equality of status; it is what equality of status means in everyday behaviour in the community itself.

Further Reading: Class

* P. ANDERSON AND R. BLACKBURN (Eds.): *Towards Socialism*, Fontana, 1965.

C. BELL: *Middle Class Families*, Routledge & Kegan Paul, 1968.

R. BENDIX AND S. M. LIPSET: *Class, Status and Power*, Routledge & Kegan Paul, 1966.

R. BLACKBURN: 'Inequality and Exploitation', *New Left Review*, No. 42, March, 1967.

* T. B. BOTTOMORE: *Classes in Modern Society*, Allen & Unwin, 1965.

* J. BURNHAM: *The Managerial Revolution*, Penguin Books, 1962.

R. DAHRENDORF: *Class and Class Conflict in Industrial Society*, Routledge & Kegan Paul, 1965.

A. GIDDENS: *Capitalism and Modern Social Theory*, Cambridge University Press, 1971.

* J. GOLDTHORPE: 'Social Stratification in Industrial Societies', *Sociological Review*, Monograph No. 8, 1964.

* JOHN H. GOLDTHORPE, D. LOCKWOOD, F. BECHHOFER AND J. PLATT: *The Affluent Worker in the Class Structure*, Cambridge University Press, 1969.

W. L. GUTTSMAN: *The English Ruling Class*, Weidenfeld & Nicolson, 1969.

C. S. HELLER: *Structured Social Inequality*, Collier-Macmillan, 1969.

* C. W. MILLS: *White Collar*, Oxford University Press, 1951.

W. G. RUNCIMAN: *Relative Deprivation and Social Justice*, Routledge & Kegan Paul, 1964.

* E. P. THOMPSON: *The Making of the English Working Class*, Gollancz, 1964.

* Available in paperback

6 Power

In many ways this chapter develops and forms a counterpoint to the themes which emerged in the section on class while some selections take up topics which were raised in the section on community.

One crucial dimension is lacking, not because it is considered unimportant, but because few sociologists have been able or have wished to undertake research in this area. There is very little which helps to explain the actual dynamics of power, how power operates in specific situations, how it is handled by the various interest- and pressure-groups involved, and what the outcomes of decision-making are. It would have been possible to include some impressionistic accounts of the experience of being involved with power and politics at first hand, but it was felt that these would not have been in tune with the remainder of this book.

In the first selection **Worsley** indicates in what ways a sociological analysis of politics involves a much broader definition of what is 'political' than does the conventional account in terms of 'what governments do'. He examines the reasons for the subordination of the power of the military and religious sectors of society to the political 'state', and for the close association between the political and the economics in Britain. Of crucial importance is the mechanism by which the ruling groups 'legitimate' their possession and exercise of power, by manipulating the symbols of authority. Clearly even an analysis in the simplest terms of 'who governs' involves explanations in terms of 'why, and how are they allowed to govern?' – 'why is it felt appropriate, and by whom is it felt appropriate that they should govern?' Thus political sociology needs to go much further than the mere examination of the correlates of specific types of voting behaviour, into an analysis of the formation of political culture.

This involves a consideration of political socialization, of how certain symbols come to be regarded as legitimate and their possession vested in representatives of particular classes

and interest groups – a theme which links this chapter to those
on ocialization, social class and the family.

Thus, in Chapter 3 Dowse and Hughes examine the extent
to which the political ideas of parents are transmitted to their
children. While it may be the case that early experiences in
the family are especially important in the development of
political values and the determination of political identification,
the type of school one attends and the socio-economic status
of one's parents may affect these issues also. In fact one
writer has suggested, when analysing the way in which young
people become socialized into the culture and values of a long-
settled homogeneous working-class community that 'the
influence of parents is not necessarily decisive, siblings and
other kin, friends, schoolmates, workmates and, later, husbands and wives may in aggregate be more important'.

Political attitudes and behaviour are not therefore a matter
simply of conscious cultural tradition, handed down from one
generation to the next. But nor are they simply a function of
the class position an individual occupies at a particular time.
The relationship between social class as it may be 'objectively'
determined by the outside observer, or as it is subjectively
assessed by the individual himself is a complex one and each
has to be taken into account.

It is certainly true as a very broad generalization that the
middle class tends to vote Conservative and the working class
to vote Labour. But when the 'working class', however narrowly defined, constitutes at least two-thirds of the population,
how are we to account for the remarkable persistence of
Conservative administrations, if the electorate is polarized on
straightforward lines of social class? (In a thorough study of
middle-class voting [admittedly published in the early fifties],
Bonham estimates that the 'middle-class vote' constitutes
30 per cent of the electorate). In practice, of course, there is a
considerable minority of working-class voters who habitually
support Conservative candidates. Most studies put the percentage of working-class Conservative voters at around one
third – or to put it another way, the Conservative party
normally derives half its support from working-class electors.
While there are certain regional differences in support for the
main parties – for instance, South-East Lancashire which had
a tradition of working-class conservatism – the national
pattern is fairly consistent.

Furthermore, the influence of class on voting is not entirely consistent in another sense too. Many studies have found that support for the Conservative Party may be strongest, not among the most affluent or powerful, but in the lower-middle class consisting mainly of clerical and white-collar workers. It may be that it is because they are in the middle of the class struggle that they need to affiliate even more determinedly with the groups in society who hold the highest status and wield the most power. Another explanation, consistent with the study of white-collar workers discussed in Chapter 5, is that it is the 'pragmatic acceptance' of the white-collar groups, rather than their involvement in what C. Wright Mills called 'the status panic', which underlies their recognition of the political facts of life. These, in terms of the political game as it has been played in Britain for most of this century, are that the Conservatives are the 'ins' while the Labour Party is the party of the 'outs'.

In a study of voting undertaken in Greenwich in 1950 by Benney, Gray and Pear, the authors conclude that the way an individual thinks of the class structure and perceives his own position within it may be a more important influence on his voting than his 'objective' class position. There is probably an element of status aspiration too, in that people tend to identify with the middle class by the very act of voting Conservative. So the relationship is a reciprocal one.

Rose goes beyond the mere association of independent variables such as social class, age or sex with the dependent variable of voting behaviour. His study looks at the association between 'working classness' and the Labour Party since 1900. As well as voting he considers the policy of the party, the recruitment of political leaders, and the party's capacity to mobilize political support. He concludes that 'no consistent relationship between class and party on these three dimensions is found, nor is there evidence of a trend towards or from convergence'. Class remains important in the explanation of political differences in British Society (indeed Alford concluded that class has a more significant effect on voting in Britain than in the United States, Canada, and Australia). But Rose suggests that this may be for a rather negative reason – that is, the absence of stronger grounds of cleavage. One of the remarkable facts of British political life since the nineteenth century has been its stability and the persistent capacity of the regime to maintain its credibility and legitimacy. Traditionally in British politics, race, religion, and nationality have not been important bases of political cleavage. Rose comments that

> . . . it appears that non-class divisions are much more likely to lead to the repudiation of a regime than are class divisions. Without going so far as to argue that class-based parties help create and maintain legitimacy, one can emphasize that such divisions are entirely consistent with the existence of a fully legitimate regime.

Nordlinger's book, recommended for Further Reading, goes further into the phenomenon of working-class conservatism, as does the study by McKenzie and Silver. Nordlinger argues that the working-class Conservative voter tends to perceive high-status individuals as possessing leadership quality and skills which their social backgrounds have developed. One group, the 'deferentials', prefer to be ruled by representatives of high-status groups because they do not believe themselves or their peers to be capable of undertaking the tasks of leadership. Another group, the 'pragmatists', argue that the high-status leaders have in practice done a better job of leadership and that this is because they have in general achieved their elevated position in life through their own efforts. So this tends to go along with a perception of the class structure as being relatively permeable and allowing scope for the individual of great capacity and talent to get to the top. McKenzie and Silver's study, though based on a more intensive and sophisticated sample, comes to broadly similar conclusions. Like Nordlinger, they find some working-class Conservatives to be 'deferential', but Nordlinger's 'pragmatists' are replaced by 'seculars'. Members of the latter group prefer leaders who have risen to high office without the benefits of inherited wealth or social standing, tend to evaluate their party's record in office in terms of policies and achievements, and support the Conservative Party on the basis of what they perceive to be its proven competence at governing the nation. Moreover, unlike the deferentials they tend to have a pragmatic view of the House of Lords, and not to see the Conservative Party as a national institution, quite different in kind from other contenders for government.

Another kind of explanation of working-class conservatism is given by **Parkin** in an article in the *British Journal of Sociology* in September, 1967. In this paper, Parkin suggests that because the dominant institutional statues – the established church, the public schools, the universities, the military and governmental elites, as well as landed capital and private business enterprise – are inextricably bound up with Conservative values and the Conservative Party, it is the working-class Labour voter who is deviant rather than his Conservative workmate. The long-settled urban working-class community represents a specific type of institutional setting in which the normative commitment to 'deviance' – that is Labour voting – can be maintained and supported. Moreover, members of the 'working class' who are not so continuously sustained in their symbolic rejection of the core values of British capitalist society will lack this 'normative protection' and may provide the basis of working-class support for the Conservative Party.

In the extract from *Middle-Class Radicalism*, reprinted in this chapter, Parkin discusses another kind of political 'deviance', that of the members of the middle class who support extreme radical causes, in this case, the Campaign for Nuclear Disarmament. 'In comparison with the working-class Conservative,' says Parkin, 'the middle-class Socialist or Radical is much more out on a limb.' He suffers more from the intense pressures exerted by the conformist majority. Thus, some of Parkin's respondents would say wryly that 'we're the black sheep of the neighbourhood', others would mark their deviance by the overt trappings of non-conformity, such as a beard, or unusual clothing.

It would be a serious mistake, however, in a discussion of power in British society, to focus attention exclusively on the electorate and their political attitudes and behaviour. Urry and Wakeford's book, recommended for Further Reading, contains a number of essays which develop the theme of power more fully.

In coming to grips with the realities of power in a modern institutionalized capitalist society, we have to face the questions posed by such writers as Mosca, Pareto, Michels, and more recently C. Wright Mills. Their common point of interest is in the ruling elite, the class or group which is involved in making the most political significant decisions.

In *The Power Elite*, Mills argues that in the complex interpretation of business, industry and government, power
may appear to be much more widely diffused than in fact
it is:

> Under the owners of property a huge and complex bureau-
> cracy of business and industry has come into existence. But
> the right to this chain of command, the legitimate access to
> the position of authority from which these bureaucracies
> are directed, is the right of private ownership.

This point is taken further in 'The Insiders' (reprinted in the
first edition of *The Sociology of Modern Britain*), which looks
critically at the thesis, propounded by Burnham, of 'The
Managerial Revolution'. Burnham had argued that the wider
spread of shareholding and the enormous increase in the
complexity of modern business and industry has created a new
group of powerful men – the managers – who owed their
power to their *control* of the resources of vast corporations,
while not being involved in share *ownership* to any great degree.
But the authors of 'The Insiders' follow Mills in seeing the
class interests of shareholders and corporate managers as being
essentially similar for 'their personal wealth and power is
intimately related to the power, stability and success of modern
business enterprise'. While the large shareholder derives his
wealth from dividends or from capital appreciation, the
manager derives his from salaries, bonuses and fringe benefits.

The relations between institutions and corporations are very
complex as **Whitley** points out.

A characteristic form of association between large concerns
is the 'interlocking directorate' and Whitley provides in
diagrammatic form a clear impression of this network interconnectedness. Often the key institution is a bank or finance
company. This study develops further the kind of research
undertaken by Lupton and Wilson which was reprinted in the
first edition of *The Sociology of Modern Britain*. The authors
of this study utilized the evidence from the Parker Tribunal
into leakages of information about changes in the Bank Rate to

> enquire whether the persons whose names appeared in the
> Tribunal evidence were linked to each other by relationships

of friendship, kinship, affinity, common membership of associations, and so on . . . In attempting to interpret the behaviour they observe sociologists look first at these 'networks' of relationships, and at the kind of training people receive to occupy positions within them.

Whitley's findings indicate that the network structures he identifies are strongly interconnected and that the group cohesion and solidarity which this indicates is supported by an extensive and deep-rooted framework of shared experiences at home, school, university and continuing into adult life.

Likewise, Guttsman's analysis of *The British Political Elite* leads him to conclude that it is misleading to try and study this elite in isolation from the upper class in which it is rooted. This group tends to come predominantly from the major public schools and the prestigious universities of Oxford and Cambridge. Guttsman's study supports the view that the ruling elite is able to maintain its position over more than one generation and this constitutes a ruling class, '. . . if we mean by it a group which provides the majority of those who occupy positions of power, and who, in their turn, can materially assist *their* sons to reach similar positions'. The gateways to elite position, even for the outstandingly able person of working-class origin tend to be through the educational system rather than through – for instance – business success.

One partial exception to this generalization is suggested by **Richards**'s study of members of Parliament. Some occupations requiring extensive education and training such as solicitors and barristers, are over-represented among members of the House of Commons but, by and large, the Parliamentary elite is sufficiently distinctive from the civil service-business-educational elite identified by Guttsman to make it reasonable to characterize it as representing an *alternative* locus of power. Indeed, Richards observes that:

Members share another attribute. Before election almost all of them were non-entities, at least in national terms . . . few men change over to politics after outstanding achievements in some other walk of life.

Many members do, however, share a common background and experience as representatives of the people in local government service. **Hampton**'s book examines local government in Sheffield, with a particular emphasis on the relations between councillors and their constituents, the people they represent. His conclusion is quite striking:

> The majority of the Councillors are not community leaders who emerge from the wards they represent; they are people interested in public affairs who seek an opportunity to represent their fellow citizens wherever it may conveniently be found.

It may be that this is an inevitable fact of political life; indeed it is only a few years since a ritual celebration of the 'apathy of the British elector' was a feature of practically all writing on the subject by political scientists. Perhaps it is only in times of crisis, that political leadership springs, like Minerva, fully-armed from the head of the local communal body politic. But in one area at least, that of planning policy, the failure to integrate local aspirations and demands with political and institutional structures may prove very destructive to the individuals concerned. In another reader in this series, *Cities in Modern Britain*, this theme is explored at some length, so it is only mentioned briefly here.

The Analysis of Power and Politics

P. M. Worsley

Reprinted with permission from 'The Distribution of Power in Industrial Society', *Sociological Review Monograph 8, The Development of Industrial Societies*, 1964, pp. 16–17, 20–6

Insofar as people's behaviour takes account of the existence of others, and is affected by expectations about others, we call it 'social'. Some of this behaviour is specifically purposive; it aims to produce effects. But not all of it is, and not all behaviour of interest to the social scientist is 'social', in Weber's sense of the term. Weber himself, indeed, emphasized that 'sociology is by no means confined to the study of "social action"; that is only . . . its central subject matter . . .' Causally determined action, as well as 'meaningfully' determined action, is part of the sociologist's subject-matter. So, although 'meaningfully' behaviour may be 'non-social', causally it can never be without social consequences.

Restricting ourselves, however, to 'social' action, we can be said to act politically whenever we exercise constraint on others to behave as we want them to. The allocation of resources to further these ends is an economic allocation. The overall assertion of values entailed is an operation of political economy.

These conceptual departure-points imply a very wide conception of politics, what we may call Politics I. By this definition, the exercise of constraint in any relationship is political. All kinds of pressure, from mass warfare and organized torture to implicit values informing inter-personal conversation, make up the political dimension. Looked at this way, there is no such thing as a special kind of behaviour called 'political'; there is only a political dimension to behaviour. Yet the vulgar (and often academic) use of the term 'politics' – what we shall call 'Politics II' – restricts the term to the specialized machinery of government, together with the administrative apparatus of state and party organization. To follow the implications of this usage through, strictly, would involve us in denying to simple undifferentiated societies the privilege of having a political system at all. Moreover, we also recognize that extra-governmental organizations within advanced societies dispose of power, and have their own constellations of power: we speak of 'university politics'. By this, we do not mean, merely and obviously that organizations like universities or trade unions, either continuously or intermittently, bring pressure to bear upon government, and are thereby behaving 'politically' – and only on such occasions. Nor do we mean that party politics emerges from and intrudes into sub-cultures. We mean, rather, that these sub-cultural groups are, latently and constantly, organized power-groupings. They have an internal system through which this power is deployed; externally, their mere existence is a fact which governments, even the most authoritarian, have to take account of. Normally, too, such power-groupings make sure governments do take account of their interests; they are not merely passive.

Power does not exist 'in itself': it flows between people. And everybody has some of it, some area of choice, of ability to affect things his way. It may only be the power to be negative, to 'vote with one's feet'; in the extreme, only to choose death – but that is a choice, and, as the study of martyrology alone shows us, one which is by no means without social consequences. But some people have overwhelming and decisive power. Power is not randomly distributed, but institutionalized.

The identification of the rulers, therefore, must involve an examination of the distribution of power generally within civil society. In British society, there are only two institutional orders, however, within which very great power is concentrated: the political order and the economic order. This is not true for all societies. In some, for example, those in control of the means of violence are specially important. In the USA, organized religion is a far more potent force than in this country, especially at the community level. The identification of the power elite, the delineation of the distribution of power, are matters for empirical investigation. But a simplistic kind of political behaviourism does not carry us very far. It is commonly assumed, for example, that the role of the military in the USA is very much more considerable than in the UK.

Only in wartime has the military successfully and seriously obtruded itself into the formation of public policy – or even tried to – but at such times, military policy is the central issue in public policy. Viscount Montgomery's public pronouncements are striking in their atypicality – and are self-consciously 'deviant' and outrageous into the bargain.

The British military, then, has never become a caste – it is too closely woven into the culture of the ruling classes. It is no longer, however, one of the major magnetic power-centres attracting the enterprising and the ambitious, probably because, increasingly, it no longer makes the key military decisions. These are made abroad, and the military machine which once coped with the Indian sub-continent, to mention no other area, finds itself stretched in dealing with Cyprus and other backwaters of the world.

Many of these features are reproduced in another formerly central institution of British society, the Church of England, which has been recently described as 'by far and away the most important social institution in the land', and 'by far and away the largest organizer of youth in the country'. Yet, in quantitative terms alone, it now exercises direct and regular influence over less than three million adult members, plus a further 1,161,000 Sunday school children aged between 3 and 14. By contrast, the *Daily Mirror* had a readership of nearly thirteen million people in 1954 – one third of the population aged 16 and over and 'Granadaland' alone embraces some eight million adults.

The Army, the Church, and the Law are not what they were. But ordination still does not mean alienation: four Oxbridge colleges produced nearly one quarter of the Church of England bishops between 1860 and 1960, and the public schools and older universities still dominate recruitment. The class connections of the lower clergy, however, have become less specifically tied to the upper classes (and 22 per cent of contemporary ordinands attended secondary modern and similar schools). Like the Army, as the Church has become less attractive to the upper classes, it increasingly finds its new recruits from formerly excluded social strata, and its senior leaders from within specifically churchly families. If the Church is no longer 'the Conservative Party at prayer', it is also still a long way from being 'that nation on Sunday'. Paradoxically, its democratization, which might well be a future source of religious strength, reflects its diminished social position. It no longer attracts those in search of decisive power; prelates have less to be proud about: education has long slipped from their grasp; morals are increasingly becoming the bailiwick of the BMA, and ideology of the mass media.

As serious centres of power, then, we are concerned predominantly with the political and economic orders. It is significant that Dahrendorf, who emphasizes, pluralistically, that all institutions carry their quantum of power, in fact only singles out economic and political power for special analysis. For Britain, the close association between the two elites at the apex of these institutional orders – the governing elite and the coalesced property-owning landed aristocracy and industrial bourgeoisie – has recently been very closely documented by Guttsman, together with the entry of 'new men' into the ranks of the governing elite (largely via the mechanisms for upward mobility presented by the Labour Movement and an extended educational system).

The uninterrupted, albeit modified, dominance, of the property-owning classes, in a society which has long been the most highly 'proletarianized' in the world, is surely one of the most striking phenomena of modern times.

The answer does not lie in the possession of machine-guns by the ruling class. In this century, only in 1926 has armed force ever been in sight. The challenge of the masses – who created a whole series of instruments of self-expression and self-assertion, from the cooperatives and the trade unions to the Labour Party – has never been a revolutionary one.

The explanation of this continuity and stability involves examination of the modification of both the ruling class and of the ruled. The former were able to accede to the demands of the masses for the vote flexibly and gradually; in the economic sphere, concessions to the 'welfare' demands of the newly-vocal enfranchised masses were also made skilfully and gradually. In the process, the theory and practice of *laissez-faire* had to be thrown overboard. Gradually, the State assumed more and more responsibility for more and more areas of social life. In an age when the nationalized sector of the economy is responsible for half the investment spending, a third of the employment income, and a quarter of the national product, Herbert Spencer's resistance to state interference, whether in the shape of the Post Office, the public mint, poor relief, 'social' legislation, colonization, organized sanitation, or state education, seems remote indeed.

The extensions of the franchise in 1832, 1867, and 1884, were the crucial steps, politically. Yet the beginnings of reform produced no sharp polarization of forces. In the crucial period

1832–68 'the classes were represented in almost the same proportions in each of the two parliamentary groupings' – 'left centre' (Liberal) and 'right-centre' (Conservative). After 1867, the new middle classes gradually crept on to the governmental scene (normally holding offices of lower prestige and 'administrative' content). Not until 1923 did a non-aristocrat hold the office of Foreign Secretary, and not until 1929 was a British government elected on full adult suffrage.

The entry of the middle classes into the centres of political power was thus a long-drawn-out process; the emerging proletariat, in its turn, only very gradually distinguished itself from the party of the middle classes.

Much more was involved in the difficult enterprise of modernization than political changes alone. On their own these might well have led to the rule of the masses so feared by sections of the elite. The modernization of British society was a much more many-sided process, the rationalization and stabilization of a whole 'political culture'. This enculturation was not accomplished by some undifferentiated 'ruling class': more specifically, many of the crucial reorganizations were the achievement of the Liberal Party, and bore the stamp of liberalism, even though that party, theoretically the repository of anti-bigness, anti-statism, and the cult of the individual, nevertheless had quite determinedly reorganized itself as a centralized, hierarchical machine, modelled on Chamberlain's Birmingham caucus system, and as a political party with a mass, extra-Parliamentary base. Self-rationalization was the climax to a long series of rationalizations of the wider society in the third quarter of the nineteenth century, a watershed between the society symbolized by Palmerston and modern mass democracy: reform of the Civil Service (the Northcote-Trevelyan reforms), of the Army (Cardwell's reforms, 1868–71), and of education, both for the elite (the development of public schools on the Rugby pattern) and for the masses (the development of primary education, 1870–80). For the newly-literate, a special literature industry was founded. Via education, a proportion of the working class could find its way into the middle classes. Convinced by their personal experience of the reality of upwards social mobility, they constituted, and constitute, an important reservoir of believers in the notion of *la carrière ouverte aux talents*; their consciousness is structured by their own experience of mobility in the 'middle levels of power', to use Mills' phrase, and generalized into a theory applicable to the society as a whole.

The persistence of patterns of deference and traditionalistic loyalty among other large segments of the lower strata cannot be documented here, nor has it yet been adequately documented anywhere. 'Deference', however, only explains part of the mass vote which the Conservative Party has been able to mobilize since modern politics began in the 1870s.

This solidarity was far more complex than any crude label like 'feudal', 'deference-pattern', or even 'traditionalism' would imply. The imperialist note, indeed, was strikingly untraditional, and was resisted for a long time in both Conservative and Liberal circles, as well as Labour. As Guttsman has pointed out, the feudal heritage was, in fact, a distant one (and had been profoundly challenged and modified via Civil War and industrialization): 'English romantic thought accepted the basic tenets of the Enlightenment: freedom of thought, equality before the law, but it reacted against the libertarian and egalitarian views of the French revolution.' The latter tradition was taken up and developed by the working class; it could not easily form a part of the self-legitimation of the ruling class.

Simple, 'objective' classification of occupations, then, or of the distribution of power, does not take us very far in explaining the success of British conservatism in attracting one-third of the trade union vote to this day. Counting heads is essential in order to establish some primary facts about who people are, but even in order to know what to count at this level, we operate with (often implicit) theoretical assumptions. To get any further, to explore deeper levels of behaviour, we have to move beyond this kind of classificatory activity into the field of 'political culture'. Of course, crude classification and correlation is analytically easier (if technically, perhaps, complicated enough) than more sophisticated exploration; it is also less controversial. The difficulties entailed in exploration arise intrinsically from the fact that human consciousness is involved, for we are dealing with attitudes, shaped by many variables. But the really fertile fields for sociological investigation lie precisely in the exploration of the interplay between the subjective and the objective. Class does not, metaphysically, mean anything 'in itself'. It is always acted upon, interpreted, mediated, by somebody, and it is the social agencies which inject meaning into class, and transmit these meanings to people, that must increasingly concern us. They concern us increasingly, both because this is the needed development in intellectual and analytical terms, and because, empirically, the mechanisms by which consciousness is manipulated are of growing importance in modern society.

Class and Party Divisions: Britain as a Test Case
Richard Rose

Reprinted with permission from *Sociology*, Vol. 2, No. 2, May 1968

Political divisions are inevitable in modern industrial societies, but social scientists disagree about the sources, signs and significance of such divisions. Students of comparative Western politics, while noting that differences in race, religion, language and regional identifications may be of special significance in particular national contexts, have usually emphasized the primary importance of class for political divisions. In such studies, Britain is often the prime empirical example of a political system based on class divisions. This assumption is shared by the great majority of specialists writing on British politics. Given the extent to which Britain approximates the ideal-type or norm for class politics, intensive examination of this case can provide a substantial although incomplete test of many generalizations in the literature of political sociology. Moreover, on one crucial point, use of explicit comparisons between Britain and other countries illustrates how Britain may be simultaneously ideal-typical and yet deviant.

The simple relationship between occupational class and voting at the 1964 general election shows, as at every election since 1945, that the middle class, and particularly the upper-middle class, has been more cohesive in voting Conservative than the working class has been Labour (Table 1 and Gallup Poll 1966). Within the class structure of Britain, one group can be singled out as of particular interest, those whose jobs differ from skilled and other manual workers, yet are not unambiguously middle class. A Nuffield voting study characterizes this group as the routine non-manual workers, placing them in the 63rd to 72nd percentiles of the class hierarchy. The Gallup Poll labels this group as shop and personal service workers, placing them in percentiles 61 to 72.

Unfortunately, the Market Research Society's classification scheme (A, B, C1, C2, DE) appears to combine this category with skilled manual workers. Both the Nuffield and the Gallup data show within this intermediate group a tendency to identify with the working class, but to vote Conservative. In order to concentrate attention upon divisions within the 'hard core' working class, persons in this intermediate category are omitted from subsequent analyses, as are the 5 per cent of Gallup respondents not assigned to any class.

Table 1. Voting by Occupational Class in Britian, 1964

Occupational Class	Percentage of Total	Con.	Lab. Percentages	Other
Professional	7	64	21	15
Business	7	75	11	14
Office workers	14	56	27	17
Shop; Personal service	12	46	37	17
Skilled workers	29	33	52	15
Semi-skilled workers	14	25	64	11
Unskilled workers	12	21	65	14
Unclassified	5	39	40	20

Given the degree of unexplained variance, the safest method of proceeding further at this stage is to examine, one at a time, the impact of working-class occupations plus a wide range of other variables. The Gallup Poll's practice of accumulating a large amount of socio-economic data on each respondent makes it practicable to test many hypotheses. The first set of three concerns the importance of subjective, psychological factors operating in conjunction with occupational position, thus combining the Lazarsfeld, Berelson and Lipset emphasis on class, with the Michigan emphasis upon the psychology of the individual elector.

(1) *Workers subjectively identifying with the working class are more likely to vote Labour than non-identifiers:* Gallup data show that 65 per cent of persons whose objective and subjective position were both working class voted Labour, 24 per cent higher than the figure for manual workers without such an identification. It is important to note that the data also strongly support the converse of this hypothesis. Middle-class identifiers in the working class divided 31 per cent Labour and 53 per cent Conservative.

(2) *Workers interested in class-salient issues are more likely to vote Labour than other workers:* This hypothesis assumes that a worker concerned with issues lacking class salience, e.g., defence or foreign affairs, will be less likely to align his vote with the party of his class than a worker concerned with such class-salient issues as labour relations or economic affairs. Notwithstanding the plausibility of this hypothesis, the data do not show substantial support. Working-class voters naming economic affairs and industrial relations as important issues do not differ significantly from the total. The converse is more strongly supported: workers naming international affairs as an important issue divide 36 per cent Conservative and 49 per cent Labour, and those concerned with defence as an issue divide 41 per cent Conservative and 49 per cent Labour.

(3) *Workers showing higher levels of political involvement are more likely to vote Labour than other workers:* This hypothesis assumes that subjective involvement in politics is more likely to make an individual align himself with the party of the majority of persons in his class. Three different indices are available – interest in the election, perception of important differences between the parties, and concern with the personal impact of the election result. On all three indices, the most involved members of the working class differ hardly at all from a cross-section of all manual workers. The most straightforward inference from this data is that as involvement in politics declines, the inclination of workers to show a preference for either of the two major parties also declines.

A second set of hypotheses can be developed, which assert the importance of material influences by combining the occupational index with another economic sub-system measure as a compound index of class. These include:

(4) *Workers belonging to a trade union are more likely to vote Labour than are non-union manual workers:* This hypothesis is supported by survey data, for among working-class respondents in a union (or in a family where the head of the household held a union card) 65 per cent favoured Labour and 22 per cent favoured the Conservatives, as against a Labour bias of 49 per cent to 35 per cent among non-union workers. Direct personal involvement in union activities appears to add little to Labour voting, since the difference in Labour support as between male respondents in trade unions and housewives whose only contact with a union is through their husband is only 7 per cent.

(5) *Workers in employment are more likely to vote Labour than those who are not in work:* This hypothesis provides a further test of the importance of face-to-face relations in work situations as an intensifier of class cohesiveness. Comparison of all members of the two groups specified in the hypothesis shows that 62 per cent in work favoured Labour and 26 per cent the Conservatives, compared to 51 per cent not in work favouring Labour and 32 per cent the Conservatives. The difference is in the predicted direction, but, in view of the importance of relatively pro-Conservative women and older persons in the not employed category, it is not great. A test comparing the party preferences of working women with those of housewives shows women in work divided 55 per cent Labour and 30 per cent Conservative; housewives favoured Labour in the proportion 51 per cent to 34 per cent Conservative.

(6) *Workers with greater insecurity of employment are more likely to vote Labour than are workers in secure jobs:* A contrary but not implausible hypothesis would be that economic security breeds self-confidence in workers, and therefore a readiness to vote against the party of the *status quo* and the employers. Both hypotheses can be tested with data on how wages are paid. Monthly wages can be regarded as most secure, weekly wages as second in security, and other forms of wages, whether hourly, daily or earned by self-employed manual workers, as least secure. The data rejects both hypotheses, for there is no regular relationship between the groups. Of monthly paid workers ($N=57$), 44 per cent are Labour, weekly paid workers are 62 per cent Labour and those in the most insecure employment are 51 per cent Labour.

(7) *Workers who are more prosperous are less likely to vote Labour than those who are less prosperous:* The thesis of working-class prosperity as a motive for voting Conservative was very popular after the 1959 general election but since then has been subjected to criticism on various grounds. In particular, small studies by Goldthorpe and Lockwood (1967) and by Nordlinger (1967) found that high wages do not bring about general *embourgeoisement*. In these studies, sample sizes and design militated against treating the findings as definitive. The large size of the Gallup sample and its comprehensive coverage provide a more appropriate group for testing this hypothesis. The omission of a direct question concerning income on these surveys is an unfortunate handicap; earnings can only be inferred from questions

concerning motor car and telephone ownership. These indices show that workers owning motor cars in 1964 divided 49 per cent Labour to 36 per cent Conservative, compared to a division of 60 per cent Labour and 26 per cent Conservative among non-vehicle owners. Telephone ownership involves even greater departure from working-class norms. Workers with telephones divided 49 per cent favouring the Conservatives as against 38 per cent favouring Labour. The findings are striking, although interpretation is difficult. It would be safest to infer that the fact of high wages is less immediately important than goods purchased with wages and their relation to life styles. Specifically, a telephone provides a means of communication outside the face-to-face boundaries of a working-class community; it is also a sign that a worker feels high confidence in his ability to communicate with the majority of telephone owners, people in middle-class statuses. A motor car provides a means of mobility outside the working-class community and can bring workers into contact with a wide variety of new experiences and individuals.

(8) *Workers with personal capital are less likely to vote Labour than those without capital:* This hypothesis is accepted not only by persons on the extreme left, but also by business propagandists for wider ownership of company shares. Gallup data provides one suitable indicator – home-ownership. This is a good index, since home-ownership, even if only of a terrace house or a pre-1914 building, is a form of capital investment within the financial means of a large number of manual workers. The implications of home-ownership differ, say, from the implications of automobile ownership, since it implies responsibilities, e.g., calculating for future repairs, rates and maintenance, more acceptable to 'respectable' workers than to the 'rough' working class. In 1964, the tendency of working-class home-owners (or, more properly speaking, mortgage-holders) to vote Labour should have been increased by the salience of the housing issue and Labour's image as a party which would keep interest rates down. Notwithstanding this situational consideration, the data show that at that election, 43 per cent of working-class home-owners voted Conservative and 42 per cent favoured Labour, compared with 64 per cent of working-class tenants supporting Labour and 22 per cent the Conservatives.

A third set of hypotheses concern the interaction of occupational class and social and environmental characteristics. These hypotheses assume, like the American concept of *socio-economic* status, that the combined impact of social and economic influences are likely to be more important than influences derived solely from the economic system.

(9) *Working-class men are more likely to vote Labour than working-class women:* In support of this hypothesis, one could advance a 'depth psychology' argument that Labour was a more 'masculine' party, or a simple sociological assertion that first-hand experience of the work situation is more likely to increase class-oriented voting than is the situation of a housewife. While there is a sex bias towards Labour among men, when one controls for age, sex becomes of limited theoretical interest. It can, of course, be of considerable practical importance in election results (Gallup Poll, 1966). The Almond-Verba study suggests that the similarities are evidence of the willingness of men and women to discuss public affairs in the home on a basis approaching political and sex equality (1963).

(10) *Workers who read pro-Labour papers are more likely to vote Labour than those who do not:* The data concerning this hypothesis, obtained from a 1967 National Opinion Poll survey, show strong relationships between newspaper reading and partisan preference, both within the middle class and the working class (Table 2). The problem is choosing between alternative

Table 2. Voting by Class and Newspaper Readership, 1967

Newspaper	N	Middle Class (ABC1)			N %	Working Class (C2DE)		
		Con.	Lab.	Other		Con.	Lab.	Other
Times	(51)	59	21	20	(22)	—	—	—
Guardian	(67)	30	30	40	(16)	—	—	—
Telegraph	(308)	69	13	18	(80)	59	30	11
Mail	(292)	66	17	17	(282)	46	40	14
Sketch	(70)	80	10	10	(176)	42	39	19
Express	(406)	64	16	21	(692)	37	42	21
Mirror	(270)	42	34	24	(964)	27	53	20
Sun	(48)	35	50	15	(251)	14	73	13
None	(121)	48	26	26	(272)	28	49	23
TOTALS		58	21	21		30	51	19

Source: National Opinion Polls, July 1967.

explanations: (a) the editorial policy of a worker's paper tends to determine his party preference; (b) party preference tends to determine choice of newspaper; or, (c) both party preference and choice of newspaper tend to be determined by a common set of underlying factors. Given the importance of intergenerational socialization influences on party preference and, by implication, on choice of newspaper, evidence that political news is not of substantial interest to most newspaper readers, and evidence of selective perception of political news, then it would be safest to accept the third explanation in default of further data. At most, newspaper reading may be important in re-inforcing previously determined partisan commitments.

(11) *The larger the proportion of workers in an area, the greater the proportion of workers voting Labour:* This assumption concerning increased residential interaction of workers with each other can best be tested by looking at the voting patterns of council house tenants, since council estates form communities or neighbourhoods most likely to intensify face-to-face contact; moreover, these estates are readily identifiable by residents and those outside as working-class areas, with very few middle-class residents. Among the working-class council tenants, 70 per cent favoured Labour and 20 per cent the Conservatives. Tenants in private housing, by contrast, divided 59 per cent Labour to 24 per cent Conservative, almost exactly the overall class average, thus indicating that spatial segregation, rather than the status of a tenant, is the chief influence here. The impact of segregation can also be seen in the fact that among the ambiguously stratified personal and service workers on council estates, a majority, 53 per cent, favoured Labour and 33 per cent the Conservatives, a major deviation from the pattern of that group as a whole. At the level of a larger territorial unit, the constituency, a multiple regression analysis of census data by Shingler (1964) found a curvilinear effect: in heavily working-class constituencies, Labour voting was higher than would be predicted by its class composition, and in constituencies in which there was a relatively small proportion of workers, Labour voting was disproportionately low. The important unit for interaction appears to be the informally bounded face-to-face community, rather than the local authority area in which an individual is formally resident, for there is no consistent relationship between town size and partisan preference. The proportion of workers voting Labour in differently sized areas was 59 per cent in rural areas; 56 per cent

in towns up to 50,000; 62 per cent in towns of 50,000 to 100,000; 62 per cent in towns of more than 100,000; and, in the seven large conurbations, 58 per cent favoured Labour.

(12) *Workers who are less mobile residentially are more likely to vote Labour than other workers:* This hypothesis assumes that a person long involved in the same community is likely to develop a much stronger sense of his place in the class structure than residentially mobile people. The data show that the relationship is more complex. Workers who have always lived in the same place tend to be lowest in Labour support (51 per cent); those who have moved since 1959 rank in the middle (56 per cent Labour), and workers who have moved at least once before then are most pro-Labour (58 per cent). Age differences do not account for this pattern, for the most pro-Labour group has the smallest proportion of young workers, and recent movers, though very disproportionately young people, are slightly below average in their Labour preferences. Age only helps account for the less Labour inclination of those who have always lived in the same house; 70 per cent are age 50 or above, an age at which Labour support declines.

(13) *Workers with above-average education are less likely to vote Labour than workers with minimum education:* Within the tenth of the working class with above-minimum education, Labour loyalties are weak. A total of 40 per cent in this group favoured the Conservatives and 41 per cent Labour in 1964. Analysis in terms of sex differences shows marked contrasts between men and women. Working-class men with further education favoured Labour as against the Conservatives, 46 per cent to 32 per cent. By contrast, educated women, most of whom will be in the working class by virtue of their husband's occupation, favoured the Conservatives as against Labour, 50 per cent to 34 per cent. Educated women in the working class are motivated perhaps partly by aspiration and partly by frustration in actively favouring the Conservatives.

Collectively, the hypotheses concerning compound influences upon working-class voting show that insofar as factors in addition to occupation are important, they are more likely to depress working-class support for Labour than increase it. This gives a little support to Parkin's thesis (1967) that the cultural strength of Conservatism is so great in Britain that even within the working class many voters are impervious to class appeals for party loyalty. Yet in compound categories in which less than a majority favour Labour, it is still infrequent for a plurality, let alone a majority of such manual workers to favour the Conservatives. A second point of considerable importance is that the bulk of influences of special strength – e.g., Welshness, Catholicism and telephone ownership – tend to affect only a very small fraction of the working class. Thus, any attempt to divide the working class into two categories based on the most potent influences would still leave a large proportion of workers unaccounted for.

Many of the problems investigated in the foregoing hypotheses are ignored because class and party loyalties are so often discussed in terms of an ideal-typical working man and his wife. In such circumstances, analysis begins with the postulation of a category of individuals all of whom have a large conglomeration of experiences and attributes in common, from a distinctive pattern of child-bearing by a working-class mum to the special burial customs of the Co-operative Society. Attitudes and behaviour are then predicted and explained by deduction. While ideal-type figures can be heuristically valuable, they will cause confusion if their quasi-empirical nature is not subjected, sooner or later, to empirical test. Ultimately, the significance of such constructs depends less on intellectual attractiveness than on the ease with which ideal-type workers can be identified in empirical research, the extent to which these workers form a substantial portion or majority of the occupational working class, and the extent to which their attitudes and behaviour conform to predicted patterns.

Gallup Poll data includes a wide variety of attributes relevant to the ideal-type or idealized worker. In order to avoid reducing the category to an esoteric group possessing say, up to twelve specified characteristics, four attributes commonly ascribed to working-class people besides occupation have been selected as the operational indicators of the 'ideal-typical' worker: subjective identification with the working class, trade union membership or membership in a family whose head is in a union, only the minimum of education, and residence in rented property. These attributes are drawn from several sub-systems of society, but sub-systems in which class is presumed to be of constant influence. The most significant data lacking are that of the class and party identification of the respondents' parents. Investigation shows that the ideal-type worker constitutes only one-quarter of the 'hard-core' working class (Table 3). If more stringent criteria had

Table 3. Ideal-Type Characteristics and Working-Class Voting

Category	Percentage of Working-Class	Con. %	Lab. %	Other %
All Characteristics (Manual worker; subjectively working-class; tenant; t.u. family; minimum education)	26	14	75	11
All but trade union family	22	22	62	16
All but tenant	10	27	61	12
All but subjectively w-c	7	24	66	10
All but minimum education	1	(56)†	(34)†	(7)†
Lack two or more characteristics of ideal-type worker	34	44	40	16

† N = 27

been employed, the fraction would have been less. The particular criteria did not constitute an unfair choice of indices, since one measure (education) eliminated only one per cent from consideration and two others together eliminated 17 per cent. It is striking that the one attribute most likely to disqualify a respondent is lack of trade union membership within the family, a connection usually assumed to be of fundamental importance in theories of working-class political action. If allowance is made for individuals with at least three of the four ideal-type attributes, another 40 per cent of working-class respondents can be said to approximate the ideal-type figure; more than one-third of the working class remain clearly remote from this category. In all, 14 per cent of the total electorate falls in the pure working-class category, and another 22 per cent in the group approximates the ideal-type. Ideal-type workers are disproportionately Labour, but possession of all the classic attributes of class makes the group no more significantly Labour than either of two non-economic attributes – Welshness or Roman Catholicism. Moreover, the absence of at least two of these four re-inforcing characteristics is positively associated with a Conservative bias. In short, Labour voting in the working class should be regarded as probable, rather than as typical or invariant.

To argue that occupational or socio-economic class is of much less importance for party loyalties than is customarily reckoned is not the same as arguing that structural influences are over-rated as determinants of partisan loyalties. The foregoing test of compositional and compound hypotheses has made it clear that subjective, psychological involvement appears less important as an influence upon working-class voters in Britain than appears to be the case in the Michigan analysis of party identification in the United States (Campbell *et al.* 1960). Among the most important influences subsidiary to occupational class, only one, subjective middle-class identification, is clearly attitudinal; the remainder refer to gross socio-economic characteristics or cultural influences such as Catholicism or Welsh nationality. One might speculate that in a country with a stable, strong class structure – in Weber's terms, 'transparent' – then objective social characteristics are likely to be more important than in America, where the extremely complex nature of the social structure allows an individual's perception of his place in society to be more fluid, and parties too are less clearly class-oriented. The analysis shows that reducing social structure to a single dimension and, further, to a single index of a position along that dimension, is both dubious in theory and, in the field of politics, much less suitable than, say, in educational sociology, where father's occupation has had a much stronger relationship with level of education achieved. Yet in a society lacking large numbers of persons distinguished by their race, religion, nationality or other such features, it is of limited utility to propose a theory of status crystallization *à la* Lenski.

More fruitful lines of enquiry require first the collection of data about a wide range of social and economic characteristics in repeated surveys, in order that tests of relationships can be made in numbers substantial enough to give confidence in the result. With such data and the employment of more sophisticated techniques of multi-variate analysis used in Germany and Austria, one would expect to find empirical verification for the existence of a politically salient model of stratification which, while primarily linked with occupation, would not be exclusively dependent upon economic indices.

In analysing the significance of class for political recruitment in contemporary Britain, one must avoid the fallacy of assuming that a whole constellation of attitudes and policy preferences can be deduced from data on social origins. The most and the least that such data can supply is evidence of symbolic values in working-class representation. The use of such gross indices as occupational class and education can be justified, however, given the system of selecting parliamentary candidates in this country, because such attributes are immediately recognizable when nominating potential Members of Parliament.

Working-class politicians are now in the minority in the Parliamentary Labour Party, but they continue to form a large category by comparison with America and Canada, which lack a major working-class party. The proportion among Labour MPs is declining, however, and among the newly elected MPs at the 1966 general election, only 14 per cent were working class, compared to 32 per cent working class in the whole PLP in 1964. Trade unions are now prepared to sponsor as MPs men whose working-class and trade union affiliations are, at best, tenuous, in order to have a spokesman in the Commons. At Cabinet level, working-class representation is even less significant in the parliamentary party as a whole, and the downward trend has extended further.

The question then arises: Are Labour MPs symbolically representative of any social group? The data in Table 4 show that the Parliamentary Labour Party is becoming representative of university graduates. Among new Labour MPs in 1966, 68 per cent were graduates, compared to a figure of 42 per cent for the whole PLP in 1964. The position in terms of Labour Cabinet ministers is intensified. In autumn, 1967 81 per cent of members of the Cabinet were graduates; 13 of the 17 were from Oxford (Table 5). The most striking feature of this evidence is the convergence of Labour and Conservative patterns of symbolic representation. Notwithstanding the relatively great obstacles that most youths from Labour homes face in attaining a higher education, the proportion of Labour Cabinet ministers with a degree is now about on a par with that in Conservative times, and the proportion of MPs with a degree is becoming more nearly equal between the parties. Within the Conservative ranks, it is almost certainly true, although difficult to demonstrate statistically, that the value placed upon the *content* of a university education is increasing, as against the *status* of having a degree from or at least having matriculated at an ancient and prestigious institution. The trend can readily be explained as a reasonable response of the parties to the growing complexity of government, and the resulting need for politicians to have the modicum of functional competence expected of a graduate, and not expected of working-class men who left school at 14. Class is not declining

Table 4. University Men in the House of Commons, 1906-1966

Year	Labour %	MPs with University Education Conservative %	Liberals and Others %	Total %
1906	0	57	49	49
1910 (Jan.)	0	58	48	52
1910 (Dec.)	0	59	45	51
1918	5	49	33	39
1922	15	48	40	39
1923	14	50	43	37
1924	14	52	48	43
1929	19	54	57	38
1931	17	55	53	51
1935	19	57	55	47
1945	32	58	62	42
1950	41	62	58	51
1951	41	65	75	54
1955	40	64	100	53
1959	39	60	100	52
1964	46	63	78	53
1966	51	67	77	58

Sources: 1906–1910: Thomas 1958:38–39
1918–1945: Ross 1955:424
1950ff.: Nuffield election studies.

Table 5. University Men in Labour Cabinets, 1924-1967

Year	Cabinet	All Universities N	Per Cent	N	Oxbridge Per Cent of University Men
1924	20	6	30	5	84
1929	19	7	37	4	57
1945	20	10	50	5	50
1950	18	9	50	6	67
1964	23	13	57	11	85
1966	23	14	61	11	79
1967 (Dec.)	21	17	81	14	82

in symbolic importance, but rather the class favoured for ruling has been redefined. No longer are MPs expected to represent an occupational class or a traditional upper-status group. Instead, they represent a class defined in terms of achieved merit and presumed performance qualities. In the contemporary social structure, however, this new 'ruling class' constitutes a minority of less than 4 per cent. It is ironically relevant that this is about the same proportion of the population as have had a public school education or otherwise qualify for inclusion in the traditional upper-status classes. Political recruitment thus continues to emphasize government by a class so defined that workers and their children are unlikely to be included.

For individuals recruited into the Parliamentary Labour Party, higher education is one stage in a process of upward social mobility. Judged by pre-university education, a fair index of family background, the great majority of Labour MPs continue to come from ordinary working-class or ordinary middle-class homes. In the current Parliamentary Labour Party, 22 per cent had only a humble elementary education, and 60 per cent a state secondary education. Among the 18 per cent at public schools (i.e. schools in the Headmasters Conference), many went to direct grant schools in the North of England, with family backgrounds more closely resembling manual workers than parents of those at major public boarding schools. For the great majority of Labour MPs, attendance at university provided an *opportunity* for considerable upward mobility, but not the certainty. After taking a degree, such individuals face a problem in sustaining their ascent, lacking the private income and family connections enjoyed by many Conservative MPs from public schools. For young graduates in prosaic occupations (the great majority), participation in party politics and standing for Parliament can confer status and become psychologically gratifying independent of the result. For example, a substantial majority of Labour candidates do not react emotionally against campaigning when they are defeated (Rose & Kavanagh, 1966). Those who succeed in entering the Commons receive enhanced status and psychological gratifications, independently of the collective performance of the party. In such circumstances, attributing a single pattern of behaviour to all graduates is likely to lead to error. University students can differ politically on many grounds, including differences arising from subjects studied at university (*Students in Society*, 1963). Oxford Union types are likely to be as common as the technocratic MP, i.e., a politician tending to recast administrative and legislative machinery in order to improve performance in terms of given goals. The style of a technocrat is moreover, as suitable to the vigorous pursuit of self-consciously calculated careerist and opportunistic goals as it is to the vigorous pursuit of macro-economic ends. The Labour Government of Harold Wilson provides examples of both types.

Judging the significance of class for policy outputs in contemporary Britain is particularly difficult at the time of writing, because the Labour government is about half-way through the life of a Parliament. Government spokesmen can argue that the years up to 1971 will differ from those since 1964. At the symbolic level, the most notable feature of policy discussions is the absence of persisting and bargainable conflicts. In opposition in the 1960s, Labour shifted from Socialism to technocracy, but in office, the technocratic style has been abandoned as opportunistically as apparently it was adopted. At both the 1964 and 1966 elections, Labour campaigns emphasized men not measures. The campaign slogans – 'Let's Go with Labour' and 'You Know Labour Government Works' – were not only devoid of class-conflict implications but also of policy implications. In both foreign and economic policy, the government has pursued policies which have often resembled those of its Conservative predecessor. In short, symbolic partisan divisions, barring an abrupt change in the Conservative Party, appear at most to be nominal or opportunistic.

In assessing material policy outputs under a Labour government, figures on welfare expenditure are available for the first part of Labour's rule. In terms of constant price, welfare expenditure rose under the Wilson government (Table 6). Examination of short-term fluctuations suggests that welfare expenditure tends to rise in advance of a general election. For example, the Conservatives prior to the 1964 election were as ready as Labour to promise greater benefits to the electorate in the late 1960s. The figures for the first two years of the Labour government may therefore be interpreted as a response to pre-election pressures, given the anticipation of a second poll, rather than as a clear-cut disjunction resulting from a change of party in office. Events since the 1966 election, including governmental policy statements, suggest that the increase in welfare expenditure over the total period 1964–70 may not be as great on average as in the

Table 6. Welfare Expenditure in Britain, 1949-1967

Government	Fiscal Year	£ mil. (Current Prices)	£ mil. (Constant Prices)
Labour	1949/50	£1,885·5	£2,553·2
Labour	1950/51	£1,963·6	£2,567·9
Labour	1951/52	£2,134·7	£2,474·4
Conservative	1952/53	£2,416·1	£2,678·9
Conservative	1953/54	£2,532·5	£2,767·7
Conservative	1954/55	£2,614·8	£2,740·3
Conservative	1955/56	£2,801·8	£2,801·8
Conservative	1956/57	£3,010·9	£2,895·1
Conservative	1957/58	£3,172·1	£2,937·1
Conservative	1958/59	£3,477·9	£3,161·7
Conservative	1959/60	£3,718·3	£3,380·3
Conservative	1960/61	£3,990·8	£3,563·2
Conservative	1961/62	£4,414·1	£3,756·7
Conservative	1962/63	£4,659·3	£3,861·2
Conservative	1963/64	£5,285·1	£4,296·8
Conservative	1964/65	£5,796·1	£4,487·7
Labour	1965/66	£6,627·2	£5,032·8
Labour	1966/67	£7,101·9	£5,187·6

Sources: Monthly Digest of Statistics (HMSO: Central Statistical Office). No. 221, May, 1964, pp. vi–vii, years 1949–1962; since 1963/64, No. 257, May, 1967, p. 6.

period 1964–66. The Labour Government's policies on the £, on bank rate, unemployment and trade union legislation further suggest that differences on policies between Labour and its Conservative predecessors may be less great in the end than once was expected. Comparison of British welfare standards with those in America and Canada, countries without working-class parties, indicates that the pressure of a Labour Party in opposition or government is not a necessary condition for high levels of welfare expenditure to be reached.

In contemporary Britain, class appears to be most significant for the mobilization of the electorate, of some significance in the recruitment of politicians, and almost certainly of least importance in decisions about policy outputs. To note this is not to argue that class is of no importance; in a comparative perspective, class is more important for British parties than it is in many European party systems. Yet the recurring pattern of cross-class voting, cross-class recruitment of politicians and cross-class policy decisions, especially within the working class and by the Labour Party, shows that the existence of class differences in politics can be a very different thing from the existence of class conflicts.

Radical Politics and Social Class
Frank Parkin

Reprinted with permission from *Middle Class Radicalism*, Manchester University Press, 1968, pp. 33–59

Indeed, the middle-class radical's position is, in many ways, more extreme than that of the working-class Conservative, in the sense that the disjunction between his own values and those of his class as a whole is considerably sharper. In fact, as McKenzie and Silver have argued, it is perhaps misleading to regard the working-class Conservative as a political deviant, since in many respects his political outlook is given strong institutional support at the social level, and even amongst his own class this outlook will not necessarily mark him off sharply from Labour voters. As McKenzie and Silver put it:

> The organic view of society, promulgated by the great Conservative spokesmen, Burke and Disraeli, finds a responsive echo in the contemporary urban working class. For such reasons, it is hard to think of working-class Conservatives in Britain as normatively deviant from working-class political culture; on the contrary, they seem to express aspects of a wide national consensus.

In comparison with the working-class Conservative the middle-class socialist or radical is much more out on a limb. Not only is his position not amenable to an appeal to the 'national consensus' – which is often the object of his protest – but also the middle class is much more homogeneous in its (right wing) political outlook than is the working class, with the consequence that the social pressures on deviants are likely to be much more concentrated. Informal interviews with CND supporters cer-

tainly suggested that this was in fact the case. It was common
for supporters to refer to tensions between themselves and their
middle-class neighbours, stemming from their different political
alignments. 'We're the black sheep of the neighbourhood', 'they
all think we're dangerous fanatics in this house' and 'anyone in
this street who isn't a staunch Tory is looked upon as a crank',
were typical statements which summed up the political isolation
which the average CND'er would probably experience in his
residential community. For women supporters at home all day
the tensions are obviously more marked, and it would seem that,
for many, social relations with their neighbours are possible only
at the price of silence on matters of politics. As a doctor's wife
explained:

> They invite me to their homes for coffee, and I've had them
> back here. If anything political is discussed I just have to sit
> mum. They have the most outrageous and reactionary views,
> and what is especially annoying is the way they assume that
> someone like myself *automatically* agrees with them. I never
> say a word, but inside I'm boiling.

An ex-schoolmistress recounted her experience in a commuter
suburb as follows:

> We moved into this house about a year ago. To begin with the
> neighbours couldn't have been more friendly and helpful. One
> day I put a Ban-the-Bomb poster in the window and from then
> on things changed. They couldn't have avoided me more if I'd
> caught the plague.

This may perhaps be an extreme case, but it seems to illustrate
the kind of situation which it is not uncommon for middle-class
radicals to be confronted with. Margaret Stacey, for example,
drew attention to similar tendencies in the political life of Banbury. She found that 'when the middle class do come across a
member who is a Labour supporter they are surprised and
shocked. They avoid social relations with the recalcitrant. When
they cannot, as with one who is both a near relative and a business associate, considerable embarrassment is caused'. Stacey
records her experience in a middle-class household on election
day, during a visit of a relative who was a Labour supporter: 'it
was impossible to keep politics out of the discussion altogether,

it was in the front of everybody's mind, and the awkwardness of the situation was only got round by a good deal of joking and back slapping'.

The comparative isolation of the middle-class radical from the political culture of his residential community is to some extent mitigated by the fact that his choice of friends is not primarily based on neighbourhood ties. Whereas working-class friendship patterns are heavily influenced by residential factors, the middle class are prone to exercise a much greater degree of selectivity in the choice of friends, and to make compatibility of interests, rather than residential propinquity, the main criterion of this choice. Because of this, the strains entailed for the middle-class radical in living in a basically hostile political environment can to some extent be lessened by the strategic selection of friends who share his own convictions. Thus 65 per cent of CND respondents reported that the majority of their closest friends approved of the Campaign, as against 23 per cent whose friends were indifferent, and only 3 per cent whose friends were hostile. The selection of politically like-minded friends seems therefore to be one important means whereby the social constraints towards conservatism in white-collar communities may be effectively countered – a process which is facilitated by the middle-class tendency to devalue the reference-group function of neighbours. As suggested above, however, this is rather more easily achieved by men than by their house-bound wives.

The ambiguities entailed in being a member of the middle class but identifying with the political aims of the radical left, and thus largely the working class, are brought out clearly in respondents' assessments of their own status position. They were asked to indicate which social class they considered themselves to belong to, and were presented with the following four possibilities: 'Upper class', 'middle class', 'working class' and 'I do not recognize classes'. The last option was included to provide some additional indication as to whether radicals whose 'objective' position was middle class subscribed to the view of society as class-stratified, or whether in view of their own relatively privileged positions, and the problematic status of the middle class amongst radicals, they would be more likely to disavow altogether the existence of classes. Their responses were as follows:

Table 1. Self-assessed social class

| | Respondents' social class (Hall-Jones scale) | | |
	1+2 %	3+4 %	5+6+7 %
Upper class/Middle class	50	39	0
Working class	8	22	70
Do not recognize classes/ No response	42	39	30
	100	100	100
	(N=96)	(N=201)	(N=44)

It is immediately noticeable that working-class respondents were more certain of their class position than middle-class respondents. None of the former identified themselves as members of the middle class – a fact which at once distinguishes them from manual workers in society at large, amongst whom there is a sizeable minority who assess themselves as middle class. In Runciman's national sample, for example, 29 per cent of manual workers classified themselves as middle class, and in Martin's sample of Greenwich and Hertford workers, a total of 24 per cent did so. It would seem therefore that the radical outlook of working-class CND supporters predisposes them to devalue the middle class as a reference group more strongly than does the manual sector as a whole. The minority of working-class CND supporters who do have doubts about their class location resolve these in favour of non-recognition of classes altogether, rather than identity with the middle class. This serves to underline the point sometimes overlooked in studies of the relationship between self-assessed social class and political choice – namely that the individual's political outlook may well decisively *influence* his class identification, and not simply be a product of that identification.

Table 1 similarly shows that the self-assessed status of middle-class CND supporters is also considerably at variance with that common to the non-manual stratum at large. Only half of those respondents in occupational classes 1 and 2 acknowledge membership of the middle class – a figure which contrasts markedly with the 93 per cent who do so in Martin's Greenwich and Hertford sample. Of these latter only 3 per cent replied 'don't know' or 'do not belong' when asked to assess their social class – a finding which squares well with other studies which have shown that the top stratum of the middle class tends to be the most 'class conscious' sector of the population. By contrast, 42 per cent of CND respondents from this stratum claimed not to recognize classes, or could not reply. Similarly, amongst occupational classes 3 and 4, only 39 per cent of CND supporters assigned themselves to the middle or upper class, against 65 per cent of the Greenwich and Hertford sample; only 3 per cent of the latter could give no answer or claimed not to belong to a class, while the comparable figure for CND respondents was 39 per cent.

Although a refusal to recognize classes is not altogether identical with the claim not to belong to any class, it is sufficiently similar to point up the discrepancy between the status alignments of the middle class in general, and those who support CND. It does again bring out the extent to which middle-class status is devalued in the eyes of radicals – not least among those who, by occupational criteria at least, share this status. This was also frequently illustrated by respondents' written comments on the questionnaire; many of those who did in fact allocate themselves to be middle class indicated that they did so with qualifications or reluctance, by entering remarks such as 'by job only', 'middle class in occupation but not in mind', or in one case simply, 'middle class – unfortunately'. The lack of identity which middle-class radicals feel with their ascribed social status might be expected to convey itself in other ways. A variety of symbolic means are available to individuals who seek to dissociate themselves in some way from the social roles and behaviour patterns which they are constrained to adopt by virtue of their occupational and other statuses. Goffman has coined the term 'role-distance' to describe the behaviour designed to convey an individual's personal withdrawal from activities which are formally required of him in certain social situations. He who personally disapproves of his role obligations is able, through appropriate gestures, intonations, and the like, to fulfil these obligations whilst at the same time conveying to others his dissociation from them; self-respect is preserved by the individual's signals that 'this is not the real me'.

It would appear that, along similar lines, the middle-class radical is often prone to exhibit what might be called 'status-

distance', by making small symbolic gestures designed to con-
vince others (as well as himself) that, despite his occupation and
income, he is not to be thought of as 'bourgeois'. One simple way
of conveying this message is by means of dress and personal
appearance. Thus, as was mentioned earlier, the wearing of
beards was far more common among CND supporters than
among men in general. And it is fair to claim that the decision to
grow a beard may be taken as a token of the individual's desire
to make a personal statement about himself and his individuality
– that he is not to be equated with the common herd. The
attitude which in our society marks out the wearer of a beard as
in some vague and unspecified ways 'different', makes it a
readily adaptable symbol for the radical wishing to convey his
dissociation from bourgeois values. No doubt differences in dress
are able to serve similar purposes. Impressionistically at least it
appears that contrasts do exist in the clothing styles of middle-
class Conservatives and radicals, although this may often be
little more than a preference for a more casual appearance on the
part of the latter. Whilst matters of dress and appearance are
only peripheral to an individual's politics it is worthwhile pointing up differences that do exist because of the way they may be
utilized by the middle-class radical to demonstrate his distance
from the middle class in general, and the political and social outlook attributed to it. By the mechanism of 'status-distance' he is
able to derive gratification and self-respect from his public dis-
avowal of bourgeois values, without at the same time taking the
drastic step of abandoning his middle-class status for one lower
in the social order. It is perhaps significant in this regard that
differences in dress and appearance are not noticeable between
Conservatives and radicals in the working class. This would
seem to support the view suggested earlier that working-class
Conservatives are not really deviant within their class in the way
that middle-class radicals are, and hence feel no need to symbolize their apartness in dress or appearance.

The City and Industry:
The Directors of Large Companies,
Their Characteristics and Connections

Richard Whitley

Reprinted with permission from Stanworth and Giddens (Eds.), *Elites in Britain*, Cambridge University Press, 1974

Introduction

Group cohesion or solidarity is often regarded as an essential pre-requisite of an elite and backgrounds of, and connections between, elite members have been studied as constituting the pre-conditions of a high degree of cohesion. To study changes in elites, defined here as sets of individuals in positions of authority over major social organizations sharing, to some minimum degree, common perceptions, beliefs and values, over time, however, and to relate these changes to the larger socio-economic environment, some indication of the degree of integration of group is required, preferably covering more than one dimension of connectedness. Lupton and Wilson examined educational background, club membership and kinship links between 'top decision makers' and Brown, among others, has discussed over-lapping directorships but connectedness between leading institutions has not been systematically analysed. A high degree of integration between leaders of major institutions has implications for their actions since it implies some common culture which mediates structural exigencies and creates the possibility of common, coordinated actions. Commonality of background and frequent opportunities for contact between leaders of similar institutions constitute favourable conditions for group solidarity, especially when combined with a considerable ownership of personal wealth. In understanding the behaviour of institutions, then, it is suggested that the degree of integration, and conditions favourable to it, are of importance since these lead to considera-tion of the group culture and rationality. Differing degrees of commonality and connectedness between leaders of institutions can be expected to lead to different responses to structural changes. Common educational backgrounds and life styles as evidenced, for example, through membership of exclusive clubs' constitute a basis for common definitions of socio-economic reality and associated actions. Similarly, structurally based connections between institutional leaders provide suitable conditions for developing and coordinating common definitions and actions. If leaders of similar social institutions are selectively recruited in terms of education, have access to prestigious social organizations and are related to the traditional aristocracy, as well as being connected through directorships, then it seems likely that they will share similar beliefs and values and so constitute an elite – although, of course, the existence of a common culture still requires direct investigation.

In an earlier paper I outlined background commonalities and connections between directors of 27 large financial institutions using published data and suggested that the basis of a common culture existed. The assumption that directors are indeed powerful in such organizations was justified by reference to their active participation in mergers and acquisitions, investment and unit trust fund management as revealed by the financial press. Although it is arguable that directors of very large industrial companies may not wield much power in terms of day to day administration, the increasing sophistication of financial control techniques and importance of major financial decisions which traditionally are the preserve of the Board of Directors make it more, rather than less, likely that directors exercise substantial control. Here, then, I extend the earlier analysis to the connections between the 'City' and very large industrial companies, to see how similar are the networks connecting directors of financial institutions and those connecting directors of industrial companies, to examine how industrial firms are connected to financial organizations, and how similar in background are their directors. This seems a necessary prelude to both differentiating industrial companies with a view to relating different types of Boards of Directors to economic variables, and to charting relations between the 'City' and industrial companies over time with a view to relating changes in these relations to changes in general financial policies. Brown has suggested a threefold classification of the top 116 companies and has related this to some common economic variables. The basis for his allocation of firms to the categories is not entirely clear, however, and by directly examining directors of financial and industrial companies it is hoped to provide a systematic basis for future work.

Procedure

The financial firms covered in the present study include the big four clearing banks, merchant banks with authorized capital of over £5m., discount houses with authorized capital of over £3m., the Bank of England and the eight largest insurance companies drawn from the 1971 *Stock Exchange Year Book*. Although some changes have taken place in individual firms through mergers and acquisitions since then it is unlikely that the general characteristics and connections of directors have altered to any great extent. The top 50 industrial companies were taken from the *Times 1,000* listing for 1970–71 and their directors similarly gathered from the *Stock Exchange Year Book*. This list is based on turnover, which is not always a reliable indicator of size since some service firms may have a large turnover in terms of paper transactions (e.g., commodity brokers) with a relatively small capital base. However, if capital employed is used as the indicator of size, only 13 companies were thereby found to be excluded from the top 50, and five of the 13 which were in the top 50 by capital employed shared directors-companies in the top 50 by turnover. Turnover, therefore, was retained as the criterion, but purely financial or brokerage firms were excluded on the grounds that they were really part of the 'City' and so more likely to be connected with leading financial institutions than non-financial concerns. In examining Boards of Directors it is also relevant to note that subsidiaries of foreign companies may well operate in different ways from companies based in this country, so foreign owned subsidiaries were also excluded. It would, of course, be of interest to analyse these companies and their policies separately. These two sets of exclusions left 40 industrial companies, which are listed, together with their turnover, capital employed and number of directors in Table 1 with the financial firms.

Data about directors' background characteristics and connections were gathered from the usual published sources. Unfortunately the proportion of directors of industrial companies for whom background data were available was not as high as for the directors of financial firms and educational and club details were located for just under a half (49 per cent) of the 'industrial' directors. Generally, information from published sources is biased towards the aristocracy and members of the traditional top-status groups, but as far as can be inferred by comparing the various sources with each other this bias is not large enough to indicate any substantial difference between the 50 per cent of directors for whom data are available and those from whom they are not. The measure of connectedness used here is based on Doreian's integration score, normalized to allow comparisons between groups of different sizes.

Background characteristics

As remarked above, educational data were available for nearly half, 261, of the directors. These are given in Table 1, together with those for the 27 financial firms reproduced for comparison purposes. As can be seen, Eton and the major public schools figure much less prominently for directors of industrial companies than is the case for directors of financial institutions. However, Eton still educated 34 industrial directors and 66 per cent attended fee-paying schools, still a substantial proportion, if not as high as the 80 per cent characteristic of directors of financial firms. This figure is, it should be noted, slightly less than the 71 per cent found by Heller in his surveys of directors of the top 200 firms. The reduction in the proportion attending fee-paying schools is, of course, largely due to the substantial number educated at grammar schools. This does not necessarily imply that all such schools were non fee-paying, simply that they were not 'independent'. Similar results occur when university education is considered. Two-thirds of the industrial directors attending institutions of higher education went to either Oxford or Cambridge, compared with 87 per cent of the financial directors. However, the proportion going to university was about the same as that for directors of the insurance companies. Overall, these results indicate a fairly selective recruitment process but not so restricted as occurred in the 'City'.

Club membership was analysed using the same prestigious and aristocratically connected clubs as in the earlier selected study from discussions in Graves, Lejeune, Matthews and Sampson, i.e., the Carlton, Boodle's, Brooks's, Buck's, the Beefsteak, Pratt's, the Turf, St James's and White's. 73 (28 per cent) of the 261 directors for whom data were available were members of at least one, and often more, of these clubs. Many more were, of course, members of other clubs such as the Athenaeum, Junior Carlton, Garrick, City of London, etc. This proportion is con-

Table 1. Educational background of directors

School	Bank of England	Clear-ing banks	Merchant banks and discount houses	Insur-ance com-panies	Indus-trial firms
Eton	1	31	37	46	34
Harrow	0	3	7	9	5
Winchester	2	11	5	6	7
Rugby	3	5	6	4	6
Charterhouse	1	2	1	2	1
Marlborough	0	2	1	0	7
Other public	3	25	25	31	110
Private	0	0	2	1	3
Total fee-paying	10	79	84	99	173
Grammar	5	18	16	17	71
No secondary	1	0	1	0	0
Overseas	2	2	5	2	8
County Secondary	0	0	0	0	9
Total	18	99	106	118	261
No data	0	16	50	48	269
Universities					
Oxford:					
Trinity	0	8	2	7	7
New	1	7	5	9	8
Magdalen	1	5	7	4	3
Other	2	11	20	11	35
Cambridge:					
Trinity	2	12	14	14	18
Magdalene	1	4	4	6	0
Other	4	13	13	13	34
Other UK	1	10	5	7	34
Military	0	2	0	3	2
Foreign	0	0	4	1	11
None	6	29	33	43	109
Total	18	101	107	118	261

siderably lower than the 46 per cent found for the direcors of large financial institutions, which suggests that industrial company directors are less associated with the traditional social elite's life style than are the 'City' directors; whether this implies a divergence in values and attitudes remains to be explored. The

Table 2. Membership of nine prestigious clubs

			Industrial companies
Club	*Financial institutions*	*No. of directors*	*Firms represented*
The Carlton	25	18	G.E.C., R.T.Z., Cadbury Schweppes, Unigate, I.C.I., Tate & Lyle, Sears, Tube Investments, Rank, Hawker Siddeley, B.I.C.C., Boots, B.P., Union International, Dunlop
Boodle's	23	12	T.I., Cadbury Schweppes, Dunlop, Bass Charrington, Burmah Oil, Shipping Industrial Holdings, Bowater, B.P., Allied Breweries, Boots
Brooks's	41	15	G.E.C., R.T.Z., Shell T. & T., Dunlop, Distillers, Rank, B.P., Burmah Oil, T.I., I.C.I., Rolls-Royce, Unilever, Bass Charrington
Buck's	4	10	I.C.I., Tate & Lyle, B.P., Burmah Oil, G.E.C., Boots, B.I.C.C., Shell T. & T., Hawker Siddeley, Rank, Hovis McDougall, Allied Breweries, Rolls-Royce, Bass Charrington
The Beefsteak	6	3	Shell T. & T., Dunlop, Distillers, Lucas, Rolls-Royce
Pratt's	20	7	I.C.I., Tate & Lyle, Shell T. & T., Dunlop. S.I H., Rolls-Royce, G.E.C., B.P.
The Turf	15	4	B.P., Burmah Oil, Marks & Spencer, Unilever, Bass Charrington, Rank, R.T.Z.
St James's	6	2	
White's	32	16	B.P., B.I., M.C., S.I.H., Bowater, Tate & Lyle, Boots, Rank, B.I.C.C., Shell T. & T., Hawker Siddeley, R.H.M., R.T.Z., Rolls-Royce, Union International

Proportion of firms in network $= 29:40 = 73\%$.
Integration score ($N = 29$) $= 0.97$.
Firms not in network: Shell Mex & B.P., Imperial Tobacco, Coats Patons, Tesco, Thorn Electric, G.K.N., Reed International, G.U.S., Courtaulds, Allied Suppliers.

firms represented by membership of the nine clubs are listed in Table 2, as is the integration score for the network which, although very high, only applies to 73 per cent of the firms under discussion. It should be noted here that this measure takes all entries in a matrix above 1 as 1 and so underestimates the actual number of connections between two firms. Unlike the 'City' firms, where the two 'newcomers' are not represented, there does not appear to be any single characteristic of the eleven excluded firms which would account for their lack of connection with these clubs. The background characteristics of the directors of industrial companies then, indicate a restricted social origin and, for a considerable minority, affiliation with prestigious social institutions.

Overlapping directorships

Direct connections between the 40 industrial companies by overlapping directorships only occur between 21 firms, and two of these, Distillers and Lucas, are not connected with the other 19. This network is not highly integrated, having in fact an integration score of 0·52. Again, these figures are much lower than in the case of the 'City' firms, where 93 per cent were directly connected by overlapping directorships with an integration score of 0·82. This picture changes rather when connections with the 'City' are taken into account. The network becomes too complicated to present figuratively and is unfortunately too large to reproduce as a matrix, 56 of the 67 firms are now included in the network, 31 industrial companies and 25 'City' ones, which indicates that a further 10 industrial companies now appear because they are directly connected to large 'City' firms and therefore included in the network. The merchant bank with the largest number of connections to industrial companies is Hill, Samuel, and the clearing bank most industrially connected is the Midland; their networks are shown in Figure 1. As can be seen ICI is the most connected industrial company. As Speigelberg points out, many of these connections are fairly recent and reflect a growth in influence on the part of the financial institutions. The firms which are not included are: Allied Suppliers, Coats Patons, Great Universal Stores, Marks and Spencer, Reed International, Tesco, Thorn, Unilever and Union International. Of these nine, six are dominated by a single man or family: only two of the other 31 appear to have this charac-

teristic – Sears Holdings, which is included because Sir Charles
Clore was on the Board of Hill, Samuel, and Tate and Lyle
which shares a director, Lord Boyd, with ICI. The comparative
isolation of the 'tycoon' and 'family' type company Board from
the 'City', the traditional elite, and other firms is reflected in
other ways. The integration score for this network of 56 firms is
0·92 which is high and, it should be noted, higher than that for
the 'City' firm taken alone: thus indicating that the cohesion of
this combined network is not solely due to the comparatively
highly interconnected 'City'. Again it should be pointed out that
very often more than one director is held in common between
two firms, but the integration score does not take this into
account.

If indirect connections between industrial companies through
overlapping directorships of other firms, obtained from the
Directory of Directors (1971), are included, 36 of the 40 firms are
connected by at least one director, showing an integration score
of 0·93. Here again, it is notable that three of the four companies
not in the network, Allied Suppliers, Marks and Spencer, Tesco
and Union International, are 'tycoon' or 'family' firms. Furthermore, Thorn Electric and Great Universal Stores each have only
one indirect connection with other firms. Distillers and Unilever
also have only one connection, with Lucas and BA Tobacco
respectively, and Unigate and Tate and Lyle have two. When the
financial institutions are included, 62 of the 67 are in the network, which has an integration score of 0·95. The omissions are:
Allied Suppliers, Marks and Spencer, Tesco, Union International
and Minster Assets. Firms only loosely connected (i.e., with only
one or two overlaps) are Great Universal Stores, Tate and Lyle
and Unilever. Thorn Electric has three connections. So again
there seems to be a large, highly connected network of most
major industrial and financial firms, with predominantly family
or 'tycoon' controlled firms remaining largely isolated from this.

Kinship connections

This picture is substantially the same for kinship connections,
except that for the industrial companies nuclear family connections are negligible. Using the same five criteria of kinship connection, based on common great-grandparents, as in my earlier
paper, fifteen of the 40 industrial companies are connected

Figure 1. Overlapping directorships: industrial connections of Hill, Samuel and the Midland Bank.

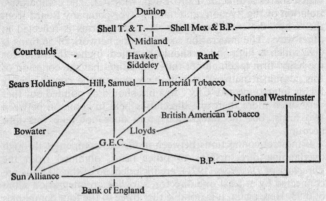

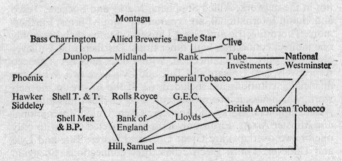

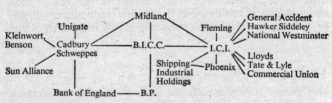

(a) Connections between Financial Institutions are omitted from this diagram for purposes of clarity.

through directors mentioned in *Burke's Peerage* and *Burke's Landed Gentry*. Only seven of these, however, form a network greater than two, and this is only loosely integrated. These numbers are very low compared with those obtained for directors of the financial institutions, where it was found that 26 of the 27 firms were connected, with an integration score of 0·91. Obviously directors of very large industrial companies are much less associated with the aristocracy than are directors of large financial institutions. When the two sets of firms are combined, 18 of the industrial firms are also included in the network to form one of 44 companies with an integration score of 0·94, which is slightly higher than that for the 'City' firms alone. Hill, Samuel, Lloyd's Bank and the Guardian Royal Exchange Insurance have the largest number of industrial kinship connections and RTZ has the largest number of total kinship connections. With the exception of Tate and Lyle, none of the 'tycoon' and 'family' firms were in the network. These results show that although Boards of the very large industrial companies are not nearly so integrated with the traditional upper status group as are those of the large financial institutions, a considerable degree of connection between many large companies and financial firms does exist through the aristocracy. This may well have increased over the last 30 or so years as the management of large sums of money has become of increasing concern to the very large firm, and the need for sophisticated financial advice has correspondingly increased in conjunction with the growth of institutional investment.

Conclusions

In comparing directors of 40 very large industrial companies with the directors of large financial institutions, both as distinct groups, and as one set, some fairly firm conclusions can be drawn. First, although the educational background of the industrial directors is not as restricted as that of the financial directors, it is still predominantly based on wealth, and a substantial number enjoy membership of an exclusive social institution, prestigious London clubs. Secondly, half of these firms share directors with at least one other in the set, although the network is not nearly so highly connected as the financial one. These connections are much increased when the 27 financial institutions are taken into account: only nine firms are not so connected. This suggests that the financial institutions play the central role in coordinating industrial companies' policies, and that seemingly disparate industries may be united through the financial elite. Obviously, however, the actual role of outside, financially expert directors remains to be determined, although according to data in Crawford merchant banks often do put one of their directors on the Boards of client companies. Spiegelberg also draws attention to the increasing influence of the merchant banks and institutions on large industrial companies. Furthermore, this network of directors from financial and industrial firms combined is highly structured. As would be expected, these figures are much increased when directorships of other firms are included, and again the 'City' and 'Industrial' seem remarkably closely linked. Thirdly, while aristocratic kinship links do not appear to be particularly relevant for the industrial companies considered alone, they are important in connecting these companies to financial institutions and in producing a large, integrated network of the two groups combined. The directorship connections between industry and financial institutions, that is, are reinforced by, or alternatively can be seen as reflections of, kinship ties. The one group of industrial companies which does not appear integrated into this combined elite is comprised of 'tycoon' or 'family' firms. It is also worth noting that 11 out of the 18 directors of Marks and Spencer, GUS, Thorn Electric, Sears and Tesco for whom educational data were available did not go to public school, a proportion much lower than that for directors of industrial companies as a whole. Not only, then, are these firms relatively unconnected through directorship, clubs or kinship to others and to the 'City', but recruitment to their Boards is not so narrowly limited as in the case of the others. Brown has already pointed to some differences in growth and profits for 'tycoon' firms in the top 116, an analysis which requires further extension. Brown also distinguishes between 'coordinator' and 'managerial' type boards, but on the basis of the evidence shown here there do not appear to be any purely 'managerial' companies in the top 40 except for Unilever and Allied Suppliers (in which, incidentally, Unilever has a substantial voting shareholding). Whether this is due to change in composition of the boards of large companies, or whether most 'managerial' boards are owned by overseas companies is not clear. A further point on these 'deviant' firms is that they are all fairly recent additions to the very large firm category. If the economists' ideas about the life cycle of the firm are applicable, then presumably these companies should eventually stabilize their growth rate and may well turn into connected companies with major institutional investors and merchant bankers on the Board.

In terms of seeing directors as an elite it appears that very large industrial and financial firms do recruit their Board members from a narrow segment in the population. These directors undergo a remarkably similar educational experience and, to some extent, have similar social circles as evidenced by club membership and kinship links. They tend, in other words, to be members of the same culture, or at any rate to have the background for sharing a common culture. The next step which needs to be taken is to ascertain to what extent these directors do, in fact, share a common view of social reality. Does, for example, the interconnectedness of financial and industrial Boards mean that the traditional opposition of the 'City' and 'Industry' has disappeared with the rise of giant companies, or do directors of merchant banks and of oil companies still see their basic interests diverging? Part of this question can be answered by finding out exactly how far the similarity of, and connections between, these directors have changed over the past 30 or 40 years. If they have indeed altered, then to what extent have these changes been associated with changes in financial and industrial strategy, and can we expect such changes to continue in the same direction? If we can ascertain the dimensions and dynamics of the culture of the financial industrial elite, we may then proceed to suggest how this culture will mediate structural exigencies of developed capitalism, by constructing an overall theory of advanced capitalism which combines sociological and economic approaches.

Members of Parliament

Peter G. Richards

Reprinted with permission from *The Backbenchers*, Faber & Faber, 1972, pp. 11–33

The United Kingdom is divided into 630 constituencies. Each returns one Member to the House of Commons: England elects 511 Members, Wales 36, Scotland 71 and Northern Ireland 12. These 630 men and women have the power to change the character of public policy and, indeed, to change the government. If the Cabinet fails to command a majority in the Commons on a vote of confidence, then the Cabinet must resign or the Prime Minister must appeal for public support at a general election. In fact, the Commons does not destroy governments, due to the strength of party loyalty and party discipline. But the threat is still there. In a less stable political situation it could become crucial. Meanwhile, the 630 Members are a vital link in the connecting chain between government and governed. They transmit opinions and help to shape attitudes. They form the pool of talent from which national leaders are chosen. They elect these leaders, either directly or indirectly. The individual backbencher is generally unimportant; collectively, backbenchers can be all-important.

What sort of people are these 630 Members? Obviously they are not, like a jury, a typical cross-section of the community. Powerful filters ensure that only certain types of individual arrive at Westminster. These filters are political, social and legal. An initial requirement is a keen interest in politics, a willingness to take up a political career and to devote much leisure time to the affairs of a political party. Such voluntary activity may lead to nomination as a parliamentary candidate. The next limitation arises from the lack of any element of proportional representation in a single-member constituency system, so political minorities are at a disadvantage and the overwhelming majority of Members are sponsored by one of the two major parties, Conservative or Labour. These parties have certain preferences as to the qualities they seek in their representatives.

Social Experience

The predominant characteristic of Members of the Commons is that almost all of them are supporters either of the Conservative Party or the Labour Party. The single-member constituency system where victory goes to the candidate with the highest number of votes is unkind to the smaller parties. So the Liberals, in spite of significant support in the country as a whole, are left with a mere handful of Members: in 1970 Liberals secured 7·5 per cent of the total vote but their six seats represented less than 1 per cent of the membership of the Commons. Other minor groups, notably the Scottish and Welsh Nationalists, suffer in the same way. An independent candidate is in a hopeless plight since he cannot combat the strength of established political organizations when trying to win support from the 60,000 voters in a typical constituency. There was one remarkable Independent victory in 1970, Stephen Davies (Merthyr Tydfil); however, the conditions were exceptional as Davies had been the local Member since 1934 and, having been rejected by the local Labour Party on grounds of advanced age, was duly re-elected on the basis of his personal reputation. The dominance of the major parties is not so firm in Northern Ireland which in 1970 returned four Members of varying opinions who fall beyond normal party groupings. The only other Members elected in 1970 outside the two-party system were the Speaker and the Scottish Nationalist who triumphed in the remote constituency of the Western Isles. Thus 617 out of the total 630 Members were either Labour or Conservative.

So the people who become Members are those who appear most suitable to local Conservative and Labour selection committees. General practice is for a constituency party to re-adopt a retiring Member. Just occasionally this does not happen because of local dissatisfaction with a Member on personal or policy grounds. Of course, sometimes a Member will wish to retire or he may be defeated at the polls when there is a 'swing' against his party. It follows that the great majority of Members of a new House of Commons will have had previous parliamentary experience. (Table 1).

The figures show that the Commons enjoy a high level of continuity. Indeed, the turnover of Members was higher in 1970 than at any election since 1945 because of the size of the movement of political opinion. So even in the least experienced

Table 1. Parliamentary Experience of Members, 1970

	Conservative	Labour	Others
First elected 1970	83	64	3
Elected pre-1970	247	223	10
Elected pre-1960	166	166	4

House since the post-war election, nearly half the Members could claim ten years' service.

To select a candidate for a seat that a party hopes to win is obviously a more serious exercise than the choice of someone to fight a hopeless seat. But to fight a hopeless contest is regarded both as good experience and as evidence of true devotion to the Party cause: the candidate for a promising constituency is often someone who has stood and lost elsewhere. The 27 Conservative Members who retired in 1970 were replaced by 11 ex-Members, 11 previously unsuccessful candidates and 5 novices. Yet local Conservative Associations do not necessarily favour the candidate with the most political experience: defeated ex-Ministers can find it very difficult to find a fresh seat. An ex-Minister is obviously a potential future Minister and, as such, local selectors may fear that he will pay less attention to constituency problems. A similar tendency has been noticeable in the Labour Party.

Table 2 shows the age distribution of Members analysed by party. It will be noticed that Labour has a higher proportion of Members above the age of 60: Labour Members are less willing to retire than Conservatives, no doubt because of less favourable financial circumstances.

The proportion of younger Members, those below 40, is very similar in the two main parties. When compared with previous Parliaments, the figures for the lowest age group, below 30, do show a major change. It used to be the case that the youngest Members were Conservatives. After the 1959 Election the ten Members below 30 were all Conservatives. In 1970 the three youngest Conservatives, Winston Churchill (Stretford), Kenneth Clarke (Rushcliffe) and John Wilkinson (Bradford, West), were all within four months of their thirtieth birthdays; had the General Election been held in October 1970, it is probable that no Conservative Member would have been below the age of thirty. It seems that Conservative selectors now require some maturity and are unwilling to accept very young men from Eton and Oxbridge with strong family connections.

Table 2. Age of Members, 1970

Age at 18.6.70	Conservative	Labour	Liberal	Others
21–29	3	5	—	2
30–39	60	53	3	—
40–49	121	87	2	3
50–59	106	78	1	—
60–69	38	59	—	1
Over 70	2	5	—	1
Totals	330	287	6	7

The number of female Members remains remarkably constant. In 1970 a total of 26 were elected, exactly the same as in 1966. There was, however, some change in the party composition of this group; the fifteen women Conservatives was an all-time record while the ten on the Labour side constituted the lowest figure since the war. As women form over half the electorate these very small numbers demand some comment. No evidence exists to show that voters discriminate against Conservative and Labour female candidates. It is impossible to show that selection committees discriminate against women because no information is available about the potential number of female parliamentary candidates. If few women wish to become Members then it is neither surprising nor unreasonable that there are few women Members. Meanwhile the total of female candidates rises slowly: Conservatives nominated 21 in 1966 and 27 in 1970 while Labour nominated 30 in 1966 and 29 in 1970. One factor to be noted is that local party selectors are unwilling to take the risk that their Member will become pregnant. It is unusual for a woman to be elected while she is in the age range when childbearing is most common. Yet this generalization is subject to a notable exception: the youngest Member of either sex elected in 1970 was Bernadette Devlin (Ind. Mid. Ulster).

The contrast between the social experiences of Conservative and Labour Members is best illustrated by a comparison of the educational and occupational backgrounds: 77 per cent of Conservative Members attended a public school; only 20 per cent of Labour Members did so. No fewer than 59 Conservatives went to Eton – nearly 20 per cent of male Tory Members. Old Etonians were also very successful at Conservative selection conferences for winnable seats: 69 Conservative candidates were old Etonians, so 85 per cent were victorious. It used to be the case that the Conservatives had a higher proportion of Members with a university education but this gap is now narrowing; the percentages after the 1970 election were Conservatives 63 per cent, Labour 53 per cent. But far more Conservatives went to Oxbridge – 82 per cent of all Conservative graduates as compared with 46 per cent of Labour graduates. At the other end of the educational scale the schooling of 20 per cent of Labour Members was 'elementary', while only a single Conservative Member fits into this category.

Certain occupations are heavily represented in the House. In 1970 there were as many as 125 lawyers; 97 barristers and 28 solicitors spread across all parties including the Liberals. There were 66 teachers; all except ten were Labour Members. All but four of 84 company directors were Conservatives. The 58 publishers and journalists were spread across the parties. 31 of 32 farmers were Conservatives. Inevitably the 22 miners were solidly Labour. While 72 Labour Members could be described as 'workers' only 2 Conservatives fell into this grouping. These occupation figures can be misleading for they refer to a Member's means of livelihood prior to election: in some cases, but not in others, a Member has continued to earn money from his original calling. Thus some lawyers continue to practise after election to Westminster but teachers cannot continue to teach. Journalists can carry on with their writing and company directors with their directing but the worker from the shop floor leaves his old environment behind. Especially with Labour Members who have been in the House for several years, something of a gap can develop between their previous occupation and their contemporary situation.

The occupational background of Labour Members is affected substantially by the practice of sponsoring candidates. This means that a trade union makes a substantial contribution to the election expenses of a local party where a member of the union has been selected as the parliamentary candidate. 112 Labour Members were sponsored in 1970. A further 17 Labour Members were financially assisted at the election by the Co-operative Party, the political wing of the Co-operative Movement.

Table 3 reveals two tendencies. Union influence has been stronger since 1964 and it also tends to be weaker when the political climate is favourable to Labour – this is because union

Table 3. Trade Union Candidates 1945–70

Year	Union candidates elected	Total of Labour Members	T.U. Members as % Labour Members
1945	120	394	30
1950	111	315	35
1951	105	295	36
1955	96	277	35
1959	92	258	35
1964	120	317	37
1966	132	363	36
1970	112	287	39

assistance is centred on seats that are likely to be won. The system helps to maintain the link between the Parliamentary Labour Party and the shop floor although an increasing number of sponsored candidates are people with professional qualifications. In the past, sponsoring arrangements have also been criticized as being responsible for the poor quality of some Labour Members.

Many Members have served on a local authority (Table 4). Selection committees seem to regard local government service as a positive merit since it means that a candidate has had experience of the welfare aspect of the work of an elected representative. This tendency is strongest in urban areas. In some large cities, especially Glasgow and Liverpool, Labour Members are almost always 'promoted' from the local council. The figures below show that it is the Labour Party which has the strongest link with local government.

Table 4. Members with Experience as Councillors: 1970

Labour	Conservative	Liberal	Others
99 (34%)	81 (25%)	0	1 (14%)

Information about the religious beliefs of Members is incomplete and possibly misleading. Some Members are not willing to publicize the nature of their faith, perhaps because they have not got any. Another difficulty is that intensity of interest in religious questions will vary: some Members are active supporters of a particular church, while for others religious affiliation is nominal. So meaningful statistics on this subject cannot be produced. Even so, a few quite important generalizations can be made. The old tag that the Church of England is the Conservative Party at prayer is, of course, an over-simplification, yet support for the Established Church is stronger among Conservatives than among Labour Members. In the case of the non-conformist churches, the reverse is true. Roman Catholics are fairly evenly spread between both sides of the House. An overwhelming preponderance of Jewish Members used to be Labour, but this disproportion was reduced substantially in 1970 when the number of Conservative Jews rose from two to nine. Atheist or humanist Members are certainly more prominent on the Labour benches. In general, it seems that a candidate's religious belief, or lack of it, does not have much influence in the selection process, although there have been individual cases where religion has been all important.

The preceding information has tended to stress differences in the social experience of Members. There are, however, common characteristics that cannot be expressed in numerical terms. Members are all politicians, party enthusiasts, with a high level of involvement in public affairs. They are forceful, vigorous and largely extrovert people. They are successful and ambitious, at least when first elected. Another common characteristic is their experience of parliamentary life. A few dislike it and drop out of the political scene. The vast majority develop a deep affection for parliamentary institutions. Despite party strife, frustrations and disappointments, Members are keen to uphold the authority of the Commons. This common attachment to Parliament does much to minimize the effect of contrasting social and cultural backgrounds.

Members share another attribute. Before election almost all of them were nonentities, at least in national terms. Political reputations are made at Westminster and few men change over to politics after outstanding achievements in some other walk of life. There have been exceptions – notably trade unionists Ernest Bevin and Frank Cousins (Lab. Nuneaton 1965–67) and John Davies (Con. Knutsford) formerly Director-General of the CBI. The trade unionists had varied achievements as Ministers: neither were successful in the Commons. Perhaps this is another reflection of Members' belief in the importance of Parliament as an institution – a feeling that Parliament should create its own leadership which should not be imported from the world outside.

Councillors and the Electorate

William Hampton

Reprinted with permission from *Democracy and Community*, Oxford University Press, 1970, pp. 197–204

In the present study we are particularly interested in the relationship between the councillors and the electorate. We do not share the view of one committee chairman who told the Maud Committee investigators that: 'the real trouble with local government is that it is far too close to the electorate'. On the contrary we are impressed by the high proportion of councillors who complain that the local electorate are not interested in their work. This attitude was much more prevalent among the Sheffield councillors than among the national sample. In addition nearly a fifth of the Sheffield councillors gave replies that could not be related to the triple categorization adopted for the national survey. The Sheffield councillors drew attention to the distinction many of the electorate make between 'the council' and individual council members, and to the occasional, but intense, interest

Table 1. Councillors' view of the attitude of the general public to the work of the council

	England and Wales		Sheffield		
	Total	C.B.	Total	Cons.	Lab.
Base	1,235	134	108	48	59
	%	%	%	%	%
Public attitude is:					
Favourable	53	44	15	4	24
Unfavourable	5	3	6	6	5
Not interested	39	47	62	77	51
Other	—	—	18	12	20
D.K./Q.N.A.	3	6	2	2	2

Note: The percentages may not add to one hundred owing to rounding.
Sources: Survey of Sheffield City Council and *M.L.G.*, II, *The Local Government Councillor*, Table 8.1.

aroused when an elector faces a personal problem. The councillors also mentioned the influence of an elector's political opinion upon his attitude towards the council. A Conservative alderman replied: 'it all depends on the end of the city, at the Labour end the present council can do no wrong, and at the other end they can do nothing right'. This opinion, as the rent rebate controversy made clear, was an exaggeration; but there is no doubt that the replies of *the councillors* were affected by their political beliefs. Only two (4 per cent) of the Conservative councillors thought the public attitude was favourable to the city council, while over three-quarters of the Conservatives thought people were not interested. The proportions of the Labour group giving comparable replies were a quarter and a half respectively. The national survey did not consider the political affiliations of the councillors interviewed and this makes it difficult to interpret their results. If a council is composed entirely of supporters of one political viewpoint, for example, then their overall view of the electorate's attitude to the council will be more favourable than if the council membership is divided between the supporters of two or more rival parties. This may explain the relatively favourable impression that rural district councillors receive of their electorate even though they have relatively little contact with them.

Councillors in urban areas are approached by their constituents more frequently than councillors in rural areas, and the response from the Sheffield councillors showed that the electorate in the city make considerable use of their representatives. A third of the Sheffield councillors had been approached by fifty or more of their electors in the four weeks before the interviews. The average number of contacts during this period was forty-five per councillor, which may be compared with an average of thirty-six per councillor in other county boroughs in England and Wales. The Labour councillors were in contact with their electors far more frequently than the Conservative councillors, and this is consistent with the different attitudes the two groups adopt towards the role of the councillor.

The frequency with which a member of the council encounters the electors is affected by their attitude as well as by that of the councillor. The middle-class electors, who form a larger proportion of the electorate in Conservative than in Labour wards, are more likely than working-class electors to approach an officer of the council instead of their ward representative. In addition a

Table 2. Councillors' contacts with electors – four-week period

Base	England and Wales		Sheffield		
	Total 1,235	C.B. 134	Total* 107	Cons. 48	Lab. 59
	%	%	%	%	%
No Contacts	10	5	6	10	2
1–4 contacts	20	11	5	6	3
5–8 contacts	18	12	7	12	3
9–12 contacts	9	10	15	21	10
13–19 contacts		31	10	10	10
20–49 contacts	40		23	23	24
50 and over contacts		27	34	17	47
Questions not answered	3	4	0	0	0
Average number of contacts in 4 weeks	26	36	45	35	53

* Excluding one independent.
Note: The percentages may not add to one hundred owing to rounding.
Sources: Survey of Sheffield City Council and *M.L.G.*, II, *The Local Government Councillor*, Table 8.11 and p. 227.

number of Conservative councillors had arrived on the council only a few months before the interviews. The longer-serving councillors were in far more frequent contact with the electorate than these 'new boys', which suggests that a councillor becomes known in his ward *after* his election rather than before.

The most frequently used method of communication between councillors and members of the electorate was the telephone. Councillors from both parties received telephone calls from members of the public fairly frequently, and a quarter of the councillors had received twenty or more such calls about council matters in the four weeks before the interviews. Letter writing was much less popular: over half the councillors received less than one letter a week from their constituents. One Labour councillor explained: 'the pattern now is for people to phone and for me to go round to see them if it is necessary. This is a changing pattern for they used to call personally at my house'. Personal visiting is still an important method of communication for many councillors. Over two-thirds of the members of the Sheffield City Council had visited a constituent within the four weeks before the

Table 3. Methods of contact between electors and councillors in Sheffield

Base	Elector visited councillor's home			Councillor visited elector's home			Telephone conversation			Councillor received letter from elector			Other ways		
	Total 108	Cons. 48	Lab. 59	Total 108	Cons. 48	Lab. 59	Total 108	Cons. 48	Lab. 59	Total 108	Cons. 48	Lab. 59	Total 108	Cons. 48	Lab. 59
	%	%	%	%	%	%	%	%	%	%	%	%	%	%	%
No. of contacts four week period:															
None	43	65	25	31	35	29	19	27	14	19	25	15	31	35	29
1 or 2	17	17	17	19	27	12	15	19	12	22	31	15	9	19	2
3 or 4	11	8	14	17	21	14	8	10	7	14	12	15	7	12	3
5–9	12	6	17	15	10	19	16	15	17	22	21	24	8	6	10
10–19	11	0	20	11	2	19	15	12	17	12	6	17	19	17	22
20 or over	6	4	7	6	4	8	26	17	34	8	2	14	20	8	31
Don't know	1	0	0	1	0	0	1	0	0	2	2	0	4	2	3

Note: The percentages may not add to one hundred owing to rounding. *Source:* Survey of Sheffield City Council.

interviews, and over half had received such a visit. In some cases several visits both by constituents and by councillors were made each week.

The Conservative councillors were far less ready than the Labour councillors to visit or to receive constituents at their homes. In most cases the Conservative councillors had received no visits from members of the public in the four weeks before the interviews, and four out of five had received less than three such visits. Many of the Labour councillors, on the other hand, spoke of their home being always open to visiting constituents. In part this reflects a cultural difference between people from middle-class and working-class backgrounds. The working-class elector, or councillor, accepts personal visits far more easily than his middle-class neighbour. This point may be illustrated by a few of the comments made in the course of the interviews. One Conservative councillor told the interviewer: 'I do not encourage people to call at my home'; and a middle-class member of the Labour group made no visits to the homes of the electors, preferring to send an officer to deal with any complaints. Another Labour councillor, a retired manual worker, took the different view that 'personal contact is the greatest service one can render'; he made seventy or eighty visits per month to the homes of his constituents. Several of the younger Conservative councillors also realized that personal visits were expected in the working-class areas of their wards, and they canvassed throughout the year to maintain contact with their electors.

In Sheffield in 1967–8 a third of the councillors lived in the ward they represented. Most of these councillors were members of the Labour group. Many of the Conservative councillors were newly elected for areas that were not traditionally Conservative in their representation; they lived in the residential suburbs, and sometimes knew little of the areas they had contested. The middle-class Labour councillors were also unlikely to live in the ward they represented, and the relatively low proportion of Sheffield councillors who have their home in their ward is due almost certainly to the sharp dichotomy of the city into middle-class and working-class areas. The proportion of Sheffield councillors who live in the ward they represent is in fact much lower than the proportions found among councillors in other areas where comparable studies have been made. In Newcastle-under-Lyme, at the time of the Keele University study, 56 per cent of the councillors lived in the wards they represented, and in

Wolverhampton Dr Jones found that the proportion was 44 per cent. In an unpublished study of forty-one local authorities in the Leeds area of the West Riding of Yorkshire, Dr Dilys Hill showed that usually at least two-thirds of the councillors lived in the ward they represented. The proportion was below this figure in only two of the thirty-five urban district councils and non-county borough councils that she studied. In the six county boroughs in her area the appropriate proportions were at least two-thirds in Dewsbury, Halifax, Huddersfield, and Wakefield; one-half in Leeds; and one-third in Bradford.

Table 4. Attachment of councillors* to ward they represent in Sheffield

| | No. of cllrs. | Proportion living in ward represented | Proportion of cllrs.' friends living in ward represented | | | | | |
			All	Most	Half	Few	None	D.K.
	No.	%	%	%	%	%	%	%
Conservative	39	18	0	12	15	52	19	2
Labour	41	46	3	12	20	44	20	0
All Cllrs.†	81	33	2	13	18	47	19	1
Cllrs. living in ward represented†	27	100	7	40	19	26	7	0

* Aldermen are not allocated to a particular ward so this Table relates to councillors only.
† Including one independent.
Note: The percentages may not add to one hundred owing to rounding.
Source: Survey of Sheffield City Council.

As a low proportion of Sheffield councillors lived in the ward they represented, it was not surprising to discover that very few of the electors knew where their councillors lived. Only 15 per cent of the Sheffield sample of the electorate claimed to have this knowledge, compared with 36 per cent of the national sample. The claims of the respondents in answer to this question were not checked, and both figures are likely 'to be somewhat inflated over the actual level of true awareness'. The Sheffield respondents also told the interviewers that if they wished to contact their local councillor they would first go to the Town Hall rather than to his home.

The simple division of councillors into those who live in the ward they represent and those who do not can exaggerate the importance of residence in determining the attachment a councillor feels for the ward he represents. The councillor who was so meticulous about visiting the homes of his constituents, for example, did not live in the ward he represented so conscientiously. The Sheffield councillors were asked, therefore, to estimate the proportion of their Sheffield friends who lived in the ward they represented. The response to this question is included in Table 4. Although the distinction between the parties is still present it is not as stark as the residence factor would suggest. Councillors from both political parties tended to draw their friends from all over the city. Two-thirds of the councillors have only a small proportion, or none, of their friends living in the ward they represent, and it is interesting to note that two of the councillors who have no friends in the ward they represent actually live in the ward.

The analysis of the place of residence of Sheffield councillors, and of the distribution of their friends throughout the city, suggests that councillors do not find their social relaxation among their ward constituents. The majority of the councillors are not community leaders who emerge from the wards they represent; they are people interested in public affairs who seek an opportunity to represent their fellow citizens wherever it may conveniently be found. The potential councillors make their friendships with people who share their interests, and it is in this way that they are encouraged to seek election to the city council. About half the councillors we interviewed were already friendly with people associated with the council before their own election.

The formal relationship which existed between many of the Sheffield councillors we interviewed and the people they represented was emphasized by their descriptions of the ways in which they got to know about the needs and attitudes of members of the public. In Table 5, the proportions of the councillors selecting each of several possible methods are given and they may be compared with the national results. The emphasis on one *main* method is somewhat artificial; most of the councillors use a variety of methods and, as one alderman complained, 'one cannot compare cheese with apple tart'; nevertheless the interviews do not suggest that the replies to this question are misleading. A very low proportion of Sheffield councillors, compared with the national sample, rely upon informal personal contacts for their

Table 5. Main way in which councillors keep in touch with the public

	In local authority area				In ward (Sheffield – Cllrs. only*)		
	England and Wales All councils	C.B.	Sheffield Total	Cllrs. only*	Total	Cons.	Lab.
Base	1,235	134	108	81	81	39	41
	%	%	%	%	%	%	%
Informal personal contacts	67	60	30	25	33	28	39
Formal approaches/ letters	8	8	17	16	16	19	13
Meeting people through vol. orgs.	6	4	4	2	1	0	2
Political parties	3	5	13	15	12	8	17
Special org. set-up for purpose	3	8	3	4	22	31	15
Local press	1	1	19	23	0	0	0
Election campaign/ canvassing	2	4	2	1	10	14	7
Reports from council depts.	2	2	4	2	0	0	0
Other ways	3	3	7	9	4	0	6
Not answered	5	5	2	1	0	0	0

* As aldermen are not allocated to a particular ward these columns refer to ward councillors only.
Note: The percentages may not add to one hundred owing to rounding.
Sources: Survey of Sheffield City Council and M.L.G., II, The Local Government Councillor, Table 8.9.

main source of information about public attitudes and needs. To compensate for this there is a greater reliance upon more formal channels of communication including the political party organization, the local press, and letters or visits received from the general public.

Further Reading: Power

R. R. ALFORD: *Party and Society*, University of Chicago Press, 1964.

V. L. ALLEN: *Power in Trade Unions*, Longmans, 1954.

* J. BURNHAM: *The Managerial Revolution*, Penguin, 1940.

R. E. DOWSE AND J. A. HUGHES: *Political Sociology*, Wiley, 1972.

W. L. GUTTSMAN: *The British Political Elite*, McGibbon & Kee, 1965.

* C. LAMBERT AND D. T. H. WEIR: *Cities in Modern Britain*, Fontana, 1975.

D. LOCKWOOD, J. GOLDTHORPE, F. BECHHOFER AND J. PLATT: *The Affluent Manual Worker: Political Attitudes and Behaviour*, Cambridge University Press, 1968.

R. MCKENZIE AND A. SILVER: *Angels in Marble*, Heinemann, 1968.

R. MILIBAND: *The State in Capitalist Society*, Weidenfeld & Nicholson, 1969.

* C. W. MILLS: *The Power Elite*, Oxford University Press, 1969.

E. A. NORDLINGER: *Working Class Tories*, McGibbon & Kee, 1967.

R. ROSE (ED.): *Studies in British Politics*, MacMillan, 1966.

* J. URRY AND J. WAKEFORD: *Power in Britain*, Heinemann, 1973.

* Available in Paperback

7 Values

Cultural values are part of the social structure. Like many of the terms used so far there is little consensus about the concept of values. It is most usefully seen as a standard against which things are compared and held to be, for example, desirable or undesirable, appropriate or inappropriate. Actions, individuals, groups, goals, ideas, beliefs and feelings may be evaluated in this way. Values provide the basis of emotional commitment. Culture is in part concerned with our ideas of the world around us and its properties and also with moral ideas involving judgements. It is more than this. Man becomes human as a member of society but the kind of human being depends largely on the culture. Our learning is always selective. It depends on group influences: our age, sex, where we live, social class, whether we are a member of an ethnic or religious minority, and many others. Within every culture there are sub-cultures distinguishable by such factors as language, clothing, occupation, gesture and behaviour.

Values extend to systems of belief of various kinds, including science and religion, but for the purposes of this chapter we shall be particularly concerned with values, current assumptions and versions of reality, which underwrite some of our social institutions. At any time there are sets of received ideas which continue to be influential long after the situations which caused them to gain acceptance have changed. In many respects we may remain prisoners of these systems of belief: two extreme examples might be those who believe that the earth is flat even now against all the evidence, and those who believe in the literal interpretation of the Bible and the acceptance of its chronology about, for instance, the Creation.

There is in the interpretation of all social life, as Galbraith has pointed out in *The Affluent Society*, 'a persistent and never-ending competition between what is relevant and what is acceptable'. He suggests three reasons for the prevalence of the 'conventional wisdom': people associate truth with convenience; we find most acceptable what contributes to self-esteem; and people approve most of what they best understand.

So we may explain the desire of some members of the middle classes to see strikes purely in terms of the irresponsibility of workers, or for people to explain the decline of Britain in terms, say, of the entry of outsiders (migrants from the Tropical Commonwealth). These simple explanations have the consequence often of removing responsibility for the state of affairs on to other groups. Sometimes they may reflect inflexible prejudgements or information which is not objective.

Our 'British culture' may be seen in relation to the norms of all sections or, as often in the image of our society abroad, in relation to the norms of the dominant group, with an emphasis on a 'public school ideal', team-spirit, playing the game, physical fitness, which has a direct relevance for only a small minority. (Norms are of two kinds: those which specify positive obligations (such as those between parent and child, worker and employer) and those which are permissive: they form a continuum, from what *must* be done, *may* or *may not* be done, to what *should* or *should not* be done.)

Some of these themes appear in the readings. There are many others for which there is not space which can be studied best by taking statements from those who believe such things and subjecting them to analysis. Three kinds of values are considered in what follows. First there are those beliefs on which our society is said to depend (social justice, or certain principles of social selection) Secondly there are the ideas about the structure of society, social processes and the place of the society in the world. Finally, there are the received ideas and the varied forms of the conventional wisdoms.

It has often been suggested that the family is declining and that the quality of the people of Britain, variously defined, is not what it used to be. **McGregor** examines some of these ideas in relation to the institution of marriage and contrasts what he calls 'theological expectations' which demand disintegrating homes with what he sees as the reality of a remarkably stable institution.

Mitchell however attacks the institution of the family because of its role in the systematic oppression of women in industrial, capitalist society. The family is, she argues 'a segmentary, monolithic unit, largely separated off from production and hence from social human activity'. It is woman's role in the family as the provider of sexual satisfaction to her male partner and as the principal agent of child rearing which imprisons her in a restricted and limiting set of routines and provides rigid limitations to what are socially acceptable manifestations of personality. Moreover, the exclusive identification of female activities with procreation and socialization may ultimately be harmful to the children as well.

There are more recent statements about the balanced community than the one by Orlans, which is the next reading, but he highlights in particular some of the assumptions which have governed the provision of housing in the kinds of settings in which many people now live. The kinds of housing provided at Stevenage, and on large numbers of the estates built by private building and local authorities after 1919, reflect in their arrangements and gardens, however inadequately executed, the ambition of Ebenezer Howard to put the best of town and country together: 'Human society and the beauty of nature are meant to be enjoyed together . . . The town is the symbol of society . . . The country is the symbol of God's love and care for man.' From their concern to provide for the town dweller some of the benefits of the country stem many of the planning conventions (about, for example, density of housing) which have been adhered to for most of the past fifty years. Orlans also raises points about leadership in the community.

There follow three readings on different aspects of the educational system. In the first we have the view of Katz, an American educator, on certain of the assumptions which in his view compose the core of our tradition. This provides an interesting and controversial perspective, especially in the way that he suggests that educational thought has avoided the recognition and resolution of conflicts between new needs and idealized traditions. In the second Cotgrove discusses some of the relationships between education and occupation and points out the distinctions between the ostensible aims of educational institutions which prepare their students for certain occupations and the actual consequences which follow from the training. There has been a 'constellation of ideas and values' strongly opposed to vocational secondary and university education. Moreover, conflicting demands on education arise from the various needs of industry and society.

Finally Halsey views the educational system in the light of the pursuit of equality in our society. This provides one statement and analysis against which others can be viewed.

The focus of the reading by **Goldthorpe** is upon what he calls 'the relatively neglected problem of the implications of inequality for social integration'. The great extent and variety of social inequality, and its pervasiveness, are indicated and this perspective shows how inequality structures virtually the whole of social life. Moreover, it is highly resistant to change. Goldthorpe concludes that social inequality poses no direct threat to the stability of the political order but that it militates seriously against stable normative regulation in the economic sphere. He discusses the views of Runciman, who is represented in the reading which follows, and of Fox and Flanders, who have argued that the British system of industrial relations is in a state of 'anomie' where disorder has developed because of breakdown of previously accepted relationships and the fact that solutions have been *ad hoc* and piecemeal and based on unrelated or divergent principles.

The argument about the quality of our society is often carried on in relation to the Welfare State and its presumed effects. Three readings on this theme are provided here. In the first **Runciman** looks at three theories of social justice which reflect, to a large extent, the political standpoint of those who hold them and poses questions about the place of ideas of social justice in our society. **Titmuss** considers the question of redistribution as an aspect of social policy and refers to the widely held misconceptions about how effective this has been in the Welfare State. **Marshall** examines the most important aspects of the Welfare State and then goes on to examine the way in which contradictory principles may be followed in different fields.

One of the most widely publicized areas of conflict in our society is that between the young and the old. The young may be held responsible for a rejection of authority and the traditions of British life. This provides a good example of the way in which stereotypes develop. The changed attitudes to parental authority also reflect changed attitudes towards 'authority' generally and **Worsley** has interesting points to make on criminality as a phase in the life cycle of the individual and the content of 'youth culture'.

Schofield hits at the 'one bad apple in the barrel' theory when he says 'it seems to be a common practice to end a criticism of adolescent sexual behaviour by adding that we all know the bad ones are an exception and that most of the youth of this country are a grand clean-living bunch of kids'. But Schofield points out crisply that 'the qualification is as wrong as the criticism is inept'. His thorough documentation of sexual behaviour among teenagers, based on systematic empirical research, indicates that the question of sexual promiscuity cannot be easily disentangled from other aspects of the teenage subculture, for which the adult world is in large measure responsible.

Lupton carries on some distinctive themes which have already emerged, such as lack of moral fibre, inadequate leadership, false ideologies, and the like. He looks at the social structure of Britain to explain some of our inadequacies but also contrasts what is commonly believed with what is the reality he has discovered. He takes up the question of economic efficiency and the consequences of technological change, and explains how, for example, more complex division of labour has posed threats to the working class and has evoked certain kinds of response.

A distinguished American observer, **Shils**, comes next with part of a general critique of British society he wrote under the title of 'Britain Awake!' He points out some of the aspects of British life which he considers to be worthwhile, as well as its disadvantages, notably what he calls a 'constrictedness' of imagination and aspiration. In his comments about the changes which have taken place, and how the apparent single-mindedness of the Victorians has given way to our self-deprecating image, he prepares the scene for the brief opinion, and historical perspective, from **Tawney**. Tawney makes a statement around which discussions about the nature and content of British society can proceed.

The Stability of the Family in the Welfare State

O. R. McGregor

Reprinted with permission from 'The Stability of the Family in the Welfare State', *Political Quarterly*, Vol. 31, No. 2, 1960, pp. 132–7

Those well-meaning persons and organizations who assume a right to tell other people how to behave now sustain a formidable indictment of the Welfare State. It rests primarily on the assertion that the admitted and always approved benefits of greater material security have been purchased at the price of a steady weakening of 'the moral fibre of the people'.

At bottom, these gloomy assessments rest on three beliefs First, that social security has made other people feel secure, thus exposing them to moral danger. Sir Keith Joseph has explained that 'it is harder for the rich or the relatively secure to be pure'. Secondly, that social provision has 'stripped the family of its functions'. This is customarily translated to mean 'they even expect the State to look after their children and aged relatives'. Thirdly, that the great rise in the number of divorces in the twentieth century measures a corresponding increase in broken homes and marital irresponsibility. This is 'the flight from stability in marriage'. The first belief reflects widespread anxiety for the relatively poor (relatively, of course, because poverty has now been abolished) in moral peril on the deep of statutory services that fail to discriminate between the deserving and undeserving. The second and third beliefs stem from historical ignorance of the social facts of life and from a simple misunderstanding of divorce statistics.

Nineteenth-century industrialism created an urban society in which only affluent families could self-helpfully discharge their functions and responsibilities. Working-class families could become going concerns only within the shelter of collective provisions that came to supply the decent houses, the schools, and the substitutes for personal thrift that such folk could not afford for themselves. This is why liberal politicians justified their social legislation in the years before 1914 as a means of buttressing the homes of the people at a time when the upper classes were pioneering new freedoms made possible by a declining birth-rate and by women's growth into citizenship. The family today is the product, on the one hand, of the diffusion of democratic habit and the destruction of Victorian domestic tyrannies and, on the other, of the extension of social policy accompanied by death and birth control.

There have also been striking changes in the community's family-forming habits during this century. The sex-ratio has altered from 962 bachelors for every 1,000 spinsters in 1901 to 1,089 at the last census. In late-Victorian days some 140 women in every thousand would be unmarried on their fiftieth birthday; today their number has fallen to fifty-five. Moreover, people are now marrying at unprecedentedly low ages: half the men and almost three-quarters of the women are married before they reach the age of twenty-five. This enthusiasm for marriage has grown persistently throughout the course of a reproductive revolution which has established the pattern of small families as it has enabled women, relieved of the burden of successive pregnancies, to participate in the general rise in the expectation of life. There is no evidence here of a flight from marriage, and it is against this experience that the asserted 'flight from stability in marriage' must be examined.

The contrast between the reality of a remarkably stable institution of marriage and the sickness perceived by moralists, though at first sight puzzling, is easily explicable. In the first place, theological expectations require disintegrating homes. All the Christian sects derive a set of rules for the regulation of the family from their interpretation of the will of God. Such rules have two characteristics. On the essential practical issues such as birth control or the permissibility of divorce, they differ irreconcilably; and they have been consistently ignored by the population for whose guidance they were promulgated. Indeed, in the last half-century, the inability of the Churches to influence behaviour has been as striking as the power of behaviour to alter theological doctrines. Thus, the Church of England was denouncing contraception in 1900 and demanding its statutory suppression: now its attitude is positively welcoming. Christians agree that God's law defines marriage as a monogamous relationship dissoluble only by the death of a spouse. This the Church of Rome asserts to be an invariable rule. The Reformed Churches, on the other hand, insist that it is an ideal standard to which earthly marriages should conform, and they all claim divine authority to permit divorce in certain circumstances which frustrate the integrity and purposes of marriage. Men equally pious, equally learned, and equally zealous for the public good have for centuries based differing conclusions about God's intentions on the same texts, and it is not to be supposed that agreement is now in sight. But there are clear signs of a marked shift of emphasis. Fifty years ago, all Churches justified their marriage disciplines in terms of distinctive theological principles. All are now prepared, like Archbishop Heenan, a contributor to a recently published and authoritative volume, *Catholics and Divorce*, to show that their teachings are 'not only true in principle but true also in social practice' and that their neglect has led to social disaster. 'Since few people now accept the Bible,' writes the Archbishop, 'either as the word of God or even as a code with binding authority . . . it will, therefore, be more useful to consider divorce as a social evil.' And he turns confidently, in company with his protestant colleagues, to the crude statistics of divorce that so conveniently measure the mounting wreckage of broken homes and social deterioration and so neatly confirm his theological expectations. Unwary ecclesiastics who venture to cross the great divide that separates the revelations of religion from the methods of the social sciences should be alive to the dangers of exposing their conclusions to the test of empirical verification.

The Position of Women

Juliet Mitchell

Reprinted with permission from *Women's Estate*, Penguin, 1971, pp. 189–97

Production

Today, automation promises the *technical* possibility of abolishing completely the physical differential between man and woman in production. But under capitalist relations of production, the *social* possibility of this abolition is permanently threatened, and can easily be turned into its opposite, the actual diminution of woman's role in production as the labour force contracts.

This concerns the future; for the present the main fact to register is that woman's role in production is virtually stationary, and has been so for a long time now. In England in 1911, 30 per cent of the workforce were women; in 1970, 37 per cent. The composition of their jobs has not changed decisively either. The jobs are very rarely 'careers'; when they are not in the lowest positions on the factory-floor they are normally white-collar auxiliary positions (such as secretaries) – supportive to masculine roles. They are often jobs with a high 'expressive' content, such as 'service' tasks. Sociologists can put it bluntly: 'Within the occupational organization they are analogous to the wife-mother role in the family.' The educational system underpins this role-structure. Seventy-five per cent of eighteen-year-old girls in England are receiving neither training nor education today. The pattern of 'instrumental' father and 'expressive' mother is not substantially changed when the woman is gainfully employed, as her job tends to be inferior to that of the man's, to which the family adapts. Thus, in all essentials, work – of the amount and type effectively available today – has not proved a salvation for women, quite the contrary.

Reproduction

Scientific advance in contraception could, as we have seen, make involuntary reproduction – which accounts for the vast majority of births in the world today, and for a major proportion even in the West – a phenomenon of the past. But oral contraception – which has so far been developed in a form which exactly repeats the sexual inequality of Western society – is only at its beginnings. It is inadequately distributed across classes and countries and awaits further technical improvements. Its main initial impact is, in the advanced countries, likely to be psychological – it will certainly free women's sexual experience from many of the anxieties and inhibitions which have always afflicted it. It will definitely divorce sexuality from procreation as a necessary complement.

The demographic pattern of reproduction in the West may or may not be widely affected by oral contraception. One of the most striking phenomena of recent years in the United States has been the sudden increase in the birth-rate. In the last decade it has been higher than that of under-developed countries such as India, Pakistan and Burma. In fact, this probably reflects simply the lesser economic burden of a large family in the richest country in the world. But it also reflects the magnification of familial ideology as a social force.

Socialization

The changes in the composition of the workforce, the size of the family, the structure of education, and other factors – however limited from an ideal standpoint – have undoubtedly diminished the social function and importance of the family. As an organization it is not a significant unit in the political power system, it plays little part in economic production and it is rarely the sole agency of integration into the larger society; thus at the macroscopic level it serves very little purpose.

The result has been a major displacement of emphasis on to the family's psycho-social function, for the infant and for the couple. I have discussed the vital nucleus of truth in the emphasis on socialization of the child. It is essential that it is acknowledged and integrated entirely into any programme for the liberation of women. It is noticeable that it was one of the first concerns of the Women's Liberation Movement. Yet there is no doubt that the need for permanent, intelligent care of children in the initial three or four years of their lives can (and has been) exploited ideologically to perpetuate the family as a total unit, when its other functions have been visibly declining. Indeed, the attempt to focus women's existence exclusively on bringing up children, is manifestly harmful to children as well. Socialization is an exceptionally delicate process which requires a serene and mature socializer – a type which the frustrations of a *purely* family role are not liable to produce. Exclusive maternity is often in this sense 'counter-productive'. The mother discharges her own frustrations and anxieties in a fixation on the child. An increased awareness of the critical importance of socialization, far from leading to a restitution of classical maternal roles, should lead to a reconsideration of them – of what makes a good socializing agent who can genuinely provide security and stability for the child.

The same arguments apply with added force to the psycho-social role of the family for the couple. The belief that the family provides an impregnable enclave of intimacy and security in an atomized and chaotic cosmos assumes the absurd – that the family can be isolated from the community, and that its internal relationships will not reproduce in their own terms the external relationships which dominate the society. The family as a refuge from society in fact becomes a reflection of it.

Sexuality

The major structure which at present is in rapid evolution is sexuality. Production, reproduction, and socialization are all more or less stationary in the West today in that they have not changed for three or more decades. Sexual repression, on the contrary, is proving less and less successful in regulating spontaneous behaviour. Marriage in its classical form is increasingly threatened by the liberalization of relationships before and after it which affects all classes today. In this sense, it is evidently the weak link in the chain – the particular structure that is the site of the most contradictions. I have already emphasized the progressive potential of these contradictions. In a context of juridical equality, the liberation of sexual experience from relations which are extraneous to it – whether procreation or property – could lead to true inter-sexual freedom. But it could also lead simply to new forms of neo-capitalist ideology and practice. For one of the forces behind the current acceleration of sexual freedom has undoubtedly been the conversion of contemporary capitalism from a production-and-work ethos to a consumption-and-fun ethos. This was already commented on in the early fifties:

> ... there is not only a growth of leisure, but work itself becomes both less interesting and less demanding for many . . . more than before, as job-mindedness declines, sex permeates the daytime as well as the playtime consciousness. It is viewed as a consumption good not only by the old leisure class, but by the modern leisure masses.

The gist of Riesman's argument is that in a society bored by work, sex is the only activity, the only reminder of one's energies, the only competitive act; the last defence against *vis inertiae*. The same insight can be found, with greater theoretical depth, in Marcuse's notion of 'repressive de-sublimation' – the freeing of sexuality for its own frustration in the service of a coordinated and drugged social machine. Society at present can well afford a play area of premarital *non*-procreative sexuality. Even marriage can save itself by increasing divorce and remarriage rates.

signifying the importance of the institution itself. These considerations make it clear that sexuality, while it could contain the potential for liberation, can equally well be organized against any increase of its human possibilities. The new forms of reification and the commercial consumption of sexuality may void sexual freedom of any meaning. This is a reminder that while one structure may be the *weak link* in a unity like that of woman's condition, there can never be a solution through it alone.

What, then, is a possible revolutionary attitude? It must include both immediate and fundamental demands, in a single critique of the *whole* of women's situation, that does not fetishize any dimension of it. Modern industrial development, as has been seen, tends towards the separating out of the originally unified function of the family – procreation, socialization, economic subsistence, etc. – even if this 'structural differentiation' has been checked and disguised by the maintenance of a powerful family ideology.

In practical terms this means a coherent system of demands. The four elements of women's condition cannot merely be considered each in isolation; they form a structure of specific interrelations. The contemporary family can be seen as a triptych of sexual, reproductive and socializatory functions (the woman's world) embraced by production (the man's world) – precisely a structure which in the final instance is determined by the economy. The exclusion of women from production – social human activity – and their confinement to a monolithic condensation of functions within a unity – the family – which is precisely unified in the *natural part* of each function, is the root cause of the contemporary *social* definition of women as *natural* beings. Any emancipation movement must still concentrate on the economic element – the entry of women fully into public industry and *the right to earn a living wage*. The error of the old socialists was to see the other elements as reducible to the economic; hence the call for the entry of women into production was accompanied by the purely abstract slogan of the abolition of the family. Economic demands must be accompanied by coherent policies for the other three elements; policies which at particular junctures may take over the primary role in immediate action.

Economically, the most elementary demand is not the right to work or receive equal pay for work – the two traditional demands – but *the right to equal work itself*. At present, women perform unskilled, uncreative, service jobs that can be regarded as 'extensions' of their expressive familial role. They are overwhelmingly waitresses, office-cleaners, hair-dressers, clerks, typists. In the working class, occupational mobility is thus sometimes easier for girls than for boys – they can enter the white-collar sector at a lower level. But only two in a hundred women are in administrative or managerial jobs, and less than five in a thousand are in the professions. Women are poorly unionized and receive far less money than men for the manual work they perform: this, among other things, represents a massive increment of exploitation for the employer.

Education

The whole pyramid of economic discrimination rests on a solid extra-economical foundation – education. The demand for equal work, in Britain, should also take the form of a demand for an *equal educational system*. In post-compulsory education there is no evidence whatever of progress. The proportion of girl university students is the same as it was in the 1920s. Until these injustices are ended, there is no chance of equal work for women. It goes without saying that the content of the educational system, which actually instils limitation of aspiration in girls, needs to be changed as much as methods of selection.

Only if it is founded on equality can production be truly differentiated from reproduction and the family; and the woman at work not bear with her the attitudes of the home. But this in turn requires a whole set of non-economic demands as a complement. Reproduction, sexuality, and socialization also need to be free from coercive forms of unification. Traditionally, the socialist movement has called for the 'abolition of the bourgeois family'. This slogan must be rejected as incorrect today. It is maximalist in the bad sense, posing a demand which is merely a negation without any coherent construction subsequent to it. The reasons for the historic weakness of the notion is that the family was never analysed structurally – in terms of its different functions. It was a hypostatized entity – just like its ideology in contemporary society. The abstraction of its abolition corresponds to the abstraction of its conception. The strategic concern is the liberation of women and the equality of the sexes, not the abolition of the family. The consequences of this demand are no less radical, but they are concrete and positive, and can be integrated into the real course of history. The family, as it exists at present is, in fact, incompatible with either women's liberation or the equality of the sexes. But equality will not come from its administrative abolition, but from the historical differentiation of its functions. The revolutionary demand should be for the liberation of these functions from an oppressive monolithic fusion. This dissociation of reproduction from sexuality frees sexuality from alienation in unwanted reproduction (and fear of it), and reproduction from subjugation to chance and uncontrollable causality. It is thus an elementary demand to press for free State provision for oral contraception. The straightforward abolition of illegitimacy as a legal notion as in Sweden and Russia has a similar implication; it would separate marriage civicly from parenthood.

The problem of socialization poses more difficult questions, as has been seen. But the need for intensive care in the early years of a child's life does not mean that the present single sanctioned form of socialization – marriage and family – is inevitable. Nor that the mother is the only possible nurse. Far from it. The fundamental characteristic of the present system of marriage and family is in our society its *monolithism*; there is only one institutionalized form of inter-sexual or intergenerational relationship possible. It is that or nothing. This is why it is essentially a denial of life. For all human experience shows that inter-sexual and intergenerational relationships are infinitely various – indeed, much of our creative literature is a celebration of the fact – while the institutionalized expression of them in our capitalist society is utterly simple and rigid. It is the poverty and simplicity of the institutions in this area which are such an oppression. Any society will require some institutionalized and social recognition of personal relationships. But there is absolutely no reason why there should be only one legitimized form – and a multitude of unlegitimized experience. What we should seek for is not the abolition of the family, but the diversification of the socially acknowledged relationships which are today forcibly and rigidly compressed into it. This would mean a plural range of institutions – where the family is only one such institution, and its abolition implies none. Couples – of the same or of different sexes – living together or not living together, long-term unions with or without children, single parents – male or female – bringing up children, children socialized by conventional rather than biological parents, extended kin groups, etc. – all these could be encompassed in a range of institutions which match the free invention and variety of men and women.

This is what we can fight for. Yet today women are confined within the family which is a segmentary, monolithic unit, largely separated off from production and hence from social human activity. The reason why this confinement is made possible is the demand for women to fulfil these three roles: they must provide sexual satisfaction for their partners and give birth to children and rear them. But the family does more than occupy the woman: it produces her. It is in the family that the psychology of men and women is founded. Here is the source of their definition. What is this definition and what is the role of the family in the ideology of it as the basic unit of society today?

The Balanced Community
H. Orlans

Reprinted with permission of Laurence Pollinger Ltd from *Stevenage*, London, Routledge & Kegan Paul, 1952, pp. 218–23

The social motives for the balanced community were ambiguous. Indeed, they sometimes seemed to represent opposing goals and forces – the classless and class societies, the Socialist and Conservative Parties and ideologies.

A high degree of class segregation in housing and social intercourse almost invariably characterizes contemporary urban society (the lower degree of segregation often prevailing in rural areas does not contradict this fact, but suggests something of the world and the century from which many planners drew inspiration). Different patterns of segregation obtain, however, in different urban areas, which influence the nature of community life and interclass relations. The middle-class suburbs and working-class slums of metropolitan areas exemplify the one-class neighbourhood which may extend over a large area, while in districts like London's Chelsea or Bloomsbury or almost any small town various social classes live together in closer proximity. A modern version of the latter type of environment was what Ministry and Corporation planners hoped to achieve in the New Towns, since they believed this induced social consequences – greater political and social stability and a broader range of social

and cultural activity -- preferable to those of one-class neighbourhoods.

Planners often try to repair with one hand what they have
damaged with the other – that is, they try to remedy conditions
which are themselves (in part) a consequence of previous
remedies. And so, to a considerable extent, the 'mixed class'
neighbourhood and town was advocated now as a reaction
against the one-class neighbourhoods which had developed
partly as a consequence of the zoning regulations of inter-war
planning legislation, under which vast districts were 'developed
at the scale of one house to the acre, eight to the acre, or twelve
to the acre, thus inevitably segregating families according to their
incomes', and partly as a consequence of previous (and continuing) housing policy which produced segregated working-
class council estates in every urban area:

> Historically, large-scale class segregation . . . is a compara-
> tively recent thing. It did not occur in the medieval city, and
> such segregation as there was in pre-Industrial Revolution
> towns was on a small scale. Even then it occurred only in the
> planned streets and squares of London, Bath and similar
> places: and it was a segregation by streets rather than by
> quarters or whole towns: there were streets of big houses and
> streets of little ones, but generally they were near to each other
> and closely associated. In the naturally growing towns larger
> houses and cottages stood . . . side by side in exactly the same
> way as they do in villages today. The split came with the rapid
> development of the new nineteenth-century industrial towns,
> and as the housing conditions of the workers became more
> and more debased the split widened, till the middle classes
> began to live in special places of their own . . .
>   The recent and present segregation . . . has arisen . . . from
> activity by government itself . . . As a result of governmental
> activity in the housing of the working classes, we have now in
> every town or city in the country whole estates devoted en-
> tirely to the housing of one particular wage-earning group.

The advantages of class segregation can readily be imagined and
are, indeed, the social part and psychological parcel of a class
system of society: in its relative isolation from others, each class
can freely enjoy the material, social, and psychological rewards
of their status much as do their opulent brethren who sprawl over

the tables of fashionable clubs, although it is not customary for the two classes to enjoy themselves together. Custom implies general, not invariant, practice; what a man elects to do one way he can also elect to do another, and no sociological or psychological law prevents a rich man from associating with a poor man if he chooses to – of course, he often does. But more often he does not; indeed, one contemporary school of sociology both defines and determines social class by the frequency and intimacy with which individuals associate together, and, in this view, a degree of contact between members of different classes as high as that between members of the same class is anomalous. It does not follow that each – or any – social class need be content with its lot; if it were, there would be no revolutions or pressure for social change. But each class must live its own life and not that of another, and nature readily conspires to make that life liveable.

In favour of encouraging social intercourse between different classes is, of course, the tradition that all men are equal before God and the gravedigger in the quantum of humanity. The opposite proposition, however, that (through birth or chance) all men are unequal, can lead to the same conclusion: charity and effective social control both require the upper and middle classes to retain contact with the lower classes. It is interesting to recall that Ebenezer Howard adduced for his balanced garden cities the same arguments that were used against the early exclusively lower-class colonization of Australia:

We send out colonies of the limbs, without the belly and the head, of needy persons, many of them mere paupers, or even criminals; colonies made up of a single class of persons in the community, and that the most helpless and the most unfit to perpetuate our national character . . . The ancients began by nominating to the honourable office of captain or leader of the colony one of the chief men . . . of the State, like the queen bee leading the workers. Monarchies provided a prince of the royal blood; an aristocracy its choicest nobleman; a democracy its most influential citizen. These naturally carried along with them some of their own station in life – their companions and friends; some of their immediate dependants also – of those between themselves and the lowest class; and were encouraged in various ways to do so. The lowest class again followed with alacrity, because they found themselves moving with and not away from the state of society in which they had been living . . .

They carried with them their gods, their festivals, their games – all, in short, that held together and kept entire the fabric of society as it existed in the parent state.

This was the opposite of a revolutionary creed, as a Stevenage Communist perceived when he dismissed the theory of a balanced community as 'not in line with the Socialist theory of a classless society', adding scornfully, 'I can't imagine people of the retired class settling down here among the working-class people of Stevenage. I'm afraid they will regard the working-class woman as very convenient labour for dinner parties and so forth'. That Ministry and Corporation officials conceived their task in benevolent and not repressive terms, and were as likely to suggest that the upper classes would benefit from contact with the lower classes as vice versa, did not contradict the conservative function of the concept. The chairman told the Press that the Corporation hoped to persuade 'some retired, fairly wealthy people' to come to the New Town 'because they are so invaluable at organizing clubs and activities'. In the same manner, the National Council of Social Service complained that because of workers' segregation on new council estates, little 'community activity' occurred there; residents had 'a large store of latent talent in the social and creative sense. This talent, however, needs some preliminary leadership to unlock it and make it available . . .' Which class would provide, or design, the key to the strangely impounded and misdirected talents of the working classes was not difficult to imagine. 'Community activity', of course, was a euphemism (and none the less a euphemism for being sincerely espoused) for 'activity congenial to the middle classes'. Boumphrey has observed that:

> The whole essence of Howard's idea was that by rehousing the working-class man in a garden city, he would be transported into a clean atmosphere and healthy surroundings . . . and instead of wasting his spare time in the gin palace, to the detriment of his health, pocket, and home life, he could spend it in the healthy and fascinating pursuit of gardening.

We conclude, then, that many garden city and New Town planners merely translated into sociological terms and architectural forms middle and upper-class ideologies of a conservative or liberal-reformist nature, and that the 'balanced community' concept thus served the forces of law and order, middle-class morality, and the social and political *status quo*.

That, for other planners (and, formally, for the Socialist Government), the 'balanced community' concept was part of a utopian Socialist creed, is too evident to require emphasis. Indeed, this was often all that the Stevenage home-owner saw.

Assumptions of British Education

M. B. Katz

Reprinted with permission from 'From Bryce to Newsom: Assumptions of British Educational Reports, 1895-1963', *International Review of Education*, 11, 1965, pp. 287-90

Educational systems reflect the dominant values and assumptions of their cultural contexts. In England, this paper contends, there is a distinct educational tradition, which can be defined in terms of certain key assumptions. To isolate some of these assumptions and, hence, to make a start towards defining the British educational tradition is one purpose of this paper. Indirectly, then, the paper hopes to shed some light on a number of persistent and deeply rooted values of British society. The twentieth century, however, has been unkind to tradition; massive economic, social and political changes have dissolved the cultural context of old beliefs while new intellectual influences have directly challenged existing assumptions. The second purpose of this paper, therefore, is to examine aspects of the impact of modern history upon the British educational tradition and to suggest the intellectual operations through which educators attempted to come to terms with the twentieth century. British educators, this paper maintains, sought to preserve the traditional and respond to the modern by avoiding the resolution of uncomfortable dilemmas, and their evasions of the essential confrontations have left British education with a number of unresolved and potentially debilitating tensions.

Ten assumptions compose the core of the British educational tradition. This section of the paper first states and then describes in more depth these ten assumptions. The second part of the paper analyses the confrontation of tradition with the challenges of the twentieth century.

(1) The duty of the school is to transmit a distinctive cultural ideal and intellectual style, which are the foundations of a genuine, or liberal education.

(2) A crucial distinction exists between education and instruction; above all, the school must avoid narrowness of outlook in curriculum, teachers and students.

(3) The school must provide training in 'character', defined as morality and religion and the 'Victorian' virtues.

(4) The school's moral responsibility implies that the 'corporate' aspects of school life are fully as important as the intellectual.

(5) The individual teacher is the most important factor in the educational process, and most of the successes of British education have been the result of inspired, individual effort.

(6) To serve the needs of the economy and society is one of the two major purposes of education.

(7) Education must also serve the needs of the individual not only by preparing him vocationally but also by affecting the 'quality' of his life. In fact, there is an identifiably superior style of life.

(8) Education should perform its functions as efficiently as possible: waste of money and individual talent must be avoided.

(9) Education reflects the values and stratification of society; schools may contribute to modifications within the existing social framework, but they cannot initiate fundamental change.

(10) The essential passivity of the school as a social institution has two implications for educational reform. First, reform must not advance beyond the limits of public opinion. Second, educational reform must follow historical development; it must rationalize the outcome of institutional evolution while altering existing institutions as little as possible.

The history of modern British educational thought is not the placid development of persistent assumptions but, rather, the development of concepts and solutions which have evaded the confrontation of tradition with the challenges of the twentieth century. Instead of recognizing and resolving confrontations, educational thought, as represented by the reports, verbalized solutions which, in reality, left unresolved and debilitating tensions to undercut and delay urgently required educational reform. Educational thought is not unique in this respect; it reflects the wider, and far from entirely successful, effort of British society to come to terms with the modern world while preserving as much as possible of an idealized past.

One tension resulted from the potentially conflicting objectives of education. Committees increasingly have been aware that they have assumed two not entirely compatible goals for education: service to society and service to the individual. The tension between the two first became explicit in the 1926 Hadow Report, and, in 1958, the Crowther Committee still wrestled with the problem. Throughout most of British history, the committee argued, the individual goal was dominant, but because of the importance of economic growth to national survival, the emphasis recently has been reversed. The report, however, avoided the difficulties of trying to resolve the two objectives by claiming that both 'are worthy and compelling, and we accept them both', and they made 'no attempt to disentangle the two purposes of education'. The Crowther solution, that education will serve both objectives simultaneously, is an evasion of the problems of resolution, and there are dangers in evasion. Britain requires many expensive educational reforms, and the necessity of choice will demand a realistic confrontation and resolution of the traditional goals of British education. In fact, the danger is that the desire to avoid theoretical conflict implies the delay and evasion of reform itself.

The oldest conflict within the educational tradition involves the tension between the cultural-intellectual ideal and the assumption that the school should serve the economic requirements of both society and the individual. This conflict between vocational and liberal education pervades virtually every report. The task was especially urgent since the economic necessity of increased technical education was more and more apparent. The solution was the concept of adaptability. Adaptable individuals were required by a rapidly changing technology, and adaptability, the antithesis of a strict and narrow vocationalism, became a key word in the reports.

Through the concept of adaptability British educators attempted to integrate the aim of serving the economy with the cultural-intellectual ideals. They identified the needs of industry with the goals of education, and the old tradition of the generalist or amateur, the man with the good liberal education who could manage any position, was extended from the Civil Servant to the manual worker. The concept of adaptability, it is clear, is based on the assumption of the inherent worth of the cultural-intellectual ideal and, as such, without empirical validation. The purpose of the concept, indeed, seems to be the evasion of the necessity for a painful evaluation of a deeply rooted assumption. The evasion, moreover, has had serious consequences; for one thing, technical education has developed with often infuriating lack of speed in Britain and has left the country with a shortage of technically skilled manpower.

The challenge to morality is a major tension that has emerged within the educational tradition since the Second World War. Earlier reports assumed a fairly stable set of moral values on which there was general consensus. But after the war the content and method of moral training in a world of rapidly altering standards emerged as a major dilemma. Men have been 'left without a generally accepted standard by which to test their own views and conduct', and, in this situation, 'men are apt to feel an undue strain'. Thus, it is 'urgent . . . that the individual should not be left indefinitely without the support he needs'. 'Everybody' is expected to have a code of morality or standards, which is partly an individual matter and partly the result of membership in society. Morals and standards, continued the report, are 'the foundations of our way of life . . . men must be able to judge for themselves what is good and what is evil, and be able to choose the good'.

The report [on 'School and Life', 1947] implies that the 'good' is capable of definition. In spite of the disintegration of morality and religion, the Committee, without rigorous consistency, implied that certain moral verities form the basis of the good life. The report identified three strands in the British moral heritage: the classical, the Christian, and the scientific. Children should be shown all three 'and absorb, as part of their moral inheritance, the virtues of each'. Yet, the children should choose their own set of values, and their choice should represent 'intellectual and moral freedom'. Here was the evasion. Children should emerge with a preconceived conception of the good life in an age when such a conception was being severely challenged. The school should provide moral training but preserve intellectual freedom. The essence of moral education was exposure. Expose children to the moral heritage, and, without coercion, the assumption appears to be, they will choose properly. Obviously, this solution is evasive. Intelligent people choose a wide variety of moral codes, some which would undoubtedly appear strange or deviant to the Committee. What guarantee, then, is there that the children will choose correctly? Intellectual freedom and moral standards surely will conflict often. Where, then, does educational authority stand? Thus, the solution is verbal only; it provides little guide for action and leaves unresolved another tension in the British educational tradition.

The tensions between the assumptions of the educational tradition were heightened by the challenge and acceptance of new intellectual assumptions. These were the assumptions of 'progressive education'. 'Progressive education' is a difficult term to define. Here, it means that body of educational theory developed in the late nineteenth and early twentieth centuries in opposition to the tradition-centred, formalistic education characteristic of most schools of the period. In particular, three key assumptions were influential in England. First, education should proceed from the interests, needs and stage of development of the child. The focus of education should be the present, not the past. Second, the most effective learning involves motor activity rather than merely passive drill and memorization, and motor activity implies the integration of subjects or disciplines. Third, education should be related to the environment of the child. Education, in other words, should be concerned with the experience of the students.

In Britain the assumptions of progressive education, restrained always by the cultural-intellectual ideal, never degenerated into anti-intellectualism. Yet, unwillingness to confront fundamental intellectual conflicts has prevented the formation of a viable and vital amalgam. Of course, no simple formulae for reform, let alone ones that are entirely intellectually and socially satisfying, will be found. Nevertheless, the confrontation and analysis of assumptions remain possible, and in such painful processes lies the most solid basis for reform.

Education and Occupation

S. F. Cotgrove

Reprinted with permission from 'Education and Occupation', *British Journal of Sociology*, Vol. 13, No. 1, 1962, pp. 33–42

In many occupations, intellectual knowledge must be accompanied by the possession of various personal qualities and skills. Two broad alternatives are possible. Occupational choice and selection may take place first, followed by the appropriate education and examinations. Alternatively, occupational selection may occur after the examination hurdle has been passed. Rejection at this stage may be very costly where the educational investment has been substantial.

There is a variety of institutional arrangements to ensure that aspirants will have suitable personal qualities. Interviewing boards for the selection of social work students may be instanced. Emphasis may be placed on the social and educational background of applicants. Medicine may well illustrate this process. Although there is a high degree of self-recruitment in the major professions, a particularly large proportion of medical students are the sons of doctors. This cannot be accounted for solely by educational criteria. The recruitment of the higher echelons of business and political elites from public school alumni provides a further example of this method to ensure the possession of the necessary personal qualities.

Any discussion of the relations between education and occupation will quickly bring to light the existence of a constellation of ideas and values which are strongly opposed to any vocational element in secondary and university education. Such values are usually asserted as self-evident, and even as 'basic moral assumptions'. F. Clarke points out that 'Often in the most ingenuous way (English writers) give vigorous expression to quite English politico-socio ideals while believing themselves to be discussing pure educational theory.' Yet these ideals influence the functioning of the educational system and constitute what Malinowski calls the 'charter' of the institutions to which they are related.

The notion that the proper role of academic man is the disinterested pursuit of knowledge for its own sake is one such notion that deserves more detailed analysis. It functions to motivate and legitimize the activities of the intellectual and shields him from any questioning of the social relevance of his functions. But such a notion is by no means self-evident, though it operates powerfully to prevent the emergence of a more socially relevant curriculum. The real task of the university it is said is 'to teach people to think'. The university is the 'gateway to knowledge, not a preparation for commerce. What graduates do after leaving is of no immediate concern to us. Our own duty is to maintain high standards of scholarship . . . not to prostitute learning to modern requirements'.

The dominant English tradition to educate for culture lies at the root of many of our current problems. The traditional solution of the classical-humanist education combined education for culture with special education for rulers and administrators. No such synthesis has yet been achieved for the education of those who will perform a much wider variety of social roles. Indeed, the notion that many branches of knowledge are banausic has hindered the development of the universities as places of preparation for a variety of occupations. Thus it is possible to receive education and training for social work in the universities, but not (generally) as an architect.

One further example of the powerful influence of ideology on education can be seen in the development of technical education in Britain. The strongly held belief that only the workshops of industry could give practical training, while the colleges should confine themselves to teaching the principles underlying trades, was a major factor in the development of a predominantly part-time system of technical education. Many of the present problems of apprenticeship can be traced to this source. Yet the belief was based on the most flimsy evidence, and many countries have in fact developed successfully college-based systems of craft training.

It is the task for the sociology of education to bring to light not only the social roots of the values and ideologies which shape the educational system, but also the social consequences of the resulting practices. The growing pressure on the university is from students seeking qualifications of vocational value, not only for the traditional functions of administration, but for a growing range of specialist functions in industry and commerce and the social services. Such students are confronted by dons, many of whom believe that the university should resist any pressure to give its activities greater social relevance. It is important to examine the resulting problems of adjustment facing the student, both as an undergraduate and after graduation.

One of the major conclusions which has emerged from the recent study of educational institutions which prepare for occupations is the important discrepancies which exist between their ostensible aims and purposes and the actual consequences which they achieve. Moreover, some of these consequences have not been intended by those responsible for educational policy, nor recognized until they were brought to light by sociological research.

Recent studies of apprenticeship provide excellent examples. The traditional and 'official' function of apprenticeship as the means for the transmission of skills has led the Ministries of Education and Labour to rely on industrial apprenticeship as the vehicle for the post-war expansion of technical education and training. Yet the researches of Lady Williams and Dr Liepmann have documented the serious inadequacies of apprenticeship. Rigid age requirements, the absence of any test of competence, the meagre facilities for practical training in most firms provide little evidence of its training function. Dr Liepmann's studies suggest that the main function of apprenticeship for the trade unions 'is that of maintaining exclusiveness of training as a means for protecting the privileges of their members'. The insistence on protracted apprenticeships is the basis for the craftsman's claim to differential wages, for job demarcation, and for regulating the supply of labour and thus providing a cushioning effect against insecurity of employment in slack times.

Apprenticeship is failing then to meet the needs of society for a trained labour force because administrators have looked only at some of its official functions. But apprenticeship is multifunctional, and in practice its regulating functions dominate its training functions. The consequences are in many respects dysfunctional for a society which relies on industrial apprenticeship as the main vehicle for increasing the supply of trained manpower. It is by bringing to light such unintended and unrecognized consequences of social action that sociology provides a basis for changes of policy.

Educational institutions perform a variety of functions. Preparation for occupational roles is only one of these, but an examination of the implications of this important function can bring to light many of the problems which will have to be taken into account in any radical examination of the future of higher education. In particular, there is need to resolve the problems which arise from the many and sometimes conflicting demands made on education by the various needs of industry and society. The traditional values of the university are in many ways in conflict with their changing role in society. It is no longer self-evident to many that the rewards of the life of scholarship are sufficient justification for the social support of educational institutions but the criterion of social utility raises fresh problems requiring the investigation of the social functions of educational ideologies and the empirical testing of many of the assumptions involved.

Education and Equality

A. H. Halsey

Reprinted with permission from 'Education and Equality', *New Society* 17 June, 1965

Some people, and I am one, want to use education as an instrument in pursuit of an egalitarian society. We tend to favour comprehensive schools, to be against public schools and to support the expansion of higher education. Our opponents want to use education for the preservation of old or the creation of new inequalities. They tend to be against comprehensives, for public schools and against expansion especially of universities.

The argument is complicated in many ways: education has other purposes than that of promoting equality. It enables us to become literate, patriotic, occupationally skilled and capable of using leisure constructively.

Above all, there are many definitions of equality and many variants of inequality, each with appropriately different educational implications. Ultimately the argument is one about values and their priorities. At this level we may never reach agreement: there is, as Tawney said, 'no agreement with the choice of a soul'. But in practice we may never need to face each other with these passionate abstractions. Certainly we can start with the facts.

The first unavoidable fact is that whatever else it does or could do, education is about equality. Education has always stood necessarily in close relation to class, status and power. In the past half century it has become part of the economic foundations of industrial society, a major avenue of social mobility and one of the principal agencies of social distribution. An advanced industrial society is inconceivable without means through which people are selected and trained for places in a highly diversified labour force. The educational system is accordingly used to establish claims and opportunities. If education is unavoidably an instrument for distributing life chances, we can only argue profitably about what kind of distribution is both desirable and possible. To recognize this is to accept that education is a proper object of political debate and a challenge to sociological analysis.

The facts of inequality have been documented by sociological research since the war. They can be summarized by considering how opportunities for education are socially distributed. This can be done by applying the concepts of 'class chances' and of 'ability' as indicated by measured intelligence.

In an enquiry into education and social selection in England in 1952, carried out by Jean Floud, F. M. Martin and myself, it was appropriate to take entry to grammar as opposed to secondary modern schools as the crucial point of educational opportunity. Using entry to grammar schools as the measure of opportunity in the early 1950s, class chances descended from nearly 1:1 for the children of the professional and business owning and managing classes, through 1:2 or 3 for the children of white-collar workers, to 1:6 for skilled workers and 1:10 for unskilled workers. During the subsequent decade a slow modification of the English secondary system has taken place with slight increase in the provision of courses of a grammar school type, either in grammar schools or comprehensive schools, and through the extension of secondary modern school courses to enable children to take GCE examinations. The proportion of 17-year-old children at school rose from 6·6 per cent in 1950 to 7·9 per cent in 1954 and 12 per cent in 1962. The proportion attaining five or more 'O' level passes in GCE rose from 10·7 per cent in 1954 to 15·3 per cent in 1961. There are no data on recent changes in class chances in British secondary education, but in discussing this issue the Robbins Report concluded that 'if there were data on the educational attainment of school children in each social class in, say, 1950 and in 1960, this would probably not show a great narrowing of social class differences'.

The trend in differential class chances of entry to full-time higher education in the period 1928 to 1960 also shows a static picture. The proportion entering universities in the period 1928–47 was 3·7 per cent and this had risen to 5·8 per cent by 1960. The chances of entry for boys of all classes had roughly doubled, leaving the situation in 1960 as it was earlier, namely one in which the child of a non-manual worker was six and a half times more likely to go to a university than a boy from the manual working class.

These class inequalities are not simply a reflection of the social distribution of measured intelligence. The Robbins Report contains evidence that at descending levels of social class, children of equal ability have reduced chances of entering higher education. For children born in 1940–41 who entered maintained grammar schools and were classified by intelligence at the 11 plus examination, it has turned out that among those with IQs of 130 or more, children of non-manual workers had twice as much chance of entering a degree course as did children of manual workers. For the group whose intelligence fell between IQ 115 and 129, the differential chance was 2·12 and for those between IQ 100 and 114, the chances of the middle-class child were three times as high as those for the working-class child.

The present organization of schooling is less than just in that, at any given level of native ability, the social and economic status of a family determines access to educational facilities. Rich men can buy educational privilege in public schools and apart from this, by and large, the better-off districts have the greater proportion of grammar school places. Wealth and residential segregation of the classes are translated into unequal educational opportunities. Clearly the abolition of purchased privilege, the integration of the private with the public sector and the alleviation of present geographical inequalities are possible roads to formal equality of educational opportunity.

Redistribution of formal opportunity is not, however, enough. The determinants of ability are also social and they are weighted in favour of the better-off classes. Redistribution of educability as well as of education is also possible. There is clear evidence that social and educational conditions have a cumulative effect on measured ability. Slum children in slum schools, whether or not they are born stupid, certainly become stupefied by their experiences, as shown for example by J. W. B. Douglas's studies of the growth of IQ among children in different social and educational circumstances.

Attractive Strategy

Educational expansion is another attractive strategy for the egalitarian. It permits reduction of injustice by reducing, or at least deferring, selection and by offering more education to everyone. Studies of the development of secondary education in France and of higher education in America both bear out this point. In France in 1953 a national survey showed that chances of secondary education varied systematically with social status, from 87 per cent among children of professionals to 13 per cent among the children of agricultural labourers. The 1959 reform of the structure of secondary education included the development of long courses in collèges d'enseignement général from which children can transfer to the lycées at a later stage. If the CEG courses are added to those at the traditional lycée, then it appears that between 1953 and 1962 the proportion of all children entering secondary courses (entrée en Sixième) rose from 30 per cent to 55 per cent. This expansion was accompanied by marked reduction in differential class chances of secondary education. Thus, comparing the professional and unskilled groups, in 1953 the chances of children in the former group were four times better and in 1962 were reduced to twice as good.

Estimates by Professor Havighurst for United States higher education over the period from 1920 to 1960 indicate a similar trend to that which has shown itself in French secondary education in the 1950s. Havighurst distinguishes four strata; comparing boys in his upper middle and upper lower strata, the differential chances in 1920 were 20:1. For the upper and upper middle class they more than doubled in the case of boys by 1960, and the differential chances between this class and the upper lower class in the same year had been reduced to something over 3:1. These statistics indicate that only great educational expansion has the power to make inroads into long standing inequalities of educational opportunity and only where, as in America, secondary education is both universal and linked comprehensively to higher education can expansion make educational selection democratic.

Social Inequality and Social Integration in Modern Britain

John H. Goldthorpe

Reprinted with permission from Wedderburn (Ed.) *Poverty, Inequality and Class Structure*, Cambridge University Press, 1974

The concern of this chapter is not to add to the detailed knowledge of the overall extent and pattern of social inequality in modern Britain, nor to produce any new synthesis of the information that exists. It is, rather, with the relatively neglected problem of the implications of inequality for social integration. Prior to broaching this problem, however, three points concerning the general nature of social inequality must be made.

First, social inequality, in societies such as ours, is manifested in a very wide variety of ways – wider than is generally recognized in public discussion of the matter. For example, in addition to great inequalities in the distribution of income and wealth, further marked inequalities are involved in the ways in which economic rewards are *actually gained* – most importantly, in the content of work tasks and roles. There is by now ample evidence to show that wide differences exist between occupations and jobs in the extent to which they offer possibilities of *intrinsic* satisfaction to the individuals engaged in them or, on the other hand, are a source of psychological or social deprivation. To take an obvious contrast, the inequalities in reward between professional employment and factory work are clearly not confined simply to the differences in their income levels.

Again, one aspect of inequality in work which it *has* of late been somewhat fashionable to point to, and to decry, is that of the status differences which operate among different categories of employee in most industrial organizations; for instance, in such matters as methods of payment, 'clocking-in' and lateness rules, toilet, canteen or car-parking arrangements, and so on. But discussion of these questions has usually been carried on without any reference to the far more basic inequality represented by the steep gradient of *authority* within such organizations – which, in fact, status distinctions serve largely to symbolize.

The tendency here illustrated to conceive of inequality in a piecemeal manner, rather than as a multiform and pervasive phenomenon, results from a failure to appreciate in what, fundamentally, social inequality consists. This leads to the second point.

Social inequality in all its manifestations can be thought of as involving differences in social power and advantage: power being defined as the capacity to mobilize resources (human and non-human) in order to bring about a desired state of affairs; and advantage as the possession of, or control over, whatever in society is valued and scarce. Power and advantage are thus closely related. Power can be used to secure advantage, while certain advantages constitute the resources that are used in the exercise of power. Moreover, different forms of power and advantage tend in their very nature to be convertible: economic resources can be used to gain status or to establish authority; status can help to reinforce authority or to create economic opportunities; positions of authority usually confer status and command high economic rewards, and so on.

In this perspective, then, the way in which inequality structures virtually the whole of social life can be readily understood. Differences in social power and advantage, simply because they imply differences across the whole range of life-chances, always tend, other things being equal, to become generalized differences. Furthermore, it is important to add that this effect operates not only from one area of social life to another but also through time. Inequalities of condition at any one point in time create inequalities of opportunity for future achievement. For example, the intergenerational aspects of this phenomenon could be said to constitute the central problem thus far for the sociology of education. The results of research in this field provide impressive evidence of how, notably through the agency of the family, the stability of social strata tends to be maintained – despite the growing importance of education to career chances and the development of policies aimed at reducing non-academic influences on educational attainment.

It has, therefore, to be recognized, thirdly, that structures of social inequality of both condition and opportunity – or, in other words, systems of social stratification – are inherently highly resistant to change. The members of higher strata have the motivation and, in general, the resources to hold on to their position and to transmit it to their children, while the members of lower strata are often caught up in vicious circles of deprivation. This is not, of course, to suggest that change in stratification systems cannot, or does not, occur; but rather that any significant reduction in the degree of inequality will require purposive, well-designed and politically forceful action to this end – that it is unlikely to come about *simply* as the unsought for consequence of technological advance, economic growth, or any such like secular trends. Such developments may well modify certain forms of inequality; but they appear just as likely to accentuate others.

Indeed, far from industrial societies having 'built-in' processes which steadily diminish inequality – as some writers have claimed – what is striking, at least in the British case, is the frequently very limited effect of even the deliberate pursuit of equality through governmental action. For example, as already implied, the egalitarian aspects of educational policy over the last half century or so have resulted in only a very slight lessening in class differentials in educational opportunity – even though over the same period an enormous expansion of educational facilities has occurred. In a similar way, major improvements in medical services and general standards of health have failed over a long period to produce any appreciable reduction in relative class differentials in infant mortality and in many kinds of morbidity. And finally in this respect the stability of inequality in income distribution over the last thirty years may be noted.

In sum, one may say that social inequality, as observed in present-day Britain, takes the general form of a substantially self-maintaining structure of social groupings differentiated multifariously and often extremely in terms of the power and advantages that their members enjoy. What, then, are the consequences of this inequality for the integration of British society; that is to say, for the extent to which the actions of individuals and groups tend regularly to comply with recognized norms, and to be thus consistent with, rather than in conflict with or unrelated to, the expectations and actions of other individuals and groups?

This question, in certain of its aspects, has in fact been examined by a number of recent writers who have adopted a similar initial approach. They have started from the observation that in Britain considerable and abiding inequality does not apparently give rise to deeply divisive conflicts in which the existing social structure, political institutions included, is frequently and fundamentally called into question. They have then gone on to infer from this, not unreasonably, that the resentment of inequality among the less favoured sections of the population is neither particularly widespread nor particularly militant – and especially if comparisons are made with the situation in certain other industrial societies. Thus, the somewhat more specific problem which emerges from this approach is the following: why is it that, given the prevailing degree of social inequality, there is no widely supported and radical opposition to the existing socio-political order, and that at all levels of the stratification hierarchy attitudes of acceptance, if not of approval, are those most commonly found? At this point, analyses tend to divide into two main types which one might conveniently label 'social psychological' and 'culturalist'. The first type is best displayed in the work of Runciman.

Briefly, Runciman's argument is that to account for the discrepancy between the objective degree of inequality in British society and the actual awareness and resentment of this inequality, we must consider the 'reference groups' in terms of which individuals in the lower social strata assess their position. That is to say, we must consider the other groups in society – real or imagined – with which members of less favoured groups habitually *compare* themselves in evaluating their rewards, opportunities and social deserts generally, and in relation to which their expectations and aspirations are formed. If, for instance, the reference groups adopted by a certain membership group are located fairly closely in the stratification hierarchy to the membership group's own position, then the degree of felt inequality is likely to be quite slight, no matter what the overall range of factual inequalities may be. A strong sense of grievance is only to be expected if reference groups are selected in a more 'ambitious' way so that considerable inequality is perceived and is then, on the basis of the comparison made, regarded as illegitimate and unjust. In other words, the degree of *relative* deprivation – deprivation which is subjectively experienced and which may thus influence political behaviour – is primarily determined *by the structure of reference groups* rather than by the structure of inequality itself as the sociologist might describe it.

Runciman's own research, using both historical and survey methods, indicates that among the British working class reference groups are, and generally have been, restricted in scope; and that while some variation in this respect can be traced over time and from one form of inequality to another, no consistent trend is evident towards wider-ranging comparisons. Consequently, the disruptive potential that social inequality might be thought to hold remains in fact suppressed: social integration is furthered through perceptual and conceptual limitations.

Turning secondly to the 'culturalist' type of analysis it should be said that this has been chiefly elaborated by American social scientists interested in the question of the social bases of stable and effective democracy. In treating Britain as one of the relatively few countries whose polity might be thus described, these investigators have been led to examine – with differing degrees of directness – such issues as the following. Why among lower social strata in Britain is there not far more alienation from a political system which is elitist in itself and under which many other forms of inequality persist? Why is there no longer in Britain, if indeed there ever was, a powerful class-based social movement seeking radical structural changes of an egalitarian kind, and prepared if necessary to challenge existing political institutions in pursuit of its objectives?

In the explanations that are offered for the absence of these possible threats to stable democracy, major emphasis is laid on the nature of British 'political culture'; that is, on the pattern or 'mix' of attitudes which research has shown to exist in British society towards political institutions and political life in general. Like other countries in which democracy flourishes, the argument runs, Britain has, in the course of her historical development, built up a political culture of a distinctive type. It is one characterized primarily by the *balance* that holds, even across lines of class and party, between participant, activist attitudes on the one hand and acquiescent, passive attitudes on the other; between emotional commitment to political principle and cool pragmatism; between consensus on matters of procedure and conflict over particular issues.

Through their socialization into this culture from childhood onwards, it is held, the majority of citizens come to feel a sense of unfanatical, but generally unquestioning, allegiance to the established political order, and one that is unlikely to be seriously disturbed by any grievances they may have over the distribution of social power and advantage. Such grievances do not lead to alienation from the political system since there is wide acceptance of the 'democratic myth' – the myth that the individual can influence political decisions and outcomes – and the system itself is not therefore seen as exploitive. Moreover, attitudes towards the political elite tend to-be ones of trust, if not of deference, and the exercise of governmental authority is generally accepted as legitimate. For example, in one study survey data are presented to show that manual workers who believe that there are inordinately powerful groups in British society (such as 'big business') are just as much prepared to allow Government a wide sphere of authority as are workers who do not share in this belief. In other words, grievances arising out of inequality do not tend to become so highly politicized that established political institutions and processes are themselves challenged. Political awareness is in any case at only a moderate level, and politics is only rarely a central life interest. Consequently, the availability of the ordinary citizen for involvement in 'unstabilizing' mass movements is low; the political culture effectively inhibits the radical political action which marked social inequality might otherwise be expected to generate.

Clearly, social-psychological and culturalist points of view on the issue in question are not incompatible: they could, rather, be represented as complementary and mutually supportive on the following lines. Because the reference groups of lower strata have remained generally restricted, political issues stemming from social inequality have tended to be relatively 'mild' and capable of being resolved or accommodated by existing political arrangements. This has, therefore, helped a basically 'allegiant' political culture to form. Reciprocally, the development of such a culture has been inimical to the spread of ideological thinking – as, say, on the matter of social justice – which could lead both to a heightened awareness of inequality and deprivation and to greater recognition of their political dimensions. In short, social psychological processes of the kind examined by Runciman could be seen as a necessary condition of the political culture of British democracy, while this culture in turn, once established, favours the persistence of these processes.

Despite the various criticisms with which they have met, the analyses reviewed do, in my opinion, go some important part of the way to explaining why the consequences of inequality in Britain are not socially divisive in an extreme degree. But what has to be kept in mind, and what should be emphasized, is that for the most part these analyses treat the problem of inequality and integration only from one particular angle. As noted earlier the focus of interest is on the possible *political* implications of inequality; and what is in effect illuminated is chiefly the question of why among the British working class there is found no significant support for political ideas and movements of a revolutionary cast, nor even the widespread *incivisme* which characterizes sections of, say, the French or Italian working class. However, there are other major aspects of the problem which may be distinguished, and ones which have been curiously neglected. In particular, I would advance the view – as the central thesis of this chapter – that the most far-reaching implications of inequality for the integration of British society occur not in the political sphere but rather in that of economic life; and that they are manifested not in a situation of fundamental class struggle but rather in a situation of anomie; that is, in a situation in which to stay close to the original Durkheimian notion, there is a lack of *moral* regulation over the wants and goals that individuals hold. This contention can best be elaborated by reference to two closely related topics of current public concern: industrial relations and incomes policy.

In a recent paper – entitled 'The Reform of Collective Bargaining: from Donovan to Durkheim' – two leading authorities, Fox and Flanders, have in fact argued explicitly and at length that the British system of industrial relations is now in an anomic state. In the post-war period, these authors observe, the wants, expectations and aspirations of industrial workers have expanded notably, and not only in regard to wage levels but also in regard to such matters as security of employment, job rights and control over work organization. At the same time, generally high levels of employment have given many groups of workers the power to pursue their new goals with some effectiveness. A frequent outcome has then been that such groups have broken through the regulation of work relationships imposed by collective agreements at a national level and have secured agreements of a more favourable kind at company, plant or shop level. Thus, Fox and Flanders argue, industrial relations have become disordered in two main ways: first, as a result of the problems involved in developing new normative systems, capable of accommodating the new issues of industrial conflict which now arise; and second, and more seriously, because the solutions arrived at so far have tended to be *ad hoc* and piecemeal ones of only limited, local application. This tendency has therefore given rise to a proliferation of normative systems based on often unrelated or divergent principles; and such a situation is one rife with anomalies, frustrations and rivalries which constantly generate new tensions and conflicts both between employers and workers and between different sorts of workers: 'Disorder feeds upon disorder.' The consequences of this anomic state are then to be seen not simply in strikes and other dislocations of the productive process, but further 'in such things as chaotic pay differentials and uncontrolled movements of earnings and labour costs'. Thus, it is claimed, threats are posed to the long-term development of the economy (apart from the aggravation of short-term balance of payments problems) and there could, furthermore, be serious political implications: increasing disorder might generate popular demands for State intervention of an authoritarian kind which would mark the end of the present pluralistic and voluntary basis of industrial relations.

The analysis offered by Fox and Flanders is insightful and important. However, I would suggest that it is one that does not go far enough in revealing just how deeply rooted in the structure of British society is the 'disorderly' situation with which it is concerned; and, further, that this limitation results precisely from the fact that Fox and Flanders do not follow Durkheim in relating the problem of anomie to the problem of inequality. This argument can best be illustrated by reference to their recommendations for reform in industrial relations – that is, for the 'reconstruction of normative order'. Briefly, what they stress is the continuing need for an incomes policy, accompanied by the regularizing and rationalizing of collective bargaining from plant and company levels upwards. In this latter respect, they point to the availability and usefulness of such techniques as productivity bargaining and job evaluation and other means of measuring and rewarding different kinds of work. Through a programme of reform on the lines in question, they see the possibility of achieving a more logical wages structure, greater control over earnings and labour costs, and industrial relations institutions which, through being more adaptable to change themselves, will be better able to manage the conflicts that change inevitably produces.

Fox and Flanders recognize that there is no guarantee that such objectives will in fact be achieved, and they refer to the 'Promethean character' of the task of reform. None the less, I would argue that they still underestimate the difficulties that are involved: in particular, in creating an area of relatively rational and orderly inequality in place of the present 'wages jungle' *when this jungle is simply part of a wider structure of inequality which has no rationale whatsoever* – other, perhaps, than the principle of 'to them that have shall more be given'. For example, at one point in their paper, Fox and Flanders remark that 'The debate on incomes policy is often conducted within the trade union movement as if collective bargaining were simply a mechanism for pursuing social justice as between capital and labour, and its function of determining the relative fortunes of different groups of labour is ignored.' This may be fair comment, but it is still highly questionable if an incomes policy of the kind they favour can be effective in establishing a less chaotic and more equitable pattern of earnings *within* the working class in the context of the *overall* degree of economic inequality which statistics on the distribution of income and wealth reveal. An industrial worker seeking a wage increase might be prepared to recognize that his claim was weak in comparison with that of, say certain of his lower-paid workmates; but he would have no difficulty in finding other groups, possibly outside the working class, in relation to whom his claim could be much better justified – even assuming that his range of reference groups was not extensive. Moreover, it should be emphasized here that while restricted reference groups may inhibit feelings of grievance over inequalities, this is not to say that they actually motivate individuals to *hold back* from attempting to improve their position, especially economically: limited social horizons are not, as Durkheim might have put it, a source of moral restraint.

Now it must be said that Fox and Flanders are well aware – indeed, they emphasize – that the normative regulation resulting from collective bargaining is unlikely ever to rest purely upon consensus; it will also be a product of the balance of power between the parties concerned and of their calculation of what, for the time being, is the most advantageous position they can achieve. What may further be involved, at least in initiating any reform, is some kind of third-party intervention – 'the forceful articulation of common norms by some authoritative source'. However, to follow Durkheim's argument closely here, one has to insist that in so far as the normative order in economic life is *not* based upon consensus, but is rather founded upon coercion or expediency, then the threat of anomie and of chronic maintegration remains – no matter what degree of internal logic or coherence normative systems may be given. For as Durkheim stresses, unless in modern society the regulation of economic life

– and, crucially, the regulation of inequality – *does* have some accepted moral basis, then it is unlikely to be effective in any continuing way. To the extent that the normative order is imposed by superior power, fundamental discontent and unrest persist if only in latent form; to the extent that it results from the calculation of advantage under given (non-moral) constraints, it is likely to be called into question as soon as these constraints vary.

Thus, while proposals for reform of the kind that Fox and Flanders put forward might well endow collective bargaining institutions and procedures with a good deal more formal rationality than they at present possess, I find it difficult to believe that such measures could go very far towards ensuring *stable* normative systems, of either a substantive or a procedural kind, at any level of industrial relations. The absence of an accepted moral basis for economic life as a whole in our kind of society must always render precarious the norms which at any time prevail in any specific area – a plant, company, industry, etc. As but one illustration of this point, taken from Durkheim's own discussion of the problem, one may consider the implications of inequalities of opportunity for attitudes towards inequalities of condition. If the former are extreme and without effective legitimation, little consensus can be expected on the latter – even supposing that some hierarchy of social positions and role is generally acknowledged. For, as Durkheim argued, 'it would be of little avail for everyone to recognize the justice of the hierarchy of functions as established by public opinion, if they did not also consider just the way in which individuals are recruited to these functions'. While ever, then, British society is characterized by the present marked degree of inequality in educational and occupational opportunity, it is difficult to see that there is any basis for the achievement of what Fox and Flanders regard as the ultimate objective of industrial relations reform; namely, 'agreed normative codes regulating the production and distribution of wealth in modern industrial society' – or, at all events, agreement will for the majority remain highly qualified, reluctant or uncertain, and thus inherently *unstable*. One need not assume that rank-and-file industrial employees resent the inferior life-chances they have been accorded as keenly as the facts might warrant in order to claim that few will feel *morally* bound by the normative codes which govern their working lives. It is sufficient to ask from what source, given the nature of the British social order, such a sense of moral commitment might stem.

The conclusion must then be that the reconstruction of normative order in British industrial relations which Fox and Flanders pursue is something of an *ignis fatuus*. Within a society in which inequality exists as brute fact – largely without moral legitimation – 'disorderly' industrial relations cannot be understood as a particular pathological development which will yield to particular remedies: rather, to maintain a Durkheimian perspective, this disorder must be seen as 'normal' – as a generalized characteristic of societies of the type in question.

The structural features of British society which stand in the way of the reform of industrial relations are at the same time obstructive, as the foregoing discussion would imply, to the effective administration of an incomes policy. The aim of incomes policy, within a market economy such as our own, is usually stated to be that of controlling the growth of incomes so that inflationary tendencies may be kept in check while still preserving relatively high levels of employment and utilized capacity. However, it is essential to appreciate that an incomes policy is not, and cannot be, just another economic instrument – despite the attempt of certain technocratically minded economists to present it in this guise. Once a Government attempts to regulate incomes, in no matter how piecemeal or partial a fashion, it is forced into the position of arbiter on particular wage levels or wage changes, and issues of social justice thus inevitably arise and have in some way or other to be resolved. Indeed, Government spokesmen in Britain have been generally prepared to acknowledge this situation and even to claim that an incomes policy is, or could be, a means of enhancing social justice; for example, by ensuring a better deal for the lowest-paid workers. But it is basically on account of this normative aspect of incomes policy that its administration runs into serious problems which have not as yet been overcome, and which may, for reasons I shall shortly suggest, be self-aggravating ones.

At the root of the difficulty is again the fact that not only is the existing distribution of income and wealth in British society 'unprincipled' – but further that there appears to be little consensus on the principles which *ought* to apply when it is a question of maintaining or altering any specific income level or relativity. Survey data are of some relevance to this argument, but more significant is the great variety of frequently conflicting considerations which are actually invoked when pay issues are debated. Some criteria, for example, would entail at least the possibility of significant change in the existing pay structure – increased productivity, job evaluation ratings, 'absolutely' low wages or persisting manpower shortages: but other criteria, such as increases in the cost of living, the need to preserve a differential or maintain the social status of a particular group, are essentially conservative in their implications. Moreover, as Professor (now Lady) Wootton has pointed out, claims for more pay based on *any* of these often conflicting criteria can be, and usually are, couched in moral terms, or at any rate the economic arguments are related back to moral premises. Thus, one is again forced to the conclusion that little basis for moral *restraint* is currently to be found in British society – that, in other words, a condition of anomie prevails. Given the diversity of moral positions that are tenable in the existing state of public opinion, virtually any occupational group seeking a pay increase is likely to be able to find some kind of legitimation for pressing its case.

From this standpoint, then, it is to be expected that the amount of 'voluntary' support for an incomes policy will be insufficient to enable it to achieve its ends; and such an expectation seems to be generally in accord with British (and other) experience. Furthermore, even when control over incomes is in some way or other 'imposed', it still appears difficult, at least within the constraints on governmental authority that liberal democracy entails, for such control to be very effective for very long. A 'norm' for pay increases may hold up for a short-run period and even a complete 'freeze' may work under crisis conditions – as in Britain, 1966–7. But in the longer term control invariably seems to break down, most notably at the level at which coercive methods are least feasible – that is, at the grass-roots level of the individual enterprise. A tendency for the actual earnings of many groups of workers to rise above the intended norm, as a result of collective agreements or other less formal arrangements locally made, has to be reckoned as the besetting problem of incomes policy administration – and even, it seems, in 'centrally planned' economies such as that of the USSR.

Thus, as one economist, John Corina, has pointed out, 'the unpalatable facts of wage drift', once recognized, pose a hard dilemma so far at any rate as Britain is concerned. Either an attempt must be made to extend the range and increase the stringency of income control, to the point at which voluntary collective bargaining ceases to exist and at risk of building up a considerable pressure of opposition; or it must be accepted that, under existing conditions, incomes policy initiatives are inherently *unstable* in their effects, and that their progressive breakdown is to be anticipated as a matter of course. Unlike some of his colleagues, Corina is prepared to recognize that 'At bottom, the crucial tangles of incomes policy stem from the intangible concept of "social justice" in income distribution', and are inseparable from issues raised both by the existing structure of inequality and by the lack of accord on what form this structure should possess. As he pertinently asks: ' . . . how can incomes policy create consent where social valuations of incomes, within a given incomes distribution, are confused and often obscure?'

Moreover, one point which Corina does not consider is that attempts to implement incomes policy may have quite unforeseen consequences which in fact tend to build up the difficulties involved. It is not simply that a 'freeze' or period of tight control over incomes may be followed by heightened militancy in wage demands, threatening greater inflationary problems than before. There is a further, yet more awkward, possibility; namely, that through increasing information about, and interest in, differences between occupational rewards and conditions, the actual operation of an incomes policy will serve to broaden comparative reference groups among the mass of the population, and at the same time bring issues of equity and fairness into greater subjective salience. Thus, following Runciman's analysis, one would expect, in the case of the working class at least, a growing sense of resentment and grievance over the *status quo* and, in turn, a yet greater unwillingness to accept 'restraint' or to hold back in any way from the direct pursuit of their own maximum advantage. In other words, what are sometimes called the 'educative' functions of incomes policy may well have the effect of undermining the viability of such policy. To the extent that evaluations of income and other economic differences do become less confused and obscure, there is little reason to suppose that what will emerge will be greater consensus from one group or stratum to another: the far more likely outcome, given the prevailing degree of inequality, is that conflicts will become more clearly defined and more widely recognized – that the anomic state of economic life will be made increasingly manifest.

To recapitulate, then, the two central arguments have been the following: first, that social inequality in Britain appears to pose no direct threat to the stability of the political order – because this is, as it were, 'insulated' from the potentially disruptive consequences of inequality by a combination of social-psychological and cultural influences; but second, that the existence of inequality, of an extreme, unyielding and largely unlegitimated kind, does militate seriously against any stable normative regulation in the economic sphere – because it militates against the possibility of effective value consensus on the distribution of economic, and other, resources and rewards.

Social Justice

W. G. Runciman

Reprinted with permission from 'Social Justice', *The Listener*, 29 July, 1965

There are, broadly speaking, three different and mutually incompatible theories of social justice: the conservative, the liberal, and the socialist. In the conservative theory, social justice consists in a social hierarchy, but a hierarchy governed by a stable system of interconnected rights and duties. Those at the top are the holders not merely of privilege but of responsibility for the welfare of those below; and through the recognition that different strata in society have different functions to fulfil, the hierarchy is accepted without dissension or envy as long as the responsibilities imposed on each class are in fact properly exercised.

In the liberal theory, by contrast, there is also a hierarchy; but this hierarchy is only legitimate if it has been arrived at from a position of initial equality. The liberal is not against inequality, but against privilege. He demands equality not of condition but of opportunity. He places a value not on an elite of caste, or inherited culture, but of individual attainment. The socialist theory, finally, is the strictly egalitarian theory. It may or may not require as a corollary that the State should play a predominant part in economic affairs. This is really only a means to an end – the maximum of social equality in any and all its aspects.

All three of these theories are persuasive, and internally consistent. How, therefore, can one adjudicate between them? How, having looked at the social structure of twentieth-century England, are we to judge it by the standard of social justice except by appealing to whichever one theory happens to suit our own interests or temperament? By what possible criterion can one be shown to be any more or less arbitrary than the other two? There is no one just distribution of the national income, no one just constitution, no one just mode of social relations. But what it is worth looking for is a principle. We may be able to find not a set of rules for the one just society but a criterion by which a set of rules as such may be assessed. We want to be able to say, not 'Is this particular inequality unjust?' but, 'Does this inequality derive from a rule which could not be defended by appeal to the notion of justice?'

The notion of justice which best enables us to assess a system of inequalities is not the conservative, or liberal, or socialist notion as such, but one which goes behind all three. It is a notion of justice which has been recently put forward by Professor John Rawls of Harvard, and which may be summarized as follows: the essence of justice is fairness, and for an understanding of the concept of fairness the most appropriate model is that of a contract between equal persons. This does not mean in any sense a reversion to the theory of a social contract which actually happened in the state of nature. It means only that when assessing particular inequalities which we find we must ask one simple question: is this an inequality defensible by a principle which we could have agreed before we had any idea which of the unequal positions we should eventually occupy?

A just system, therefore, is a system to which people would have agreed if they had had to decide on the principles by which social systems were to be regulated before they knew either what their own system would be or what would be their own place in it. Suppose I had to decide on the principles by which education was to be run in my eventual society before I knew either where I would be placed in the social hierarchy or what the abilities or temperaments of myself or my children would be. Would I agree that the best education should go to the children of the richest parents? I think there is no doubt that I would not; and by this token any educational system of such a kind is demonstrably unjust.

Should no Inequality be Justified?

It might seem that this line of argument leads directly to the socialist view of social justice. You may feel that we would all, in the state of nature, have agreed that no inequality should be justified – that all jobs should be equally rewarded, that everyone should treat everyone else as a social equal, and that nobody should have more power than anybody else. But one of the virtues of Rawls's model is that it shows that what would have been agreed is not a total egalitarianism. In Rawls's state of nature, we should only have agreed that no inequality could be justified in our eventual society unless it followed from a principle agreed in advance of vested interest. The contract model is, therefore, fundamentally egalitarian, but only in this special sense. It requires all inequalities to be justified. But among those which it justifies there may well be some which would be justified also by the conservative or liberal theories of social justice.

The suggestion that everyone should receive an equal reward breaks down at once. If, as far as I know, I may turn out to be a man doing a difficult and responsible job with long hours, and to have in addition many dependents to support, I will surely want to be able to claim a higher reward than will be allotted to a man who has no dependents and an easy half-time job. I will, conversely, be prepared to concede this even if I in fact turn out to be the second man (having had, as far as I knew, an equal chance of being either). In fact, I shall be prepared to agree on three principles by which I shall be willing, if it so turns out, to be the loser. These principles, which in their various forms are familiar throughout the history of political theory, are need, merit, and contribution to the common good. By merit I do not, of course, mean moral virtue, but things like danger money; and the criterion of merit must also be linked with the third criterion: contribution to the common good – it would be absurd to suggest that, say, an outstanding solver of crosswords should be paid an extravagant income unless the solving of crosswords contributed in some widely accepted sense to the national welfare. But these three principles, however difficult their application in practice, would surely be agreed by people in the state of nature who did not yet know what their position in the social structure would turn out to be.

No Acceptable Formula

This argument obviously is not enough to show whether a coal-miner contributes more to the national welfare than an architect, whether a laboratory technician should be paid more than a policeman, or whether the state should provide a family allowance for the first as well as subsequent children. But there is never going to be a formula which will answer such questions as these. The concept of social justice can only be brought to bear at a different level – the level at which we can establish the principles by appeal to which any divergence from strict equality can be justified.

If we picture ourselves in a state of nature, we can agree for a start that jobs requiring a long training and a high degree of skill and fulfilling an essential need should be accorded higher reward than where this is not so. We can also agree that any unemployed person willing to work should have a claim on the communal resources on the grounds of need; if I know that I have as good a chance of finding myself in this position as in any other, I shall surely want to stipulate in advance that I should have a claim on the communal resources even at the price of conceding this claim if I should turn out to be among the employed. This much might be agreed on any theory of justice; even the more extreme versions of the conservative or liberal theories do not nowadays require the unemployed to starve. But there are three consequences which follow from Rawls's theory of justice which are rather more important. The first is the importance of needs. The second is the irrelevance of conventional comparisons. The third is the requirement of redistribution.

The most obvious provisions that follow from this are hardly at issue in contemporary Britain. We have freedom of speech, restrictions on theft or assault, and universal suffrage. But there is still a case to be made for saying that there is less equality of power in our social structure than would be consonant with what would have been agreed from the state of nature. Whatever position I turned out to occupy in twentieth-century Britain, I would surely want a maximum of say in the decisions by which my life was governed; and any inequality of power would have to be justified in the light of this injunction. Would it not therefore be just that workers should have a greater say in management? The reasons why such demands have not been more strongly pressed is largely – perhaps even entirely – because they are impracticable. But because justice is impracticable it does not cease to be justice; and if the ordinary worker has less say in the decisions by which his working life is governed than we should all have wished to stipulate before knowing what our own location would be in the economy of industrialized Britain, then this is a social injustice.

But – and it is a big but – to show that a social structure is unjust is not to show either how it ought to be changed or even that it ought to. Would more people be happier in a just society? Even if they would, might not more unhappiness than happiness be caused in the transition to justice? Inequalities are always least resented when expectations are low; and, conversely, deprivations are most strongly felt when a previous expectation has been disappointed. This much, indeed, is a truism. But it has the important consequence that the reformer, in attempting to make society just, may risk causing as much unhappiness as he will cure. Whether a system is just or not has nothing to do with people's attitudes towards it; even if slaves preferred to be slaves, this would not make slavery just, and even if everyone was miserable under a just regime, this would not make it unjust. In the same way, the efficiency or even the workability of a system has no necessary connection with its justice. It never follows, from the fact that a system is unjust, that it must be undone, and it is only by recognizing this that a clear and useful appeal to the notion of social justice can be made.

The Welfare State

R. M. Titmuss

Reprinted with permission from *Commitment to Welfare*, Allen & Unwin, 1968, pp. 195–8.

The major positive achievement which has resulted from the creation of direct, universalist, social services in kind has been the erosion of formal discriminatory barriers. One publicly approved standard of service, irrespective of income, class or race, replaced the double standard which invariably meant second-class services for second-class citizens. This has been most clearly seen in the National Health Service. Despite strict controls over expenditure on the Service by Conservative Governments for many years it has maintained the principle of equality of access by all citizens to all branches of medical care. Viewed solely in terms of the welfare objective of non-discriminatory, non-judgemental service this is the signal achievement of the National Health Service. In part this is due to the fact that the middle classes, invited to enter the Service in 1948, did so and have since largely stayed with the Service. They have not contracted out of socialized medical care as they have done in other fields like secondary education and retirement pensions. Their continuing participation, and their more articulate demands for improvements, have been an important factor in a general rise in standards of service – particularly in hospital care.

But, as some students of social policy in Britain and the United States are beginning to learn, equality of access is not the same thing as equality of outcome. We have to ask statistical and sociological questions about the utilization of the high-cost quality sectors of social welfare and the low-cost sectors of social welfare. We have to ask similar questions about the ways in which professional people (doctors, teachers, social workers and many others) discharge their roles in diagnosing need and in selecting or rejecting patients, clients and students for this or that service. In the modern world, the professions are increasingly becoming the arbiters of our welfare fate; they are the keyholders to equality of outcome; they help to determine the pattern of redistribution in social policy.

These generalizations apply particularly when services in kind are organized on a universalist, free-on-demand basis When this is so we substitute, in effect, the professional decision-maker for the crude decisions of the economic market-place. And we also make much more explicit – an important gain in itself – the fact that the poor have great difficulties in manipulating the wider society, in managing change, in choosing between alternatives, in finding their way around a complex world of welfare.

We have learnt from fifteen years' experience of the Health Service that the higher income groups know how to make better use of the Service; they tend to receive more specialist attention; occupy more of the beds in better equipped and staffed hospitals; receive more elective surgery; have better maternity care; and are more likely to get psychiatric help and psychotherapy than low-income groups – particularly the unskilled.

These are all factors which are essential to an understanding of the redistributive role played by one of the major direct welfare services in kind. They are not arguments against a comprehensive free-on-demand service. But they do serve to underline one conclusion. Universalism in social welfare, though a needed prerequisite towards reducing and removing formal barriers of social and economic discrimination, does not by itself solve the problem of how to reach the more-difficult-to-reach with better medical care, especially preventive medical care.

Much the same kind of general conclusion can be drawn from Britain's experience in the field of education. Despite reforms and expansion during the past fifteen years it is a fact that the proportion of male undergraduates who are the sons of manual workers is today about one per cent lower than it was between 1928 and 1947. Although we have doubled the number of University students the proportion coming from working-class homes has remained fairly constant at just over a quarter.

The major beneficiaries of the high-cost sectors of the educational system in 'The Welfare State' have been the higher income groups. They have been helped to so benefit by the continued existence of a prosperous private sector in secondary education (partly subsidized by the State in a variety of ways including tax deductibles), and by developments since 1948 in provisions for child dependency in the category of fiscal welfare. Take, for example, the case of two fathers each with two children, one earning $60,000 a year, the other $1,500 a year. In combining the effect of direct social welfare expenditures for children and indirect fiscal welfare expenditures for children the result is that the rich father now gets thirteen times more from the State than the poor father in recognition of the dependent needs of childhood.

Housing is another field of social policy which merits analysis from the point of view of redistribution. Here we have to take account of the complex interlocking effects of local rate payments, public housing subsidies, interest rates, tax deductibles for mortgage interest and other factors. When we have done so we find that the subsidy paid by the State to many middle-class families buying their own homes is greater than that received by poor tenants of public housing (local government) schemes.

These are no more than illustrations of the need to study the redistributive effects of social policy in a wider frame of reference. Hitherto, our techniques of social diagnosis and our conceptual frameworks have been too narrow. We have compartmentalized social welfare as we have compartmentalized the poor. The analytic model of social policy that has been fashioned on only the phenomena that are clearly visible, direct and immediately measurable is an inadequate one. It fails to tell us about the realities of redistribution which are being generated by the processes of technological and social change and by the combined effects of social welfare, fiscal welfare and occupational welfare.

How far and to what extent should redistribution take place through welfare channels on the principle of achieved status, inherited status or need? This is the kind of question which, fundamentally, is being asked in Britain today. And it is being directed, in particular, at two major areas of social policy – social security and housing. Both these instruments of change and redistribution have been neglected for a decade or more. We have gone in search of new gods or no gods at all. It is time we returned to consider their roles afresh and with new vision. Perhaps we might then entitle our journey 'Ways of Extending the Welfare State to the Poor'.

Social Selection in the Welfare State

T. H. Marshall

Reprinted with permission from 'Social Selection in the Welfare State', *Eugenics Review*, Vol. XLV, No. 2, 1953

It would be difficult to find any definition of the Welfare State acceptable to both its friends and to its enemies – or even to all its friends. Fortunately I needn't try to define it; I have only to explain what are the characteristics of the Welfare State which seem to me to provide a distinctive setting to the problem of social selection. I take the most relevant aspect of the Welfare State, in this context, to be the following.

First, its intense individualism. The claim of the individual to welfare is sacred and irrefutable and partakes of the character of a natural right. It would, no doubt, figure in the new Declaration of the Rights of Man if the supporters of the Welfare State were minded to issue anything so pithily dramatic. It would replace property in those early French and American testaments which speak of life, liberty and property; this trinity now becomes life, liberty and welfare. It is to be found among the Four Freedoms in the guise of 'Freedom from Want' – but that is too negative a version. The welfare of the Welfare State is more positive and has more substance. It was lurking in the Declaration of Independence, which listed the inalienable rights of man as 'Life, Liberty and the Pursuit of Happiness'. Happiness is a positive concept closely related to welfare, but the citizen of the Welfare State does not merely have the right to pursue welfare, he has the right to receive it, even if the pursuit has not been particularly hot. And so we promise to each child an education suited to its individual qualities, we try to make the punishment (or treatment) fit the individual criminal rather than the crime, we hold that in all but the simplest of the social services individual case study and family case work should precede and accompany the giving of advice or assistance, and we uphold the principle of equal opportunity, which is perhaps the most completely individualistic of all.

But if we put individualism first, we must put collectivism second. The Welfare State is the responsible promoter and guardian of the welfare of the whole community, which is something more complex than the sum total of the welfare of all its individual members arrived at by simple addition. The claims of the individual must always be defined and limited so as to fit into the complex and balanced pattern of the welfare of the community, and that is why the right to welfare can never have the full stature of a natural right. The harmonizing of individual rights with the common good is a problem which faces all human societies.

In trying to solve it, the Welfare State must choose means which are in harmony with its principles. It believes in planning – not of everything but over a wide area. It must therefore clearly formulate its objectives and carefully select its methods with a full sense of its power and its responsibility. It believes in equality, and its plans must therefore start from the assumption that every person is potentially a candidate for every position in society. This complicates matters; it is easier to cope with things if society is divided into a number of non-competing social classes. It believes in personal liberty because, as I choose to define it, it is a democratic form of society. So although, of course, like all States, it uses some compulsion, it must rely on individual choice and motivation for the fulfilment of its purposes in all their details.

How do these principles apply to selection through the educational system? The general social good, in this context, requires a balanced supply of persons with different skills and aptitudes who have been so trained as to maximize the contribution they can make to the common welfare. We have, in recent years, seen the Welfare State estimating the need for natural scientists, social scientists and technicians, for doctors, teachers and nurses, and then trying to stimulate the educational system to produce what is required. It must also be careful to see that the national resources are used economically and to the best advantage, that there is no waste of individual capacities, by denying them the chance of development and use, and no waste of money and effort, by giving education and training to those who cannot get enough out of them to justify the cost.

On the other side, the side of individualism, is the right of each child to receive an education suited to its character and abilities. It is peculiar, in that the child cannot exercise the right for itself, because it is not expected to know what its character and abilities are. Nor can its parents wholly represent its interests, because they cannot be certain of knowing either. But they have a rather ambiguous right at least to have their wishes considered, and in some circumstances to have them granted. The status of parental rights in the English educational system is somewhat obscure at the moment. There is no reason to assume that the independent operation of the two principles, of individual rights and general social needs, would lead to the same results. The State has the responsibility of harmonizing the one with the other.

So far I have merely been trying to explain the general meaning which I have discovered in the title of this lecture. As I have already said, I shall first limit this broad field by concentrating on selection through the educational system. I shall then limit it further to the two following aspects of the problem. I shall look first at the selection of children for secondary education and try to see what is involved in bringing it into harmony with the principles of the Welfare State. I choose this particular point in the selection process partly because of its intrinsic and often decisive importance, and partly because so much has recently been written about it. I shall look in the second place rather at the social structure and consider how far it is possible to achieve the aims of the Welfare State in this field – particularly the aim of equal opportunity – in a society in which there still exists considerable inequality of wealth and social status. In doing this I shall be able to draw on some of the still unpublished results of researches carried out at the London School of Economics over the past four years, chiefly with the aid of a generous grant from the Nuffield Foundation.

The Welfare State, as I see it, is in danger of tying itself in knots in an attempt to do things which are self-contradictory. One example, I submit, is the proposal to assign children to different schools, largely on the basis of general ability, and then to pretend that the schools are all of equal status. If this means that we shall take equal trouble to make all schools as good as possible, treat all the children with equal respect and try to make them all equally happy, I heartily endorse the idea. But the notion of parity of esteem does not always stop there; and I feel it really is necessary to assert that some children are more able than others, that some forms of education are higher than others, and that some occupations demand qualities that are rarer than others and need longer and more skilled training to come to full maturity, and that they will therefore probably continue to enjoy higher social prestige.

I conclude that competitive selection through the educational system must remain with us to a considerable extent. The Welfare State is bound to pick the children of high ability for higher education and for higher jobs, and to do this with the interest of the community as well as the rights of the children in mind. But the more use it can at the same time make of allocation to courses suited to special tastes and abilities the better. It further seems to be that, for the purpose of selection on grounds of general ability, the objective tests are already accurate enough to do all that we should ever ask them to do, while, so far as 'allocation' is concerned, they will never be able to give a decisive verdict in more than a minority of cases, although they can be of great value in helping to decide what advice to give.

The problem which now faces us is more administrative than psychological. There is less to be gained by trying to perfect the tests and examinations than by thinking how to shape the structure of our educational and employment systems. It is better to minimize the effects of our decisions in doubtful cases than to imagine that, if we only try hard enough, we can ensure that all our decisions in such cases are correct. The word 'correct' has no meaning in this context; it is a bureaucratic fiction borrowed from the office where there is a correct file for every document.

By 'minimizing the effects of our decisions' I mean refrain from adding unnecessary and artificial consequences to acts whose real meaning and necessary consequences I have been urging that we should frankly recognize. A system of direction into distinct 'types of secondary school' rather than 'courses of secondary education' (to use the titles I quoted earlier) must, I think, intensify rather than minimize the consequences. I am aware of the educational arguments on the other side, but do not intend to enter into a controversy for which I have no equipment. The other point at which artificial consequences may be added is the point of passage from education to employment. The snobbery of the educational label, certificate or degree when, as often, the prestige of the title bears little or no relation to the value of the content, is a pernicious thing against which I should like to wage a major war.

There is another matter on which the Welfare State can easily try to follow contradictory principles. It relates to occupational prestige, social class and the distribution of power in society.

Although the Welfare State must, I believe, recognize some measure of economic inequality as legitimate and acceptable, its principles are opposed to rigid class divisions, and to anything which favours the preservation or formation of sharply distinguished culture patterns at different social levels. The segregation when at school of those destined for different social levels is bound to have some effect of this kind and is acceptable only if there are irrefutable arguments on the other side. Further, a system which sorts children by general ability and then passes them through appropriate schools to appropriate grades of employment will intensify the homogeneity within each occupational status group and the differences between groups. And, in so far as intelligence is hereditary and as educational chances are influenced by family background (and I have produced evidence to show that they are), the correlation between social class and type of school will become closer among the children.

Finally, the Welfare State, more than most forms of democracy, cannot tolerate a governing class. Leadership and power are exercised from many stations in life, by politicians, judges, ecclesiastics, business men, trade unionists, intellectuals and others. If these were all selected in childhood and groomed in the same stable, we should have what Raymond Aron calls the characteristic feature of a totalitarian society – a unified elite. These leaders must really belong to and represent in a distinctive way the circles in and through which their power is exercised. We need politicians from all classes and occupational levels, and it is good that some captains of industry should have started life at the bench, and that trade unions should be led by genuine members, men of outstanding general ability who have climbed a ladder other than the educational one. It is important to preserve these other ladders, and it is fortunate that the selection net has some pretty big holes in it. It is fortunate too, perhaps, that human affairs cannot be handled with perfect mechanical precision, even in the Welfare State.

Authority and the Young

P. M. Worsley

Reprinted with permission from 'Authority and the Young', *New Society*, 22 July, 1965

It seems universally agreed among publicists and guardians of public morality that we are in the midst of a crisis, in which traditional values and institutional controls have been rejected, and that nothing has emerged to replace them. This decay of authority is believed to be most visible among young people, not only in Britain, but in all developed countries, whatever their cultural and ideological differences. T. R. Fyvel, for example, has described the 'Teddy boy international': Soviet stilyagi, Swedish skinnknuttar, French blousons noirs, Australian 'bodgies' and 'widgies', Japanese taiyozoku, West German Halbstarken, and so on – a new generation (of vipers) whose language is jazz, who dress alike, who share the same style of non-work life, and who though not radical ideologically, are detached from official society to the point of constituting a delinquent international sub-culture.

Impressionistic as this may be, it is not without some foundation in reality. Yet we lack adequate studies of inter-war youth against which we might more accurately assess just how different post-1945 youth is in fact. The quite limited literature on contemporary youth, too, by no means supports the thesis that the end of World War II inaugurated an era of social disorganization.

Barbara Wootton, in her study of criminality published in 1959, for example, pointed out that the UK statistics of indictable offences of all kinds (with all their acknowledged limitations) exhibited a remarkable stability: 787,482 in 1938; 753,012 in 1952; and 735,288 in 1955. Taking youthful crime separately, young people were responsible for 36 per cent of all indictable offences in 1938, and in 1955 – 33 per cent. Subsequently there has been a distinct rise, the significance of which is still being debated. What is of particular interest to us in all this, however, is that when the figures are looked at within the processual analytical framework of age, rather than globally, they suggest that criminality is a phase in the life-cycle of the individual rather than a phase in the 'life' of the whole society.

Changed attitudes to parental authority go hand in hand with changed attitudes to 'the authorities' in general. But it was the parents themselves who started the rot (if 'rot' it is): they overthrew the old Victorian paterfamilias; they urged youth to be free, experimented with bottle feeding, struggled so that 'the kids' could have better homes, more rewarding (in every sense) jobs, better education than themselves. And now, confusingly, 'the kids' are biting the hands that fed them. The 'scholarship boys', absorbed into middle-class ways, can't even find anything to talk to their parents about. On all sides, the laments rise up.

If they are radical, however, this is scarcely a radicalism of ideas and beliefs, it is a radicalism of personal independence: a manifestation of the normal structural phenomenon of intergenerational separation of experience, exacerbated in an era in which the Depression and the War are only historical events to the children of parents for whom these were crucial experiences.

The fact that youthful criminality exhibits a marked sexual division of labour alone suggests that we are dealing with patterns of behaviour that cannot be explained merely as the adding together of thousands of idiosyncratic cases, each one unique. There are very distinctive styles of crime, too. Crime, here, is not a mode of production, or a career: it is more commonly a mode of expression, or a phase during which personality needs are satisfied in precisely the ways held out as desirable by respectable society in other contexts. It is frequently opportunity-crime, or by rationalistic standards, purely destructive. It yields microscopic returns. And, classically, it is often oriented towards the acquisition or use of consumption goods, such as clothes and cars. Its values are the values of a consumption-oriented society, not those generated by basic poverty.

The emergence of a specialized 'youth industry', engaged in

selling goods to young people, obviously reflects the fact, as we are always being reminded, that youth can now afford to buy what it wants, or is led to want. Teenagers' real earnings have risen faster than those of adults (though as Mark Abrams has noted, their share of the national wealth is 'very modest . . . (and) . . . scarcely sustains a picture of an extremely prosperous body of young people'). It becomes profitable to exploit this market. This is indeed a necessary departure point in analysis, but it does not tell us why these kinds of goods are produced and consumed and not others. Clothes, for example, are important because they make the man: they express a personality, buttress a personality if it needs it, provide an artificial one if a real one is effectively lacking. So young people are interested in what they look like, how they project an image of themselves (for they are not too sure of themselves yet), particularly to the opposite sex they have so marvellously discovered. They are so insecure, in exchanging the controlled and hierarchical regularities of school for what is, for so many, visibly a dead-end job at the bottom of the ladder, in changing their status within the family (and soon in leaving it altogether), that they cling together and create a new world which quickly becomes powerfully normative.

Nothing is more striking than the way in which the very revolt of youth is so standardized. 'Deviance', indeed, has its quite prescriptive uniform and regalia, and fashion exercises as authoritative a sway over the beatniks as it does over the readers of *Vogue*. Hence the dictatorship of the 'Top Twenty' reflects and responds to far deeper wants than could ever be artificially induced by the most ingenious or unscrupulous public relations teams. Yet the media do command very considerable power, and the values they purvey are importantly internalized: when the young audience says that they'll buy it 'because it'll be a hit', they are at once internalizing commercial values (it will sell), and the social values of identification and solidarity with the culture of the peer-group: their friends will be playing it, dancing to it, and talking about it.

If youth is 'materialistic', this is precisely the path pioneered for them by their parents, and in particular by those who run the world in which their parents are pretty powerless and confused, too . . . The inculcation of dispositions and values starts very early – and the parents start it. The middle-class striver, for example, has his 'deferred gratification' pattern well built into his psyche during that brief period between potty and primary school: his life is a career-pattern – and he sees it as such – long before he enters the world of work.

For him, the phase of independent 'youth culture' is less defined. He can never be as 'free' as the young worker, anyhow, since he is still financially dependent on the state or parents, and socially is pressurized to remain sexually immature: he is not supposed to have an adult sex life, and is highly discouraged from marrying (particularly if he is attracted to a girl of the wrong class). At a time when the age of puberty begins earlier, and in a society in which working-class youth are marrying ever younger, the conflicts and contrasts are immense and full of tensions.

Those at the top pass from the private sector of the educational system through to the universities, scooping up the Oxbridge open scholarships with the confidence that has characterized the modern public schoolboy since he was invented in the mid-nineteenth century. At the other end, the doors are closed: 2 per cent of the children of semi- and un-skilled manual workers reach the universities. Even so, every fourth student in the provincial universities comes from quite modest origins. They often identify powerfully with the 'Opportunity State': after all, they themselves have 'made it', so they know it to be true. They do not need to internalize an ideology of social mobility: it is the story of their success by referring to 'intelligence', 'personality', 'hard work', or 'ambition'. Those who didn't, 'explain' their failure as due to lack of 'influence', or 'contacts', or lack of education.

The 'failures' adapt, not necessarily by challenging society's criteria of what 'failure' or 'success' consists in, but by 'explaining' their 'failure' within the 'rules of the game' – they weren't taught to play properly, or other people cheated, but the game is, in principle, a fair one. Equality of opportunity is accepted as equality. Even so, since they know that money can 'buy' brains, and thereby re-engender wealth, status, and power, there is a chronic bitterness. They also adapt by lowering their threshold of aspirations.

The Sexual Behaviour of Young People
Michael Schofield

Reprinted with permission from *The Sexual Behaviour of Young People*, Longmans, 1965, pp. 253–7

It seems to be common practice to end a criticism of adolescent sexual behaviour by adding that we all know the bad ones are an exception and that most of the youth of this country are a grand clean-living bunch of lads. But this qualification is as wrong as the criticism is inept. For the results of this research show clearly that those who are having sexual intercourse are not a tiny minority. In round figures something over 350,000 boys and girls under the age of twenty have had experience of premarital intercourse.

But although it is not a small minority, it is not a majority, and those who are concerned about this problem might begin by asking why, in view of the great strength of the sexual drive, there are not more teenagers who are sexually experienced. Young men under the age of twenty are at their highest sexual potential and social pressures are by no means all on the side of restraint.

We found that many of the teenagers gave moral reasons for not going further, although few gave specific religious reasons. Many appeals to youth either assume Christian values or explicitly state Christian doctrines, but most of the young people we interviewed were not interested in Christianity. It is possible that many young people find their way of living incompatible with the moral teaching of Christianity and the Church's emphasis on sexual morality may make the experienced teenager feel that there is no room for him in the Christian Church.

Despite the social and physiological pressures towards sexual intercourse, many teenagers manage to resist these influences. This research has found several differences between those who do and those who do not have sexual intercourse . . . These differences do not reveal serious anti-social tendencies in those teenagers with experience of sexual intercourse. The experienced boys were gregarious and outgoing, even hedonistic, but they were not misfits. Sexual experience among teenage girls is closely associated with a desire for freedom and independence from the family, but they were not debauched.

Nor is there any evidence that premarital sexual intercourse leads to or encourages adulterous relations after marriage. Most of the young people in this sample disapproved of extramarital relations and this is as true of the experienced teenagers as of the others.

Those who are worried about the extent of premarital sexual intercourse among teenagers must accept that these activities cannot be eliminated altogether in the foreseeable future. The most effective way to prevent teenage sexual activities would be to decrease the opportunities by reintroducing ideas like chaperonage of girls and further segregation of the sexes. But if this is what is required, we shall also have to accept a measure of Communist discipline and a reduction in personal freedom.

Many people will have noticed that this research has found an association between sex experience and lack of parental discipline. There is a danger that some people will seize upon this as if it is the most important finding in the report because it fits in with their preconceived ideas and because it appears to be easy to remedy. But it is not certain that further restrictions will be of value. The report of a symposium on adolescents warns about the dangers of 'scrupulosity' – a tendency to make an individual see evil where there is no evil, serious sin where there is no sin and obligation where there is no obligation.

In face of much of the uninformed criticism about teenage sexual activities, it is tempting to spend too much time in pointing out that many of the generalizations are without factual foundation, that there are no signs of moral collapse, that more thought should be given to adult immorality, that many teenage attitudes are refreshing and stimulating, that there are many serious young people with great intellectual curiosity and high aspirations. But these assertions of good sense are not a substitute for factual information.

Indeed a disinterested look at the teenage cult will reveal several facets which are quite depressing and many signs that the least valuable and shabbiest aspects of adult society have been adopted with enthusiasm. The particular facet which concerns this research is the pressure towards conformity within the teenage cult and the formation of a teenage mythology. A typical example is teenage fashions which may seem daringly different from adult society, but in reality they are an illustration of strict conformism within the teenage subculture.

Four out of five people in Great Britain now live in urban areas, some of immense size. This urbanism has made possible the growth of teenage subcultures which are often at variance with adult standards. The improved economic position of the teenagers has given them more independence and greater mobility. But for many it has become a confused world as they revolt against an imposed middle-class morality and at the same time lose the assurance of their own working-class environment.

Within these urban conditions has grown up the teenage mythology, built up by the press, the advertisers and the special teenage and pop music magazines. This has created an image of how the teenager is supposed to behave. Here is an organized system of behaviour expectations and attitudes, and the young person acts out his role, largely learnt from the teenage group to which he belongs.

The sexual behaviour of young people is influenced by this teenage subculture. There is a danger that a teenager may feel he is exceptional because he has not had sexual intercourse. In the same chapter we found that half the boys and two-thirds of the girls did not enjoy their first experience of sexual intercourse, but nearly all of them tried it again fairly soon. Yet at the time of the interview there were still 28 per cent of the experienced boys and 39 per cent of the experienced girls who did not always enjoy it.

We envisaged a situation in which the boy and girl engaged in sexual intercourse although neither of them wanted to do this. We found that many teenagers felt their friends were having more sex than they were and we noted that the most enthusiastic advocates of teenage conformity were the sexually experienced boys and girls.

We found that the sexually experienced were the ones who had the least respect for adult standards. Consequently the time that these people spend with adults is cut to a minimum and there is no interaction between the adult and teenage worlds. The young people no longer have what the Americans call 'corrective feedback' from adults, and youth becomes, not 'an ephemeral privilege' as Cocteau thought it ought to be, but 'a separate hardy race setting itself up in opposition to the decaying race of the old'.

Yet it is obvious that this teenage subculture has been created by the adult world, not by the young people themselves. For example, the sexually experienced went to the cinema more often than the others and therefore could see that sexual satisfaction is all important in most films, and premarital sex is acceptable in many. The teenagers with the most sexual experience were also those with the most money to spend and therefore the quarry for the very active salesmen of the teenage commercial market. Incidentally the only group of teenagers that sets out to resist the blandishments of the marketeers are the Beats, and they come in for an extra measure of social hostility.

The adult world, unlike the Beats, cannot contract out. It is our responsibility for it is our society that has created the modern teenager. No matter what measures are taken to restrict or control or change or influence the activities of our young people, it is certain that in the immediate future a not inconsiderable number of teenagers will engage in premarital sexual intercourse. These sexually experienced teenagers are every bit as much our responsibility as the others. Whatever the long-term answer may be, there is an urgent short-term task, and that is to make youthful sex activities less harmful. This may be done by increasing the amount of knowledge and enlightenment on sexual matters, by introducing more and better sex education in the widest sense, and by providing individual counselling which on some occasions will mean making available methods of birth control to those who need them. Above all it is vital that future programmes of advice, help and restraint should be based, less on unsubstantiated impressions, and more on the demonstrable facts.

The Culture is Wrong

T. Lupton

Reprinted with permission from 'The Culture is Wrong', *New Society*, 22 September, 1966

Economic explanations of Britain's inability to maintain even a moderate rate of economic growth are nowadays frequently accompanied by reference to lack of moral fibre, absence of positive leadership, false ideologies, petty sectional interests, and latterday Luddism. Politicians refer nostalgically to the 'Dunkirk spirit'. We hear of 'wreckers' who promote class warfare and spread false economic doctrines. Managers are urged to show more initiative and to learn imported skills from Harvard professors at summer schools. Even a sympathetic observer like Edward Shils can write of a 'construction of imagination and aspiration' in contemporary Britain.

All this shows a growing awareness that some obstacles to growth are non-economic. It would be wrong to conclude, however, in an excess of George-Brownism, that mass conversion to the doctrine of national salvation through individual effort is possible, or a solution. Since economic nostrums also have limited effect, it might be of use to attempt to identify socio-cultural obstacles to higher productivity and healthy growth.

British social structure is demonstrably highly resistant to shifts towards greater equality of wealth, power, and educational career opportunity. Yet it is commonly thought that educational and career opportunities have greatly improved in the last 50 years. This gap between fact and belief could well be at the root of much of the dissatisfaction, frustration and cynicism which can be found in the 'lower' strata of British society, and which affect responses to appeals for greater effort, and attitudes to new machinery and administrative methods.

At the top of British society, access to key positions is based too much on family connection and type of school and university, and not enough on intrinsic merit and educational and economic achievement, irrespective of social background. This has often been stated and as often challenged. My own inquiries show there is more hard evidence to back it up than to contradict it. Its effect could be a plethora of polished duffers in seats of power, or of able men ill-equipped to run the institutions of a technically complex siege economy, or both. Traditional values perpetuated by educational exclusiveness, inherited leadership, amateur 'all-roundism', continuity, cultured leisure and leisured enquiry and what Tawney once referred to as 'the sentimental aroma of an aristocratic legend' – all these may be thought to suffocate the urge for radical reform and the growth of specialized professional competences.

The importance for economic development of having the right kind of elites has often been emphasized. Perhaps we have inherited the wrong kind. It is true that our traditional elites are highly absorbent, but so pervasive is the 'sentimental aroma' that it mellows the absorbed, and sours the rejected. The extent to which our economic performance has been inhibited by these factors merits closer enquiry.

The increasing traffic between Whitehall and the business world is usually thought of either as an example of pressure group activity, or as evidence of growing consensus – both healthy symptoms. In a persuasive article J. P. Nettl has thrown serious doubts on these interpretations. The facts he adduces, and the logic of the situations he describes, suggest rather that big business is infected by bureaucratic values and procedures and that business men are weaned from their proper concerns. They, too, play the Whitehall game and become amateur all-rounders. Another example, it would appear, of the propensity of our institutions, and the values which suffuse them, to blunt the qualities needed for highly specialized performance, and to misuse talent.

Again, it would be difficult, on present evidence, to prove a direct causal connection in the wrong direction between the processes of economic decision-making in Whitehall and business efficiency, productivity and growth; but the idea is worth following up.

From a different perspective McLelland provides theoretical backing for the general line of argument pursued so far. Careful psychological experiments and thorough international comparisons together lead him to the view that economic development depends upon individuals with 'high achievement need' – which is, put crudely, a mental state which induces vigorous pursuit of self-generated standards of excellence, a kind of lay Puritan ethic.

Traditional values stifle it. McLelland's remedy is to arrange the primary socialization of children and subsequent social experience to increase the supply of persons with high achievement need, and to alter social arrangements to create opportunities for its full expression. It might be that Britain produces too many who complacently accept traditional standards, and discourages those who do not.

The sociological evidence about top people is thin, perhaps because sociologists, whose nosing around is an implied threat to the *status quo*, are unwelcome among them. Much more is known about the lesser folk. Little and Westergaard have recently reviewed the state of knowledge. They conclude that, though inequalities of access to secondary education have been (expectably) reduced in the last half century, the reduction has been small. Increased opportunity has been given to working-class children, but many of them, for class-cultural and economic reasons, have been unable to benefit fully. For the same reasons many bright ones fail even to gain entrance. The significant increase in university places has been taken up mainly by middle-class children.

Over the same period, rates of social mobility have altered hardly at all. This indicates perhaps that what we have gained by a limited increase in educational opportunity has been lost by the closing up of extra-educational channels of mobility as some sectors of economic life have become increasingly bureaucratic and professional.

Plainly, at all levels, despite the movement of some individuals, the structure of our class system has remained so far impervious to radical reform. This is more than just a matter of occupational inertia. Class differences are also differences in life chances and styles of living. The classes are separated by social and geographical distance, by barriers of communication, by differences of speech idiom and techniques of culture transmission, of intellectual climate, in patterns of consumption, and in leisure pursuits. It is a moot point whether the mass media, reflecting and emphasizing as they do distinctions in the social structure, make a desirable impact.

A favourite theme of after-dinner speakers is the need in the interests of economic efficiency to end once and for all the talk of 'two sides' in industry. We are all in the same boat now, they say, and in a rough sea we ought not to rock it. A more refined version of the same theme says that the separation of industrial ownership and control has given rise to a new breed of professional managers, efficient and dedicated to the public weal. Entry to the new technocracy is open, it is said, to the humblest if the talent is there. No one wants to grind the faces of the poor any more for the sake of profit. So Marx was wrong, and Burnham was right, and trade unions are an anachronism and declarations by business men about industrial relations make sense.

It sounds good. Unfortunately, the facts do not point in that direction. In the first place, technological advance and increases in scale of business operation have emphasized career discontinuities between managers and non-managers – which are already implicit in the social structure, as Lloyd Warner showed long ago. The professionalization of the middling ranks of management, and the growth of large-scale national and international organizations has now produced what Watson has called the 'spiralist', a mobile man with no firm social roots, a very different animal from the working man tied by kin, occupation and life style to the local community. There are few, if any, crosscutting ties between the two groups to moderate the conflicts between them which arise from division of function and cultural incongruence, and the quarrels over access to scarce power, cash and satisfaction at work.

The working class has not escaped the consequence of technical change. A more complex and minute division of labour has threatened many traditional occupational interests and allegiances, and hallowed working practices. For this reason, among others, the increased power and security brought by full employment has seen a tightening, rather than a relaxation of protective practices, and increasing conflicts of interest between occupational groups. It is misleading to consider that these processes, when taken together with the growth of technical and white-collar occupations, are evidence of the break-up of the working class and its cultures and institutions. Common patterns of residence and style of life, an oral tradition of culture transmission, and common experience of relative deprivation and the expectation of deference to one's 'betters' preserve solidarity and an egalitarian ethos. All this is in sharp contrast to the competitive culture of the career professional, and the ways of the traditional 'cultured' elite.

This analysis helps to explain the persistence of restrictive practices, and the alienation of union leaders from rank-and-file difficulties of geographical redeployment of the labour force and retraining.

It might be comforting if, in the middle ranks of society, the managerial revolutionaries were on the march – dedicated technocrats and super-organizers moving into the seats of power. But some evidence from a recent study reveals that if the separation of ownership and control has produced a new breed of trained salaried managers, they are strangely absent from the boardrooms of British industry, where the cult of the amateur still persists. It is not difficult to see why education for management is so difficult to get off the ground.

If our social class structure, with its fairly distinct and discrepant subcultures, stifles movement and change, and produces conflict, there is at least one positive goal the politicians and the advertisers have got us all to agree about – that to accumulate material possessions is good, and that a man is judged and socially categorized as much by these as by his intrinsic worth or proven achievement. This being so, barriers to accumulation arising from doubtfully legitimated social inequalities, may well channel energies into doubtfully legitimated means of accumulation in attempts to buy intangible signs of social prestige. This is a partial explanation of the increase in crime. Taken together with the boring and uninteresting work which technical progress brings for working men and women, it serves also as a partial explanation of fiddles, restrictive practices, 'instrumental' attitudes to work, and a resentment of technical and administrative pushes to higher effort and efficiency.

We seem, in short, to be suffering from severe cultural 'lag'. Our social structure and institutions and their values on the one hand, and our economic goals on the other, are strangely but perhaps understandably incongruent. We have no social regulators to prevent cultural hangovers, to compare with the post-Keynesian economic regulators we now confidently and hopefully deploy. Perhaps, as some suggest, drastic wage freezes and stiff central controls will force a change of attitudes and set off the required social changes. Experience does not bear this out.

Patient research, enlightened administration, better (or more appropriate) education and training, improved occupational selection, the encouragement of talent, and a campaign against snobbery, privilege and incompetence – all these combined might help. But one sometimes wonders whether we have been irrevocably entranced by the fatal charms of social continuity, tolerant and civilized incompetence, and a moderately growing material affluence.

British Society

E. Shils

Reprinted with permission from P. Hall (Ed.), *Labour's New Frontiers*, André Deutsch, 1964, pp. 6–16

British society today certainly is no paradise. Yet as human societies go, its attainments, in recent decades, are very considerable. It has made great progress in the present century towards the moral equality which is a *sine qua non* of a good society. The level of material well-being of previously horribly, impoverished strata has been greatly improved. The weak, the defenceless, the young, the failures are better cared for than ever before, and even where the actual care remains markedly insufficient, solicitous concern exists and promises real improvement in the future. Educational opportunity is diffusing more widely than ever before the capacity to share in the cultural inheritance, to broaden the range of intellectual and aesthetic experience and to acquire the skills and qualifications necessary for occupational and professional achievement. It has continued to remain in the front ranks of the pioneers of scientific research. It has renounced with relatively good grace its empire which was until quite recently, among its greatest glories, and among the greatest creations of world history. The country has had stable government and the government has remained democratic. The institutional machinery for the public conduct of conflict and for the peaceful adjudication of contention is likewise fairly good by any realistic standard. Civility remains high. The manners of public life are relatively gentle and considerate. The political system, although far from meeting ideal standards, has at least not collapsed as it has in France. Public liberties have remained more or less intact. There are no large parties which are so alienated from the rest of the political system that they are committed to the subversion of the existing constitution, as in Italy and France. Its immunity from ideological fevers has not had to be acquired, as in contemporary Germany, by recuperation from a long bout of murderous madness.

Yet the situation in Britain today distresses many who contemplate it. They are, quite reasonably, not content that there should be no growth in virtues already acquired. Sometimes distress over present shortcomings blinds critics to the accomplishments, persisting and recent, of British society, but our awareness of their blindness does not invalidate their criticisms. There still remain, despite the transformation of the public appearance of the ancient regime, very deep strata of 'darkest England', of hierarchical harshness, of contemptuous hostility towards the weak and unsuccessful. There are still pockets of misery particularly among the aged. A 'race problem' is beginning to emerge in and at the edges of the Negro and Indian ghettoes in some of the larger cities. The educational system at nearly every level is unable to cope with the increased numbers who should be educated, and it is contorted by its inegalitarian inheritance. The inter-university hierarchy and the inferior dignity of technological studies, both of which are related to the class system of this country, are still alive and injurious to the fruitfulness in life and in society of those who suffer at the lower strata of these hierarchies. Much of the urban physical environment – especially housing accommodation and amenities – is inconvenient far past the point necessitated by modern technology, and it is hideously ugly. The major provincial centres are dreary and boring. Political and economical leadership, although generally virtuous and mild mannered, is unimaginative and inspires little confidence; it is lacking in initiative and self-confidence. The British economy, which must provide the wherewithal for the next necessary improvements, is encumbered by archaic practices and arrangements, and both at its top and at its bottom it shows the constraints and distortions of its hierarchical traditions. The enormous progress that has been made in the movement towards moral equality only makes more evident the crippling inequality and the powerful snobbery which still exist. The power of the aristocracy and gentry has been largely broken, but the aura of deference which attended that power still persists. This manifests itself in many ways, the most important of which is the inhibition of individuality and initiative.

One of the features of British society which impresses a foreign observer is its constrictedness of imagination and aspiration. There is a lack of vigour and daring in the conception of new possibilities of life and a too narrow radius of aspiration. In its older industries, there is an anxious adherence to past practices.

Foreign models dominate the vision of those who would leave the British past behind. Those who try to break away into some new sphere seem to lack self-confidence and innovators are distrusted. Too little is expected of life and too little is expected from oneself and from others in the discovery of new ways of doing things. The demand for pleasure is too restricted; curiosity too confined to conventional paths.

It is true that there are variations in this picture of the situation. Certain industries do attempt to find better techniques through research; there are great scientists at the height of their power, at work in the country. Some new universities are trying out new syllabi; certain local education authorities introduce innovations. But on the whole, they stand out by their rarity. It is in the younger generation throughout British society that the compression of desire which the traditions of British society demand is less willingly accepted. The 'youth culture' which includes pop music, sartorial elegance, early sexual intercourse, motor-bikes and juvenile delinquency, is part of this refusal. These all express a new aesthetic sensitivity, a greater appreciation of more diverse experiences and a livelier contact with other human beings. Yet there too, in this most notable manifestation of spirit, one perceives a readiness to retract under the pressure of adulthood, into a more confined 'life-space', more like that in which the elders have been living.

The class system which took form in the nineteenth and early twentieth centuries in this country demanded a lot both from those who were its obvious beneficiaries and those who were its obvious victims. From those at the bottom, it demanded more than obedience, it demanded respectability. There were many who did not conform but they were outcasts; they were expected neither to 'get on' nor even to hold their own before the universal dangers of unemployment, dependence on charity and base impulse. An iron discipline which looked straight ahead and not very far and a steady attendance to obligation did not leave much room for the opening of imagination or sensibility. The religion of respectability and the religious beliefs of the respectable reinforced what was necessitated by private property, scarcity and the police. Respectability entailed not only self-restraint, it entailed deference to one's betters, which involved self-derogation.

The obvious beneficiaries had their own religion of respectability too. It was a respectability which was less confining but it was acquired by a discipline in institutions which restricted the range of experience and narrowed the imagination. It had the great advantages that those who survived it felt themselves qualified for anything. It was a discipline which was integral to ruling. Those who passed through it went on to the Civil Service, the Indian Civil Service, the Colonial Service, politics, the law, and the Anglican clergy which in those days was much closer to the atmosphere of ruling than it is today when it lives in miasmal depression. Those who followed none of these paths still inhaled the air which is breathed by rulers.

Had Britain been a rather rich, hierarchical society without an empire, like Sweden, those at the top might not have felt so ascendant. But having an empire meant that India and Africa, and parts of the Middle and Far East, were also in a sense the lower strata of British society, the peak of which was the destined inheritance of the successful survivors of institutional discipline. The 'effortless superiority of the Balliol man' or of any man who had successfully passed other parts of the institutional system was the product of a sense of confidence. Their mere 'being' qualified them to do what had to be done – to administer, to do research, to understand the essentials of any problem and to take the action called for.

The great changes within national societies and between them in the present century have eroded the ascendancy of the beneficiaries of the British system of stratification. Within Britain the continuous growth of democracy has almost obliterated the power of the aristocracy and it has especially diminished its symbolic grandeur; and the growth of trade union power and the nationalization of major industries has restricted the power of the plutocracy. The dissolution of the Empire and increasing real independence of the English-speaking dominions have contracted the size of the society over which the British elite – and British society as a whole – were superordinated.

These two simultaneous diminutions of the power of the British elite have had tremendous consequences for the life of present-day Britain. The elite have lost that sense of effortless superiority which came from 'being' what they were. Their diminution has laid them open to self-criticism and to criticism by those who shared in their glory. Those over whom they ruled at home are now no longer so impressed by the standard which they represented or by the ideal of respectability which was its immediate derivative. Humiliated pride and once repressed resentment both come forward now.

British society is no longer regarded by those who live in it as a repository of a charismatic quality which exalted its members and imposed itself on the world. Pride in being British is no longer what it was. There is little confidence that one's inherited pattern of institutions and culture or one's own party has the answers to important questions. There is a critical spirit abroad. Much of it is a nagging criticism and offers only archaic solutions to real problems.

The Acquisitive Society

R. H. Tawney

Reprinted with permission from R. H. Tawney, *The Acquisitive Society*, Victor Gollancz, 1937, pp. 9–10

It is a commonplace that the characteristic virtue of Englishmen is their power of sustained practical activity, and their characteristic vice a reluctance to test the quality of that activity by reference to principles. They are incurious as to theory, take fundamentals for granted, and are more interested in the state of the roads than their place on the map. And it might fairly be argued that in ordinary times that combination of intellectual tameness with practical energy is sufficiently serviceable to explain, if not to justify, the equanimity with which its possessors bear the criticism of more mentally adventurous nations. It is the mood of those who have made their bargain with fate and are content to take what it offers without re-opening the deal. It leaves the mind free to concentrate undisturbed upon profitable activities, because it is not distracted by a taste for unprofitable speculations. Most generations, it might be said, walk in a path which they neither make nor discover, but accept; the main thing is that they should march. The blinkers worn by Englishmen enable them to trot all the more steadily along the beaten road, without being disturbed by curiosity as to their destination.

But if the medicine of the constitution ought not to be made its daily food, neither can its daily food be made medicine. There are times which are not ordinary, and in such times it is not enough to follow the road. It is necessary to know where it leads, and, if it leads nowhere, to follow another. The search for another involves reflection, which is uncongenial to the bustling people who describe themselves as practical, because they take things as they are and leave them as they are. But the practical thing for a traveller who is uncertain of his path is not to proceed with the utmost rapidity in the wrong direction: it is to consider how to find the right one. And the practical thing for a nation which has stumbled upon one of the turning points of history is not to behave as though nothing very important were involved, as if it did not matter whether it turned to the right or to the left, went up hill or down dale, provided that it continued doing with a little more energy what it has done hitherto; but to consider whether what it has done hitherto is wise, and, if it is not wise, to alter it.

When the broken ends of its industry, its politics, its social organization, have to be pieced together after a catastrophe, it must make a decision; for it makes a decision even if it refuses to decide. If it is to make a decision which will wear, it must travel beyond the philosophy momentarily in favour with the proprietors of its newspapers. Unless it is to move with the energetic futility of a squirrel in a revolving cage, it must have a clear apprehension both of the deficiency of what is, and of the character of what ought to be. And to obtain this apprehension it must appeal to some standard more stable than the momentary exigencies of its commerce or industry or social life, and judge them by it. It must, in short, have recourse to Principles.

Further Reading: Values

R. ATKINSON: *Orthodox Consensus and Radical Alternative*, Heinemann, 1971.

T. BOTTOMORE: *Classes in Modern Society*, Allen & Unwin, 1965.

S. BOX: *Deviance, Reality and Society*, Holt, Rinehart & Winston, 1971.

* E. BUTTERWORTH AND R. HOLMAN (Eds.): *Social Welfare in Modern Britain*, Fontana, 1975.

* E. BUTTERWORTH AND D. T. H. WEIR (Eds.): *Social Problems of Modern Britain*, Fontana, 1972.

J. E. T. ELDRIDGE: *Industrial Disputes*, Routledge & Kegan Paul, 1968.

* B. JACKSON: *Working Class Community*, Routledge & Kegan Paul, 1968.

E. RUBINGTON AND M. S. WEINBERG: *The Study of Social Problems*, Oxford University Press, 1971.

P. TOWNSEND: *The Last Refuge*, Routledge & Kegan Paul, 1962.

J. URRY AND J. WAKEFORD (Eds.): *Power in Britain*, Heinemann, 1973.

* P. M. WORSLEY (Ed.): *Problems in Modern Society*, Penguin Books, 1972.

* J. YOUNG: *The Drugtakers*, Paladin, 1971.

* Available in paperback

Textbook Reference

As we pointed out in the Introduction, this book of readings is not intended as a substitute for conventional textbooks, any more than it is hoped to supplant the reading of original materials

The aims and intentions are that the easy availability of original material in the form of a reader will increase the value of courses, organized round one or other of the major textbooks in the field, or a basic lecture course on Modern Britain.

Accordingly we compiled a list of the textbooks which seemed to be in most common use in teaching courses of this type, and in introductory sociology generally. We then traced out the major themes which seemed to be important within the institutional areas which form the framework of this book of readings, whether we had been able to select readings in these areas or not. Although there are doubtless many other texts which could be included and many more will be on the market within a short time, there seem to be advantages for the student in having a readily accessible summary of the comparative coverage of the major textbooks, and of the areas within which one is substitutable for another. In our experience, a good deal of disillusion and disappointment on the part of students can be associated with inappropriate advice about textbooks, and a lack of guidance about which texts are relevant for particular sections of a course.

The annotations are derived from a systematic and comprehensive survey of the contents of each book. The roman numerals refer to chapters and the arabic numerals to pages in the relevant textbooks. Not all of these books, as will be noted, cover precisely similar ground, and some, for instance Halsey, are not strictly *textbooks* in the commonly-accepted sense: all however, provide introductory and reference material for courses on Modern Britain.

Textbooks

V. AUBERT: *Elements of Sociology*, Heinemann, 1967

T. B. BOTTOMORE: *Sociology: A Guide to Problems and Literature*, George Allen & Unwin, 1962

E. CHINOY: *Society: An Introduction to Sociology*, Random House, 1961

S. F. COTGROVE: *The Science of Society*, George Allen & Unwin, 1967

B. GREEN AND E. A. JOHNS: *An Introduction to Sociology*, Pergamon, 1966

A. H. HALSEY (Ed.): *Trends in British Society Since 1900*, Macmillan, 1972

E. A. JOHNS: *The Social Structure of Modern Britain*, Pergamon, 1965

H. M. JOHNSON: *Sociology: A Systematic Introduction*, Routledge & Kegan Paul, 1961

G. D. MITCHELL: *Sociology: The Study of Social Systems*, University Tutorial Press, 1959

J. RYDER AND H. SILVER: *Modern English Society*, Methuen, 1970

G. SERGEANT: *A Textbook of Sociology*, Macmillan, 1971

E. J. WILKINS: *An Introduction to Sociology*, MacDonald & Evans, 1970

P. M. WORSLEY (Ed.): *Introducing Sociology*, Penguin Books, 1970 (Worsley 1).

P. M. WORSLEY (Ed.): *Modern Sociology: Introductory Readings*, Penguin Books, 1970 (Worsley 2)

Textbook References

* Chapter references are in roman numerals, page references in arabic numerals.

The Sociology of Modern Britain	1. Family	2. Community	3. Socialization	4. Work	5. Class	6. Power
Aubert	15, 47–8, 83–8, 92–6, 141, 211, 223	210–29	87, 91, 96, 163, 176, 190, 203, 215, 223–4	87, 95, 159–70	V	10, 29, 33, 86, 103, 167, 199–200, 213, 225
Bottomore	165–74	82–3, 93–7	110–44, 548–51	130–46, 315–16	93–7, 147–54 179–96	140, 155–7 147–61, 191–2
Chinoy	110–17, 128, 156	85, 87, 154, 202–23	334–8	IV, 131–66, 227–45	207–21, 257–8	—
Cotgrove	43–64	—	70–100, 104–8	IV, 15–16, 27, 57, 130, 242–67	210–41	92–5, 154–82, 206–7, 220–1, 277–82
Green & Johns	39, 55, 59, 68, 73, 77, 80–5, 96–101, 145	52–4	54–6, 120–31, 133–46	V, 80–91	109–10, 117, 129	64–6, 76–9, 91–6

The Sociology of Modern Britain	1. Family	2. Community	3. Socialization	4. Work	5. Class	6. Power
Halsey	II	IX	VI, VII	IV	V	VIII, IX
Johns	II	—	IV	—	III	VI
Johnson	147-49, 155-60, 171-200	—	120-44	215-18, 235-45, 280-312	XVII, IXIX, 469-92, 516-35	XIII, XIV, 280-312, 587-624
Mitchell	53-76	40-50	140-50	115-16, 126-39	109-32	77-92, 126-34
Ryder & Silver	IX, 107-16	II, 102-17	VI	VI	VII	III, X
Sergeant	III	—	IV	—	II	VI
Wilkins	VII, XII	XIII	X	IX	VI	VIII
Worsley 1	III	VI	IV	V	VII	VII
Worsley 2	III	VII	IV	V, VI	VIII	IX, 265-74

Index

Ronald Meek

Figuring Out Society

This book is the first comprehensive non-technical introduction to the use of quantitative methods in the social sciences. It is written with the needs of the non-mathematical student and general reader very much in mind, and in fact the book grew out of a series of highly successful voluntary lectures in the University of Leicester.

Figuring Out Society provides a highly individual approach to social and economic models, regression analysis, sampling, the theory of games, cost benefit analysis, and much more.

Not only is the mathematical content kept to a minimum, but a special mathematical appendix is added. There are numerous diagrams, and all points are made clear, interesting, and often amusing, by means of brilliantly chosen examples.